Journeymen for Jesus

The Kenneth Scott Latourette Prize in Religion and Modern History

The Conference on Faith and History, an organization of more than six hundred scholars devoted to exploring the relation of faith to historical study, sponsors a series of historical monographs that assess religion's role in modern culture. These books are the prize winners of an annual manuscript competition conducted by the Conference.

With this series, we honor the memory of a founding member of the Conference on Faith and History, Kenneth Scott Latourette (1884–1968). Latourette was Sterling Professor of Missions and Oriental History at Yale University and the author of more than a score of books on Asian history and on the history of Christianity. Recognized as a preeminent authority on the history of Christianity, of its development in non-Western cultures, and of the history of East Asia, Professor Latourette served as president of the American Historical Association, the Association of Asian Studies, and the American Society of Church History. His deep interest in the study of modern religious and cultural history, his gracious example as a Christian historian, and his outstanding scholarly accomplishments make him our obvious choice for naming the prize.

Religious and cultural history, as Professor Latourette demonstrated throughout his work, is much broader than church history. Indeed, the unifying theme for this competition is the historical study of religion's interplay with other elements of modern culture. The period of history since 1500 has brought a complex of social and cultural developments that provide the common reference point for this series. Religion provides another, for this series will focus on the profoundly human propensity to ground one's identity and life's meaning in a transcendent purpose or force. A historical approach is a fitting way to explore the interaction of religion and modern culture since it allows scholars to address the element so characteristic of modernity, namely, change.

It is the hope of the Conference on Faith and History that these books will stimulate further scholarly interest in a field that has already produced path-breaking work, and that they will provide exciting and worthwhile insights for anyone interested in the complex dynamics of religion and modern culture.

WILLIAM R. SUTTON

Journeymen for Jesus

Evangelical Artisans Confront Capitalism in Jacksonian Baltimore

The Pennsylvania State University Press
University Park, Pennsylvania

Library of Congress Cataloging-in-Publication Data

Sutton, William R., 1949–
Journeymen for Jesus : Evangelical artisans confront capitalism in Jacksonian Baltimore / William R. Sutton.
p. cm.
Includes bibliographical references and index.
ISBN 0-271-01772-4 (cloth : alk. paper)
ISBN 0-271-01773-2 (pbk. : alk. paper)
1. Evangelicalism—Maryland—Baltimore—History—19th century. 2. Artisans—Religious life—Maryland—Baltimore—History—19th century. 3. Capitalism—Religious aspects—Protestant churches—History—19th century. 4. Baltimore (Md.)—Church history—19th century. I. Title.
BV3775.B2S38 1998
305.5′62′097527109034—dc21 97-49128
CIP

Printed in the United States of America
Published by The Pennsylvania State University Press,
University Park, PA 16802–1003

It is the policy of The Pennsylvania State University Press to use acid-free paper for the first printing of all clothbound books. Publications on uncoated stock satisfy the minimum requirements of American National Standard for Information Sciences—Permanence of Paper for Printed Library Materials, ANSI Z39.48-1992.

To Ben, Matt, and Zak

CONTENTS

PREFACE

This book examines a specific group of early nineteenth-century common men and women—artisans, in particular, but also petty merchants and consumers, who were evangelical Protestants. Their beliefs and actions reflected a distinctive perspective on the socioeconomic and cultural transformation generated by the market revolution in America. These people were an integral part of what was known as the producing class. "Producerism" is actually an old interpretive construct, used by nineteenth-century skilled workers and small manufacturers themselves to explain their work experiences in and attitudes toward preindustrial and industrialized settings. Recently it has been refurbished by such historians as Ronald Schultz, Christopher Lasch, and Victoria Hattam to describe artisan contributions to broader Anglo-American culture. Nineteenth-century producers took pride in their work; recognized their responsibilities to fellow workers, employers, and the community at large; and emphasized the central importance of living and working without being dependent on the power and authority of others. But producerism as a tradition also mandated obligations for masters and consumers, with all acknowledging, or at least paying lip service to the idea, that working men and women deserve fair pay, livable working conditions, limited upward mobility, and input into production decisions—

in other words, in the popular religious expression of the day: the worker was to be considered and treated as worthy of his or her hire.

In general, American artisans were deeply ambivalent toward the industrial and capitalist innovations sweeping American society. They saw opportunities for advancement and material accumulation in these changes, but they also recognized the potential for dislocation and exploitation. In opposition to the organizing concept of the "natural" law of supply and demand, the fundamental consciousness of producers was built upon ideals of socio-economic justice: antimonopolist limits to power and accumulation, independence for the nonprivileged, and cooperative control of work. In this sense, producerism was oftentimes explicitly anticapitalist. This nineteenth-century reality, however, causes confusion for contemporary readers because American cultural understandings are still bound by McCarthyite polarities, insisting that anticapitalism equals communism, the perceived antithesis of the American republican tradition. Such Manichean dualism has greatly obscured the broad spectrum of anticapitalist sentiment that existed before the time of Karl Marx. Artisans said nothing about expropriating public property or welcoming the dictatorship of the proletariat; rather, they embraced the notions that their labor was their property and that upward mobility within limits was a socially progressive incentive for sustained effort. In the process, producers provided a potent language and ethic inspiring early American suspicions of capitalist transformation. This is the mentality Christopher Lasch describes in *The True and Only Heaven* as "anticapitalist but not socialist or social democratic, at once radical, even revolutionary, and deeply conservative; and it deserves a more attentive hearing, on its own terms, than it has usually received."

As critical as the ideals of producerism are to this book, it is equally concerned with the goals and aspirations of nineteenth-century evangelicals. And while American producer culture is often considered separately from evangelicalism, the two are by no means incompatible, nor were they seen as such in the nineteenth century. Nineteenth-century evangelicals across the board shared traditional Protestant understandings of original sin, need for atonement, justification by faith (realized in a personal experience of the saving grace of Christ), authority of Scripture, and the vital importance of church communities. Individually, evangelical consciousness revolved around ideals of religious significance: divine affirmation, personal character building, some sense of communal responsibilities, intolerance toward any behavior deemed sinful, and an awareness of God's authority in all walks of human life. Collectively, evangelicalism was a dynamic process, integrating personal searches for existential meaningfulness with communal attempts to impose moral order in an open but confusing environment as the early American republic certainly was. As a contemporary member put it, an evangelical was "ardent in his devotions, . . . scrupulous in his conduct" and "tenderly concerned for the salvation of his neighbor."

Undergirding the theological and experiential superstructure, however, was a cosmological foundation: a powerful, often unarticulated sense of how the world was ordered. In short, evangelical cosmology emphasized human limitations, both in activity and understanding—God was God (the Cause of and Reason for all Being) and humankind was not. Traditionally, evangelicals held that the ways of God were at times clearly discernible but never fully comprehensible, though as evangelicals became more Enlightenment-oriented, Arminian, and optimistic in the nineteenth century, that critical distinction became blurred. This broad sense of divine restrictions on human initiative—referred to as the cosmology of limits—included perspectives on economic morality, provided evangelicals with boundaries circumscribing accumulations of wealth and power, and lay at the heart of evangelical producerism. As Joseph Pilmore, one of the first American Methodists, summarized the common-sense doctrine of limits: "How happy would it be with religious Merchants in general, if they knew when they had enough." In Jacksonian America, evangelical producerism provided a potent counterbalance to unregulated capitalist innovation.

This book began in embryonic form ten years ago in a labor history class taught by Professor James Barrett at the University of Illinois. The very fact that I had enrolled in the class was serendipitous if not providential, given that I was studying American Protestant theology in an intellectual and cultural history program, but graduate offerings for Americanists were slim that year. In this class, as a direct result of Jim's teaching excellence and passion, I forgot the New England divines long enough to become captivated by the ongoing struggle of America's workers to make the promise of the nation their own in the face of internal fragmentation, external persecution, and a dominant culture that was often hostile to their concerns. The theoretical and moral implications of this struggle were fascinating, but I quickly realized that the personal dimensions of the topic were equally interesting. As Jim described the artisan culture and workplace environment—the sense of pride and independence as well as inherent conflicts between workers and owners over control and profit—I was constantly reminded of my own experience during the previous nine years when I had worked at a custom cabinetmaking shop. In the men and women with whom I worked, I recognized tremendous creativity, devotion to hard work, and a fierce desire to be left alone in their work. In my boss (who was also a friend), I recognized serious internal conflicts regarding his genuine concern for the welfare of his workers and his (sometimes unwelcome) desire to closely monitor the quantity, quality, and pace of production. In myself and others, I recognized tension related to control issues, even when all involved were trying to be conscious of the interests of those around them. And among our customers, I recognized a tremendous disparity in attitude—some viewed us as inconsequential hired help, existing to satisfy their every whim at the cheapest cost, while others saw us as quality workmen, possessing skills to be respected and paid for accordingly. As my history class explored the lifestyles and ethics of artisan culture, I realized that I had lived some of that experience, making me even more appreciative of the craftspeople with whom I had worked.

As personally exhilarating as the discovery of labor history was for me, however, I soon found myself troubled by two questionable assumptions that seemed to pervade the secondary literature I was reading. The first was a romanticized view of laboring-class culture, in which only proud and politically precocious artisans operated in a prelapsarian environment devoid of incompetence, discomfort, greed, dishonesty, or boredom. Having experienced something of this artisan life myself (albeit in a late-twentieth-century context), I was suspicious of attempts to paint too rosy a picture of artisan labor and lifestyles. I remembered all to well the realities of shop work: sweating through ninety-five-degree temperatures (only minimally relieved by fans), participating in morally ambiguous shopfloor practices, and recalling major mistakes we made. (Once we stained an entire kitchen's worth of cabinets the wrong color and had to build another kitchen for no compensation.)

Such experiences have always kept me cognizant of the down sides of small-scale craft work. In fact, my own personal epiphany—when I decided that I might actually be better suited to a life of mental rather than manual labor—came as I rolled around the filthy floor of a kitchen-under-construction, applying contact cement to formica kickboards and wondering if Excedrin could produce enough aspirin substitute to deal with my headache. (It was years before I learned that Cotton Mather considered such habitual grovelling to be spiritually beneficial—I found it merely dirty and uncomfortable, my disgust only exacerbated by the ubiquitous and potent glue fumes I was constantly inhaling.) Although the satisfactions of custom cabinetmaking jobs well done were certainly significant, the work could also be tedious, difficult, and less than romantic—a reality as true for nineteenth-century artisans as for us.

The other assumption that surprised and then increasingly disturbed me concerned the religious culture of artisans. Social and labor historians used the term "evangelical" as a pejorative gloss on all artisan spirituality, perceiving religious artisans to be the scum, not the salt, of the earth. Evangelicalism itself was portrayed as either an attempt to create a malleable work force enervated by the straitjacket of "Christian submission," or an attempt to create an emotionally emasculated community entranced and distracted by visions of blissed-out transcendence. In either case, the historical picture of evangelicalism as presented in otherwise exemplary labor histories was unremittingly negative. In their interpretations, evangelicalism became the ideological sibling of religious fundamentalism and the psychological parent of all manner of social pathology: sexual repression, political intolerance, self-righteous moralism, and elite domination. Whereas these descriptions are accurate at times for some evangelicals, the subculture they constructed was more complex than is evident from academic caricatures, which really say more about the privileged status of intellectual scepticism in the late twentieth century than they do about artisan life and religion in the early nineteenth. Given the modern academy's barely concealed contempt for any expression of religious commitment, especially Christian, and the popular acceptance of the simplistic "religion is the opiate of the people" reductionism, this should not perhaps have amazed me as much as it did.

This set of assumptions also engaged me personally because for even longer than I had been a cabinetmaker, I had been an active member of an "evangelical" (if one uses the term loosely and recognizes that not all evangelicals are card-carrying members of the Religious Right) congregation trying to come to grips with a broad vision of personal empowerment, character building, democratic inclusion, and social justice within an orthodox Protestant framework. Without overglorifying this collective experience of spiritual struggle, I found these apparently unexamined presumptions regarding alleged religious quietism and inauthenticity at best questionable and at worst downright offensive. Most pressing for me as a budding historian, however, the question remained: was this picture accurate? And so, as a response to that question and in reaction to the set of stereotypes surrounding it, this book has gradually taken shape.

To recover the experiences of evangelical producers has not been an easy task. In the first place, any study of the intellectual histories and interior lives of common Americans is made difficult by the paucity of sources left (or, more accurately, not left) by those with neither the time nor the inclination to leave records of their thoughts and actions. In this light, I have long visualized a possible cartoon of a simple artisan family with all their earthly belongings filling a handcart outside a humble dwelling. As they are leaving whatever comforts their home had provided, the wife says to the husband, "Let's be sure to drop the memoirs off at the historical society on the way out of town." Since such scenarios occur only in overly caffeined imaginations, however, I was forced to seek out other sources. Fortunately, improved printing technologies in the early nineteenth century provided common Americans with unimagined opportunities to share their private, often profound, thoughts publicly, and they gratefully appropriated this potential by publishing handbills, group resolutions, short treatises or books on any subject, and, especially, periodicals and newspapers. These sources, then, proved invaluable in recovering the world of evangelical artisans.

Secondly, difficulties in assessing primary sources for this book were further complicated because of the potentially distinctive trajectories followed by producers and evangelicals—a producer could be a Catholic, a freethinker, or a marginal Protestant, just as an evangelical could be a capitalist, a consumer preoccupied with cheap prices only, or an owner determined to control and exploit his workers. In fact, one of my early concerns was that discovering representative evangelical producers might prove to be impossible. Readers can perhaps imagine my excitement when I recognized that the William Stilwell who had had his hand in every expression of Methodist egalitarian radicalism in the 1820s was the same William Stilwell who had participated in a seminal anticapitalist organization, the New York Society for Promoting Communities, and had helped provide the most thoroughgoing scriptural critique of capitalism in the early national period. Equally exciting was the realization that the John H. W. Hawkins who had agitated for the democratic reform of Methodist organization was the same John Hawkins who had led an important hatters' strike in Baltimore and had later emerged as the preeminent Washingtonian temperance missionary in the country. Similar discoveries convinced me that prevailing assumptions regarding artisan evangelicals and capitalist transformation were critically insufficient.

In the process of exploring the permutations of evangelical producerism, I have enjoyed a great deal of help and encouragement. From the beginning, Jim Barrett has shared advice, encouragement, expertise, and correction. Even more involved, as appropriate, was my adviser, Winton Solberg, whose painstaking supervision and high standards are legendary; not only did he read and reread every word of the dissertation from which this book has grown, he offered constructive criticism that continues to prove indispensable. If I were to thank all those who have supported me both inside and outside the university, this would become a two-volume work, but special thanks are due Walter Arnstein, John F. W. ("Pookie") Beeler (whose unique sense of humor was exceeded only by his precocious aging), Chris Butler, Bob Ubriaco (and all the Angry Wheezers), Steve Vaughan, and Cathy Entner Wright as well as Judson Chubbuck, Vic Fein (my cabinetmaking mentor), Don Kurtz, and Peter and Ashley Goldhor-Wilcock (the latter two also graciously housing me during my research trips to Baltimore). Along the way, others have offered their personal support and historical expertise. Richard Carwardine, Donald Dayton, Nathan Hatch, Mark Noll, Dick Shiels, and John Wigger were particularly supportive in the context of the Conference on Early American Methodism held in October 1994. Ronald Schultz read the entire manuscript, and his suggestions from the perspective of a legitimate labor historian were extremely valuable. Equally appreciated were the comments and suggestions sent me by Nick Salvatore and Bruce Laurie, whose expressed anticipation for the book both encouraged me and scared me witless (the latter being an unintended result, I'm sure). Former students Mark Foley, Seth Kerlin, and Abby Davis Warfel, besides helping to make teaching the most fulfilling calling imaginable, saved me from an inexcusably inaccessible introduction among their other valued contributions, and Casey Smith performed computer miracles to bail me out at a crucial point in the project. During my work in Baltimore, the Reverend Edwin Schell and Betty Ammons made available the wonderful resources of Lovely Lane Methodist Museum, Michael Franch shared with me his voluminous research on Baltimore religious leaders, John McGrain made available his extensive scrapbook on early Baltimore-area factories, and George DuBois provided transcripts of relevant newspaper articles. I would also like to thank Jim Lewis and Jim Wind of the Congregational History Project at the University of Chicago for their financial support through a dissertation fellowship, Judith Pinch of the Charlotte Newcombe Fellowship Foundation for fellowship aid and initiative in presenting the project to various publishers even before it reached final dissertation form, Dick Pierard of the Conference on Faith and History who gave me the opportunity to share a much abbreviated version of this story at the annual meeting in 1995, and, of course, the anonymous reviewers of the Kenneth Scott Latourette Prize Committee who graciously granted this book their prize. Finally, I would like to thank Peter J. Potter of the Penn State Press and

Eliza Childs, whose insightful editorial contributions were exceeded only by their unfailing patience.

As everyone knows, at least theoretically, the completion of a book requires, if I may use the expression, an ungodly amount of time. No people are more aware of this reality than the members of my family. My parents, Bob and Betty Sutton (both historians themselves) and my mother-in-law Ethel Shindle, have my undying gratitude for the moral and financial support they have offered over the years. I thank my children, Ben, Matt, and Zak, for what they have unconsciously but lovingly made accessible over the years—themselves. I never cease to delight in them, and every time I needed a break from the manuscript they were always ready to play ball with me. In very important ways this book really is for them because we want them, as children raised in the context of a faith community, to see that spiritual inspiration and social justice activism are not mutually exclusive. But, of course, my deepest debt is to my wife and friend, Jane, who has never had the slightest personal interest in this project yet has unfailingly supported me throughout the long years taken for its completion. In the nineteen years of our marriage we have made cabinets, built community, canoed rivers, worked on houses, and raised kids together, and this is the only area in which I have worked without her. Because of that, we welcome the end of this project. But I, at least, also hope that it can inspire similar investigations for other historians to pursue.

Introduction

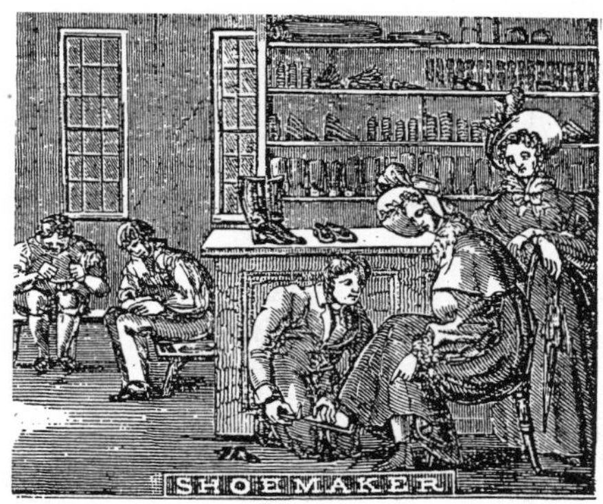

At the end of 1829, an article praising the industrial developments of the previous decade appeared in a Baltimore-area newspaper. The 1820s, according to the anonymous booster, was "not an heroical, devotional, philosophical or moral age, but above all others, the mechanical age." This, of course, was no startling revelation; technological innovation had been transforming the city's productive industries, especially the consumer finishing work carried out by tailors, cordwainers, cabinetmakers, chairmakers, and seamstresses, but by the 1820s the pace of change was clearly increasing. So, too, was the social tension caused by such transformations, and the author of this paean to modernization readily acknowledged that the mechanical age presented mixed blessings: "Our old modes of exertion are all discredited and thrown out," he noted. "On every hand, the living artizan [*sic*] is driven from the workshop, to make room for a speedier, inanimate one." Despite this dramatic shift, which affected the lives of many Americans, optimism prevailed: "We war with rude nature; and by our restless engines, come off always victorious, and loaded with spoils."[1]

This newspaper article illuminates the process of modernization as it was experienced by American artisans in the early nineteenth century. Modern-

1. *Banner of the Constitution,* Dec. 19, 1829, 1:18.

ization of course affected all areas of life. In addition to bringing higher standards of living and opening opportunities, it changed a society previously marked by social and political deference, religious establishment, preindustrial labor relations, and protocapitalist economic exchange. For many, modernization became an unambiguous and inevitable aspect of progress, to be celebrated without question. But this article brings into sharp focus a set of moral conflicts related to issues of power and authority: who was to enjoy the spoils of this mechanical and organizational innovation and what recourse was available to the "living artizan," who was increasingly alienated from skilled work as well as from the spoils and independence it engendered? Evangelical producers—the subjects of this book—formed their often ambivalent response from both preindustrial artisan culture and Protestant moral traditions.

Shared power relations and mutual decision making characterized preindustrial, producerist work processes involving the various members of the artisan community: apprentices, journeymen, and master craftsmen. The legally bound apprentice lived with and learned from his master; upon becoming skilled and mature, he became a free journeyman and received a full set of tools from the master as a rite of passage. The journeyman worked as he could find employment, with the ultimate goal of saving enough to achieve his "competence"—sufficient economic success and craft skill to become a master. But he attained this independence within the camaraderie and context of the larger craft community. Journeymen and apprentices were expected to work diligently and effectively, but masters also had obligations, with all participating in jointly established pay rates, hours, and workshop customs. They were small producers and their collective pride, identity, and craft solidarity were expressed in rituals, parades, and trade organizations.[2]

The small producer tradition, however, was more than just work. It engaged both those journeymen and masters who created quality goods and services through physical labor, mental skill, and shared decision making,

2. Ronald Schultz, "The Small Producer Tradition and the Moral Origins of Artisan Radicalism in Philadelphia, 1720–1810," *Past and Present* 127 (May 1990): 84–108; Christopher Lasch, *The True and Only Heaven: Progress and Its Critics* (New York: W. W. Norton, 1991), 201–24, 265–70, 302–3, 486; Victoria C. Hattam, *Labor Visions and State Power: The Origins of Business Unionism in the United States* (Princeton: Princeton University Press, 1993), 17–18, 76–111, esp. 96–99; Bruce Laurie, *Working People of Philadelphia, 1800–1850* (Philadelphia: Temple University Press, 1980), 168–77; and Tony A. Freyer, *Producers Versus Capitalists: Constitutional Conflict in Antebellum America* (Charlottesville: University Press of Virginia, 1994), 5–11, 39–43.

and their customers who observed certain ethical traditions when purchasing those products. Producerism as a sensibility operating to protect workers' self-respect, economic independence, and community status was not confined to workers; like the republican ideology with which it often coexisted, the maintenance of communal harmony and economic morality were explicit goals shared across class lines. Americans devoted to a preindustrial producerist work regime, then, were the skilled journeymen who made the shoes and built the houses. They were the hard-working small manufacturers who worked alongside journeymen cabinetmakers and provided "outwork" for weavers performing the initial stages of production in their own homes. And they were the appreciative customers who paid "just prices" (reflecting the labor theory of value, or the belief that products have worth based on the labor that has gone into them, not on what the market will bear) for the beaver hats and personal coaches they were purchasing.[3]

Industrialization and conversion to a market economy (what can be termed "industrial capitalist development") threw this producerist operation into turmoil. With machines and division of labor displacing skilled labor, with hourly wages replacing mutually established piece rates, and with employers usurping more authority over shop behavior and pace of work, industrial capitalist development often exacerbated the conflict over control of work and distribution of profits. Although it is true, as Thomas Cochran notes, that the "classic question of whether or nor industrialization benefited the worker . . . is not amenable to a single, comprehensive answer," it is also clear that many artisans found their situations deteriorating.[4] Mechanization and efforts to improve efficiency encouraged the division of labor and the bastardization of craft, with workers beginning to mass-produce parts of clothing, shoes, and chairs as outwork. The reduction of the necessity of craft skills eventuated in the replacement of skilled journeymen with semiskilled machine tenders or laborers locked into repetitive tasks. Further eroding traditional relations was the growing practice of using apprentices as helpers rather than as trainees in skilled operations. In all this, artisans faced a dilemma—should they try to take advantage of industrial innovations and capitalist reorganization, or should they resist the phenomenon of "the living artizan . . . driven from the workshop?"

3. Sean Wilentz, *Chants Democratic: New York City and the Rise of the American Working Class* (New York: Oxford University Press, 1984), 157–58.

4. Thomas C. Cochran, *Frontiers of Change: Early Industrialism in America* (New York: Oxford University Press, 1981), 137; see also Paul Gilje, ed., *Wages of Independence: Capitalism in the Early American Republic* (Madison, Wis.: Madison House, 1997).

The rise of merchant capitalism accompanied transformations in productive processes. The new system shifted the ownership of tools, raw materials, and the workplace itself from the master craftsmen to capitalists whose contribution lay not in any familiarity with production but rather in a surplus of investment wealth. This led to the gradual replacement of mutually established price lists with fluctuating wage rates, resulting in "free labor" being treated not as workers' property but as just another market commodity. Thus, both production and remuneration became impersonal elements of the market economy, the effects of which greatly eroded artisanal independence and status.[5] At the same time, artisans able to capitalize on the opportunities offered by small-scale capitalism became petty proprietors, thereby moving unintentionally but inexorably away from their artisan roots and values.[6] In the process, however, they faced the same compelling moral issue: should they opt for financial success even if it necessitated the expropriation of the labor of others?

By the nineteenth century, evangelicalism was in the midst of a transition similar to that faced by artisans. Between the Arminian assertion that humans retained a spark of divinity despite the Fall, the Scottish Common Sense reliance on natural theology to ward off the religious skepticism engendered by the Enlightenment, and the challenges and possibilities effected by disestablishment, Calvinist evangelicalism was undergoing serious revision. Emerging in its place was a hybrid Protestant theology that deemphasized or rejected predestination in order to assert through Arminianism the innate power of individuals to choose salvation, to strive for moral perfection, and to create a society ready to become the millennial Kingdom of God on earth. At the same time, the Calvinist legacy remained strong, especially in its insistence on punishing individuals whose pursuit of selfish or sinful interests threatened the communal covenant with God. The new

5. Eric Foner "Free Labor and Nineteenth-Century Political Ideology," in Melvyn Stokes and Stephen Conway, eds., *The Market Revolution in America: Social, Political, and Religious Expressions, 1800–1880* (Charlottesville: University of Virginia Press, 1996), 99–127.

6. Raphael Samuel, "Workshop of the World: Steam Power and Hand Technology in Mid-Victorian Britain," *History Workshop* 3 (spring 1977): 7–13; Wilentz, *Chants Democratic*, 17, 27–33; idem, "The Rise of the American Working Class, 1776–1877," in J. Carroll Moody and Alice Kessler-Harris, eds., *Perspectives on American Labor History: The Problems of Synthesis* (DeKalb: Northern Illinois University Press, 1989), 85–109; Bruce Laurie, *Artisans into Workers: Labor in Nineteenth-Century America* (New York: Noonday Press, 1989), 15–16, 35–36; David M. Gordon, Richard Edwards, and Michael Reich, *Segmented Work, Divided Workers: The Historical Transformation of Labor in the United States* (Cambridge: Cambridge University Press, 1982), 18–20, 64–67; Billy G. Smith, *The Lower Sort: Philadelphia's Laboring People, 1750–1800* (Ithaca: Cornell University Press, 1990), 200.

evangelicalism provided empowering self-discipline for individuals and sanctions for maintaining moral communities, but it exhibited profound ambivalence toward matters of economic morality.[7]

The colonial Puritans had incorporated medieval Catholic practices into what can be called traditional economic morality. Part of this sensibility, reflecting the cosmology of limits, condemned the sinfulness of individuals who had made faith in and dependence on God's provision irrelevant through their accumulations of wealth and power. But there was more to the tradition than a simple antiwealth message. Traditional economic morality promoted the ideal of the just price, condemned usury and dishonest trade practices, and recognized the immorality of profiting from another's ignorance, distress, or powerlessness.[8] As one evangelical put it, "All that course of stratagem . . . which aims to conceal the truth from men by taking advantage of their ignorance, their passions, or their fears, has in it the essence of lying, and ought to be discouraged among all peoples as having a pernicious influence upon the best interests of society."[9] This perspective identified vices that violated both community-oriented and masculinist ideals of self-denial deemed essential to preserve justice and order. Such sins included exploiting workers in order to afford luxuries, embracing economic individualism in order to enjoy unlimited mobility, and avoiding productive labor in favor of indulging amusements or idleness. And those evading the biblical order to earn one's keep by the sweat of one's brow were considered effeminate as well.[10]

7. Mark Valeri, *Law and Providence in Joseph Bellamy's New England: The Origins of the New Divinity in Revolutionary America* (New York: Oxford University Press, 1994), 77–82, 88–93; Randolph A. Roth, *The Democratic Dilemma: Religion, Reform, and the Social Order in the Connecticut River Valley of Vermont, 1791–1850* (Cambridge: Cambridge University Press, 1987), 6.

8. John E. Crowley, *This Sheba, Self: The Conceptualization of Economic Life in Eighteenth-Century America* (Baltimore: Johns Hopkins University Press, 1974), 17–20, 51–62; Jonathan A. Glickstein, *Concepts of Free Labor in Antebellum America* (New Haven: Yale University Press, 1991), 315n16; Jesper Rosenmeier, "John Cotton on Usury," *William and Mary Quarterly*, 3d series, 47 (Oct. 1990): 548–65; Morton J. Horwitz, *The Transformation of American Law*, 1780–1860 (Cambridge: Harvard University Press, 1977), 237–45. For articulation of the cosmology of limits, see Lasch, *True and Only Heaven*, 17; and Philip Scranton, *Proprietary Capitalism: The Textile Manufacture of Philadelphia, 1800–1885* (New York: Cambridge University Press, 1983), 69.

9. *Mutual Rights* 3 (Aug. 1827) cited in D. S. Stephens, comp., *Defense of the Views of the Reformers* (Indianapolis, 1884), no. 2, 12.

10. Richard Rabinowitz, *The Spiritual Self in Everyday Life: The Transformation of Personal Religious Experience in Nineteenth-Century New England* (Boston: Northeastern University Press, 1989), 224–29; Crowley, *This Sheba, Self*, 76, 96–105; Joyce Appleby, *Capitalism and a New Social Order: The Republican Vision of the 1790s* (New York: New York University Press, 1984), 8; and Steven Watts, *The Republic Reborn: War and the Making of Liberal America, 1790–1820* (Baltimore: Johns Hopkins University Press, 1987), 70–86.

Continued evangelical acceptance of traditional economic morality (and the producerism it supported) faced three serious challenges in the era of the market revolution. In the first place, evangelicals were beginning to embrace, through natural theology, the Enlightenment notion that God had created a universe run by natural laws, established for humans to investigate, understand, and learn to manipulate.[11] The purpose here, according to the evangelical theologians, was to generate awe and worship of a creator so generous with children. But God's laws, natural as well as moral, were not to be trifled with. In a bit of a stretch, evangelical philosophers began to equate scientific laws (e.g., the law of supply and demand) with scriptural injunctions. Thus, market practices, even those that contradicted traditional understandings of economic morality, could be sanctified by those with a mind to do so. At the same time, many evangelicals developed an entrepreneurial spirit and a high level of comfort with the emerging market culture and its ways of gaining wealth.[12] In fact, disestablishment almost mandated such attitudes, as Protestant denominations competed with each other for the allegiance of potential converts, and as Protestant congregations came to depend, under the doctrine of stewardship, on the largesse of its more prosperous members. Finally, evangelicalism insisted on self-discipline and promoted an appreciation for deferred gratification. For evangelicals, these were quintessentially spiritual values, part of their dynamic relationship with God. But they also proved to be highly effective survival skills in a culture divesting itself of traditional restrictions. Although these values were undeniably compatible to the new "industrial morality," the initial connection was an unintended result, not a self-conscious preoccupation.[13]

11. Although the focus here is somewhat narrow, this intellectual transition had implications ranging far beyond economic ethics. Whereas older traditions had emphasized knowing God through the paradox and mystery of internal spiritual experience and external "providences," natural theology insisted that the character and nature of God be apprehended through the proofs of divine wisdom, power, and benevolence clearly evident in his material and moral order. Although natural theology proved helpful in reconciling Christianity and the Enlightenment, its peculiar insistence on the scientific proof of Christian revelation opened a Pandora's box. James Turner, *Without God, Without Creed: The Origins of Unbelief in America* (Baltimore: Johns Hopkins University Press, 1985); Mark Noll, "Common Sense Traditions and American Evangelical Thought," *American Quarterly* 37 (summer 1985): 216–38; William R. Sutton, "Benevolent Calvinism and the Moral Government of God: The Influence of Nathaniel William Taylor on Revivalism in the Second Great Awakening," *Religion and American Culture* 2 (Feb. 1992): 23–47.

12. Richard Carwardine, "'Antinomians' and 'Arminians': Methodists and the Market Revolution," in Stokes and Conway, eds., *Market Revolution*, 282–307.

13. Paul G. Faler, "Cultural Aspects of the Industrial Revolution," *Labor History* 15 (summer 1974): 367–94. For alternative interpretations, describing worker willingness to adopt aspects

But this was a very contested process, especially for those described by Nathan Hatch as "populist evangelicals."[14]

Populist evangelicals, according to Hatch, were the common Protestants who shared a disdain for clerical domination, for hierarchical and deferential social ordering, for restrictions on individual interpretation of Scripture or spiritual exercises, and for any sense of second-class citizenship. Whereas artisans gained identities from their labor skills, evangelicals gained theirs from a personal conviction of divine affirmation, often through an empowering conversion experience, but the two identities were by no means mutually exclusive. Thus evangelical commitment could easily (and often did) coexist with producerist sensibilities. The operative variables were real-life experience, socioeconomic circumstances, and religious standards. Evangelical producerism flourished in situations where socioeconomic dislocation was obvious and faith commitments to traditional tenets of Christian social justice were strong. Its significance in the artisan culture of the early nineteenth century cannot be overemphasized.

The argument offered here is that the small producer tradition maintained a critique of the "ambition, jealousy, cupidity, and the blind love of innovation" that accompanied unchecked capitalist development.[15] Furthermore, a core element of that producerist opposition was provided by populist evangelicals who continued to maintain the tenets of traditional economic morality. This should not be surprising; in ecclesiastical matters, these same people had overthrown the religious domination enjoyed by clerical elites, and in political matters, they had eagerly embraced democratic participation. Both populist evangelicals and artisan producers were active agents in shaping American culture by demonstrating their unwillingness to submit to any illegitimate authority and by defining the moral limitations to be placed on industrial capitalist transformation.[16] In the

---

of "industrial morality" as survival skills and means of upward mobility, see Charles Stephenson, "'There's Plenty Waitin' at the Gates': Mobility, Opportunity, and the American Worker," in Charles Stephenson and Robert Asher, eds., *Life and Labor: Dimensions of American Working-Class History* (Albany: State University of New York Press, 1986), 72–91; and Richard Stott, "Artisans and Capitalist Development," *Journal of the Early Republic* 16 (summer 1996), 257–71.

14. Nathan Hatch, *The Democratization of American Christianity* (New Haven: Yale University Press, 1989).

15. The descriptions were those of producerist leader Joseph McConnell during a Philadelphia-area strike in 1842, quoted in Anthony F. C. Wallace, *Rockdale: The Growth of an American Village in the Industrial Revolution* (New York: Alfred A. Knopf, 1978), 369. For similar sentiments, see *Methodist Magazine and Quarterly Review* 16, n.s., no. 5 (Oct. 1834): 454.

16. David Grimsted has traced "the cross-class acceptance of democratic-religious values" that inspired much of the violent opposition to capitalist dislocation in the nineteenth century.

circumstances of evangelical producerism, religious and occupational activism could flow together in a powerful expression of counterhegemony. Yet because both artisans and evangelicals also had access to the material fruits and occupational opportunities of the emergent capitalist culture, their opposition was rarely marked by the furious focus of, say, Luddite radicals. Indeed, many were grateful to be able to buy previously unavailable or unaffordable goods and were pleased to work as factory hands, clerks, or managers.[17] Neither militant revolutionaries nor meek accommodationists, evangelical artisans offered power and consolation to a wide range of Americans through democratized denominations, vigorous trade union organizations, and a plethora of self-help alternatives. In these efforts, they provided an oppositional language and legacy to challenge the rising hegemony of laissez-faire economics and industrial capitalism.

In this book, I use the Jacksonian label as a convenient categorization for the era from the mid-1820s to the early 1840s that promised expanded social, political, and economic opportunity for free Americans, especially white males. The age of Jackson witnessed the market revolution, political democratization, and the series of Protestant revivals known as the Second Great Awakening. This activity indicated that as the Revolution grew more distant, Americans were willing to relax socioeconomic limits and to challenge power structures. But of course new centers of power were quick to emerge, and those comfortable with the market enjoyed clear access to them. Workers had to face industrial capitalism at its most basic level, and their critiques of capitalist transformation set precedents for generations of American workers to follow. To understand the ongoing struggle between capitalist culture in America and the workers who sought to find a place within it, one must understand the early antecedents that, I believe, became obvious on a large scale for the first time in the Jacksonian years. This resistance and negotiation occurred in the context of the ever-malleable set of beliefs and attitudes known as liberal republicanism.[18]

David Grimsted, "Ante-bellum Labor: Violence, Strike, and Communal Arbitration," *Journal of Social History* 18 (fall 1985): 5–28, quote from 17.

17. Gary J. Kornblith, "The Artisanal Response to Capitalist Transformation," *Journal of the Early Republic* 10 (fall 1990): 315–21; Carol N. Toner, *Persisting Traditions: Artisan Work and Culture in Bangor, Maine, 1828–1860* (New York: Garland Press, 1995); Freyer, *Producers Versus Capitalists*, 8.

18. "Republicanism in the United States evolved as a *bifurcated* ideology that had a fairly clear political side and a very murky economic component." Stephen J. Ross, "The Transformation of Republican Ideology," *Journal of the Early Republic* 10 (fall 1990): 326, his emphasis.

The very conceptualization of "liberal republicanism" might seem oxymoronic for this book. As Stephen Ross has argued, "what separated liberals from republicans was their attitudes toward the *limits* of acquisitiveness and unfettered individualism."[19] This distinction was near to the hearts of producers, but it tended to become blurred in their real-life existences. To be sure, "liberal" in the nineteenth-century vernacular referred to the removal of "unnatural" restrictions to free individuals in all areas of human activity. But the anarchic potential of liberalism was offset by the sober demands of "republicanism," which insisted that the well-being of the whole was more important than individual aggrandizement. Thus liberal republicanism mandated the maintenance of a precarious balance between the pursuit of self-interest and the protection of community welfare. Americans recognized that achieving such a balance was difficult, but they lived in a hopeful age, and they would have argued that the rampant individualism and materialism that came to characterize American society in the twentieth century was neither enviable nor inevitable.

Because the pace at which industrial capitalism transformed America was uneven across the country, one can see the experience of Baltimore as both typical and distinctive.[20] Like Philadelphia and New York but more slowly, Baltimore was moving into a period of rapid industrial growth following the War of 1812 and the panic of 1819. There were indications, however, that this transition was less than smooth. As Samuel G. Smith (a New Englander hired in 1831 to make profitable the Warren Factory just outside Baltimore) complained to his wife, "The people in this part of the country are ignorant of the management of a factory, the duty of an agent, etc., etc. . . . There never has been a manufacturing company here but has lost money."[21]

An important debate between Lance Banning and Joyce Appleby contrasts the classical republican tradition to the liberal one. Lance Banning, "Jeffersonian Ideology Revisited: Liberal and Classical Ideas in the New American Republic" and Joyce Appleby, "Republicanism in Old and New Contexts," *William and Mary Quarterly*, 3d ser., 43 (Jan. 1986): 3–34, esp. 23–25.

19. Ross, "Transformation of Republican Ideology," 328, his emphasis; Lasch, *True and Only Heaven*, 22–24.

20. Robert Gray, "The Languages of Factory Reform," in Patrick Joyce, ed., *The Historical Meanings of Work* (Cambridge: Cambridge University Press, 1987), 143. The best monograph treatments of early Baltimore are Charles Steffen, *The Mechanics of Baltimore: Workers and Politics in the Age of Revolution, 1763–1812* (Urbana: University of Illinois Press, 1984), and Gary L. Browne, *Baltimore in the Nation, 1789–1861* (Chapel Hill: University of North Carolina Press, 1980).

21. Samuel G. Smith, letter to his wife, Mar. 13, 1831, in Warren Factory Papers, MS #2308, Maryland Historical Society, Baltimore; Steffen, *Mechanics of Baltimore*, 4–6.

Baltimore. Wards, districts, and approximate location of other significant sites, 1830–1845

1. Original terminal, B & O Railroad
2. Columbia Street Methodist Episcopal Church
3. Howland-Woolen steam-planing mill
4. Chase's Tavern (founding place of Washington Temperance Society)
5. Charles Street Methodist Episcopal Church
6. George Quail hat manufactory
7. Thomas Sappington hat factory
8. Battle Monument (site of Reverdy Johnson's mansion and the court house)
9. Baltimore *Republican*
10. Trades' Union Hall
11. Bank of Maryland
12. Washington Temperance Society Hall
13. Jacob Daley's bazaar
14. Pitt Street Methodist Protestant Church (meetingplace of seamstresses union)
15. Seamen's Bethel

Baltimore's cultural homogeneity was also a factor. Populated largely by citizens of German and British stock, with a sizable community of African-Americans, both slave and free, Jacksonian Baltimore retained a sense of preindustrial solidarity and corporatist ethics not yet fragmented by immigration and the industrial relocations of the 1840s. The result was a city in only the initial stages of modernization, with cultural adjustments proving to be as problematic as economic ones.

The arrival of capitalist culture was not the only story of historical interest in Jacksonian Baltimore. The city was also a center of populist evangelical activity and, among the urban centers, the undisputed heart of American Methodism. Numerically, the Methodists were the most explosive of the evangelical sects in America and processed the negotiation of economic morality carefully. Between 1770 and 1830, American Methodism had grown from an inconsequential group of one thousand members to a powerful cultural force of nearly half a million.[22] A secular newspaper in 1834 reported that one in every twelve Baltimoreans was a member of a Methodist congregation,[23] with adherence rate estimated at twice that figure (because the strictness of Methodist discipline kept some from achieving full "connection"), making Baltimore Methodists significantly more numerous than Methodists living in other large cities. Congregational ratios were equally significant—in 1830, roughly 6 percent of all Boston congregations were Methodist, 12 percent in New York, 13 percent in Philadelphia, but fully 25 percent in Baltimore.[24]

22. John H. Wigger, "Taking Heaven by Storm: Methodism and the Popularization of American Christianity, 1770–1820" (Ph.D. diss., University of Notre Dame, 1994), 1–3. Wigger provides a wealth of material on the growth and experience of the early Methodists in the United States. Equally impressive was Methodist growth vis-à-vis other Protestant denominations; on the eve of the Revolution, Methodists accounted for 2 percent of church membership in America, but by 1850 their share was 34 percent. Roger Finke and Rodney Stark, "How the Upstart Sects Won America: 1776–1850," *Journal for the Scientific Study of Religion* 28 (1989): 27–44. For religion in Baltimore before and after the Jacksonian era, see Terry D. Bilhartz, *Urban Religion and the Second Great Awakening: Church and Society in Early National Baltimore* (Rutherford, N.J.: Fairleigh Dickinson University Press, 1986), and Michael S. Franch, "Congregation and Community in Baltimore, 1840–1860" (Ph.D diss., University of Maryland, 1984).

23. Other statistics for Methodist membership in proportion to the general population for 1834: in Boston, 1 in 71; in New York, 1 in 44; and in Philadelphia, 1 in 30. *Baltimore American*, Feb. 4, 1834.

24. For the high adherence rates, particularly among skilled artisans and small proprietors, see Bilhartz, *Urban Religion*, 19–27. The figures on congregational percentages are based on reports in *Mutual Rights and Methodist Protestant* 1 (Jan. 21, 1831): 2; 1 (Feb. 4, 1831): 37; 1 (Feb. 17, 1831): 45; Franch, "Congregation and Community," 113. The problems with

As significant as the rise of American Methodism was, however, the movement defies easy generalizations. Theologically, Methodists sublimated doctrine to experience while insisting on a strict code of personal behavior to foster character building. Methodists also celebrated emotional release and direct access to divine empowerment while maintaining the necessity of submitting to legitimate authority. Finally, Methodists epitomized populist challenges to traditions of deference while supporting hierarchical organization.[25] In a similar paradox, Methodists straddled economic modernization. Emphasizing self-discipline in all areas of life, they heeded the call of their founder John Wesley to earn all they could in order to give all they could; as a result, Methodists could and did excel in a wide-open economic environment. Yet they also remained hypersensitive to the inherent immorality of unequal and exploitative power relations, especially obvious in certain capitalist practices. And, since Methodism pervaded Baltimore society and its artisan communities, Baltimore is a logical choice for recovering the legacies of evangelical producerism.

Although succeeding chapters describe events involving a significant portion of the Baltimore populace, this book is not a complete history of Jacksonian Baltimore. The research concentrates on the experience of

estimating the extent of religious adherence and its concomitant level of influence in Jacksonian America are well known; nevertheless, the historiographical assumption has been that, for artisans, evangelical influence was negligible. Laurie, *Artisans into Workers*, 212; Wilentz, *Chants Democratic*, 227. The most exhaustive recent efforts regarding American religious adherence, however, suggest that since colonial times from 35 to 40 percent of the population have regularly attended, with official membership perhaps one-third that level. The greatest increase in membership and congregational establishments occurred in the first four decades of the nineteenth century, largely as a result of evangelical revival efforts. E. Brooks Holifield, "Toward a History of American Congregations," in James P. Wind and James W. Lewis, eds. *American Congregations*, 2 vols. (Chicago: University of Chicago Press, 1994), 2:24, 33–34. See also Roger Finke and Roger Stark, *The Churching of America, 1776–1990: Winners and Losers in Our Religious Economy* (New Brunswick: Rutgers University Press, 1992).

25. As Paul Bassett notes, in describing the relative importances of experience and doctrine for American Methodists, "The theological authority of the Bible follows from its sufficiency for salvation. . . . More specifically, it is the love of God for us to which the Spirit witnesses, and scripture is authoritative because it alone calls us (the Spirit speaking through it) to that love, guides us into it, and instructs us in how we should love." Paul M. Bassett, "The Theological Identity of the North American Holiness Movement: Its Understanding of the Nature and Role of the Bible," in Donald W. Dayton and Robert K. Johnston, eds., *The Variety of American Evangelicalism* (Knoxville: University of Tennessee Press, 1991), 78–79. See also Paul K. Conkin, *The Uneasy Center: Reformed Christianity in Antebellum America* (Chapel Hill: University of North Carolina Press, 1995), 63–89; Russell E. Richey, *Early American Methodism* (Bloomington: Indiana University Press, 1991); and Richard Carwardine, "The Second Great Awakening in the Urban Centers: An Examination of Methodism and the 'New Measures,'" *Journal of American History* 59 (1972): 331–33.

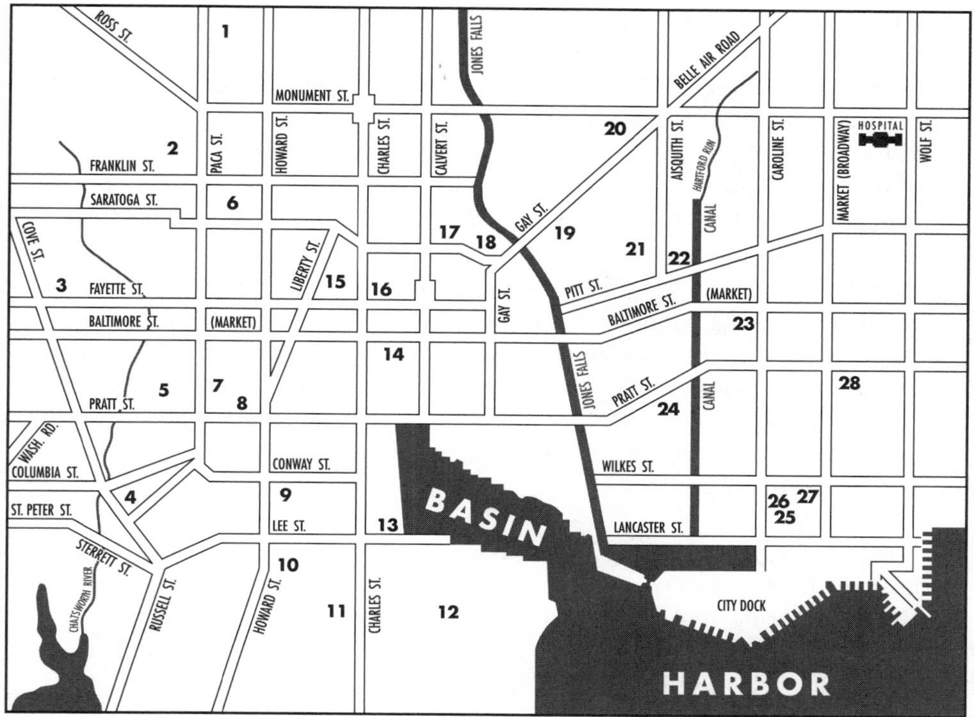

Baltimore's Methodist churches, 1840s (white Methodist Episcopal unless otherwise noted). Map prepared with the help of the Rev. Edwin Schell of the United Methodist Historical Society at Lovely Lane, and Tom Bassett, University of Illinois.

1. Strawbridge
2. Orchard Street (M. E. colored)
3. Fayette Street
4. Columbia Street
5. West Baltimore (Methodist Protestant)
6. Eutaw Street
7. McKendrean Chapel
8. Sharp Street (M. E. colored)
9. Wesley Chapel
10. John Wesley
11. Ebenezer (African Methodist Episcopal)
12. William Street
13. Sailor's Bethel (Methodist-supported)
14. Light Street
15. St. John's (Methodist Protestant)
16. Charles Street
17. "African meeting," North and Saratoga streets (M. E. colored)
18. Bethel (African Methodist Episcopal)
19. Exeter Street
20. Monument Street
21. Asbury Chapel (M. E. colored)
22. Pitt Street (Methodist Protestant)
23. Caroline Street
24. High Street
25. Seamen's Bethel (Methodist-supported)
26. Strawberry Alley (M. E. colored)
27. Wilkes Street
28. Broadway

artisans and small masters, but this is neither the history of technological innovation nor of the Baltimore working class (if such an entity can be said to exist in the fluid social relations of the early republic). Although the work is driven by considerations of the beliefs and practices of one strata of evangelical society, this is not a comprehensive denominational nor a theological study. In addition, although African-Americans and women workers have certainly played key roles in Baltimore labor relations, the dearth of appropriate sources for this early period mandates that this study largely misses their contributions. Instead, this work describes the persistence and evolution of a residual and oppositional subculture (evangelical producerism) and populist religious language (the traditional Protestant economic morality of producerism) as both operated within an increasing dominant liberal culture. In this sense, it is the intellectual history of a set of popular religious and ethical propositions shared by a significant number of Americans in or sympathetic to the producing classes.

The historiography of evangelical artisans in industrializing milieus has been, at best, uneven. Only sporadically have historians recognized that, as Eileen Yeo noted, evangelical Christianity was not limited to any one social group but that its responses to industrialism lay in "contested territory."[26] Dominated by a generally pejorative interpretation presented by labor historians and until recently left unchallenged by religious and other historians,[27] an "orthodox" historiography of artisan evangelicalism has emerged (most clearly obvious

26. Eileen Yeo, "Christianity in Chartist Struggle, 1838–1842," *Past and Present* 91 (May 1981): 109. For an extended discussion of this historiography, see William R. Sutton, "To Grind the Faces of the Poor: Journeymen for Jesus in Jacksonian Baltimore" (Ph.D. diss., University of Illinois, 1993), 50–70, and idem, "Tied to the Whipping Post: New Labor History and Evangelical Artisans in the Early Republic," *Labor History* 36 (spring 1995): 251–65.

27. Recent exceptions include Jama Lazerow, "A Good Time Coming: Religion and the Emergence of Labor Activism in Antebellum New England" (Ph.D. diss., Brandeis University, 1982); idem, "Religion and Labor Reform in Antebellum America: The World of William Field Young," *American Quarterly* 38 (summer 1986): 265–86; idem, "Religion and the New England Mill Girl," *New England Quarterly* 60 (Sept. 1987): 429–53; idem, "Spokesmen for the Working Class: Protestant Clergy and the Labor Movement in Antebellum New England," *Journal of the Early Republic* 13 (fall 1993): 323–54; idem, *Religion and the Working Class in Antebellum America* (Washington: Smithsonian Institution Press, 1995); Teresa A. Murphy, *Ten Hours' Labor: Religion, Reform, and Gender in Early New England* (Ithaca: Cornell University Press, 1992); Ronald Schultz, "God and Workingmen: Popular Religion and the Formation of Philadelphia's Working Class, 1790–1830," in Ronald Hoffman and Peter J. Albert, eds., *Religion in a Revolutionary Age* (Charlottesville: University of Virginia Press, 1993), 125–55. See also Herbert Gutman's inexplicably ignored recognition of evangelical contributions to labor activism in the late nineteenth century. Herbert G. Gutman, "Protestantism and the American

in the works of Bruce Laurie, Sean Wilentz, and Paul Johnson),[28] presenting evangelical contributions to changing capitalist social relations as either a top down expression of elite manipulation and control of artisans or as a bottom up manifestation of collective lobotomization of those same artisans. This view has reduced evangelical artisans to a quivering mass of obsequious quietists, has failed to grant agency to the historical actors involved, has underappreciated the contemporary perspectives of a broad producerist class, has ignored the possibility of evangelical opposition to the emerging system, and, according to Nathan Hatch, has foreclosed "the broad range of questions about popular Christianity in the early republic."[29]

Similar problems occur in historiographical attempts to fit evangelical artisans into discussions of class, possibly because the class dynamics of evangelical artisan experience often transcend convenient boundaries. Evangelicalism, following Paul Johnson, has been delimited as "a middle-class solution to problems of class, legitimacy, and order generated in the early stages of manufacturing," with laboring-class or producerist evangelicalism by definition oxymoronic. Since much of the early work on American labor stressed the Marxian preoccupation with the formation of an identifiable working class and the emergence of a distinctive working-class consciousness

---

Labor Movement: The Christian Spirit in the Gilded Age," *American Historical Review* 72 (Oct. 1966): 74–101.

28. This triumvirate, including Paul E. Johnson, *A Shopkeeper's Millenniun: Society and Revivals in Rochester, New York, 1815–1837* (New York: Hill and Wang, 1978), has been identified by Ken Fones-Wolf in his review of Teresa Murphy's *Ten Hours Labor* in *Labor History* 34 (winter 1993): 138. For the reliance of these three authors on the work of the others, see Wilentz, *Chants Democratic*, 429; idem, "Artisan Origins of the American Working Class," *International Labor and Working Class History*, no. 19 (spring 1981): 14, 17; Laurie, *Working People of Philadelphia*, 216; and Paul E. Johnson and Sean Wilentz, *The Kingdom of Matthias: A Story of Sex and Salvation in 19th-Century America* (New York: Oxford University Press, 1994).

29. Hatch, *Democratization of Christianity*, 225. As an example of this historiography, Bruce Laurie pictures artisan "revivalists" as thoroughly feminized, sitting "in nervous expectation" in the company of their wives and daughters, and "breaking down into tears or flailing their arms about in fits of uncontrolled emotion" under the "intimidating" onslaught of the "evangelist's fiery words." Laurie, *Working People of Philadelphia*, 33–34. Laurie's subsequent treatment of "radical revivalists," emerging in the 1840s in Philadelphia is more balanced. George Marsden has placed this tendency into historical perspective in his essay, "The Soul of the American University: A Historical Overview," in Marsden and Bradley J. Longfield, eds., *The Secularization of the Academy* (New York: Oxford University Press, 1992), 9–45. As Christopher Lasch noted in his lecture "The Soul of Man Under Secularism," presented at the Jewish Theological Seminary, Apr. 1991, "Religion is consistently treated as a source of intellectual and emotional security, not as a challenge to complacency and pride." Quoted by Peter Steinfels, "Beliefs: A Social Critic Rejects the Modernists' Relegation of Religion to the Childhood of Humanity," *New York Times*, Apr. 27, 1991.

(as opposed to the broader producerist or laboring-class sensibilities), the familiar Marxian animus toward religious influence seemed automatic. Evangelicalism, as an ambiguous phenomenon operating across class lines, was eliminated as a factor with countervailing potential; instead, it was seen simply as an inhibiting factor in the development of authentic class consciousness and labor militancy. Despite noteworthy attempts in recent years to disassociate themselves from such theoretical constraints, labor historians still seem locked into Marxian presuppositions toward the allegedly opiative influence of evangelical religion and its appeal, seeing it as limited to those of middle-class privilege.[30]

Increasingly, these assumptions are being called into question; no less an authority than E. P. Thompson recently challenged the tendency to make class a unitary and authoritative interpretive construct.[31] Particularly problematic is the insistent but elusive search for a nineteenth-century working-class consciousness. Despite the valiant efforts of Sean Wilentz and others, it is anachronistic to speak of a recognizable working class in the Jacksonian period. In this light, David Grimsted presents a wide-ranging critique of "the search for a separatist working-class culture" throughout the nineteenth century. Similarly, Nick Salvatore has taken exception to Wilentz's formulations of class formation by citing "the very real ambiguity at the core of the nineteenth century working-class experience," in which artisans could share in the prevailing ideological consensus without precluding the possibilities of genuine conflict related to which elements of the common republican ideology would predominate. Salvatore's hypothesis of "conflict-within-consensus" best describes the experience of artisans in Baltimore in the 1830s.[32] Their perceptions were those of threatened producers rather than incipient prole-

30. Johnson, *Shopkeeper's Millennium*, 138; Sutton, "Tied to the Whipping Post," 261–64. For related critiques, see Lazerow, "Spokesmen for the Working Class," 325.

31. "'Class' was perhaps overworked in the 1960s and 1970s, and it has become merely boring. It is a concept long past its sell-by date." E. P. Thompson, "The Making of a Ruling Class," *Dissent* 40 (summer 1993): 380. I am grateful to Nick Salvatore for alerting me to this reference.

32. Grimsted, "Ante-bellum Labor," 17; Nick Salvatore, "Response to Sean Wilentz, 'Against Exceptionalism': Class Consciousness and the American Labor Movement, 1790–1920," *International Labor and Working Class History*, no. 26 (fall 1984): 30. Helpful here is Victoria Hattam's insistence on "historicizing the concept of class" by realizing that "different conceptions of class were at once a product of both the changing economic conditions and the interpretive frames individuals and organizations brought to those changes." Hattam, *Labor Visions*, 204–8, 88. For an interpretation taking Wilentz's side in the discussion but emphasizing the role of religion in the creation of an American working-class consciousness, see Lazerow, *Religion and the Working Class in Antebellum America*, 11 and 232n52.

tarians; since the transition from journeyman to small proprietor was very fluid, shopkeepers, artisans, and sympathetic professional and commercial interests could easily unite to oppose perceived immorality in the excesses of industrial capitalist development.

The suspicions of capitalist transformation, then, occurred within the parameters of a producerist consciousness not confined to artisans and resonant with other elements within the "middling classes."[33] Similarly, early national evangelicals also described themselves as occupying an amorphous middle ground, but that perception had little to do with the market nexus. Rather, evangelicals constructed a social spectrum that rejected, on the one end, the indolence and immorality of the rough elements within the laboring classes and, on the other end, the wastefulness and worldliness of the aristocratic class. Considering themselves a respectable middle group, evangelicals condemned the rowdy as spiritually deficient and the elite as spiritually comatose, but they welcomed the hard working, disciplined, and "deserving" across Marxian class lines. As Charles Sellers points out, "The so-called middle class was constituted not by mode and relations of production, but by ideology. . . . Scorning the handful of idle rich and the multitude of dissolute poor, they apotheosized a virtuous middle class of the effortful."[34] Such a middle class could and did cast a suspicious eye on the entire process of embourgeoisment and could as easily manifest producerist allegiances as capitalist ties. Simply put, producerist interests do not lend themselves easily to orthodox class characterizations. Thus, a more nuanced discussion of class as it operated for evangelical artisans and others in the nineteenth century is appropriate, not only because their experiences deserve to be taken seriously on their own merits but also, as E. P. Thompson so eloquently put it, because their insights may help illuminate "social evils which we have yet to cure."[35]

33. Stuart M. Blumin, *The Emergence of the Middle Class: Social Experience in the City, 1760–1900* (Cambridge: Cambridge University Press, 1990), 2–12; Bruce Laurie, "Spavined Ministrers, Lying Toothpullers, and Buggering Priests: Third-Partyism and the Search for Security in the Antebellum North," in Howard B. Rock, Paul A. Gilje, and Robert Asher, eds., *American Artisans: Crafting Social Identity, 1750–1850* (Baltimore: Johns Hopkins University Press, 1995), 99–100.

34. Charles Sellers, *The Market Revolution: Jacksonian America, 1815–1846* (New York: Oxford University Press, 1991), 237. See also Thomas W. Laqueur, *Religion and Respectability: Sunday Schools and Working Class Culture, 1780–1850* (New Haven: Yale University Press, 1976); Michael Zweig, *Religion and Economic Justice* (Philadelphia: Temple University Press, 1991), 29; and Rhys Isaac, *The Transformation of Virginia, 1740–1790* (Chapel Hill: University of North Carolina Press, 1982), 172–77, 321–22.

35. Edward P. Thompson, *The Making of the English Working Class* (New York: Vintage Books, 1966, first published 1963), 13. For an attempt to explore those insights in the late

If the recovery of the contributions of artisan evangelicalism has languished due to the prejudgments of labor history, it has also suffered from the inability or unwillingness of religious historians to recognize class tensions and contradictory cultural impulses within the Second Great Awakening. Until recently, American religious historians have concentrated on following the triumphal progress from sect to church in denominational histories, on celebrating evangelical contributions to a distinctively vibrant antebellum culture(s),[36] and tracing doctrinal developments, often separated from their social contexts. Such "consensus" history failed to take seriously the categories of race and gender,[37] nor did it recognize the existence of evangelical critiques of liberal republicanism, industrial capitalism, and bourgeois attitudes, and as a result it has obscured the contested nature of early national Protestantism, especially among evangelical artisans. The efforts of Nathan Hatch, Laurence Moore, Jon Butler, and Mark Hanley to reverse that trend have reopened many questions.[38] Thus the well-documented emergence of the bourgeois strain of evangelicalism in the mid-nineteenth

---

nineteenth century, see Robert Craig, "The Underside of History: American Methodism, Capitalism and Popular Struggle," *Methodist History* 24 (Jan. 1989): 73–88.

36. James D. Bratt, "Religious Alienation and American Culture," *Evangelical Studies Bulletin* 3 (Oct. 1986): 1. An important exception remains Donald W. Dayton, *Discovering an Evangelical Heritage* (New York: Harper and Row, 1976).

37. This is, of course, no longer the case, as the evangelical influence on the creation of African-American culture has created significant debate. Orlando Patterson, *Slavery and Social Death: A Comparative Study* (Cambridge: Harvard University Press, 1982); Olli Alho, *The Religion of the Slaves: A Study of the Religious Tradition and Behaviour of Plantation Slaves in the United States 1830–1865* (Helsinki: Suomalainen Tiedeakatemia Academia Scientiarum Fennica, 1976); Albert Raboteau, *Slave Religion: The "Invisible Institution" in the Antebellum South* (New York: Oxford University Press, 1978); Theophus H. Smith, *Conjuring Culture: Biblical Formations of Black America* (New York: Oxford University Press, 1994); Eugene D. Genovese, *Roll, Jordan, Roll: The World the Slaves Made* (New York: Pantheon, 1974). Similarly, evangelical experience was mediated by gender in terms of the nature of conversion as well as in subsequent activity. Although disparate patterns are discernible, it remains important to recognize the ambivalent, almost androgynous nature of gender-ordered evangelicalism; women could use evangelical piety to seek power in ecclesiastical and, later, other public spheres, and men could appropriate spiritual consolations to strengthen their secular involvements. Susan Juster, "'In a Different Voice': Male and Female Narratives of Religious Conversion in Post-Revolutionary America," *American Quarterly* 41 (1989): 34–62; Catherine Brekus, "Female Evangelism in the Early Methodist Movement, 1784–1845," paper presented at the Conference on Methodism and the Shaping of American Culture, 1760–1860, Oct. 7–8, 1994, Asbury Theological Seminary, Wilmore, Ky.

38. Hatch, *Democratization of Christianity*; Jon Butler, *Awash in a Sea of Faith* (Cambridge: Harvard University Press, 1990); R. Laurence Moore, *Religious Outsiders and the Making of Americans* (New York: Oxford University Press, 1986), 3–21; Mark Y. Hanley, *Beyond a Christian Commonwealth: The Protestant Quarrel with the American Republic, 1830–1860* (Chapel Hill,

century has obscured the dynamic and conflictive nature of Jacksonian evangelicalism, particularly among American artisans.[39]

To correct these historiographical oversights, and to take seriously the perspectives of evangelical artisans themselves, I have used both the usual secular labor sources (newspapers, trade union publications, and anti-capitalist manifestos) and the writings, sermons, and memoirs of populist evangelicals who either were artisans themselves or who ministered to artisan congregations. To provide an interpretive framework, I have adopted the insights of cultural hegemony theory to assert that populist evangelical reactions to incipient industrial capitalism were complex, contradictory, and often oppositional. As Raymond Williams has developed the theory (an alternative to cruder conceptions of "social control"), the process of collective intellectual change is carried out gradually through the dynamic interaction of "dominant," "residual," and "emergent" aspects of culture.[40] In terms of the economic ethics of the republican paradigm dominant during the Jacksonian era, emergent liberalism challenged both the constraints of the formerly dominant republicanism and the restrictions of the increasingly residual small producer tradition. In their place, liberalism presented a new commonsensical consciousness that sanctified individualism, that presented the dislocations of capitalist competition as the unavoidable byproduct of unchangeable laws of nature, and that, for the rising bourgeoisie, made the possibility of challenging such liberal constructions simply out of the question.[41]

University of North Carolina Press, 1994). For a review that attempts to interpret Hatch's *Democratization of Christianity* as a mere refurbishment of consensus views, see Paul E. Johnson, "Review Essay: Democracy, Patriarchy, and American Revivals, 1780–1830," *Journal of Social History* 24 (1991): 845–50.

39. See the excellent discussions of this historiographical trend in Hatch, *Democratization of Christianity*, 221–25, and Moore, *Religious Outsiders*, vii–xv.

40. Raymond Williams, "Base and Superstructure in Marxist Cultural Theory," *New Left Review* 82 (Nov.-Dec. 1973): 3–16; T. J. Jackson Lears, "The Concept of Cultural Hegemony: Problems and Possibilities," *American Historical Review* 90 (June 1985): 567–93; Watts, *The Republic Reborn*, xv–xxiii, 14–16; Leon Fink, "The New Labor History and the Powers of Historical Pessimism: Consensus, Hegemony, and the Case of the Knights of Labor," *Journal of American History* 75 (June 1988): 115–36; Dwight B. Billings, "Religion As Opposition: A Gramscian Analysis," *Journal of American Sociology* 96 (July 1990): 1–31.

41. As Mark Noll notes, "The intellectual history of the United States in the early national period is complex, especially for the connections between religion and public thought. Nonetheless, it now seems clear that between the ratification of the Constitution and the election of William Henry Harrison in 1840, the assumptions of the nation's public philosophy evolved, or completed their evolution, from a basic republicanism to a basic, if not exclusive, liberalism." Mark A. Noll, "Revival, Enlightenment, Civic Humanism, and the Development of Dogma: Scotland and America, 1735–1843," *Tyndale Bulletin* 40 (1988): 56.

The clear implications of this hegemonic reorientation led evangelical producers to develop oppositional strategies (antagonistic, alternative, or qualifiedly accommodative) along a spectrum from reluctant assimilation to violent rejection of industrial capitalism.[42]

Although evangelical practice could indeed reinforce liberalism, producer-oriented evangelicals in the early republic used such disparate scriptural teachings as the Levitical Jubilee,[43] the Sermon on the Mount, and Isaiah's judgments on the disobedient children of Israel to condemn the commercial deceit and exploitation they believed characterized emergent capitalism. Methodist reformer Thomas Stockton alluded to such perspectives in 1821 when he wrote, "there is perhaps no subject so imperfectly understood as the liberty christians have to extract poison from the blessings of God's providence, and to gain perishing treasure at the expense of temporal and eternal good [when] . . . the christian gets rich by being . . . in fact a profiting copartner in ruining . . . immortal beings."[44] Radical evangelical anticapitalist critiques suggested sophisticated schemes to redistribute land and wealth along the lines of legislation outlawing primogeniture, governmental ceilings on profit accumulation, restrictions on interest rates, and community-sanctioned pressure to force employers and consumers to honor the moral

42. Patrick Joyce, "The Historical Meanings of Work: An Introduction," in Joyce, ed., *Historical Meanings of Work*, 7. At one end of the spectrum, antagonistic reactions included writings and activity designed to resist capitalist culture through moral suasion, legal maneuvering, political activity, and spontaneous militancy. At the other end of the spectrum, the qualifiedly accommodative reactions introduced the transition from challenge to integration. But Robert Fowler rejects the opposing sociological traditions of "integration" and "challenge," neither of which are adequate as models. Instead, "religion in America has been . . . an alternative to the liberal order, a refuge from our society and its pervasive values." Robert Booth Fowler, *Unconventional Partners: Religion and Liberal Culture in the United States* (Grand Rapids, Mich.: William B. Eerdmans, 1989), 3–4. Alternative reactions referred to writings and activity designed to meliorate the worst effects of endemic abuses, consciously or unwillingly inflicted in the changes accompanying the emergent culture.

43. See Peter Linebaugh, "Jubilating; Or, How the Atlantic Working Class Used the Biblical Jubilee against Capitalism, with Some Success," *Radical History Review*, no. 50 (1991): 143–80. I am indebted to Steve Vaughan and Toby Higbie for this reference.

44. *Wesleyan Repository and Religious Intelligencer* 1 (Aug. 30, 1821): 163. Samuel Harris also preached along antiliberal lines, claiming that only Christianity could "extract the poison which the liberty tree sucks up from its roots of sin." Samuel Harris, "The Dependence of Popular Progress on Christianity," *New Englander* 5 (July 1847): 433–51, cited in Hanley, *Beyond a Christian Commonwealth*, 42. The evangelical understanding of "liberty" was "self-determination in one's appropriate ethical sphere," not necessarily "freedom to defy established conventions." A. Gregory Schneider, "Social Religion, the Christian Home, and Republican Spirituality in Antebellum Methodism," *Journal of the Early Republic* 10 (summer 1990): 168.

imperatives of producerism.[45] These critiques emerged from a variety of loosely connected sources but shared a foundational concern with an aesthetic of limited accumulation. Their widespread currency indicated a general evangelical predilection for such ideas. Though relatively few created or joined militant organizations (and those that did often saw their radical positions altered by age, institutional compromise or indifference, or partial success), other less antagonistic avenues of opposition remained viable among American populist evangelicals. Continued suspicions of the ramifications of industrial capitalist hegemony led to a plethora of counterhegemonic responses in Jacksonian Baltimore, including evangelical participation in Jacksonian trade union and anticapitalist militancy, artisan temperance and other self-help activity, and evangelism and congregation building in artisan and emerging factory neighborhoods.

45. Craig, "Underside of History," 73–88; William R. Sutton, "To Extract Poison from the Blessings of God's Providence: Radical Methodist Suspicions of the Market Revolution," paper presented at the Conference on Methodism and the Shaping of American Culture, 1760–1860, Oct. 7–8, 1994, Asbury Theological Seminary, Wilmore, Ky.

Chapter One

The World of Baltimore's Evangelical Artisans

In January 1834 the barrel makers of Baltimore went on strike. In an initial explanation of the strike, entitled "Appeal of the Journeymen Coopers to the Citizens of Baltimore" and published in a local newspaper, the coopers complained that their employers—the merchants and millers—had used the slack winter season to renege on the list of prices agreed upon by both parties six months earlier, thereby threatening to impoverish the journeymen. The coopers, in response to this "associated" effort on the part of the employers, called upon the Baltimore community to boycott the offending masters.[1] Their arguments and the popular response to them reveal a great deal about the world of Jacksonian artisans.

Although financial considerations were critical to the coopers ("can a man and his family even live and have the necessaries of life, upon this

1. Baltimore *Republican*, Jan. 13, 15, 1834. As David Grimsted notes, relative to similar Jacksonian labor conflicts, "Success, failure, or compromise depended on a multitude of local and personal variables: specific conditions, worker options, general economic realities, and the degree of worker-manager trust and flexibility. An additional variable seemingly mattered much more in antebellum conflicts than in later ones: the degree of communal sympathy or support for worker demands." Grimsted, "Ante-bellum Labor," 6.

pittance?"), the journeymen framed their appeal in the complementary languages of political rights and religious morality. This naturally led these workers to identify with the suffering of the Old Testament people of Israel. They introduced their appeal with a quotation from Isa. 3:15: "What mean ye * * that ye grind the faces of the poor, saith the Lord God of Hosts?" Such appeals, using religious language to describe practical predicaments, were not unusual for Jacksonian artisans, who were increasingly pressured by the changes brought about by industrial capitalism. In fact, their situation was not all that different from late twentieth-century workers facing dislocation from deindustrialization and globalization.

The coopers' announcement highlights a conflict that divided Americans in the early republic over the benefits and dangers of economic modernization. Three key developments were at the heart of this conflict: industrial technology, centralized capitalist organization, and liberal ideology. Industrial technology replaced human labor with machine work, and it promised to free workers from dangerous and tedious tasks. But, in an era when unemployment was more devastating than low wages, it also threatened to eliminate jobs for certain workers and to make others dependent on owners of large machines. Similarly, capitalist organization involved new banking practices, made possible market expansion, widened occupational opportunities for workers, and broadened investment possibilities. But it also threatened to destroy personalized economic relations where sellers knew their consumers, where employers and employees observed mutual obligations owed to each other, and where all recognized the overriding interests of the community.

These technological and economic developments reflected a profound intellectual departure. Liberal ideology presented a distinctive challenge to the status quo because liberalism celebrated the scientifically discoverable laws of nature (chief among them being laws of supply and demand) and the conviction that the pursuit of self-interest would lead to freedom and prosperity for all except the unworthy.[2] As a result, liberalism undermined the social, political, ecclesiastical and economic restrictions that had characterized preindustrial society, but it also threatened to remove economics and social relations from the realm of moral consideration. Common folk worried about the future of the American experiment, particularly when industrial capitalism threatened to subordinate skilled workers to the

2. John Rule, "The Property of Skill in the Period of Manufacture," in Joyce, ed., *Historical Meanings of Work*, 117. For artisan willingness to embrace liberal economics and industrialization for their own self-interest, see Kornblith, "Artisanal Response to Capitalist Transformation," 315–21, and Stott, "Artisans and Capitalist Development," 270.

decisions made by entrepreneurs operating outside the normal constraints of classical republican culture, where theoretically the maintenance of communal welfare was more important than the success of ambitious individuals.[3]

From the Baltimore coopers' perspective, the possibilities for advancement promised by economic modernization were being compromised by the greed of unscrupulous masters. Aware that poverty, exploitation, and domination could as easily accompany modernization as opportunity, they appealed to a set of Christian socioeconomic ethics to protect themselves. According to this tradition, in the vernacular of the nineteenth century, to exploit those who were dependent, powerless, or poverty stricken was "to grind the faces of the poor." This expression, from the Book of Isaiah, was used by a wide range of Jacksonian social justice advocates. For instance, humanitarian philanthropist Mathew Carey used it to excoriate capitalists whose practices forced seamstresses to live on starvation wages, and radical Methodist William Stilwell cited it when describing commercial practices that exploited workers in an unregulated economy.

For Americans living in the early republic, Isa. 3:15 embodied the moral power of the community to enforce limits on the ambitious, and given the high rate of biblical literacy at the time, its scriptural context was no doubt familiar. Explicit in this biblical passage was the idea of judgment: Israel had been violating the Old Testament covenants by increasing the levels of poverty and subjecting its most vulnerable members to exploitation. Inherent in the scripture was the conviction that such treatment warranted prophetic condemnation and, if left unaddressed, divine punishment. The message of conditional judgment went beyond immediate circumstances to threaten the prosperity and blessing of the larger community. "Grinding the faces of the poor" was, in the eyes of many nineteenth-century Americans, as dangerous as any other social sin and called into question the alleged moral superiority of the ongoing "city upon the hill" experiment in nineteenth-century America.

Questions, however, remain: what groups were likely to use this moral discourse, and why was this language meaningful to so many Americans? Those who decried the increasing prevalence of "grinding" operations were invariably common folk—farmers, artisans, small merchants, and professionals of the middling sort—whose livelihoods were at risk from capitalist dislocation and whose sense of economic justice was rooted in producerist ethics promoting nondependence, limited upward mobility, and the dignity of labor. Although populist evangelicals were most familiar with the scriptural

3. Lasch, *True and Only Heaven*, 13–17.

foundations of the critique, the entire culture of the early republic was grounded in Protestant sensibilities; therefore, "grinding" was anathema to a broad spectrum of Americans. More precisely, this discourse was an integral part of early nineteenth-century producerist culture—those journeymen and small masters whose livelihoods, autonomy, and pride depended on having some control over craft production and profit distribution.[4] In the midst of transformations praised by celebrants of the mechanical age, antagonism toward "grinding" practices persisted, leaving artisans as a whole in a state of deep ambivalence regarding the implications of industrialism. As long as they could share in the fruits of progress, they were satisfied, but when they were denied prosperity, status, and opportunity, their opposition was almost guaranteed.

The immediate context of the coopers' strike was the vicious competition between merchants in Baltimore and Philadelphia to dominate the prosperous Middle Atlantic wheat flour trade. In the late eighteenth and early nineteenth centuries, Baltimore had grown from a sleepy backwater into a thriving metropolis primarily because of its successful wheat and tobacco trade with the West Indies. By 1830 it had passed Boston to become, behind New York and Philadelphia, the third largest American city. At the same time, the increasingly commercialized farmers of central Pennsylvania and western Maryland were sending great quantities of wheat to the flour mills springing up along the various streams flowing into the Chesapeake near Baltimore. As the economy boomed in the years following the War of 1812, the competition for this wheat increased. Thus the Middle Atlantic flour trade exemplified the broader structural factors of the market revolution, with expanded opportunities for capital investment, innovations in credit arrangements, and demands on reducing costs all featured prominently in the new economic configurations. The establishment of the Baltimore and Ohio Railroad in 1829 was emblematic of Baltimore's aggressive push to dominate the economy of the region.[5]

The demands of market competition had forced changes in the processes of flour milling, which Baltimore's more ambitious millers were successfully embracing. By the 1830s, there existed a clear distinction between the small, neighborhood "custom mills," regulated by state law and custom for local

4. Rule, "The Property of Skill," in Joyce, ed., *Historical Meanings of Work*, 104–13.

5. James W. Livengood, *The Philadelphia-Baltimore Trade Rivalry, 1780–1860* (New York: Arno Press, 1970), 13–15, 26.

producers and consumers in a nexus of personalized exchange, and the new "merchant mills," established for the benefit of farmers with surplus grain and adventurous investors with excess capital in a context of nationalized competition and speculation. The unregulated nature of this latter arrangement necessitated aggressive cost containment, the factor which dragged the coopers into the vortex of capitalist expansion: their hand-crafted oak barrels transported the milled flour to its ultimate destinations, which, for Baltimore mills was often the West Indies.[6]

Coopers drew on personal skill, specialized implements, and a long craft tradition to produce various barrels, tubs, and casks. Depending to a great degree on well-practiced hand-eye coordination and tools like frows, curved drawing knives, and crussets, coopers, like other preindustrial artisans, jealously guarded the secrets of their trade as well as their independence. In a typical preindustrial arrangement, Baltimore's coopers and their employers jointly established prices for various products. But, by the 1830s, the coopers, too, were involved in the industrializing innovations of outwork: the division of labor into specialized tasks, and mass production of standardized pieces. Besides contributing the oak barrels used to transport flour to the West Indies, Baltimore's coopers were also sending prefabricated staves and heads for assembly overseas. Although increasing their production and profit, especially in slack times, their willing participation in these changes was not without problems; as the merchant millers and certain master coopers sought to control and reduce their costs, they came into direct conflict with others in the trade. It was only after a period of unsuccessful negotiation in winter 1833–34 that the journeymen coopers resorted to publicly portraying their antagonists as oppressive, greedy, and sinful, violating not only their rights but the divine prerogatives of the biblical God of righteousness and judgment.[7]

The masters did not take such vilification without protest; their response appeared a week later in the *Republican.* Twenty-two employers, including one Joshua Stinchcomb, claimed that the slack season wages being proposed were higher than they had been at any time in the previous ten years and that when business was brisk, the traditional "harmony of interests" between masters and journeymen had prevailed. The masters expressed annoyance at the journeymen's religious effrontery, "as if" they had been "authorized by

6. Edward Hazen, *The Panorama of Professions and Trades; or Every Man's Book* (Philadelphia, 1836), 24–26; Livengood, *Philadelphia-Baltimore Trade Rivalry,* 13.

7. Hazen, *Panorama of Trades,* 230–31.

the Great Ruler of the Universe" to offer the scriptural challenge. The masters were equally familiar with their Bibles (if not properly appreciative of the importance of context). They selectively quoted Matt. 20:6–7 to condemn their ungrateful employees: "Why stand ye all the day idle?" "Because no man will hire us." To close their case, the masters resorted to the new emphases on tightly regulated industry and hyperindividualism; citing the emergent "industrial morality," they blamed the coopers' refusal to work on laziness, not moral indignation, and accused them of extortion for appealing to the collective conscience of "brother mechanics."[8]

Neither overawed by such questionable scriptural exegesis nor impressed by the appeal to industrial morality, the journeymen responded three days later: "we stand idle . . . because . . . unprincipled men, who have brought certain quotations from a holy and good book, to subserve their own purpose, have attempted to deprive us of the reward for our labour, and thereby rob our families of that sustenance to which they are entitled by our exertions." Because their wages had not been adjusted to rising costs of living over the past decade, they had been underpaid for years, resulting in constant anxiety that, despite their diligence, they and their families would go "'supperless to bed.'" The journeymen concluded: "But, thank God, we live in a land where we can be heard—where by the censure of a just and enlightened public, these would-be-masters can be brought into subjection, and their perfidious designs . . . will recoil with redoubled force upon their own heads. They ought to know, and we hope will feel the censures, if they still pursue their course which followed a like transaction in this city some time ago. The spirit that was aroused at that time in favour of the operatives . . . has not entirely subsided, and if it had, we see no reason why it will not be brightened by this attempt to oppress us." Maintaining the biblical basis for their collective action without wavering, the striking journeymen confidently expected that the community would uphold their just cause.[9]

The coopers were not disappointed; the hatters of Baltimore responded immediately and favorably with money and a published exhortation to the community. In an archetypical employment of traditional Protestant economic morality, the hatters condemned the "innovations" of the masters "as a dictation of the love of wealth; as originating from . . . selfish considerations; having no resting place for its grasping desires; and which, if

8. *Republican*, Jan. 21, 1834.

9. *Republican*, Jan. 24, 1834. The allusion, implied by the term "some time ago," is probably to the weavers' strike in 1829 or to the hatters' strike in 1833.

permitted . . . by the labouring classes . . . will eventually subject them . . . to the condition of European vassalage."[10] The hatters' contribution was fitting; just six months earlier, they had, with significant public support, successfully resisted an attempt by their masters to depress wages by 25 percent and to undercut the traditional autonomy of the journeymen. This hatters' strike, in fact, inaugurated the most volatile season of labor activism that Baltimore had ever seen; at least eleven strikes or threatened turnouts had erupted in 1833 and nearly thirty journeymen's craft organizations had formed, as well as a central organization to coordinate artisan activity.[11] For four years following the hatters' strike, Baltimore's journeymen rallied to support each other and joined national efforts to challenge the dislocations of industrial capitalism.

The hatters were facing economic and cultural pressures similar to those experienced by the coopers. When the effects of outside competition and the desire for investment capital led three large-scale manufacturers to reduce their pay scales in June 1833, the hatters resorted to moral arguments. In their public communique, the workers cited the greed of the employers, denied any desire for unearned gain, and complained that they were not benefiting from the wealth their labor had produced; in fact, they reminded the masters that, during the eleven years since the masters had last associated, journeymen's wages had stagnated while profits had increased dramatically. In addition, they drew attention to plans made by the masters to splinter artisan unity and pleaded with fellow mechanics for class solidarity. A distinctive ethic reflecting the labor theory of value inspired their note: "We hold . . . that every man should be rewarded according to the amount of labour by him performed; creating thereby stronger incentives to industry." Finally, the aggrieved hatters equated their plight with the concomitant degeneration of American institutions which, if left unchallenged, would inevitably lead to the spiritual and political demise of the nation. Their public manifesto had been signed by six officers of the

10. *Republican*, Jan. 17, 1834. The hatters also sent $77.50 to the coopers through a committee headed by Joshua Vansant.

11. John R. Commons et al., *History of Labour in the United States*, 2 vols., (New York: MacMillan, 1918), 1:478. For 1833, Commons mentions only strikes or threats by the hatters, machinists, bricklayers, coachmakers, combmakers, painters, and seamstresses. According to contemporary papers, other strikers included house carpenters; plasterers; blacksmiths; and copper, tin plate, and sheet iron workers. The broad range of artisan organizations included male, skilled workers threatened by the deskilling of industrialism, such as cordwainers, carpenters, and tailors, as well as semiskilled carters, female chair-caners, ornamental painters, and other groups of workers.

United Journeymen Hatters' Society, including John H. W. Hawkins, Philip Adams, Dennis Wagner, and Adrian Posey.[12]

The final resolution of the journeymen coopers' strike in 1834 remains unclear. What is clear is that the producer culture of Jacksonian artisans was subject to severe socioeconomic and ideological pressures brought to bear by the transformations of industrialism, capitalism, and liberalism—transformations celebrated by many, both then and now, as the keys to American success and triumphalism. In addition to increased reliance on outwork, new systems involving "sweated" labor, and the deskilling of craft work, intense competition in national and international markets demanded a level of external work discipline previously unheard of—discipline that entrepreneurs on the make often proved willing to impose. At stake for artisans caught in this process were serious questions of power and control.

Capitalist change in the early republic, as made clear in the coopers' and hatters' struggles, involved three interconnected groups: employers (masters), workers (journeymen), and consumers (the public). In preindustrial communities, there was an explicit recognition that the rights and needs of the producer were of paramount importance in any economic exchange, a recognition that formed the basis of artisan culture. But industrial capitalism challenged artisan culture on a broad front. The preindustrial artisan regime approximated the work rhythms of agricultural labor, with periods of intense labor interspersed with times of more casual diligence and both formal and informal opportunities for rest and leisure. Work in many industries was seasonal, sporadic, and subject to the vagaries of both nature and competition—realities that some artisans welcomed as breaks from routine. Production rates, as well as prices, were often set by prearrangement between masters and journeymen, thereby reducing the temptation for competitive overachievement. Workplace tensions were not eliminated in this system, but discipline emanated as much from craft tradition, internal values, and family needs as from the unilateral coercive power of the master. This situation reflected the artisan preoccupation with relatively equal power relations within the craft and a decentralized pattern of economic expansion.[13]

Artisan culture, through the traditions, practices, and rituals of the various crafts, also provided a context of common socialization for workers. Each

12. *Republican*, July 30, 1833.

13. Edward P. Thompson, "Time, Work Discipline, and Industrial Capitalism" *Past and Present* 38 (Dec. 1967): 56–97; Hattam, *Labor Visions*, 76–78, 101.

trade necessitated particularized work experiences and encouraged the development of unique terminology. Artisan parades featured banners with distinctive mottoes, provided demonstrations of the mysteries of the trades, and encouraged craft solidarity. In ceremonial rites of passage, apprentices became journeymen and were given sets of tools by their masters, a ritual often followed by an alcoholic celebration thrown by the communities of journeymen. For many artisans, inclusion in a distinctive craft culture formed an important aspect of self-identity and existential pride. Equally operative, however, was the belief that the products of their labor were viewed by all as significant contributions to the larger community. Self-restraint was as important as self-motivation, and monopolizing the finite resources and opportunities within a given community was as socially destructive as failing to produce a sufficient quantity of quality work. In this sense, artisan culture deplored parasitic nonproducers on both ends of the socioeconomic spectrum: entrenched elites and unskilled transients. In contrast, artisans saw themselves as "laboring-class" bulwarks of the all-important "middling classes."[14]

At the heart of this producerist system was a recognized interdependence among workers, employees, and consumers. Mutual obligations obtained throughout this system, with journeymen and masters participating in jointly established wage rates, hours, work rules, and informal social customs. Moreover, the producerist insistence on the harmony of interests extended to employers and consumers as well, with the popular ideal insisting that "every able-bodied man willing to work should find employment at a rate of wages sufficient to insure him the necessities and conveniences of life." Employers' responsibilities to workers included maintaining livable working conditions, resisting the temptation to accumulate excessive percentages of profits, and acknowledging the basic humanity and nondependence of artisans. Consumers were to recognize the necessary reciprocity between the quality of worker's products and their price; they were expected to avoid making purchases based on mere cheapness. Finally, violations would warrant communal sanctions: damage to reputations, ostracization, public humiliation, and, in extreme cases, rioting.[15] As artisan culture informed the ethics of the larger community, personal relations involved in the processes of producing and selling goods were of central importance.

14. Blumin, *Emergence of the Middle Class*, 12, 17–65.

15. *Bangor Daily Whig and Courier*, July 31, 1841; *Journal of the American Temperance Union* 6 (Sept. 1842), 136.

This mutuality of work, rituals, and parades was also evident in trade organizations. Initially resembling benefit societies and fraternal groups, craft societies provided welfare protection for sick or injured workers as well as security for their families, opportunities for education and socializing, and contexts for resolving internal trade-related disagreements; as such, these organizations included masters and journeymen alike. By the 1820s, however, as capitalist competition began to erode connections among artisans and some trade societies became dominated by entrepreneurial masters, journeymen increasingly formed separate organizations. In times of early labor conflict, these new journeymen's organizations often evolved into militant protective unions and, occasionally, political organizations designed specifically to resist the dislocations of capitalist development.[16] Thus, as more ambitious masters abandoned the old traditions in favor of liberalized economic arrangements, journeymen and sympathetic small masters (either unwilling or unable to adapt to capitalist innovation) were left to defend the traditions of producerism by organizing resistance to offending employers and by appealing to the larger community for support.

Traditional Protestant economic morality and religious understanding of work were central to artisan culture. In achieving their competences, producers were expected to be just in their dealings and limited in their ambitions. In the Anglo-American culture operative throughout the colonial period and beyond, the intersection of economics and religious morality was perceived as part of the seamless web of the created universe. Although church adherence rates fluctuated and popular levels of religiosity ebbed and flowed,[17] the workings of the universe for most were explained by an amalgamation of traditional folk beliefs and Reformed Protestant theology.[18] Even for artisans with no explicit religious commitments, Protestant understandings of work and economic justice were highly significant and, like other aspects of artisan producerism, were challenged by the liberal ideologies of the Enlightenment.

Despised by medieval scholastics but redeemed by radical Protestants in the Reformed tradition, labor had become a sacred undertaking because it

16. Laurie, *Artisans into Workers,* 50–52; Wilentz, *Chants Democratic,* 56–57; David Bensman, *The Practice of Solidarity: American Hat Finishers in the Nineteenth Century* (Urbana: University of Illinois Press, 1985), 50; Hattam, *Labor Visions,* 78.

17. Patricia Bonomi, *Under the Cope of Heaven: Religion, Society, and Politics in Colonial America* (New York: Oxford University Press, 1986), 87–92, 123–27; Isaac, *Transformation of Virginia,* 243–69.

18. David D. Hall, *Worlds of Wonder, Days of Judgment: Popular Religious Belief in Early New England* (Cambridge: Harvard University Press, 1989), 71–116; Sellers, Market Revolution, 29.

presented believers with opportunities for reflecting God's glory, for pursuing various calling, and for relieving the poor through proper stewardship. Work was as appropriate an arena for experiencing the presence of God as any other, but it also contained possibilities for indulging selfishness and greed. Economic practices then, like all human activity, were accountable to the religious demands of holy living. The mutual obligations between master and journeyman held explicitly religious dimensions mirroring the social ones. Traditional Protestant economic morality prohibited evangelical masters from ill treating or underpaying workers, just as it commanded evangelical workers to work diligently. Under the usual understanding of covenants and contracts, if one party circumvented the obligations of the agreement, righteousness and justice demanded that the other draw attention to that fact and insist on community support in the correction of those abuses. Ideas of traditional economic justice that placed social and moral considerations over economic ones were central to the Reformed conceptualization of work.[19]

Yet Protestant economic morality was not the full-blown ideology of sophisticated economic theorists, rather it suggested that "the moral consequences of economic malfeasance were only too immediately apparent in the community."[20] Traditional economic morality was firmly grounded in the Reformed disgust with extremes of wealth and poverty, which were believed to inculcate degeneracy or effeminacy and were condemned as leading to greed or indolence. The Reformed preoccupation with the fallenness of human nature—with sin defined as selfishness and with virtue equated with self-denial—resulted in ecclesiastical insistence that the good of the community prevail over individual desire. Even with the onset of secularization and the challenge of Arminianism, which stressed the spiritual autonomy of individuals, two assumptions for evangelical Protestants remained: one was an understanding that labor was to be amenable to Christian discipline, and the other was a recognition that social harmony was to be achieved through the mutuality of economic benefits.[21] In addition, the belief persisted that by

19. Stephen Innes, *Creating the Commonwealth: The Economic Culture of Puritan New England* (New York: W. W. Norton, 1995), 5–38 (esp. 25–30) and 113–15. See also Bernard Bailyn, ed., *The Apologia of Robert Keayne* (New York: Harper and Row, 1964); David DeLeon, *The American As Anarchist: Reflections on Indigenous Radicalism* (Baltimore: Johns Hopkins University Press, 1978), 26–31; and Innes, *Creating the Commonwealth*, 160–91.

20. Crowley, *This Sheba, Self*, 50, 53; Rabinowitz, *Spiritual Self*, 224.

21. Crowley, *This Sheba, Self*, 17–20, 51–62; Glickstein, *Concepts of Free Labor*, 315n16; Mark Valeri, "The Economic Thought of Jonathan Edwards," *Church History* 60 (Mar. 1991): 37–54.

diligent and honest work one would succeed, yet restrictions on the enjoyment of that success remained operative, and society could only suffer "from the impatience of growing rich by the gradual accumulation of moderate gains" when individuals transgressed such limits. The resulting conception of prosperity suggested models of honesty, industry, and frugality and was to be understood as a corporate, not an individual, blessing.[22]

The Enlightenment-inspired loosening of corporate restrictions coupled with emphasis on the primacy of religious experience in the Great Awakening marked a change, especially among the commercial Calvinists of New England. Prosperous and well-educated Puritan merchants and commercial farmers joined their less fervent Anglican and Quaker fellows in embracing the laws of supply and demand and demanding legal protection for investment adventuring; for them, the traditional strictures of economic morality had long proven unenforceable by secular authorities and were increasingly unnecessary nuisances.[23] From the other direction, "Awakened" Protestants who stressed human depravity understood the individual's propensity for economic transgression and consequent social disruption, yet, by minimizing the role of clerical power, they depended on sanctified self-discipline to protect social order. Increasingly, the force of traditional economic morality was reduced to vigorous yet unenforceable denunciations of commercial transgressions, but it retained currency among agrarians and artisans, as well as among influential clergy like Jonathan Edwards who were willing to condemn the antisocial practices of emerging economic elites. No longer recognized as problematic by capitalist-minded merchants, these economic vices included sins of consumptive excess referred to as "luxury" and "needless self-indulgence," sins of exploitation referred to as "avarice" and "oppression," sins of nonproductivity referred to as "idleness" and "indolence," and such sins of social destructiveness as rapid mobility, accumulations of wealth, and economic individualism; all of these, according to traditional economic morality, violated the community-oriented self-denial necessary to preserve justice and order.[24]

22. "Memorial of Farmers, Mechanics, and Others of Anne Arundel and Baltimore County against an Increase on Imported Manufactures," U.S. Congress, House, 20th Cong., 1st sess., Mar. 10, 1828, Doc. no. 110, cited in Neal A. Brooks and Eric G. Rockel, *A History of Baltimore County* (Towson, Md.: Friends of the Towson Library, 1979), 194.

23. Innes, *Creating the Commonwealth*, 172.

24. Rabinowitz, *Spiritual Self*, 224–29; Crowley, *This Sheba, Self*, 76, 96–105; Valeri, "Economic Thought of Jonathan Edwards," 37–54. For more on the contemporary notion of the sins of avarice, see Appleby, *Capitalism and New Social Order*, 8, and Watts, *Republic Reborn*, 70–86. Stephen Innes adds to this list "excessive calculations," a practice that early on

The importance of the Protestant moral tradition throughout the eighteenth century, however, cannot be overemphasized. Resembling but by no means identical to the "moral capitalism" of the Massachusetts Bay Colony and John Cotton's seventeenth-century reworking of the just price ideal,[25] producerist morality underwrote artisanal critiques of insufficient wages, arbitrary exercises of control at the workplace, and accumulation of power among the wealthy. Grounded in notions that monopolies of wealth and power mandated oppression for the rest of the community and that unrestrained self-aggrandizement presented an almost blasphemous challenge to the prerogatives of God, traditional economic morality provided a powerful critique of capitalist innovation. By the early nineteenth century, the thrust of this understanding was reactive rather than proactive and was only intermittently translated into specific programs, dependent as it was on communal, not ecclesiastical or governmental, coercion and voluntary assent. Still, this quintessentially Protestant sensibility continued to proscribe a wide range of activities increasingly popular within liberal economic schemes, including market-driven lending and monetary practices, unchecked competition, taking advantage of circumstances to increase gain, unlimited accumulation, and consumer purchases based solely on the impersonal criterion of cheapness.

The circumstances surrounding the coopers' and hatters' strikes was symptomatic of conditions in the 1820s and 1830s, as capitalist work relations gradually superseded the mutual arrangements of craft producerism. In the expanding economy of the mid-1820s,[26] increasing competition and a growing desire by employers for control of production and commercial exchange made preoccupation with reducing labor costs a central focus. But other forces were at work as well, one of which was the advent of large-scale and far-reaching technological innovations. By the early 1830s, the issues surrounding technological modernization initiated a number of heated discussions among Baltimoreans. Representative of this conflict was the proposed extension of the Baltimore and Ohio Railroad (B & O) into the center of the city in late 1833. When the first tracks were laid just west of

---

distinguished Puritan protocapitalists from other New England merchants. Innes, *Creating the Commonwealth*, 185.

25. Innes, *Creating the Commonwealth*, 7, 169–71.

26. Bruce Laurie notes a fifteen-year economic resurgence beginning in the early 1820s, but Charles Sellers cites specifically the jubilee year of 1826 as initiating the "decisive phase of market revolution." Laurie, *Artisans into Workers*, 38; Sellers, *Market Revolution*, 237.

Baltimore to tap into the commercial farming areas of western Maryland and southern Pennsylvania and to neutralize the economic advantages New York and Philadelphia enjoyed through access to the Erie Canal, Baltimoreans were jubilant.[27] But when the B & O proposed to extend the railroad into Baltimore itself, thereby jeopardizing the employment of hundreds of workers in the carrying trades, resistance quickly crystallized.[28]

A letter from "One of the People" to the editor of the *Republican*, backing City Council candidates who opposed the planned extension, laid out the controversy: "Working men look to your interests," the author wrote; extending the railroad would eliminate employment at good wages for "hundreds of honest cartmen, draymen, labourers, &c," for the sake of the "'favoured few.'" Arguing that such innovations would impoverish families and make saving "something for . . . the decline of life" impossible for the displaced workers, the author concluded, "I say be united and let your watchword be 'down with all monopolies.'"[29] Samuel Harker, the prolabor editor of the *Republican*, endorsed these sentiments. A few days later he printed a similar letter, where arguments against the railroad were cast in the rhetoric of traditional economic morality. "One of the hard Working People" declared: "But we hear a voice in the wilderness crying aloud for 'help, help, help.' Let us not commence our work by skimming off the surface, and thus feed the last ear to those who are already fattened, and are rolling in affluence (which their monopoly has sapped from our hard earnings,) and thus try to appease their squealings. No! fellow-citizens, this is not our spirit—we will look first to the needy, then there is time to promote the interests of those who are already too rich—but let's us to the bottom and rout out this rotten fraternity from their stronghold." He too called for political action to halt the planned extension.[30]

These two letters elicited a favorable response among the *Republican* readership. Indicating that for some political partisanship was a peripheral concern, "A No Jackson Man," portrayed the conflict over railroad extension as one linking the "middle and poorer classes" against the rich and exploitative monopolists. "One of the People" had noted that proextension arguments based on consumer convenience, resource availability, and market accessibility for outlying farmers were not unreasonable in them-

27. Anita Gorochow, "Baltimore Labor in the Age of Jackson" (master's thesis, Columbia University, 1949), 4–5; Browne, *Baltimore in the Nation*, 84, 112.

28. *Republican*, Oct. 11, 16, 19, 1833; *American*, Oct. 11, 22, 1833.

29. *Republican*, Oct. 8, 1833.

30. *Republican*, Oct. 12, 1833.

selves, but he favored bringing products to "the margin of our city" whereupon they would be transported into the city by carters and others. Another respondent extended the argument against transportation "improvements" and urged the paper to oppose the proposed widening and dredging of the harbor, a process that would throw large numbers of haulers out of work as well as raise city taxes.[31] Concern for employment opportunities for honest workmen should take precedence over the convenience of commercial giants.

Such protectionist perspectives were quickly challenged by others who saw development in a positive light. Writing as "A Friend to Improvement," one man was flabbergasted by the opposition: "I thought," he moaned, "that this was considered the age of improvement and that the word of the day was onward." His modernist sensibilities outraged, the author asked if all labor-saving inventions, including the horse and cart used by the draymen and more efficient planes used by carpenters, were to be rejected in the interest of saving jobs. Equally unworthy was the idea of keeping prisoners in the penitentiary idle so that they would not encroach upon the employment opportunities of Baltimore workers, "as if our wide spreed [*sic*] land presented us so very little labour to perform that we must covet it for ourselves." The author concluded that all technological innovation was to be embraced as inherently progressive.[32]

The cause of improvement was also taken up by "Fair Play," who drew attention to the financial losses suffered by the largest B & O investors. But "Fair Play" was not content to accept the debate as one between greedy monopolists and exploited workers. Instead, he described tensions between workers themselves as resulting from the allegedly high prices (three to five dollars per day) charged by draymen, and the large profits made by carrying-trade employers at the expense of artisans who were forced to pay dearly for needed supplies. Finally, appealing to broader consumer concerns, he pointed out that during the previous winter, because of the availability of wood made possible by the railroad, Baltimoreans paid four to five dollars per cord whereas Philadelphians paid twelve dollars. "Fair Play" concluded that "any thing which will cheapen the price of carriage and facilitate the expidition [*sic*] of every sort of produce" which the railroad would ostensibly do, "is . . . of great public utility."[33]

31. *Republican*, Oct. 14, 15, 1833.

32. *Republican*, Oct. 15, 1833.

33. *Republican*, Oct. 15, 16, 1833. One candidate in the Sixth Ward, Thomas Morse, ran for City Council on an antirailroad plank but was soundly defeated. The Sixth Ward was not,

The debate over the B & O (which was in fact soon extended into the city) was not the only public controversy related to technological improvement. Soon after the railroad extension discussion, a dispute arose between enterprising manufacturer John Howland and disgruntled house carpenters. In early October 1833, the carpenters—employers and journeymen—called an open meeting to publicize "the evils that resulted from the late steam plaining mill" that had just burned down. They complained that machine-planed boards were often not uniform because of the machine's inability to differentiate between softer wood and knots and other anomalies that effected the planing process. Noting that hand planing eliminated those problems, which they otherwise had to correct on the job, the carpenters also pointed out that hand planing kept them employed in the slow winter season. Finally they promised, "by all lawful means" to prevent Howland from replacing the destroyed mill.[34] Once again, disagreements related to economic modernization were crystallized as consumer and investment concerns clashed with attempts to protect jobs and to avoid perceived monopolies.

The complaints of the carpenters did not go unnoticed in the local press. An anonymous defender of economic liberalism and technological improvement attacked their "primitive" reasoning which, if taken to its logical conclusions, would eliminate plows, sails, and other inventions "by which human exertion may be economized or the produce of it increased." Appealing to the language of liberal republicanism, the writer condemned as "unpatriotic" any citizen who, "in this Athenian day of American intelligence, improvement, and refinement," would refuse to yield his or her own benefits for the sake of "the general good and prosperity." Citing the ultimate republican authority, the author concluded, "As the Father of our country said, whoever causes another blade of grass to grow, was a public benefactor, so is he who by invention increases the produce of the labor of man's hands is benefactor to his race, and assists in elevating the scale of human existence."[35] In this response, the author described a factor that became

---

however, predominantly working class. Gorochow, "Baltimore Labor," 15. Morse received 84 votes, while his opponents gathered 475, 353, and 266, respectively. *Republican*, Oct. 22, 1833.

34. Baltimore *American*, Oct. 22, 1833; Baltimore Republican, Oct. 11, 1833. At this time there were an estimated forty master carpenters in Baltimore, along with about five hundred journeymen. The new mill was capable of turning out eight to ten thousand feet of boards per day. Charles Varle, *A Complete View of Baltimore As It Is with a Statistical Sketch* (Baltimore, 1833), 88, 145. For similar artisan antimachine sentiments, see *National Trades' Union*, Nov. 29, 1834, and J. Thomas Scharf, *The Chronicles of Baltimore: Being a Complete History of "Baltimore Town" and Baltimore City from the Earliest Period to the Present Time* (Baltimore, 1874), 429.

35. *American*, Oct. 22, 1833; *Republican*, Oct. 15, 1833.

increasingly significant in the public acceptance of industrial change: a generally higher standard of living for many in the middling classes. When the growing desire for creature comforts came into conflict with traditional community standards of economic morality, upheaval was almost inevitable.

Since Jacksonian Baltimoreans were by no means ignorant of this cultural tension, a quick response was to be expected, and "J. S.," a self-described "MECHANIC and a very hard WORKING MAN" provided it. Acknowledging the benefits (less arduous and dangerous work) accruing from the introduction of labor-saving machinery, J. S. nevertheless decried "the great evils which usually attend the immediate introduction" (e.g., deskilling, unemployment, and reduced wages) of such innovations. The question, then, was not whether labor-saving machinery should be allowed, but "what can be done to counteract the evils . . . upon those who are . . . affected by it and who are . . . least able to contend against them."[36] Throughout the Jacksonian period, Baltimore artisans wrestled with the ambivalence generated by these issues. Their suggested solutions were varied, but they all tended to embrace the necessity of protective organization, maintenance of producerist morality, and involvement of community sanctions to enforce those ethics. As "J. S." indicated, concern for potentially dislocated artisans was a moral issue that had to be taken seriously by the entire community.

Such a recognition of the complexities brought by technological and capitalist innovation was by no means unique, nor was this concern limited to journeymen. Ambitious masters still ambivalent about the moral trajectories (or lack thereof) of capitalist competition recognized that some compromise in ethics might be necessary to remain economically viable. In many instances, of course, the rationalization of capitalist practices was quick and easy. When Baltimore-area factory owner Michael McBlair was confronted with the fact that his female textile operatives simply could not live on his low wages, for instance, he claimed he had only agreed to pay them what their labor was worth, as determined by market forces, and if they suffered it was none of his concern.[37] But other masters pursued more ambiguous courses. Accepting the entrepreneurial ideal that business acumen was superior to the traditional dignity imparted by skilled labor and rejecting some of the restraints of traditional economic morality, Baltimore masters like Jacob Rogers practiced impressive feats of ethical legerdemain.[38]

36. *American*, Oct. 11, 1833; *Republican*, Oct. 16, 19, 1833.

37. Brooks and Rockel, *History of Baltimore County*, 202.

38. Browne, *Baltimore in the Nation*, 92, 267.

Rogers was a master hatter reputed to be "feared, respected and loved for his strict sense of honor, justice and propriety." He had risen from apprentice to ownership of the largest hat manufactory in the country in the 1830s.[39] He was apparently among the first to discover how to make "a prime beaver-napped hat" with only "the slightest sprinkling of the valuable beaver fur." When asked if they were "genuine beaver," Rogers replied, "I pledge my word that the best part of the material in that hat is pure beaver." The customer bought the hat and left, and a friend rebuked Rogers for his dishonesty. Rogers protested, "I made no misrepresentation. I told my customer . . . that the best part of the material of which the hat was made was pure beaver, and so it was."[40] Such rationalization was all too typical among masters on the rise, yet Rogers retained other aspects of producerist traditions; in 1833, Rogers apparently refused to join the aggressive master hatters in cutting journeymen's wages and, eleven years later, when another hatters' strike broke out to maintain wages, his firm (run by his sons after his death in 1842) was publicly cited for keeping the wage agreement.[41] Rogers's producerist ethics, while failing to remain pristine, persisted through the industrializing era.

Other masters, reflecting conservatism, conscience, or both, were likewise troubled by the ramifications of economic competition and depersonalized consumption. An advertisement for the work of John Cur[t]lett revealed the ambiguities facing ambitious artisans working within skilled craft traditions. Curlett was a master coachmaker who had presumably passed through the artisan stages of apprentice and journeyman before achieving his competence in 1812. In the notice, Curlett identified himself as "being a practical Coach Maker," indicating that he labored alongside his workers. Being intimately involved in all processes of production allowed Curlett to promise work that "will reflect credit upon himself and his workmen."[42] Coachmaking was a complex and highly skilled operation that required the talents of wheelwrights, cabinetmakers, and ornamental painters, and by the 1830s, production was subdivided to employ all three artisan trades. Wheels were made by hand, using a lathe to shape the center and saws, axes, knives, spokeshavers, chisels, and sandpaper to form the spokes and outer rim. The

39. Philip Kahn Jr., *A Stitch in Time: The Four Seasons of Baltimore's Needle Trades* (Baltimore: Maryland Historical Society, 1989), 37.

40. William T. Brigham, *Baltimore Hats, Past and Present* (Baltimore, 1890), 55–57. For changes in the hatting trade, see ibid., 62–74.

41. *Republican,* July 30, 1833; *Baltimore Sun,* Feb. 10, 1844.

42. *Republican,* Oct. 12, 1835.

wheel was then sent to a blacksmith who bound it with hoops of iron nailed to the wooden rim. Axles were wrought iron, and at this time, reflecting the changes in the industry, they were either individually crafted by the blacksmith working on the wheels or they were bought from a mass production outlet. Constructing the coach body was similar to making cabinets: using ash rails and poplar panels cut according to pine patterns (also capable of being mass produced), the body was carefully glued together and then puttied for painting. The final step—finishing the coach—was performed by workmen skilled in the art of ornamental painting. After five tediously applied coats of filling and polishing, the body was ready for several layers of paint.[43] The end result was a functioning work of art, but because so much work had gone into production, only the wealthy could afford coaches. Only by simplifying the process could coachmakers lower the cost sufficiently to attract a broader clientele. Equally important for the coachmaker, expanding prosperity and upper- and middle-class willingness to indulge in luxuries was a precondition for his occupational success; otherwise his market was extremely limited.

Lowering costs and appealing to a wealthy market were central to success in the coachmaking trade. Yet John Curlett remained bound by producerist ethics as he declared himself "prepared to execute all orders . . . with neatness and dispatch, and with the most scrupulous regard to rendering justice."[44] "Rendering justice" in the producerist idiom was a far-reaching concept. It included presenting the customer with a quality product, it implied that the customer would be willing to pay an honest price (not necessarily a cheap price), and it necessitated the master paying his workers a reasonable percentage of the profits realized. To do anything other than following these three steps would warrant communal sanction in the form of refusal to patronize Curlett's establishment. Thus the coachmaker had identified and called on all three groups to honor their respective producerist obligations. In his appeal for business, Curlett presented his operation to the public in terms of meeting the demands of justice. He and his son, who followed him into the trade, were rewarded with great success, extending well into the 1850s.[45]

In 1837, George Holtzman found himself facing similar issues. Holtzman was a Baltimore tailor who had worked his way up from journeyman to small

43. Hazen, *Panorama of Trades*, 232–33.

44. *Republican*, Oct. 12, 1835.

45. John C. Gobright, *City Rambles, or, Baltimore As It Is* (Baltimore, 1857), 42–43.

master. His operation at 147 Baltimore Street was in the heart of the downtown clothing district area and typified the preindustrial work regime that was threatened by premade clothing manufacturers who utilized outwork or the notorious sweating system, in which underpaid labor, often female, performed increasingly specialized and repetitive tasks.[46] In an advertisement, Holtzman claimed to have "some of the very best workmen employed" and reminded readers that, in terms of prices, "the best work cannot be had without the best prices, for every man of experience knows that workmanship and materials must of necessity correspond to the prices given for them." Acknowledging market pressures, Holtzman concluded, "But this much he will say that as every exertion shall be made to have his work of the first order, it shall be furnished as cheap as it can be had of the same quality elsewhere."[47] Thus, Holtzman tried to balance the master's need for profit, the producerist obligation to pay worker's reasonable wages, and the consumer demand for quality products. And, alluding to the problems faced by artisans and small masters at this time, he suggested a solution: the recognition by consumers and the public that such workmen (and their employing small masters), according to the familiar and still relevant set of ethics embodied in traditional economic morality, deserved their patronage and support.

Master hatters, coachmakers, and tailors were not the only ones forced to deal with changing and ambiguous circumstances. Although journeymen coopers found expanded markets for their barrels as merchant millers pioneered new flour grinding techniques, they were at the mercy of those same millers during slack seasons. Journeymen hatters enjoyed the consistent employment guaranteed by the demand for beaver hats and welcomed any relief from the tedious and sometimes backbreaking work of ruffing, waterproofing, and shaping, but they resented the large-scale hat manufactories where machines and semiskilled laborers dominated production and corporate owners monopolized profits. Journeymen printers took advantage

46. Varle, *Complete View of Baltimore*, 147; Edward K. Muller and Paul Groves, "The Changing Location of the Clothing Industry: A Link to the Social Geography of Baltimore in the Nineteenth Century," *Maryland Historical Magazine* 71 (fall 1976): 405. For excellent discussions of the implications of sweating, outwork, and the extreme division of labor, see Laurie, *Artisans into Workers*, 39–43. For a discussion of the changes facing tailors and the description of the occupation of merchant tailor, see Muller and Groves, "The Changing Location of the Clothing Industry," 404–5. For a description of how these changes worked out in textile factories, see William A. Sisson, "Bell Hours: Work Values and Discipline in the American Textile Industry, 1787–1880" (Ph.D. diss., University of Delaware, 1984), 40–48.

47. *Republican*, Apr. 17, 1837.

of the dynamic book culture in the highly literate early republic, but their opportunities to gain master status were constantly shrinking as competition from large printing concerns squeezed smaller operations. Seamstresses—married, widowed, or single—found outwork opportunities in the burgeoning markets for ready-made clothing a godsend, as long as they were able to maintain some control over their labor, to enjoy livable wages, and to avoid the exploitation of sweatshops.[48] The story was the same for the majority of American artisans, as capitalist modernization continued to bring both dislocation and opportunity. When producerist norms were violated, however, evangelical artisans and others voiced religious criticisms of the emerging capitalist status quo.

This was certainly the case with the Baltimore hatters and coopers in 1833–34, as seen in their producer-oriented critiques of industrial capitalism. The entrepreneurial master coopers and millers, for their part, presented evidence indicative of the alleged laziness or backwardness of challenged workers in comparison to their own ambition and skill, with the merchants enjoying the prerogatives of the newfound prosperity their abilities alone had presumably made possible. For the striking journeymen, however, the strike was about independence, self-pride, and appropriate distributions of wealth and power in the community. In a cultural environment still under construction, the coopers' militancy reflected both producerist and republican strains; "determined to resist . . . every . . . attempt to circumscribe their rights" in this "struggle of the few to govern the many," they denounced their employers' actions as violations of "the progress of liberal principles," as challenges to the ongoing "march of liberty," and as abuses of "those rights 'which God and nature gave.'" In addition, the "harmony of interests" informed their decision; before the strike, they had gone "along harmoniously, acting in perfect unison, . . . believing and hoping that our prices were giving perfect satisfaction to our employers." Finally, popular religious sensibilities were evident as the coopers accused their employers of violating the fundamental proposition of traditional economic morality that forbid any member of the

48. Representative of outwork efforts prospering both employer and worker (at least at first) was the experience of William Dickey who immigrated to Baltimore from Ireland as a child. Disappointed in attempts to become a Presbyterian minister, Dickey eventually left his father's woolen shop in Baltimore in the late 1830s to establish his own competence. He succeeded by distributing wool to Baltimore weavers who lived in his neighborhood along Saratoga Street and then selling on the open market the wool they produced. In time Dickey became successful enough to buy the mill town of Wetheredsville (renamed Dickeyville), where his Ashland Manufacturing Company prospered. Brooks and Rockel, *History of Baltimore County*, 199.

community from taking advantage of the unfortunate circumstances of others: "as soon as business became dull . . . they aimed a blow at us, . . . while there is an extensive pressure in the money market, and a general stagnation of business, to bring us down in our prices, and thereby deprive us and our families of a living." Likewise, the hatters' complaint six months later reflected the sense of appropriate limits to wealth and power that informed the economic ethics of producerist evangelicalism.[49] The journeymen hatters and coopers shared a common solution: to seek the help of fellow mechanics and the support of the community in boycotting the offending masters.

Other than representing relatively isolated instances of social tension related to economic modernization, what do these vignettes have in common? Significantly, all the individuals mentioned by name in these examples except Michael McBlair were evangelical Protestants, indicating that activist evangelicals lined up on both sides of the conflicts. The master cooper Joshua Stinchcomb,[50] the steam-planing manufacturer John Howland, and the master hatter Jacob Rogers were all up-and-coming Methodist laymen, and Howland and Rogers had played a prominent role in the expulsion of dissident Methodists (see chapters 2 and 3) disenchanted by the undemocratic nature of Methodist polity. The journeyman hatter John H. W. Hawkins was one of Baltimore's earliest Sunday School teachers and one of the rebellious Methodists expelled by Howland, Rogers, and others in 1828. Master coachmaker John Curlett's religious affiliation in the 1830s remains unknown, but by 1850 he was a member of Baltimore's low church Episcopalian congregation and enjoyed continued success without compromising his producerist ethics. Finally, the master tailor George Holtzman was a Methodist class leader who apparently took seriously his denomination's expectations that their lay authorities would be models of "personal industry . . . , honest . . . [and] clean and innocent from every just charge of indolence, oppression,

49. *Republican*, Jan. 13, 15, 1834; July 30, 1833.

50. Mention of Stinchcomb appears in the Isaac Cook Papers, Lovely Lane Museum, Baltimore. Affiliations of the journeymen are subject to the usual difficulties of fragmentary evidence. John Mackinghamer (Mackenheimer or Mackenhammer) was one of the signers of the rebuttal to the masters. An artisan by the same name had long been active in labor associations and politics, as well as in the Methodist church, although by 1834, he would have been fairly old. Mackinghamer was originally a carpenter by trade and active in anti-Federalist politics in the early nineteenth century, and he was one of the original cooper delegates selected to form a city central union (named the United Trade Society initially) in Sept. 1833. If this is indeed the same man, his signature on only the second appeal may have been another attempt to marshal support by employing the endorsement of a well-known public figure. *Baltimore Saturday Visiter*, Sept. 7, 1833; Steffen, *Mechanics of Baltimore*, 147, 162, 174, 202–7, 230.

and unjust gain."[51] Holtzman's attention to balancing producerist demands with capitalist realities (like Curlett's) succeeded in guaranteeing his continuing independence; at least, his uninterrupted stint as class leader through the disruptions following the panic of 1837 indicates a certain level of success. Although they differed significantly in their understandings of economic morality, each of these men epitomized the activism and moral fervor characteristic of evangelical empowerment.

The final set of questions to be addressed in this chapter center on the experience of artisan religion itself: how, in the volatile religious environment of Jacksonian America, did the religious perspectives of producerist evangelicals operate and how did evangelical spiritual experience affect the ways in which believers built self-identities, created communities, and interacted with the larger culture around them? While Protestant evangelicalism could inspire all manner of eccentric behavior and esoteric theology, the argument here is that the religious beliefs and spiritual experiences of many evangelical artisans provided the inspiration, consolation, and meaningfulness necessary to navigate the troubled waters of capitalist transformation. Far from uniformly inculcating pious docility, otherworldly transcendence, or feminized obedience, evangelicalism turned out activist believers from all classes ready and willing to construct a new nation in line with their sensibilities regarding justice and morality.[52] This concerted evangelical effort has become known as the Second Great Awakening.

Although periodization is often problematic, what can be characterized as a first phase of the Second Great Awakening began in the mid-1790s as theologically similar revival efforts among four relatively distinctive audiences: itinerant missionaries presenting Methodism in the large cities and later into the countryside; populist ministers preaching an explosive salvation message in frontier camp meetings; moderate Calvinist elites attempting to soften traditional doctrines and to reestablish their hegemony among the people of New England; and African-American Christians synthesizing biblical liberation and deliverance themes with African spiritual traditions and rituals.[53] As

51. *Mutual Rights and Methodist Protestant* 2 (Nov. 23, 1832): 372.

52. See Johnson and Wilentz, *Kingdom of Matthias* for these presuppositions that lead the authors to present Second Great Awakening revivalism as a Yankee middle-class phenomenon featuring capitalist business practices and a "feminized spirituality of restraint." Johnson and Wilentz, *Kingdom of Matthias,* 3–11, quote from p. 9.

53. Carwardine, "Second Great Awakening," 327–40; Charles A. Johnson, *The Frontier Camp Meeting: Religion's Harvest Time* (Dallas: Southern Methodist University Press, 1956);

the movements began to overlap in the early decades of the nineteenth century, a distinctive evangelical ethos began to emerge, with a new emphasis on human initiative, emotional spiritual experience, and egalitarianism significantly modifying (but not eliminating) the old emphases on ratiocinative theology, "hopeful" conversions, and social hierarchy. In this environment, although the endemic racism of American culture was already beginning to sunder African-American Christianity from the white mainstream, black evangelicals drew support from some of their white brethren even as the former continued to contribute liberationist doctrine and vibrant worship to American Protestantism. And revived men in all walks of life discovered the initiative and accepted the responsibility to reshape the American republic according to a wide range of evangelical moral schemes.

The first phase of the Second Great Awakening began largely though not exclusively as a populist counterculture, but by the late 1820s, a second, consolidating phase was clearly underway. With an identifiable rapprochement being reached among the various white evangelical groups and with Second Great Awakening revivalism moving from the cultural periphery toward centers of power and respectability, the larger movement distanced itself from its earlier and more radical evangelical understandings of equality and opportunity.[54] Formerly marginalized Methodists and Baptists were following Presbyterians and Congregationalist standards, as expensive churches replaced humble meetinghouses, camp meetings metamorphosed from soul-saving exercises to family-oriented vacation getaways, patriarchal power

---

Conrad Cherry, *Nature and Religious Imagination: From Edwards to Bushnell* (Philadelphia: Fortress Press, 1980); George M. Marsden, *The Evangelical Mind and the New School Presbyterian Experience* (New Haven: Yale University Press, 1970); Gayraud Wilmore, *Black Religion and Black Radicalism: An Interpretation of the Religious History of Afro-American People*, 2d ed., (Maryknoll N.Y.: Orbis Books, 1983).

54. In 1827, the quintessential frontier revivalist Charles Finney had reached a shaky alliance with moderate Calvinist and Yale divine Lyman Beecher. From 1828 to 1830, radically democratic Methodists had challenged the episcopal polity of the denomination, with both groups settling on a more democratic respectability. During this period as well, white antislavery evangelical groups backed off from their earlier denunciations of slavery as sin. See Richard J. Carwardine, *Evangelicals and Politics in Antebellum America* (New Haven: Yale University Press, 1992), 2; idem, *Transatlantic Revivalism: Popular Evangelicalism in Britain and America, 1790–1865* (Westport, Conn.: Greenwood Press, 1978); Donald G. Mathews, *Religion and the Old South* (Chicago: University of Chicago Press, 1977); idem, "The Second Great Awakening As an Organizing Process, 1780–1830," *American Quarterly* 21 (spring 1969): 23–43; William G. McLoughlin, *Modern Revivalism: Charles Grandison Finney to Billy Graham* (New York: Ronald Press, 1959), 3–121; Marsden, *Evangelical Mind*, 31–58. For the "allure of respectability" as it played out in the life of antipopulist Methodist Nathan Bangs, see Hatch, *Democratization of Christianity*, 201–4.

structures discouraged female itinerants, women's energies were channeled into domestic responsibilities and reform voluntarism, and lay preaching gave way to the establishment of evangelical universities created to produce polished ministers. By the mid-1840s, as this second phase ended, all denominational expressions of American evangelicalism could be viewed as "branches of one great body," informed by a common theology, preoccupied with institutionalization, and espousing a social ethos that emphasized domesticity, individual initiative, social order, and respectability.[55] The increasingly refined evangelical mainstream of the 1840s and beyond was a far cry from its primitive origins among the plain, the ragged, and the disempowered in the early nineteenth century and there remained loud dissenting voices to this process of privileging respectability.

The revivalism of the Second Great Awakening was a unique blend of logic and emotion, but the evangelical theology undergirding it suggested thoughtful solutions to age-old questions: were humans powerless in a deterministic universe or did they enjoy free will, and was the universe created for humans to explore and manipulate for their own ends or were humans to find fulfillment in submitting to the natural and moral laws of its Creator? At times evangelical answers to these questions were profound and liberating, at other times they were simplistic and repressive, but throughout this early modern period, those providing the answers were confident in their abilities to explain the ways of God to humankind. By the turn of the nineteenth century, however, all Western religious doctrines had to respond to the intellectual challenges of Enlightenment rationalism. Where hegemony existed (mostly in New England), it lay in various permutations of Puritanism, and educated clergy followed Jonathan Edwards to extravagant lengths to reconcile the older Calvinism to the demands of the Enlightenment. On a doctrinal level, the Enlightenment offered serious alternatives to the fundamental Calvinist premises of revelation through Scripture, divine sovereignty, and human powerlessness ("original sin" or "human moral inability" in the Calvinist vernacular). According to the more radical claims of the Enlightenment, reason superseded revelation, although Enlightened

55. Robert Baird, *Religion in America,* (New York, 1856), 370, cited in Carwardine, *Evangelicals and Politics,* 2. A number of factors point to the mid-1840s as the end of a unified Second Great Awakening: numbers of revival converts dropped after peaking in 1843; the strongest denominations were splintering over the question of slavery; and many immigrants—who arrived in great numbers beginning in 1846—did not resonate with the peculiar combination of republicanism and Arminianized Calvinism that drove Second Great Awakening revivalism. Carwardine, *Transatlantic Revivalism,* 48–52. Laurie, *Artisans into Workers,* 26.

Calvinists tried desperately to finesse this transformation through prodigious (if not ultimately unconvincing and possibly counterproductive) efforts to prove biblical faith claims through scientific evidence and rationalist logic. The result was a modernized Calvinism that substituted a reasonable and nurturing deity for a stern and authoritative God.[56] The taming of the Calvinist God was furthered by the demands of republicanism, the popular ideology of the age,[57] which rejected, even on the cosmic level, any hint of tyranny or abuse of power. Instead, revivalist theologians like Nathaniel William Taylor and Charles Finney presented a Calvinist God shorn of his omnipotence and soteriological authority, although they were quick to point out that these newly discovered divine limitations were self-imposed. Providing a doctrinal system consistent with a self-limited God, the alternative theology of Arminianism replaced Calvinist election with human free agency, wherein individuals were responsible for choosing or rejecting salvation.

The end result of this transformation was a popular Arminianized Calvinism, which dominated American religious thought until Darwinism and the revolt against formalism shattered its hegemonic influence late in the nineteenth century.[58] The new willingness to define the workings of the universe in terms of humanly discernible and manipulable natural laws and to include the natural laws within the parameters of morally neutral aspects of human existence limited the prerogatives of God even as it increased the possibilities for human activity and innovation.[59] Although this metamorphosis was still

56. Allen C. Guelzo, "An Heir or a Rebel? Charles Grandison Finney and the New England Theology," *Journal of the Early Republic* 17 (spring 1997): 61–94; Marsden, *Evangelical Mind*, 6. For Methodist spirituality emphasizing divine nurturing, see Schneider, "Social Religion and Republican Spirituality," 163–89.

57. Robert E. Shalhope, "Toward a Republican Synthesis: The Emergence of an Understanding of Republicanism in American Historiography," *William and Mary Quarterly*, 3d ser., 29 (1972): 49–80; idem, "Republicanism and Early American Historiography," *William and Mary Quarterly*, 3d ser. 39 (Apr. 1982): 334–56; Robert Kelley, "Ideology and Political Culture from Jefferson to Nixon," *American Historical Review* 82 (1977): 536–37, 544; Wilentz, *Chants Democratic*, 14–15. The most thorough treatment of classical republicanism is J. G. A. Pocock, *The Machiavellian Moment: Florentine Political Thought and the Atlantic Republican Tradition* (Princeton: Princeton University Press, 1975).

58. Grimsted, "Ante-bellum Labor," 18–19.

59. Henry F. May, *The Enlightenment in America* (New York: Oxford University Press, 1976); Cherry, *Nature and Religious Imagination*; Turner, *Without God, Without Creed*; Herbert Hovenkamp, *Science and Religion in America, 1800–1860* (Philadelphia: University of Pennsylvania Press, 1978); Theodore D. Bozeman, *Protestants in an Age of Science* (Chapel Hill: University of North Carolina Press, 1977); Daniel Walker Howe, "The Evangelical Movement and Political Culture in the North during the Second Party System," *Journal of American History* 77 (Mar.

developing in the Jacksonian period, it was already recognizable. As the Congregationalist Samuel Goodrich summarized this transition in retrospect, "Orthodoxy [i.e., Calvinist Congregationalism] was in considerable degrees methodized and Methodism in due time became orthodoxed."[60] In fact, Lyman Beecher and other prominent evangelical Protestants in the early republic had begun to recognize the cultural influence accessible to them if they could accommodate and shape emergent liberal republicanism; by mid-century, under the broad umbrella of the Second Great Awakening, like-minded evangelicals had banded together sufficiently to create "the most formidable subculture" of the antebellum period.[61] But this claim is somewhat misleading, given evangelical ambivalence toward liberalized economics, allegedly redemptive politics, and a social egalitarianism that might include immigrants, Catholics, and nonbelievers. The seemingly easy accommodation of Arminianized Calvinism to liberal principles was illusory; instead, strife was endemic within the evangelical subculture. Mirroring what Nathan Hatch has described as the "cultural ferment over the meaning of freedom" in the early national period,[62] Arminianized Calvinists struggled with the rational logic of "gospel liberty" for socioeconomic relations, disempowered groups, and the political order. What was clear however, was that humanity had moved inexorably to the center of the created universe, and as a result the traditionally theistic cosmology of limits was under attack.

For all the effort put into establishing tight theological systems, correct doctrine and moral order had rarely been sufficient for evangelicals; individual spiritual experience involving human emotions and divine intervention was more often the attraction.[63] This orientation was reinforced in the early

1991): 1218, 1230; Ronald Wells, *History through the Eyes of Faith: Western Civilization and the Kingdom of God* (San Francisco: Harper and Row, 1989), 126–37.

60. Goodrich, quoted in Richard Shiels, "The Methodist Invasion of New England," paper presented at the Conference on Methodism and the Shaping of American Culture, 1760–1860, Oct. 7–8, 1994, Asbury Theological Seminary, Wilmore, Ky.

61. Carwardine, *Evangelicals and Politics*, 42–45.

62. Hatch, *Democratization of Christianity*, 6.

63. In Wesleyan theology, for instance, doctrine has followed experience. Bassett, "Theological Identity of the North American Holiness Movement," 78–79. The Reformed approach, in contrast, subjected personal experience to orthodox doctrines of a Calvinist worldview. Rabinowitz, *Spiritual Self*, xxix, 220–21. For the varieties of spiritual experience influencing Methodism, see John Wigger's excellent "Taking Heaven by Storm: Enthusiasm and Early American Methodism, 1770–1820," *Journal of the Early Republic* (summer 1994): 167–94. See also Caroline Franks Davis, *The Evidential Force of Religious Experience* (Oxford: Clarendon Press, 1989).

republic where republican antihierarchicalism and disestablishment had eliminated many of the normally operative reasons for joining churches and where evangelical clergy were particularly conscious of the necessity of devising new ways to evangelize their communities. According to the evangelical doctrines of the Second Great Awakening, spiritual experience took two forms: the immediate and life-changing sense of acceptance and affirmation accompanying conversion ("justification"), and the subsequent series of encounters with the divine, which empowered individuals to resist sin and maintain holy lives ("sanctification").[64] While examples of revivalists celebrating emotion exclusively certainly existed within the evangelical tradition, the more accepted goal, stemming from the revival successes of Calvinists Jonathan Edwards and George Whitefield, was to meld "head" religion (rational assent to orthodox doctrinal tenets) with "heart" religion (emotional experience corroborating those tenets). The centrality of emotion in this process did not preclude the importance of rationality; rather, the evangelical synthesis of the two was designed to eschew vacuous sentimentality as it liberated converts from fear, anxiety, and existential meaninglessness. The point was to convince individuals of their ability to influence their own lives, as well as the social networks in which they participated.[65] It was also to provide a context for the trials and misfortunes of life, which were rationally explained either as rearguard actions of a defeated devil or as purifying work of a demanding God. The revivalist legacy fit well with the Arminianized Calvinism bursting forth during the Second Great Awakening.

The Second Great Awakening revival was successful because it exposed and assuaged deeply felt anxieties experienced by men and women who appreciated the opportunities offered in the American experiment but who still lived lives often beyond their control. This psychic tension went beyond the usual (though still operative) concerns with health, safety, security, and purpose; in the early republic people struggled with the propriety of abandoning

64. Edmund S. Morgan, *Visible Saints: The History of a Puritan Idea* (Ithaca: Cornell University Press, 1963), 68–70; Charles L. Cohen, *God's Caress: The Psychology of Puritan Religious Experience* (New York: Oxford University Press, 1986), 3–22; David S. Lovejoy, *Religious Enthusiasm and the Great Awakening* (Englewood Cliffs, N.J.: Prentice-Hall, 1969), 8–9; Marsden, *Evangelical Mind*, 32; William G. McLoughlin, "Revivalism," in Edwin S. Gaustad, ed., *The Rise of Adventism: Religion and Society in Mid-Nineteenth-Century America* (New York: Harper and Row, 1974), 119–49.

65. Cohen, *God's Caress*, 133; Rabinowitz, *Spiritual Self*, 94–96; Lorne Dawson, "Self-Affirmation, Freedom, and Rationality: Theoretically Elaborating 'Active' Conversions," *Journal for the Scientific Study of Religion* 29 (June 1990): 159.

extended families, community ties, and traditional mores in their various pursuits of happiness. In the most successful and authentic revivals, the experiential component of Christian conversion involved a difficult internal struggle (often an extended process) to abandon deep-seated identities and attachments, recognized as no longer efficacious to overcome self-condemnation or to inspire self-love, in the hope of realizing immediately superior psychic replacements. The evangelical gospel was a combination of bad news (human sinfulness practiced in the presence of holiness leading to judgment) and good news (divine grace presented in the person of Jesus resulting in forgiveness), with the former tapping into an individual's deepest self-doubts unmediated by the normal protective processes of denial and ego support; hence, the effective revivalist's emphasis on sin, or self-centeredness, as an inherent condition corrupting every moral action. But condemnation was merely a prelude to a more uplifting message, and revival audiences knew that. In this light, Methodist itinerant Stephen Roszel urged those attending his revival to lift their "hearts in humble prayer to God that he may now pour the Holy Ghost upon us. . . . God is on the giving hand—you feel his divine influence, and are encouraged to ask, that your joys may be full; that your peace may be as a river, and your righteousness as the waters of the sea. . . . Look to experience the glory of Jesus!" But, Roszel went on to warn the congregation, if people refuse to accept this grace, serious consequences would occur. "Our God has his fan in his hand . . . [and] the chaff, the ungodly hypocrite, and unbelievers of all discriptions, he will burn with unquenchable fire." He ended in characteristic revival fashion by reminding his listeners to allow "no more delay . . . tomorrow may be too late."[66] Second Great Awakening revivalists consistently pounded home to revival audiences that their lives had eternal significance and that their moral choices mattered.

As seen in Roszel's efforts, the good news of revival preaching was profoundly paradoxical; at the moment an individual acknowledged his or her utter inability to merit divine approval by meeting the demands of the moral code, the affirmation of a forgiving God could be immediately experienced, often in emotionally overwhelming fashion. Evangelical revivalists, however, were rarely satisfied with relief from moral culpability; they also insisted that their converts avail themselves of the spiritual resources present to avoid returning to their former sinful behaviors, which were understood as mere manifestations of an unredeemed center. Evangelical life after

66. Stephen George Roszel, *The Substance of a Sermon Delivered in the White Marsh Meeting House, Lancaster City, Virginia, on the 15th of May, 1825* (Baltimore, 1826).

conversion, therefore, was an ongoing struggle to achieve holiness, but perfectionist teachings promised the spiritual support necessary to succeed. This message was not particularly subtle or nuanced, and evangelicals were confident that not only could they overcome sin but that they could also define and identify its presence in others, across time and cultures; hence, the low level of toleration for the allegedly aberrant behavior of others. The result was an aggressive, at times arrogant and resented, moral impulse, by no means unaware of the effect of environment on religious choices but preoccupied with the possibilities for permanent social change through persuasion, preferably, or legislation if necessary. This evangelical passion for social melioration ran the gamut from abolitionism to nativism, with some evangelicals favoring influence and others coercion.

Individual capacity to appreciate sin-damaged psyches, socioeconomic anxieties, and theological paradox were crucial in the revival context. For some Americans who enjoyed privileged existences or experienced negative Christian influence in their lives, the suggestion of a healthy self-abasement was oxymoronic and the suggestion of a positive life in Christ seemed chimerical at best; for others, addressing spiritual concerns simply had less resonance than meeting the demands of everyday life. But for those convinced of their limitations or not yet conditioned by modernist illusions of boundless human potential for wielding power and controlling nature without repercussions, the necessity of "dying to self" in order to live the "victorious life," though difficult, was not inconceivable. And since evangelical conversion required more than the prerequisite of individual crisis, receptivity to divine affirmation was also indispensable. Thus revival psychology was a double-edged phenomenon. The potential convert needed both an openness to the potential friendliness of God and sufficient self-esteem to make believable the possibility of becoming morally acceptable and existentially meaningful. The revivalist, meanwhile, had to effectively present a system in which all human behavior was at the same time ultimately significant and doomed to fail to merit divine approval, but also amenable to some kind of redemption. Even though the evangelical life relied on a supernatural act that was afforded, according to Christian theology, only through the death and resurrection of Jesus and the subsequent activity of the Holy Spirit, both the appropriate ministrations of an effective revivalist and the correct response of a receptive audience were fundamental to revival success.[67]

67. For a similar discussion of these themes, see Christopher Lasch's interpretation of William James's *The Varieties of Religious Experience* in Lasch, *True and Only Heaven*, 289–92.

The necessary *precondition*, then, for evangelical conversion, rested on a general acceptance of the notions that God existed and that he rewarded those who sought him. Conversion success turned on three interrelated propositions: one needed to acknowledge the limitations on human ability (particularly in the area of moral perfection), one needed to understand the importance of submitting to the will of a personal yet transcendent God who alone imbued individuals with worth and righteousness, and one needed to entertain the hope that such a deity could stand meaningfully in the gap between (holy) ideals and (sinful) reality. The paradoxical *result* of this evangelical submission, however, was the empowering realization that former mental orientations and boundaries ceased to exist; in this experience lay the ecstatic, "liminal," element of evangelical conversion, wherein the initiate could experience a transcendent view into the divine mysteries and could cease, at least briefly, to care for social norms and respectable behavior. The ecstatic expressions accompanying the liminal experience—the jerks, unfocused hilarity, barking, glossolalia, swooning—caught the attention of those suspicious of charismatic or hyperemotional experience. Fear of these implicitly dangerous behaviors (because those so converted might very well no longer care for any order, decorum, or deference) led to the disparagement of revivalist excesses.[68] Despite the anarchic potential, however, Protestant social traditions and cultural restraints were still operative, and the moral discipline and attention to communal welfare noted in the lives of many revival converts attracted, at times, even the skeptical.[69]

Instructive here are the conversion accounts left by Methodists Thomas Branagan and Thomas Rutherford. Branagan was an Irish seamen and adventurer, initially part of a privateering crew and later a slave overseer on the Caribbean island of Antigua. Raised as a Catholic, he converted to a vital if generic Protestant evangelicalism through a series of dreams and revelations, after which he joined a Methodist connection. Branagan's conversion progressed through rather typical stages: from awakening (the recognition of personal sinfulness, or as Branagan described himself, operating as an

68. This discussion of liminality comes from Victor W. Turner, *Dramas, Fields, and Metaphors: Symbolic Action in Human Society* (Ithaca: Cornell University Press, 1974), 272–99; see Donald G. Mathews, "Evangelical America—The Methodist Ideology," in Russell E. Richey and Kenneth E. Rowe, eds., *Rethinking Methodist History: A Bicentennial Historical Consultation* (Nashville: Kingswood Books, 1985), 95. See also James Hoopes, *Consciousness in New England* (Baltimore: Johns Hopkins University Press, 1989), 4–30; Isaac, *Transformation of Virginia*, 260–64.

69. Schneider, "Social Religion and Republican Spirituality," 172–74.

"enlightened heathen") to purgation (the unsuccessful, even futile, attempt to attain righteousness through one's own efforts) to illumination (the experience of moral helplessness, followed by intense affirmation through, according to Branagan, "the mediatorial office of Christ") to sanctification (the ongoing experience of empowerment precluding religious complacency and demanding personal devotion to character-building and religious activism).[70] While many evangelicals came to spiritual enlightenment gradually through family training and church instruction, and others through revival preaching, and still others received illumination unmediated by family, ministers, or congregations.[71] Branagan was representative of the third group.

As he described it, while bound for the West Indies, Branagan began to worry about the state of his soul. One night he had a powerful dream in which he saw Jesus intervening with God on his behalf. When Branagan awoke, he was "dissolved in joy, love, and gratitude" and determined to devote his life, as much as possible, to the realization of the Kingdom of God on earth. His Catholic relatives were not as pleased with this quintessentially mystical experience; when they discovered his switch in religious orientation, they disinherited him. Now permanently isolated both emotionally and financially, Branagan soon departed for the United States, never to return to Ireland. Arriving penniless in Philadelphia in 1799, he fell in love with the city, which he "admired . . . more than any one I visited" because it had abolished slavery and because it included only "one capitalist, two banks, comparatively few brothels, grog shops, apothecary shops, and not one pawnbroker's shop in the whole city."[72] For the rest of his life, Branagan worked as an itinerant preacher, based in Philadelphia.

70. The stages are set forth and described in Doris E. Andrews, "Popular Religion in the Middle Atlantic Ports: The Rise of the Methodists, 1770–1800," (Ph.D. diss., University of Pennsylvania, 1986), 144n77.

71. For charismatic Methodist experience in the early republic, see Wigger, "Taking Heaven by Storm," 167–94.

72. Thomas Branagan, *The Guardian Genius of the Federal Union; or, Patriotic Admonitions on the Signs of the Times, in Relation to the Evil Spirit of Party, Arising from the Root of All Our Evils, Human Slavery* (New York, 1839); idem, *The Penitential Tyrant; or, Slave Trader Reformed: A Pathetic Poem in Four Cantos* (New York, 1807), 11, 15, 27–28. Branagan's career and literary work are described in Lewis Leary, "Thomas Branagan: Republican Rhetoric and Romanticism in America," *Pennsylvania Magazine of History and Biography* 77 (July 1953): 332–52, and his contributions are mentioned in James D. Essig, *The Bonds of Wickedness: Americans Evangelicals against Slavery, 1770–1808* (Philadelphia: Temple University Press, 1982), 154–56, and Gary B. Nash, *Forging Freedom: The Formation of Philadelphia's Black Community, 1720–1840* (Cambridge: Harvard University Press, 1988), 178–80.

Thomas Rutherford's conversion account both resembles and diverges from Branagan's. Rutherford was a late-eighteenth-century British Methodist. An account of his conversion experience and subsequent Methodist service appeared in book form in 1807 and was published in Baltimore sometime later. Rutherford was born in 1752 and raised in the rigid Calvinism of British Presbyterianism. As a young man he was drawn somewhat to religion, but his attempts to pray met with "coldness and formality" because of his self-admitted addiction to the "horrid vice" of swearing. Probably equally salient to his sense of psychic distress, however, were the deaths of his mother and sister when he was fifteen. Throughout the summer after those tragedies, he heard his first Methodist preaching. Young Rutherford was moved, not by fear of fire and brimstone, but by a desire to love Jesus as, according to the Methodists, Jesus was loving him. Steeped in the dour doctrines of the Presbyterians, he remained suspicious of Methodists and watched carefully to observe their practice. They proved to be diligent in their work and seemed to "manage all their secular affairs in the very same spirit in which they went to church, heard preaching, read the Scriptures, sung hymns, and poured out their souls in prayer to God." Revealing the Wesleyan preference for the practical over the doctrinal, Rutherford concluded that "whatever might be wrong in their principles" according to his Calvinist precepts, "their practice was right."[73]

Under the continued influence of Presbyterian preaching, Rutherford experienced feelings of "deep depravity." At his first communion, he felt "divine peace" but "no rapturous joy." Even this comfort, however, soon eluded him, presumably because he did not have the practical spiritual knowledge necessary to "preserve the blessing" and because he lacked the support of fellow believers. Soon thereafter one of Rutherford's friends was "set at liberty and filled with joy and peace in believing," having simultaneously experienced justification ("the full deliverance both from the guilt and power of sin") and partial sanctification ("the abiding sense of the divine presence"). Upon hearing the first-person witness of the recent convert, he, too, "felt all the darkness, barrenness and depression of soul, which for near two months I had laboured under, entirely removed" and was filled with "love and joy" because he was now completely convinced that God "was altogether lovely, and infinitely precious. I could do nothing, from

73. Henry Moore, *An Account of the Lord's Dealings with the Rev. Thomas Rutherford, The Greater Part Written by Himself* (Baltimore, n.d.), 7–26. Moore also authored a biography of John Wesley in 1826.

morning to night, but wonder, rejoice, and adore." His conversion, by his own admission, was not the result of any voice, vision, or scripture (although those occurrences were not unusual in evangelical experience); it was simply "a conviction or evidence in my soul . . . as well as . . . assurance . . . not produced in the way of reasoning or argument," but rather "by direct, immediate, and instantaneous, and also clear and unequivocal" divine inspiration. Rutherford continued, "I went to Him as my Father . . . with filial confidence . . . and found him always ready to . . . help me." He joined the Methodists immediately, and "his highest wish in the world" became "to live and die a simple, humble, earnest, holy, happy, primitive Methodist." For Rutherford, the liberating aspects of a Wesleyan (Arminian) relationship with God superseded the formal creedalism of his Reformed (Calvinist) background (without seriously challenging the major points of its doctrine), empowering him with an optimistic evangelical faith for a lifetime of service. Moreover, a distinctive communal aspect pervaded his evangelical experience; "the whole of our economy furnish us with . . . frequent and multiplied opportunities of bearing each other's burdens, lifting up the hands that hang down, and confirming the feeble knees."[74]

Despite the different channels through which the Holy Spirit reached Branagan and Rutherford, their conversion and postconversion experiences of love and joy testify to the most significant element of evangelical life—the liminal power of Arminianized evangelicalism. Rutherford immediately sought to exercise evangelical empowerment within established channels of church and social activity and he maintained his normal secular pursuits, but in a redeemed manner. Rutherford's remarks concerning the self-discipline of Methodism and his observations on the centrality of Methodist fellowship clearly indicate that disorder, Christian anarchy, or hyperindividualism were never the ultimate evangelical goal; like Rutherford, many converts sought out evangelical camaraderie and avenues of "voluntary usefulness" in the church and the larger society without changing occupations.[75] In contrast, Branagan's postconversion metamorphosis transformed both his spiritual consciousness and his worldly preoccupations. Though the progression was gradual, Branagan's heightened sense of divine love and awareness of the debilitating effects of human selfishness and unlimited control led him to

74. Ibid., 27–43.

75. When James Finley experienced conversion, his first thought was for an evangelical community: "I sighed for Church privileges and communion with the people of God." Holifield, "Toward a History of American Congregations," in Wind and Lewis, eds. *American Congregations*, 2:23.

forsake the lucrative career of a slave overseer. This decision set him on a long pilgrimage as an itinerant preacher and radical polemicist, dedicated to presenting the demands of social justice as a Christian duty to as wide an audience as he could reach. For forty-four years until his death in 1843, and in some twenty published volumes, Branagan championed a broadly progressive evangelical program of republican reform, emphasizing the abolition of slavery but also espousing producerist anticapitalism, nonfeminist protection of women's rights, celebration of cultural diversity, and even recognition of animal rights.[76] Branagan's understanding of sanctification made his personal life less settled than Rutherford's and his radical Methodism was less institutionally oriented, but both remained inspired by their ongoing experences of divine forgiveness and affirmation.

For evangelicals like Branagan and Rutherford, conversion has historically been tied to group-mediated concepts of holiness and moral behavior, characterized by the centrality of obedience in evangelical thought.[77] Like the notion of submission, however, Christian obedience did not mean undifferentiated obsequiousness; rather, it demanded agreement to a specific message and participation in living out its precepts, thereby galvanizing believers to action. Activism could move in either positive or negative channels, in the latter case condemning specific sins or opposing pretensions to overweening human authority. As Thomas Branagan expressed it: "POWER, though limited by written laws, in the hands of mortal men, poorly educated, and surrounded by sycophants and flatterers, who wish, by partaking the power, to partake also of its profits and distinctions, and thus gratify at once their pride and avarice, is always endeavoring to extend itself beyond the limitations; and requires to be watched with the most jealous eye, by all who

76. Although his earlier works emphasized racial equality and prospered only through the support of African-American ministers like Richard Allen and Absalom Jones, for a time at least Branagan lapsed into a racist diatribe against the proliferation of African-American black males in Philadelphia who, he argued, threatened the employment of white immigrant workers and the alleged purity of lower-class white women. Thomas Branagan, *Serious Remonstrances, Addressed to the Citizens of the Northern States, and Their Representatives* (Philadelphia, 1805), cited in Nash, *Forging Freedom*, 178–80. Such a conflation of racism and nativism in producerist arguments to protect workers dislocated by capitalist transformation was not unusual in American labor history. See David R. Roediger, *The Wages of Whiteness: Race and the Making of the American Working Class* (London: Verso, 1991). Consideration of Branagan's position in 1805, however, needs to balanced by the recognition that Branagan published his epic antislavery poem, *Avenia, or a Tragical Poem, on the Oppression of the Human Species; and Infringement on the Rights of Man in Five Books with Notes Explanatory and Miscellaneous. Written in Imitation of Homer's Iliad*, (Philadelphia, 1810), five years later.

77. Essig, *Bonds of Wickedness*, 6–9, 26–28.

are subject to it, and to be restrained within its bounds by the manifest efforts, and the most determined resolution of virtue."[78]

Evangelical activism could also mandate social action in the form of various reform efforts. Although evangelicals maintained much of Calvinist theology regarding individual sin and social justice, the combination of Arminian assurance and empowerment was offered as an antidote to Calvinist paralysis and fatalism. As popular Methodist itinerant Nicholas Snethen noted, the Calvinist "hope of distant mercy" had only led him to "the spirit of bondage to fear" and inaction which his conversion to Methodism had cured. Similarly, the *Christian Recorder*, an official organ of Arminianized Calvinism, denigrated the "stern and self-denying virtues" of Calvinist tradition and espoused the "amiable and pacific" attitudes of liberalism. In an archetypical Arminian perspective, Methodist Henry Slicer encouraged his audiences to avoid being "anxious to get out of the world," because the promises of God were "great in the good they offer temporal [and] spiritual; for [this] time and eternity."[79] At issue was not activism per se, but rather the distinctive directions activism was to take in the early nineteenth century in light of the tensions created by the conflicts between tradition and modernity. In this respect, the liminal potency of evangelical conversion was invariably channeled in particular directions according to religious traditions and shifting cultural factors as well as individual predilections.

The predominant characteristic of American society in the early republic was its openness to cultural reconstructions. While Americans were quick to seize the obvious opportunities made possible by independence, the reality of modernity could foster anxiety as well as ambition, especially as the protection provided by traditional social networks and arrangements eroded. This anxiety, moreover, was authentic; frontier circumstances and challenges were as real to those caught up in the transformations of the market revolution as they were to those moving west or trying to extend slave-holding culture. To succeed in this upheaval required new perspectives and

78. Thomas Branagan, *The Beauties of Philanthropy, Extracted from the Writings of Its Disciple* (New York, 1839), 190–91.

79. *Mutual Rights* 1 (Nov. 1824): 125; *Christian Recorder* (1829), cited in Lasch, *True and Only Heaven*, 260; Henry Slicer, *Journal*, 3 vols. (unpublished) 1:53, Lovely Lane Museum, Baltimore. Holy living was much more than humiliation: "I endeavored to show that the greatest efforts of the will, when exerted only over the appetites and passions with a view to self-denial or self-punishment, have been found inefficacious . . . to improve the mental faculties and have not facilitated the discovery of religious truth." *Wesleyan Repository* 3 (Jan. 1824): 356.

social skills, and evangelical empowerment proved particularly pertinent because it offered self-disciplined strategies for this life as well as for the hereafter. To be sure, evangelical preoccupation with the spiritual transcendence of mundane earthly problems could inculcate fatalistic or quietistic expressions of devotional piety, but, in the heady days of the early republic, activism regarding the creation of godly social structures or oppositionalism in the face of impious social constructions were more likely. Most relevant in this regard was the evangelical emphasis on instilling self-discipline and character as a religious duty, on maintaining Calvinist notions concerning the importance of "redeeming time" by eschewing frivolity and luxury, on transforming as well as transcending the world through organized resistance to oppression and through voluntarist reform organizations, on insisting that politics reflect covenant responsibilities, and on establishing alternative religious communities wherever the breakdown of traditional sources of security left individuals isolated and alienated.[80]

Disciplined social activism among Second Great Awakening evangelicals was often reinforced by an aggressive, biblicist egalitarianism that was limited only by the deep-seated prevalence of race and gender restrictions in American society, and even these were not safe from evangelical attack. Faith commitments empowered people, by "taking their deepest spiritual impulses at face value," to challenge existing power relations and status distinctions. Unquestioned allegiance to the doctrines of educated theologians and the discipline of trained clergy weakened in light of a general reluctance to trust the so-called lessons of the past to instruct the possibilities of the future. In keeping with the prevailing individualism evident in populist interpretations of sola scriptura, one evangelical wrote, "I could say in truth that the gospel that was preached to me, was not after man; for I neither received it of man, neither was I taught it by man, but by revelation of Jesus Christ, through the medium of the Holy Spirit in opening my understanding to understand the scripture."[81] Politically and socially, populist evangelicals dared to imagine any number of ways in which social harmony could be built, and they celebrated the virtue of the common working people whose labors would

80. George M. Marsden, *Fundamentalism and American Culture: The Shaping of Twentieth-Century Evangelicalism, 1870–1925* (New York: Oxford University Press, 1980), 85–93; Carwardine, *Evangelicals and Politics*, 331–32n35; Winton U. Solberg, *Redeem the Time* (Cambridge: Cambridge University Press, 1977); Stephen E. Berk, *Calvinism Versus Democracy: Timothy Dwight and the Origins of American Evangelical Orthodoxy* (Hamden, Conn.: Archon Press, 1974).

81. Hatch, *Democratization*, 10, quote from p. 41.

make the new nation prosperous and godly, as well as the decentralization which would protect that virtue. Authority and tradition remained legitimate, but to be morally binding they had to meet standards which evangelicals were ready to reshape, articulate, and enforce. Surrendering to the will of God was by no means the same as submitting to the whim of man, and populist evangelicals, through the agencies of biblical and personal revelation, were able to differentiate between the two.

The economic opportunities available to populist evangelicals in the early republic were myriad, and the initiative inherent in their faith commitments enabled them to reject traditional restraints and to take advantage of new options. In this sense, populist evangelicals were transparently modern, with an enhanced (at times, overweening) sense of self-importance and ability. As "average people on the make," capitalism and liberal economics appealed mightily to them.[82] The capitalist attraction was heightened by evangelical shapers of public opinion like Francis Wayland. Wayland, a product of populist evangelical upbringing, a Baptist preacher/educator, and a professor at Brown University, authored an influential defense of liberal economics in his widely read *The Elements of Moral Science* (1835) and *The Elements of Political Economy* (1837). His economic philosophy, based on liberal republican tenets, emphasized the dual sacrosanctity of individual freedom and private property, with the former subordinated to the latter. The individual right to use and exploit private property (including labor), coupled with the natural laws of supply and demand, led Wayland to reject traditionalist proscriptions against usury, price controls, unfair competition, and exploitation. According to his modernist dogma, unfettered competition would correct outrageous interest rates, poor laws were offensive because they ran contrary to the salutary impetus of self-interest, and exploited workers were to obey and submit to their masters, even as they worked to improve individual moral behavior. With personal restrictions no longer operative in the morally neutral arena of Enlightened economics, Wayland gave implicit religious sanction to unrestrained acquisitiveness and the elevation of individual economic concerns over community interests.[83]

But Francis Wayland was no Henry Ward Beecher, and few evangelicals in the early nineteenth century were ready to assert the crass Social Darwinism that would mar upper-class evangelicalism in the Gilded Age. By 1837, in the

82. Idem, "The Puzzle of American Methodism," Bartlett Lecture delivered at Yale University, Feb. 9, 1993, 15.

83. Joseph Dorfman, *The Economic Mind in American Civilization, 1606–1865*, 2 vols. (New York: Viking Press, 1946) 2:758–61.

wake of a devastating panic, Wayland was modifying his position to reiterate the importance of producerist limitations on capitalist expansion. In a sermon preached to the First Baptist Church in Providence on May 14, Wayland condemned the rampant speculative and monopolizing characteristics of emergent capitalism. "Instead of using his capital for a blessing, he is using it for a curse to his neighbor. . . . He has no right to use his capital as an instrument for grinding the faces of the poor. . . . 'He that withholdeth corn, the people shall curse him.'" But Wayland offered no systemic alternative and instead proposed individualized solutions.[84] Such a defense, moreover, had serious unintended ramifications. As Nathan Hatch emphasizes, "the modern and individualistic" tenor of populist evangelicalism could and often did have "the ironic effect of accelerating the break-up of traditional society and the advent of a social order of competition, self-expression, and free enterprise," in which "grasping entrepreneurs could erect new forms of tyranny in religious, political, and economic institutions."[85] In its sundering of the bonds of mercantilism and social economic privilege as well as political hierarchicalism, laissez-faire liberalism had much in common with the populist evangelical challenge to established authority and the search for individual independence. Much has been made of this compatibility between liberalism and evangelicalism, as indicated by the individualistic nature of conversion through revivalism as well as the emphasis on the ascetic moralism of empowered, yet circumscribed, evangelicals. This reality, according to Richard Rabinowitz, revealed the "idolatry of the isolated self," which included a this-worldly moralism, sufficient ability todefer gratification in order to plan for the future, and the acknowledgement that risk taking was morally acceptable.[86] Underlying all this was an emphasis on individual will and the practicality of virtue, so crucial in the process of elevating individual character over social ethics.

The process of achieving success through liberalized economics, however, should be understood in the context of the psychic distress that accompanied it for devout evangelicals. Here is where the tension between modern options and traditional restrictions became most acute, as evangelical demands for holy living encountered the ambition and competition necessitated by the

84. *Sun*, May 30, 1837. The scriptural reference is to Prov. 11:26. Wayland was even more condemnatory of contemporary financial practices following the panic occurring in 1857. Hanley, *Beyond a Christian Commonwealth*, 101–2.

85. Hatch, *Democratization of Christianity*, 14. By the 1830s, according to George Marsden, evangelicals "optimistically affirmed that men's moral standards (if not their natures) were steadily improving." Marsden, *Evangelical Mind*, 235.

86. Rabinowitz, *Spiritual Self*, xxvii, 86–123

as such claim legitimate moral authority. The insistence on Christian submission to legitimate authority had inspired much Revolutionary rhetoric, was undergirding the populist evangelicalism of the early republic, and would provide a moral base for much subsequent evangelical anticapitalism. But constructions of legitimate moral and socioeconomic authority were fraught with ambiguity—a fact readily discernible in the ecclesiastical tensions and cultural alignments generated by the Methodist Protestant schism. This schism, the focus of chapter 2, erupted in Baltimore in the latter half of the 1820s and became institutionalized as a new denomination by the early 1830s.[94] Although the predominant issue pertained to democratizing the Methodist polity, this upheaval and its aftermath also featured the populist limits of submission to established authority and revealed a great deal concerning the ongoing evangelical debate over liberal innovations in light of the traditional proscriptions against, as the prophet Isaiah put it, "grinding the faces of the poor."

94. Such schisms were by no means unusual for Methodists in the early republic, nor were their ambivalent social implications hidden. The furious debate related to Thomas Jefferson's successful candidacy for the presidency in 1800 that divided Philadelphia's Methodists "revealed the ongoing issue of how a popular movement might be a harbinger of working class and middle class culture at one and the same time." Andrews, "Popular Religion in the Middle Atlantic Ports," 272.

Methodist Protestant Reform 1820–1835

Chapter Two

Methodist Dissent and the Limits of Christian Submission to Authority

The April 16, 1836, edition of the *National Trades' Union*, published under the auspices of the General Trades' Union of New York City and distributed to artisans in urban centers throughout the United States, carried an article entitled "Prayer for Kings." This filler mentioned the dilemma Paul's command to pray for rulers (1 Tim. 2:1–2) presented to contemporary Methodists: how could republicans pray for kings? Answering his own question, the minister continued, "I have thought of a way to get over this hard spot, without violence to our principles and feelings as republicans. I would recommend . . . to all on whom it may be incumbent to pray for kings, to ask the Lord to give them short lives, happy deaths, convert their souls, and take them home to heaven, and send no more such." His Methodist audience heartily agreed, and according to a contemporary, this petition was afterward presented as a toast on various public occasions. The purported author of these sentiments was the Methodist itinerant and erstwhile presiding elder, Jacob Gruber, who was stationed in Baltimore in 1814 when this "blessing" was originally uttered and was called back in 1834 and 1835 to fill the pulpits of the Asbury and Sharp Street African-American Methodist congregations.[1]

This anecdote provides a window into the interplay between artisan militancy and populist evangelicalism, particularly Methodism, in the early republic. The very choice of sermon topic is instructive: Americans no longer lived under monarchy, and so scriptural demands regarding temporal authority had to be recast. Both preacher and audience were cognizant of the potential for tyranny incumbent in any nonrepublican polity; while oppression was unacceptable, neither was violent reaction. Instead, the preacher suggested a kind of benevolent curse, asking God to initiate the corrective action and limiting the need for the unwilling ruled to take matters into their own hands. Within this traditional sensibility, however, the strong response of the congregation indicated that there were limits to the notion of Christian submission to authority and clearly suggested an openness to more militant action if necessary. Finally, by appearing in a leading labor journal, this sermon calls into question the prevailing historiographical assumption that evangelicalism and artisan activism were mutually exclusive and that evangelicalism, despite its emphasis on equality, operated solely as the inculcator of individualistic and quiescent mentalities necessary to create a submissive, pliable work force. It is these unquestioned assertions that have led Sean Wilentz to identify "at Methodism's core" its definitive tension "between submissiveness and egalitarianism."[2]

Defining American Methodism (and populist evangelicalism in general) in terms of these interpretive polarities is problematic. Whereas the egalitarian emphasis certainly helped make common folk welcome in Methodist communities and enabled evangelicals to create their own subculture, the authoritarian power structure governing those communities was contested, early on and often. In evangelical experience, submission to authority meant, first of all, submission to God and the demands of Scripture. But Scripture made clear that duly constituted and divinely appointed authority could indeed be guilty of immorality, for which the entire community would pay; that, in fact, was a fundamental message of the Old Testament. The question for believers was how were they to respond? This question was crucial in the early republic—not just for Methodist polity but also for Methodist response to threats to producerist ethics.

1. *National Trades' Union*, Apr. 16, 1836. Jacob Gruber also had a reputation for strongly rebuking any evidence of "luxury of superfluity" in his Methodist charges. William B. Sprague, *Annals of the American Pulpit*, 7 vols. (New York, 1859), 7:342–46.

2. Wilentz, *Chants Democratic*, 80.

Ever since the English Civil War, Anglo-American Protestants had been presented with dichotomous religio-political answers—for the privileged and the pacifistic, passive obedience and nonresistance were prescribed, but for the disempowered and the militant, resistance to illegitimate authority became a religious duty. The debate was not theoretical for Methodists. During the Revolution, the tiny band of American Methodists had pursued the former course, with some reflecting the political conservatism of John Wesley and others revealing a genuine commitment to Christian pacifism. For their pains, Methodists were reviled as cowards and persecuted as loyalists, both epithets that Methodist itinerants and their growing legions of populist followers in the post-Revolutionary years were eager to disprove. Under the ubiquitous influence of republicanism and driven by their experience of harassment from established authorities, Methodists accepted the proposition that submission to authority referred to legitimate authority only, and with this submission came the responsibility to challenge and resist immoral leadership in any area.[3] This rejection of passive obedience was interpreted broadly and was not restricted to Methodism. Tensions over what properly constituted authority were relevant to all evangelical commoners, including artisans caught up in the transformation from the producerist mode to the increasingly unilateral control exercised by some large-scale capitalist entrepreneurs. And the populist evangelical understanding of the doctrine of submission to authority was, in short, the antithesis of submissiveness.

This debate over power and authority was most readily apparent among America's Methodists who had undergone, from their origins in the late eighteenth century, serious conflicts over the issues of ecclesiastical representation and intradenominational power relations, with undertones related to traditional Methodist primitivism and producerism.[4] Despite his popularity as the father of Methodism, John Wesley was noted for notoriously autocratic tendencies, as was his English-born disciple Francis Asbury, the father of American Methodism—realities not lost on Americans prone to nativism and republicanism.[5] Under the dynamic and indefatigable Asbury, the authoritarian ecclesiastical organization denominated the Methodist Episcopal

3. Harry S. Stout, *The New England Soul: Preaching and Religious Culture in Colonial New England* (New York: Oxford University Press, 1986), 241–44; Wigger, "Taking Heaven by Storm," 100–4.

4. Richey, *Early American Methodism*, 90–91 and passim.

5. Pronounced Anglophobia was not unusual in early national Methodism. The popular Methodist itinerant Nicholas Snethen ("Dokemasius") dismissed Asbury, for instance, as little more than an Englishman with an Englishman's proclivity for aristocratical governance (*Mutual Rights* 1 [Apr. 1825]: 342), and another Methodist local preacher—Samuel Jennings—

Church monopolized power in the General Conference, which consisted of itinerants and bishops only, met once every four years, assigned itinerants to established circuits on a rotating basis, determined the rules of the *Discipline*, and did business with no official input from local preachers and laity. From 1772 on, American Methodists in agreement with Robert Strawbridge, James O'Kelly, and William Hammett chafed under the domination of bishops and itinerants within the Methodist Episcopal Church, with followers of the latter two leaving to found short-lived alternative organizations.[6] Adding to popular suspicion of the power of bishops and the new presiding elders in the first quarter of the nineteenth century was the fact that many traveling preachers were "locating," or abandoning the rigors of the itinerancy for the stability of settled lay ministry, thereby effectively removing themselves from the structures of power within the church.[7] Further aggravating these grievances, attempts by leaders like Nathan Bangs to make Methodism socially respectable led primitive Methodists to conclude that such leadership might no longer warrant obedience.[8] And if Methodist authority was judged illegitimate, resistance was a religious duty.

---

referred derogatorily to the earliest Methodists in America as "those six Englishmen." Samuel K. Jennings, *An Exposition of the Late Controversy in the Methodist Episcopal Church* . . . (Baltimore, 1831), 124; R. F. Shinn, *A Tribute to Our Fathers: Being A Vindication of the Founders of the Methodist Protestant Church* (Cincinnati and Baltimore, 1854), 60–61.

6. The Methodist Episcopal Church was the official name of the organization popularly referred to in the United States as "the Methodist Church." Gordon Pratt Baker, ed., *Those Incredible Methodists: A History of the Baltimore Annual Conference of the United Methodist Church* (Baltimore: Commission on Archives and History, The Baltimore Conference, 1972), 12, 16; The first General Conference included all the itinerants. Later the conference was composed of delegates—by 1808, one delegate for every seven licensed preachers—"to be appointed by seniority or choice [of the bishops]." Emora T. Brannan, "The Presiding Elder Question: Its Critical Nature in American Methodism, 1820–1824, and Its Impact upon Ecclesiastical Institutions" (Ph.D. diss., Duke University, 1974), 48–50; *Wesleyan Repository* 2 (July 1822): 88. For the O'Kellyite and Hammettite schisms, see Frederick A. Norwood, "The Church Takes Shape," and Frederick E. Maser and George A. Singleton, "Further Branches of Methodism Are Founded," in Emory Stevens Bucke, ed., *The History of American Methodism*, 3 vols. (New York: Abingdon Press, 1964), 1:433–52, 1:617–22. For Methodist Protestantism, see Douglas R. Chandler, "The Formation of the Methodist Protestant Church," in ibid., 1:636–65.

7. "Locating" referred to the practice of preachers leaving the itinerancy to pursue secular callings, retaining only the limited privileges of local preachers. Brannan, "Presiding Elder Question," 24–28; Stephen J. Novak, "The Perils of Respectability: Methodist Schisms of the 1820s," paper presented to the American Historical Association, 1980, 14.

8. Bangs's efforts were severely criticized by Methodists without social pretensions. New York artisan Michael Floy wrote an article in 1834, referring derogatorily to Bangs and exposing "the Doctor's sophistry." Richard A. E. Brooks, ed., *The Diary of Michael Floy Jr., Bowery Village, 1833–1837* (New Haven: Yale University Press, 1941), 123. See also Hatch, *Democratization of Christianity*, 201–6, and attacks on Bangs in the *Wesleyan Repository*, in which offense was

In 1820, such opposition to established Methodist authority erupted simultaneously in the major urban centers and drew scattered support from various backcountry areas. In New York City, James Varick and Abraham Thompson, following the example of Richard Allen in Philadelphia, led African-American Methodists in challenging the control of the white General Conference. The black Methodists were supported by white Methodist leaders William Stilwell and James Covel, whose thoroughgoing devotion to primitive Methodist egalitarianism led them to resist the innovations of socially conscious modernizers within the denomination. In Philadelphia, opposition was more focussed on power relations between the General Conference (the itinerants and bishops) and local preachers and lay members. Inaugurated by Ezekiel Cooper in the pages of the *Reformer* and popularized by Methodist layman William Stockton in his *Wesleyan Repository*, the Philadelphia agitation concentrated on decentralizing the powers of decision making to include the input of local preachers and laypeople. The challenge emanating from Philadelphia was immediately embraced by a cadre of located itinerants in Baltimore, including Alexander McCaine, Samuel Jennings, and William Kesley, all of whom were incensed by their experience at the 1820 national meeting held in Baltimore. Frustrated by the political manipulation and high-handed rejection of their suggestions for limited reform, the Baltimore dissidents became vocal and organized.

Although these movements all reflected a determination to religiously resist illegitimate authority, the results epitomized the ambiguities inherent in populist evangelical efforts to negotiate the demands of liberal culture. Each of these expressions of activism followed the internal logic of their own particular local dynamics and led to a variety of reform suggestions and new organizations, but only in Baltimore was an alternative Methodist denomination permanently established, when the currents of Methodist dissent crystallized during the following decade into a national phenomenon known as the Methodist Protestant schism. This division came to fruition in three stages, each concerned with the manner in which all governing power within Methodism lay in the hands of the itinerant ministers and the bishops. The initial stage, from 1820 to 1827, was marked by agitation and internal reform, during which a number of dissidents attempted to transform Methodist

taken to Bangs's statement that "the government of the church of God is somewhat different from 'civil society' and . . . those ministers whom God selects . . . possess the right of governing themselves in religious matters, and all those committed to their care." *Wesleyan Repository* 2 (Feb. 1823): 373, quoted in Richard M. Cameron, *Methodism and Society in Historical Perspective* (New York: Abingdon Press, 1961), 117.

polity not only in keeping with their visions of evangelical republicanism, but also in keeping with their understandings of its radical liberative potential for the disempowered. During these years, three separate issues (the process of selection of the presiding eldership, lay participation in the affairs of the denomination, and membership of local preachers in the General Conference)[9] dominated the discussion, eventually coming together under the heading of "lay representation." Although other aspects of radical challenge—in the form of abolitionist, anticapitalist, and gender-equal sentiments—were also present, the internal focus on lay representation within Methodism overshadowed broader radical agendas.[10]

The middle stage of Methodist Protestant development, from 1827 to 1830, was one of ever more heated debate, during which Methodists on both sides elevated the public abuse of their opponents to an art form.[11] Attempts at conciliation ultimately failed, and after reluctant withdrawal, individuals who were expelled from Methodist connections for forming protective union societies and for disseminating periodicals discussing the implications of their dissent formed preliminary organizations. During this period, specific critiques of elements of liberal culture persisted, but the radical elements interested in redefining Methodism as consciously countercultural

9. In 1792 the office of presiding elder was added. Bishop-appointed, these officials helped supervise itinerant stationing and local appointments. Many itinerants, as well as local preachers (unpaid workers with secular occupations who were licensed by the General Conference to preach, exhort, and superintend class meetings), resented this concentration of power, but it remained part of the Wesley-inspired *Discipline* in 1820. By 1825, the religious duties of the local preachers varied; they were to preach (on Sundays and occasional weekdays), to perform baptisms and marriages, to conduct the Lord's Supper, to lead class meetings and prayer meetings, to support the itinerants financially, to build meeting houses, and to "labour diligently, with their hands, or pursue some worldly business, to maintain themselves and their families." *Mutual Rights* 1 (June 1825): 420.

10. For most of the Methodist Protestant leaders, especially those who took over leadership after the expulsions (as opposed to the Stilwellite leadership), the term "radical" is appropriate but, according to differentiations described by James Henretta, because they were acting out of a struggle with orthodox beliefs or practices, not because they were ready to undertake major shifts in social thought and behavior patterns. James Henretta, "Commentary," in Margaret Jacob and James Jacob, eds., *The Origin of Anglo-American Radicalism* (London: George Allen and Unwin, 1984), 271.

11. In this, Methodists in the 1820s were carrying on a longstanding American Protestant tradition in which the self-righteous condemnation of those who differed on a few points of doctrine was apparently considered a major virtue. For examples of this dubious practice on either chronological side of this dispute, see William K. Breitenbach, "New Divinity Theology and the Idea of Moral Accountability," (Ph.D. diss., Yale University, 1978), 273, and Richard Carwardine, "Unity, Pluralism, and the Spiritual Market-Place: Interdenominational Competition in the Early American Republic," in R. N. Swanson, ed., *Unity and Diversity in the Church* (London: Blackwell, 1996), 324–25.

were gradually marginalized, as the main force of the movement tried in vain to stay within the mother denomination. The final stage, following the significant expulsions and withdrawals around 1830, was marked by consolidation and institutionalization, during which the expelled reformers created a new institution, the Methodist Protestant Church, with its greatest strength in Maryland and Ohio.[12] In the institutionalizing phase, as preoccupation with internal matters waned, Methodist Protestant leaders began to evaluate the liberal republican concerns of Jacksonian society, including paying closer attention to the problems of social disorder ("anarchy") and espousing the positive potential of capitalist development in respect to both the demands of disestablishment and to the traditional limitations of producerism. Although Methodist Protestantism clearly revealed the nonsubmissive nature of the Protestant doctrine of submission to authority and was potentially inspirational to all who felt cut off from access to power (particularly in its recognition of the efficacy of associated efforts to ward off oppression), the movement as an organized entity exhibited ambivalence toward the changes and challenges of liberal culture, as well as toward producerist critiques of those transformations.

In New York City, resistance to Methodist authority coalesced around one man: William Stilwell. Stilwell was a native New Yorker; his father, Stephen, was an inventor of some success, and the American branch of the family was descended, according to family legend, from an ancestor of radical Puritan sympathies who was directly involved in the treason trial and beheading of Charles I. After the Restoration, this ancestor fled incognito and, upon safe arrival in New York, took the aptly descriptive surname to signify his continued well-being.[13] William Stilwell had joined the Methodists (New York Conference) in 1814 and soon become a licensed itinerant. With the support of his uncle Samuel,[14] fellow radical and local preacher Dr. James Covel

12. Methodist Protestantism, while never enjoying the numerical success of the initial Methodist organization, continued to be significant denominationally until the two branches reunited more than one hundred years later. Montgomery J. Shroyer, "Mutual Rights and Wrongs," in Baker, ed., *Those Incredible Methodists*, 164.

13. Maser and Singleton, "Further Branches of Methodism Are Founded," in Bucke, ed., *History of American Methodism*, 1:610–11, 625–29; and Samuel Stilwell Doughty, *The Life of Samuel Stilwell, with Notices of Some of His Contemporaries* (New York, 1877), 5.

14. Samuel A. Seaman, *Annals of New York Methodism, Being a History of the Methodist Episcopal Church in the City of New York* (New York, 1892), 221, 226–27. Samuel Stilwell was every bit the radical evangelical activist that his nephew was. In 1794, to rebuke the infidelity of Thomas Paine, he published a pamphlet entitled *A Guide to Reason; or, An Examination of*

(Covell or Corvel),[15] and African-American leaders James Varick, Abraham Thompson, and Christopher Rush,[16] William Stilwell proved a rallying point for New York City Methodists dissatisfied with the growing penchant for centralized bureaucracy and social respectability. His radicalism was not limited to internal issues of Methodist practice; he and Covel were founding members, along with Quaker radical Cornelius Blatchly, of the scripturally anticapitalist organization the New York Society for Promoting for Communities.

The Stilwells and Covel were members of the John Street Church, the oldest and most important New York City Methodist church, long renowned for its independent spirit. In 1820, a long-simmering conflict related to remodeling the church building boiled over. The trustees of the church were divided, with those supporting the addition of a carpeted altar and expensive renovations backed by a majority of the itinerants in the New York Conference and by those who looked with favor upon the social attainments of prosperous Methodists. Their opponents were supported by common lay members and a few itinerants who viewed the architectural improvements as sinful pride and who saw the influence of the itinerant-dominated trustees as an indication of an imbalance of power favoring the Conference.[17] At issue, beyond ownership and control of the property, was the future cultural trajectory of the Methodist Church in New York City.

As the conflict deepened, the New York Conference appealed to the state legislature to support the move of the modernizers. This suit turned out to be unsuccessful, but the traditionalists had had enough: under the leadership of the Stilwells and Covel, a group of four hundred whites and eight hundred blacks protested vigorously. "To seek for legislative aid to enforce the discipline of a church," wrote Samuel Stilwell, "is a step toward popery, that in this enlightened day we should suppose would hardly be submitted to, *except* by those who have lost the spirit of Christianity and of freemen."

Thomas Paine's "Age of Reason." He was close friends with prominent New York politicians (including Silas Wood, the National Republican legislator and moderate candidate of the Working Man's Party in New York City in 1829). Doughty, *Life of Samuel Stilwell*, 24, 12, 22; Wilentz, *Chants Democratic*, 196–97. For information on the dispute over the furnishings of the John Street Church, see Seaman, *Annals of New York Methodism*, 219.

15. Seaman, *Annals of New York Methodism*, 227; and Sprague, *Annals of the American Pulpit*, 7:564.

16. In 1819, then an ordained elder, Stilwell was appointed to serve two black Methodist churches in New York City, Asbury and Zion. Zion, in an old account, was noted as "the first church edifice built expressly for the people of color in New York." J. B. Wakeley, *Lost Chapters Recovered from the Early History of American Methodism* (New York, 1889), 444.

17. Seaman, *Annals of New York Methodism*, 215–29.

Complaining about the unethical nature of taking property from the people and granting it to a highly centralized and increasingly powerful bureaucracy, and decrying the lack of lay representation in the conferences, the discontented faction formally withdrew from the Methodist Episcopal Church. The black Methodists, who had suffered decades of official interference from the white bureaucracy, asked William Stilwell and James Covel to ordain their elders and went on to form the African Methodist Episcopal Zion Church. The whites, recognized nationally as the Stilwellites, organized the short-lived but important Methodist Society in the City of New York, "founded . . . on Scripture and the equal rights of mankind."[18]

The Methodist Society's Articles of Association adopted in early 1820 were as doctrinally simple as they were radically egalitarian:

I. The Bible will be their rule of Discipline.
II. Each member, male and female, shall have a vote in the choice of preachers, and the allowance to be made for their services.
III. Disputes or disagreements between members, to be settled by three, five, or seven members of the Society, as may be agreed upon. If the dispute is between men, it shall be left to men to settle: if between women, to be left to women.
IV. Persons to be tried for transgressing against the good order of the Society, shall have the fairest opportunity possible of obtaining an impartial jury.
V. The members will all be classed in classes of about twenty members each, and will be met once a week by a leader of their own choice.
VI. The members, having equal rights, may form such rules for regulating and promoting the good of the society as may be thought expedient by a majority of the members.[19]

Particularly noticeable here was the equality of power extended to women in the Methodist Society.

18. Samuel Stilwell, "Rise and Progress of the Methodist Society, in the City of New York," *Friendly Visitor* 1 (Nov. 23, 1825): 372; (Nov. 1, 1825): 348. The African-American leaders continued to look to Stilwell for leadership as they established their denominational autonomy. As in the Methodist Society, both men and women voted on preaching appointments, and on July 17, 1822, Stilwell and Covel ordained Abraham Thompson, James Varick, and Levin Smith as elders. David Henry Bradley, *A History of the A. M. E. Zion Church: Part 1, 1796–1872* (Nashville: Parthenon Press, 1956), 63, 71–79, 82, 95; Wilmore, *Black Religion and Black Radicalism*, 85.

19. Seaman, *Annals of New York Methodism*, 227–28.

The Articles of Association were followed, in August 1820, by the Articles of Faith and General Rules. The Articles of Faith included the doctrinally orthodox Apostle's Creed, an Arminian Christology, and a relaxed sacramentalism, while the General Rules reflected the radical as well as producerist propensities of the membership. Retaining the inclusivity of the original Methodist invitation (that all were to be welcomed who expressed a "*desire to flee from the wrath to come, and to be saved from their sins*"), the rules proscribed "drinking spiritous liquors, except in cases of necessity," any involvement in the slave trade, "brother going to law with brother," smuggling, "*using the weapons of war for the purpose of depriving any person or persons of their rights, life, liberty, or property*," "giving or taking things on unlawful interest," violating the Golden Rule, "borrowing or buying without a probability of paying," luxurious fashions, and, as a catchall for the remainder, "needless self-indulgence." The rules ended with a call for members to take up their crosses, "submitting to bear the reproach of Christ when men say . . . evil of them falsely for the Lord's sake," and a threat to discipline members who insisted on continuing their transgressions.[20] Clearly evident in the Methodist Society's rules was a collective consciousness advocating limitations on individual endeavors, espousing elements of traditional economic morality, and preaching the virtues of self-discipline.

Agitation reflecting rank-and-file concern with an undemocratic polity and embourgeoisement was not limited to New York City; as the decade progressed, Baltimore became the epicenter of reformist activity. Baltimore was a natural arena for such a contest. Lacking the traditions of a strong established church or an exclusive theological system and open to the ministrations of populist itinerants, the Chesapeake region was especially amenable to Methodist preaching; in Baltimore, the humble meetinghouses of neighborhood Methodist congregations attracted significant numbers of congregants from the 1780s on. Recent estimates indicate that, by 1790, nearly half the city's population were nominal churchgoers, with Methodists a growing minority. Baltimore seemed to avoid the religious apathy that characterized other urban centers at that time.[21]

Originally, Episcopalians and Presbyterians were most numerous in Baltimore, but in the wake of disestablishment and the explosion of the Second Great Awakening in the 1820s, the quintessentially populist Methodists

20. *Friendly Visitor* 1 (Nov. 16, 1825): 364–65; Seaman, *Annals of New York Methodism*, 229.

21. Russell E. Richey, "The Chesapeake Coloration of American Methodism," paper delivered at the Conference on Methodism and the Shaping of American Culture, 1760–1860, Oct. 7–8, 1994, Asbury Theological Seminary, Wilmore, Ky.; Franch, "Congregation and

enjoyed enormous growth, particularly in Maryland, Delaware, Virginia, and Ohio. In the adolescence of their success, Baltimore's Methodists remained low in social status and marginally influential, but by the 1820s their burgeoning numbers and gradual economic success mandated that their dual concern for soul-saving and social justice permeate Baltimore society.[22] By 1830, 50 percent of Baltimoreans attended some Christian church, and one in six of these church-goers were Methodists.[23] Baltimore was unique among American cities in terms of the depth of populist religious influence; contemporaries estimated Methodism to be significantly stronger in Baltimore than in any other urban center. But how would this strong influence and the traditional social concerns accompanying it be affected by the intellectual and cultural challenge of liberalism?

At the same time that William Stilwell and his allies were repudiating the Methodist establishment in New York City, an article condemning the Methodist policy of excluding "the members from any participation in the government of the church whatever" appeared in the April 1820 edition of a Philadelphia periodical, the *Reformer.* The anonymous author extolled Methodism for its populist successes in "reforming mankind, especially the middle and lower classes" at a time when "infidelity had nearly overspread England." But now, unfortunately, "like all other societies, we have had our rise, our zenith or flourishing state, and our gradual decline, 'making way for the departure of light.'" The problem for American Methodists was the coexistence of a powerless laity and clerical declension; if "our ministers once become worldly, avaricious, high minded and overbearing . . . we shall see what dreadful havock [*sic*] will ensue, by an undo exercise of that power, over which we have no more control, than we have over the elements of the natural world." But all was not yet lost for the Methodists: the article ended with an impassioned plea for "the adoption of a LAY REPRESENTATION."[24]

Community." Terry Bilhartz arrives at high numbers for evangelical participation in Baltimore. Bilhartz, *Urban Religion,* 19–27. See also Finke and Stark, *Churching of America.*

22. Mathews, "Methodist Ideology," in Richey and Rowe, eds., *Rethinking Methodist History,* 91.

23. These estimates come from Bilhartz, *Urban Religion,* 19–25; See also Steffen, *Mechanics of Baltimore,* 253–58, 267; Andrews, "Popular Religion in the Middle Atlantic Ports."

24. *The Reformer: A Religious Work, Published Monthly* 1 (Apr. 1, 1820): 93, 89. The *Reformer* was published by the iconoclastic, anticlerical Christian populist Theophilus Gates, and the article was signed "a Methodist," most likely Ezekiel Cooper, a well-respected itinerant stationed in Philadelphia. Emora T. Brannan, "From Right to Expedience: Lay Representation and Thomas Emerson Bond," *Methodist History/A. M. E. Z. Quarterly Review* (Apr. 1975):

One month later, at the General Conference meeting in the Eutaw Street Methodist Church in Baltimore, delegates wrestled with the issues raised in the *Reformer* article. The conservative legacy of Asbury, who was buried beneath the pulpit in the church, was apparent. The major reform proposed at this conference was a new selection process for presiding elders, in which the bishops would nominate three times the number of necessary presiding elders, from which the General Conference would make the final selections.[25] The choice of a new bishop was also critical. The delegates reached a compromise on the presiding elder question, but their efforts were thwarted by the newly elected bishop, the archconservative Joshua Soule. Soule, claiming that the compromise on the presiding eldership issue violated the unwritten constitution of the Methodist Episcopal Church, cleverly refused his election until the compromise was repudiated. In a series of backroom maneuvers that would have made Martin Van Buren blush, Soule's supporters prevailed upon a bare majority of those still in attendance to suspend the earlier compromise for four years, ostensibly to maintain the unity of the church. In the words of Baltimore reformer, Dr. Samuel Jennings, the conference reaffirmed the exclusive power of the itinerants "to make laws for the church, whereby the local ministry and the laity are excluded from . . . representation." The frustrated reformers now had firsthand experience with the overweening power of the conservative Methodist bishopric.[26]

William Stockton, a layman and frequent contributor to the *Reformer*, was one such frustrated reformer. On April 12, 1821, he published the first number of the *Wesleyan Repository and Religious Intelligencer*, a semimonthly periodical dedicated to an open discussion of the issues surrounding reform of the Methodist polity. Stockton was a bookseller; an early temperance advocate; a regular commentator for the political paper, the *People's Advocate*; and periodically (dependent on the exigencies of party patronage) the superintendent of the Blockely Almshouse outside Philadelphia. He wrote many of the articles in the *Wesleyan Repository*, but he had ample support

---

125–26. For more on Gates and the *Reformer*, see Brannan, "Presiding Elder Question," 70–76, and Hatch, *Democratization of Christianity*, 176–79.

25. Edward J. Drinkhouse, *History of Methodist Reform, Synoptical of General Methodism, 1703 to 1898, with Special and Comprehensive Reference to Its Most Salient Exhibition in the History of the Methodist Protestant Church*, 2 vols. (Baltimore and Pittsburgh, 1899), 2:5–6.

26. Ironically, Soule insisted on maintaining his resignation because he had been so embarrassed by the vocal opposition to his autocratic ways. Drinkhouse, *History of Methodist Reform*, 2:5–16; Jennings, *Exposition of the Late Controversy*, 106. In the four years between General Conferences, however, Soule and his supporters managed to build a sufficient power base to insure his election without controversy in 1824.

from longtime Methodists, who wrote anonymously because they feared ecclesiastical discipline and socioeconomic repercussions. For the next three years, the pages of the *Wesleyan Repository* were filled with reform propositions on all manner of institutional policy—presiding eldership, lay representation, individual rights, disciplinary and trial procedures—as well as works advocating temperance and abolition of slavery.[27] Underlying this agitation, however, was a determination to avoid schism and an explicit refusal to follow the lead of the Stilwellite Methodist Society because such divisions were "of very doubtful value as examples."[28]

Preeminent among the Methodist authors featured in the *Wesleyan Repository* were Nicholas Snethen, Asa Shinn, Dr. Samuel Jennings, and Alexander McCaine.[29] Born in 1769, Nicholas Snethen became an itinerant in 1794; he most completely wedded the reformers' concerns to the republican discourse of the day. By 1800 he was a rising star in the Methodist connection and was selected by Asbury as his traveling companion.[30] Snethen was an exceptional revivalist; one camp meeting he led outside Baltimore in 1803 was known forever after as "Happy Monday" because of the number of converts and the depth of the experience. From 1809 to 1810 he was stationed in Baltimore, and three years later, he was elected chaplain to the U.S. House of Representatives. In 1814, married with children, he retired from the itineracy. In 1816, he ran for Congress as a Federalist but lost badly. Highly respected across the Methodist social spectrum, Snethen exemplified the ambiguities of Methodism in regard to political allegiance, social privilege, and the contest for hegemony between producerism and economic liberalism.[31]

Snethen's choice of political party was in marked contrast to the overwhelming preference for Jeffersonian Republicanism among American

27. While employed at the Alms House, Stockton eliminated such abuses as treadmills, showers used as punishment, and the chained isolation of the insane. He took his responsibilities toward the poor seriously, and he distinguished himself by being one of the few to remain in the city through the cholera epidemic of 1832. *Wesleyan Repository* was originally published in Trenton, then Philadelphia, where it became a monthly. T[homas] H. Colhouer, *Sketches of the Founders of the Methodist Protestant Church, and Its Bibliography* (Pittsburgh, 1880), 53–54; Drinkhouse, *History of Methodist Reform,* 2:30, 34; T[homas] H. Stockton, *A Discourse on the Life and Character of the Rev. Samuel K. Jennings, M.D.* (Baltimore, 1855), 15; *Wesleyan Repository* 1 (July 19, 1821): 123; 2 (June 1822): 43.

28. *Wesleyan Repository* 1 (Dec. 20, 1821): 306.

29. Drinkhouse, *History of Methodist Reform,* 2:34; *Wesleyan Repository* 2 (June 1822): 43; Brannan, "Presiding Elder Question," xii.

30. Colhouer, *Sketches of the Founders,* 15–17.

31. Bilhartz, *Urban Religion,* 88–89.

Methodists into the 1830s. He was comfortable in the company of the politically powerful, he was outspoken in his opposition to the more flamboyant Methodist circuit riders like Lorenzo Dow, and, after locating, he enjoyed financial security. His views on artisan culture were those of an outsider; he endorsed "habits of diligence and industry, and moderate wages" because "plentiful wages enable men to relax their exertions" and "experience abundantly proves that these intervals are devoted to intoxication."[32] But he also recognized the potential for disestablished churches to become dependent on the largesse of the wealthy and, in the process, lose much of their prophetic power to call the community to economic righteousness. He expressed this fear when he opposed the push for the establishment of denominational colleges and seminaries, repeating John Wesley's warnings against the influence of wealth and concluding:

> The money all comes of the laity, and will the poor never complain? But what was that Methodist discipline, which the necessity for rich men might oblige travelling preachers to bid farewell to? . . . Would there be nothing like bribes, or bartering; no tacit understanding, like, if you will not discipline me, I will pay? Who can help seeing the difference between birth right liberty, and liberty so purchased? . . . When the rich of their abundance shall have cast their millions into the college treasury, can you believe, that . . . learned gentlemen, and gentlemen's sons, will be expelled from these seminaries of learning for speaking evil of travelling preachers, and all the wealthy contributors, say amen, to it?[33]

Samuel Jennings, one of Baltimore's leading physicians as well as a popular preacher, was a son of privilege. Educated at Rutgers, he had written *The Married Lady's Companion or the Poor Man's Friend*, a self-explanatory medical handbook that borrowed heavily from the writings of Dr. Benjamin Rush and Princeton president John Witherspoon and was published by Lorenzo Dow. Born in 1771 in New Jersey, Jennings was raised Presbyterian but was converted

32. Richard Carwardine, "Methodist Ministers and the Second Party System," in Richey and Rowe, eds., *Rethinking Methodist History*, 139; Nicholas Snethen, *Snethen on Lay Representation, or Essays on Lay Representation and Church Government, Collected from the* Wesleyan Repository, *the* Mutual Rights, *and the* Mutual Rights and Christian Intelligencer, *from 1820 to 1829 Inclusive, Now Republished in a Chronological Order, with an Introduction by the Rev. Nicholas Snethen* (Baltimore, 1835), xx; *Wesleyan Repository* 2 (July 1822): 93.

33. Snethen, *Essays on Lay Representation*, xxv–xxvi; quoted in Rick Nutt, "'The Advantages of Liberty': Democratic Thought in the Formation of the Methodist Protestant Church," *Methodist History* 31 (Oct. 1992): 23.

by Methodist preaching when he was twenty-three. Earlier skeptical about religious faith, he maintained, as was fashionable for the educated, a vague deism, which was not openly infidel but rejected both the authority of the Bible and the relevance of the Christian mysteries. After a chance meeting with an uneducated but perceptive Methodist itinerant, Jennings was faced with an empirical challenge to test the power of God as experienced in evangelical conversion. A product of the Enlightenment, Jennings determined to put the question to the test in prayer—was the God of nature the same as the God of the Christian revelation? He was rewarded for his pains a short time later with a vision of Jesus, and his deism vanished in an intense and long-lasting experience of assurance of salvation. His dramatic conversion made him a lifelong believer, and his subsequent experience of what Methodists called sanctification effectively removed forever both skepticism and "the desire to accumulate . . . riches and [worldly] pleasures," although it did not disabuse him of the pursuit of social mobility or the notion of the efficacy of personal power within republican limitations.[34] By 1822 Jennings had become a subscriber, and, a year later, a contributor to the *Wesleyan Repository*.[35]

Whereas Snethen and Jennings utilized the advantages of social privileges to revel in controversy, Asa Shinn was the epitome of moderation and conciliation as he tried desperately to keep the reform-minded Methodist factions united. The son of poor Quaker farmers, he was born in New Jersey in 1781 and grew up, unsophisticated and ignorant, under frontier conditions in western Virginia. Converted at seventeen, he was chosen by his presiding elder to itinerate two years later; he preached with great success in Baltimore from 1810 to 1812 and from 1820 to 1822. As an itinerant and presiding elder he was a member of the General Conferences during the agitation of reform issues and contributed numerous articles to the *Wesleyan Repository* under the pseudonym of "Bartimaeus."[36] Shinn's health was fragile and he

34. Samuel K. Jennings, *The Married Lady's Companion or the Poor Man's Friend* (New York, 1808). Quoting Rush, Jennings asserted, "A christian . . . cannot fail of being a republican, for every precept of the gospel inculcates those degrees of humility, self-denial, and brotherly kindness, which are directly opposed to the pride of monarchy and the pageantry of a court. A christian cannot fail of being useful to the republic, for his religion teacheth him, that no man liveth to himself." Jennings also expressed the typical populist distrust of Protestant scholasticism; referring to much of doctrinal orthodoxy as "the deep mysteries of . . . scholastic systems, which cannot be understood even by those who teach them." Ibid., 181, 184. See also Stockton, *Discourse on Jennings*, 6–12; Colhouer, *Sketches of the Founders*, 80–81.

35. Colhouer, *Sketches of the Founders*, 70–71; Stockton, *Discourse on Jennings*, 16.

36. Colhouer, *Sketches of the Founders*, 120–24; James E. Armstrong, *History of the Old Baltimore Conference from the Planting of Methodism in 1773 to the Division of the Conference in 1857* (Baltimore: King Brothers, 1907), 167; Drinkhouse, *History of Methodist Reform*, 2:38.

periodically suffered mental breakdowns; when lucid, however, he was very effective. Always moderate, Shinn was as quick to ridicule the conservatives' espousal of "the consolations of passive obedience and non-resistance" as he was to warn of democratic excesses. Where Snethen and Jennings agitated, following their consciences wherever they might lead, Shinn mediated, dutifully striving to maintain the republican unity of the Methodist community and trying to minimize the growing hostility between reformers and conservatives.[37]

A fourth important leader of the Methodist Protestants was educator Alexander McCaine. Born in Ireland in 1768 and trained for the Roman Catholic priesthood, McCaine arrived in Charleston, South Carolina, in 1797, where he converted to Methodism after encountering the populist preaching of William Hammett, who was in the process of being rebuked by the General Conference for his interference with episcopal prerogative. As the Hammettite conflict wound down, McCaine began preaching on his own, becoming one of Asbury's favorite itinerants. He continued in the traveling connection intermittently until 1821, when he retired to teach school in Baltimore.[38] Among others, he taught the young John H. W. Hawkins, later leader in the journeymen hatters' strike of 1833. By locating in Baltimore, McCaine removed himself from his accustomed position close to the sources of power within the conference. But McCaine had no family or financial connections, so he continued to scrape by as a teacher and author of Methodist polemics. According to his own testimony, in his preaching travels and reform agitation, he had "convened with the high and the low, the rich and the poor; and have conversed with all ranks in the community, from the governor down to the day laborer." Throughout his long Methodist service, he stayed close to his commoner roots.[39]

More than the other Methodist Protestant spokesmen, McCaine was philosophically comfortable with the populist radicalism that was informing

37. Colhouer, *Sketches of the Founders*, 125–26, 146. Shinn's plain style was described as "nothing Frenchified or Latinized"; if ever a man "knew how to use pure Anglo-Saxon words to advantage, he was that man." C[ornelius] Cooke, *Discourse on the Life and Death of the Rev. Asa Shinn*, (Pittsburgh, 1853), 14. Drinkhouse, *History of Methodist Reform*, 2:108; *Mutual Rights* 3 (Sept. 1827): 43, 46–47.

38. For comments on McCaine's pedagogical style, see William G. Hawkins, *The Life of John Hawkins* (Boston, 1859), 3–5.

39. McCaine enjoyed the personal if not the financial support of some of America's leading citizens. When he undertook, in 1827, a trip south to improve his health and to sell books, he carried with him the personal endorsements of a number of influential men, including Attorney General William Wirt and Postmaster General and Judge John McLean. Colhouer, *Sketches of the Founders*, 112, 116.

artisan resistance to capitalist change. He publicly endorsed the textbooks of Jesse Torrey Jr., whose predilection for artisan republicanism and producerism was also applauded by British radical William Cobbett.[40] McCaine did not shrink from identifying with the political radicalism of those whose religious sentiments he vigorously opposed. Despite his personal affinity for Francis Asbury, McCaine came to despise Asbury's authoritarian ecclesiastical polity, claiming that Asbury in this respect had done more damage than Thomas Paine.[41] Although his name appeared as secretary on some of the documents reading the Stilwellites out of the Methodist connection in 1820, McCaine later took great pains to point out that signing decisions reached by official committee, in his position as secretary, did not necessarily indicate his agreement.[42]

Featuring the writings of Stockton, Snethen, Shinn, Jennings, and McCaine, the *Wesleyan Repository* was evangelical populism at its purest. Although its main target was the antirepublicanism of institutional Methodism, producerist sensibilities permeated the arguments. Its authors condemned the economic oppression manifested in the exploitation of the powerless and ignorant, the effeminacy of luxury and indolence, the unrestrained consumerism inspired by industrial capitalism, and the sinfulness of status differentiations based on wealth and power.[43] The reformers insisted on

40. Torrey's *Moral Instructor* was permeated with populist sentiments, artisan republicanism, producerism, and general comments supportive and appreciative of labor. Torrey also espoused the virtues of industry, self-improvement, and traditional economic morality. The advertisement for Torrey's work featuring McCaine's endorsement (from 1823) appeared in *National Trades' Union*, Feb. 21, 1835. Also advertised in *National Trades' Union* was *Torrey's American School Library*, which included such suggestive titles as "William and Thomas, or the Contrast Between Industry and Indolence." *National Trades' Union*, Jan. 10, 1835.

41. Colhouer, *Sketches of the Founders*, 91–92; Bucke, ed., *History of American Methodism*, 1:433, 618. Typical of the antireformers' rejection of McCaine were the comments of Dr. Thomas E. Bond; he characterized McCaine's writings as works "which for malignity of purpose, shrewd cunning, misrepresentation of facts, and misstatement of circumstances, has no parallel among the productions of modern times, on a similar subject, except the far-famed Cobbett's History of the Reformation." Bond, quoted in Alexander McCaine, *A Defence of the Truth, As Set Forth in the "History and Mystery of Methodist Episcopacy," Being a Reply to John Emory's "Defence of Our Fathers"* (Baltimore, 1829), v–vi. As late as 1876, mainstream Methodists were still claiming that "if such writers as McCaine and Cobbett are to be received as authority, then whose church or personal character is safe in this land?" J. M. Boland in *Nashville Christian Advocate*, August 5, 1876, cited in Colhouer, *Sketches of the Founders*, 114.

42. Seaman, *Annals of New York Methodism*, 221; McCaine, *Defence of the Truth*, 56.

43. The populist sensibility cut both ways. A leading antireformer who had once been friendly to the cause, Thomas Bond, upon becoming editor of the *Methodist Magazine*, claimed an affinity for the reformers' principles but felt they were not presented in a sufficiently deferential form; he objected to the "manner" of the *Wesleyan Repository*. *Wesleyan Repository* 2

biblically inspired activism as the only acceptable alternative to the ever-present polarities of infidelity and passive religiosity: "the vice of the free-thinker is presumptuousness; that of the devotee to authority, contemptible timidity." Moreover, such activism was the antidote to the most objectionable feature of the Methodist Episcopal polity: the attempt to instill "unqualified submission to the powers that be" through "the doctrine of passive obedience and non-resistance."[44] For the Methodist reformers, quietism was anathema.

Equally unthinkable for the populists was the residual hierarchicalism of the Methodist scheme. Alexander McCaine ("Veritas") went to the heart of reform egalitarianism: "No doctrines of the new testament are plainer than these:—GOD is the Creator of all men: all men are created equal: revealed religion confirms natural rights." The preservation of these natural rights were threatened by existing conditions; somehow the Methodist Church must steer between the dangers, described by classical republicanism, of despotism and anarchy. But anarchy in the 1820s was not yet the threat that tyranny was. Defined as "undivided, unlimited and uncontrollable power in the hands of any number of men, as well as in the hand of any single individual," despotism was clearly recognized to dwell at the heart of the system of bishop, presiding elders, and General Conferences. Even though in the distant past the clergy had been unfriendly to the rights of the people, the coming of American democracy had changed matters. Strongly implying a negative response, "Episcopius" asked, "And if it be lawful for the greater to oppose the less, is it unlawful for the less to use all the means in their power, offensively and defensively, against the greater?" In spite of its powerful advocates, reform did not progress without setbacks. Stockton's *Wesleyan Repository* went under in 1824; its five hundred permanent subscribers were not enough to sustain it.[45]

(June 1822): 43. Stockton took Bond to task publicly for the patronizing flavor of this comment. *Wesleyan Repository* 1 (Dec. 20, 1821): 299–300. On their side, the reformers resented "the dictatorial manner" of some Methodist authorities, which "furnishes melancholy evidence of the tendency of undefined power to supplant brotherly love," noting caustically that "more learning and less power would have been better for them." *Wesleyan Repository* 1 (Dec. 20, 1821).

44. *Mutual Rights and Methodist Protestant* 1 (Dec. 23, 1831): 421; Snethen cited in Stephens, *Defense of Our Fathers*, no. 1, 19.

45. *Wesleyan Repository* 3 (May 1823): 26. "Veritas" was writing to refute "infidel writers" who claimed that revealed religion destroyed natural rights. *Wesleyan Repository* 1 (Nov. 8, 1821); 279; 3 (Jan. 1824); 360; 2 (Jan. 1822): 19; Bucke, ed., *History of American Methodism*, 1:651.

At the same time, further disaffection with the Methodist status quo was evident in Baltimore, based on the treatment of certain local preachers, nearly all of whom were "inchoate reformers."[46] In 1821, William Kesley, a Baltimore teacher and local preacher, was recommended by his Local Preacher's District Conference for deacon's orders. Kelsey was rejected by the Baltimore Annual Conference, which consisted of itinerants assigned to the Baltimore area, for no stated reason. Born into a poor farming family in 1788, Kesley was orphaned eight years later. His adoptive family sent him to school in the winter, and Kesley soon became the archetypical autodidact. Converted at thirteen, he was licensed as a local preacher a few years later. He left no written record, but his endorsement (like that of Alexander McCaine) of Jesse Torrey's schoolbooks indicated his close sympathy with the egalitarian and producerist teachings of that author.[47] By all accounts he was a popular and respected teacher and preacher. Following his rejection by the itinerants, the members of Kesley's class meeting petitioned the conference, asking them to reconsider their decision. In response several members of the conference expressed their "disapprobation" at the effrontery of the petitioners, who were offered the opportunity to withdraw their request. The petition was indeed withdrawn, but the tension between populists and conservatives remained. The efforts of Kesley's friends, moreover, were not fruitless; at the Annual Conference the following year, Kesley attained deacon's orders.[48]

William Kesley was not alone; Daniel Reese, another local preacher and educator of populist sentiments, was similarly rejected for elder's orders, again despite the recommendation of his District Conference. A preacher in Baltimore since 1799, Reese was a good friend of radical evangelical Thomas Branagan, whose many published works condemned, on scriptural grounds, slavery, violation of women's rights, political tyranny anywhere in the world, Indian genocide, and capitalist exploitation.[49] It was not necessarily his

46. Drinkhouse, *History of Methodist Reform,* 2:34, 17–18; Brannan, "Presiding Elder Question," 44–48.

47. *Journal of the Baltimore Annual Conference* (Baltimore, 1821), 139; The biography of Kelsey in *Sketches of the Founders* emphasizes his populism. Colhouer, *Sketches of the Founders,* 226–27. Kesley's endorsement of Torrey was dated 1823. *National Trades' Union,* Feb. 21, 1835.

48. *Journal of the Baltimore Annual Conference* (1821), 148.

49. In 1839, Branagan dedicated *Guardian Genius* to the anonymous "brave Baltimoreans were my most generous and numerous patrons, . . . with grateful affection to the children, for the generosity, liberality, and hospitality with which their parents treated me before they were born" (p. 85). For similar sentiments, see idem, *The Pleasures of Contemplation, Being a Desultory Investigation of the Harmonies, Beauties, Benefits of Nature: Including a Justification of the Ways of God to Man, and a Glimpse of His Sovereign Beauty* (Philadelphia, 1817), 222.

radical proclivities that precluded Reese's promotion (no record explained his rejection), but, unlike Kesley, the next year, Reese was again turned down, his recommendation mysteriously "dismissed for informality."[50] Two years later, just before the next quadrennial General Conference, Baltimore lay ministers produced a circular, signed by Jennings, McCaine, and James Williams (a Baltimore dyer), which drew particular attention to the desires of local preachers like Kesley, Reese, and themselves for more power within the polity. Hopes for widespread dissemination of their views, however, were dashed, when the official *Methodist Magazine* refused to print the circular because it might "disturb the peace and harmony of the Church."[51] The pace of reform agitation was quickening and its focus was in Baltimore.

The General Conference of 1824 met in Baltimore on May 1. Those who favored lay representation remained isolated from power, but seventeen of them, led by Jennings and McCaine, met in the latter's schoolroom on the evening of May 21. Their agenda was "to obtain, by a voice of a majority of the ministry and membership, a representative form of church government, which shall extend to the people as well as to the preachers." The result of the meeting was threefold: the reformers decided to publish another periodical to replace the defunct *Wesleyan Repository*; to organize societies to propagate the populist program of religious liberty; and to send to all ministers and members a circular explaining their actions in light of the fundamental rights and liberties of American citizens. At the end of the conference, Bishops William McKendree, Enoch George, and Robert Roberts rejected the circular on the grounds that it threatened Methodist harmony by creating ecclesiastical class conflict (a "distinction of interests") and denied that the pattern of American civil government had anything to do with Methodist practice.[52] With this, official reform of the Methodist polity was dismissed, at least for another four years.

50. *Journal of the Baltimore Annual Conference* (1821), 148. Interestingly enough, no mention of this action against Kesley and Reese appears in Drinkhouse's otherwise exhaustive treatment of the reform movement. This disciplinary action was the beginning of the discrimination Reese suffered, culminating in the official refusal to allow him to preach in any of the city pulpits by 1827. Daniel E. Reese, *Rev. D. E. Reese's Protests, Arguments, and Address, Against the Whole of the Proceedings of His Prosecutors, &c. in the Baltimore City Station, Who Have Combined to Prefer Charges Against Him and Others* (Baltimore, 1827), iii, 12.

51. Bucke, ed., *History of American Methodism*, 1:651; *Methodist Magazine*, Sept. 1823, cited in Drinkhouse, *History of Methodist Reform*, 2:34.

52. Drinkhouse, *History of Methodist Reform*, 2:47. "Minutes of the First General Meeting of Reformers" in *Journal of the General Conference of the M. P. Church* (Baltimore, 1831), 4; Bucke, ed., *History of American Methodism*, 1:651; "Minutes of the Reformers," in *Journal of the M. P. Church* (1831), 7; *Mutual Rights* 1 (Aug. 1824): 5–7.

Despite the bishops' cavalier dismissal of the offending circular, many rank-and-file members responded favorably to it. A society in line with its suggestion was formed in Baltimore in summer 1824. Officially denominated "The Union Society of the Methodist Episcopal Church in the City of Baltimore," it was referred to as the Baltimore Union Society. Led by Jennings, McCaine, and Reese, it included a number of Baltimore artisans, small merchants, and local educators, including John H. W. Hawkins (journeyman hatter), Lambert Thomas (master cabinetmaker), Wesley Starr (grocer and former carpenter), John J. Harrod (printer), John Chappell, (druggist), and William Kesley. A model constitution for similar union societies was printed in the new periodical, known simply as *Mutual Rights.* In this publication, the purpose (and protective nature) of the Baltimore Union Society was made explicit: to associate together for support, to foster mutual encouragement, and to exchange information. More significant was the language used and sense of collective consciousness revealed; explicitly producerist in tone and language, the Baltimore Union Society, with a key component of artisan support, called for the recognition of "class" interests and community intervention on behalf of the oppressed. Specifically, the protection of union societies meant that "no reformer can be persecuted, even in a corner, without its being speedily known to all the reformers in the United States. They provide a mutual support; for if the members of one Union society are persecuted or maltreated, they make common cause with the sufferers, and use their utmost effort to obtain for them redress of grievances." Samuel Jennings later summed up the significance of this protection, asserting, "This was one of the chief reasons wherefore the men in power desired their destruction." Although by forming the union societies reformers recognized the existence of a conflict of interests, they continued to hope for restoration of a harmony of interests.[53]

Mutual Rights, a forty-page monthly, was first published in August 1824. Unlike its broader-based predecessor, *Wesleyan Repository, Mutual Rights* was devoted exclusively to discussion of lay representation and religious liberty, and it was open to opponents as well as proponents of reform. Led by Nicholas Snethen and Asa Shinn, many contributed to a line of argument that emphasized the inherently corruptible nature of unregulated power as it pertained to evangelical Christianity. "Are not the leaves of the Holy Bible," Snethen wrote, "written . . . with the admonition . . . *beware of power?*" Shinn

53. *Mutual Rights* 1 (Aug. 1824): 20; Jennings, *Exposition of the Late Controversy,* 143; "Minutes of the Reformers," in *Journal of the M. P. Church* (1831), 5.

echoed Snethen's distrust of power; in answer to the claim that reformers lusted after power simply because they lacked it, he replied that the reformers wanted to see power "circulate" so that it would not become "permanently established in a few hands" because an unhealthy love of power was "too common and too deep in human nature" to be successfully eradicated. Citing Matt. 23:6–10, Shinn added, "The inordinate desire of power" was the "most destructive, perhaps," in "human nature." "Its dreadful effects" had "caused the earth to be filled with violence." Referring again to the polarities so familiar to populist evangelicals, Shinn summated his evaluation of power: "Its pernicious influence over all orders of society" filled some with "dictatorial self-sufficiency and others with a spirit of servile and dastardly submission." Men must be free, he concluded, "both from the desire of power and from the dread of it."[54]

Like most Christian populists and many reformers, Snethen extolled the virtues of the early church and deplored the Constantinian heresy of uniting church and state. He also refuted Sir Robert Filmer's "patriarchal scheme" of social theory on the grounds that it fostered submissiveness. The reformers favorably compared the Glorious Revolution of 1688 to the schism in Britain of the New Connexion Methodists under Alexander Kilham over this very issue of representation. The reformers' identification of corruption within the Methodist Episcopal polity was not restricted to political theory;[55] they were equally opposed to the passive attitude that subsequent Methodist Protestants ridiculed as "pray, pay, and obey." Snethen wrote: "When parents and magistrates teach, or command directly, or indirectly, to disobey God, . . . the moral order of the human and divine obligation, is subverted. . . . Then it is . . . most clear [that] good men may with caution and prudence . . . disobey parents and magistrates." Moreover, according to Cornelius Springer ("Cincinnatus"), "It may be as much a duty, at one time, to resist government, as it is, at another, to obey it; to wit, whenever more advantage will, in

54. Drinkhouse, *History of Methodist Reform,* 2:69. The *Methodist Magazine* was explicitly closed to any topic its conservative editors deemed controversial. Ibid., 71. *Mutual Rights* 1 (Mar. 1825): 309. Snethen, *On Lay Representation,* vi, x; *Mutual Rights* 1 (July 1825): 459–61. These principles were so critical to the reformers that Alexander McCaine resigned from the editorial board of *Mutual Rights,* not "in consequence of any change in my mind respecting representation for the local ministry and laity; but because I am an advocate for rotation in office." *Mutual Rights* 2 (Aug. 1825): 17. For a similar argument expressed in political terms, see *Republican,* Apr. 19, 1837.

55. "The claims of the hierarchy, or the patriarchate, gain one essential point, viz: the docility of all." *Mutual Rights* 1 (Oct. 1824): 105, 107; (Feb. 1825): 263–64; Snethen, *On Lay Representation,* xxvi.

our opinion, accrue to the community, from resistance, than mischief." The reformers were similarly concerned with the control of church property, which was held by the itinerants and bishops of the General Conference or by trustees appointed for life. This practice was characterized by Snethen as "one of the essential principles of an absolute government" because of the inherently autocratic nature of lifetime office holding. This issue, along with concern over socioeconomic inequalities among the faithful, had sparked the Stilwellite secession in New York in 1820. Such actions reflected the reformers' stated preoccupation with principle over expediency—a stance that emerged as one of the key differences within the controversy and provided Thomas Bond, their former ally, with a most effective weapon for turning moderate reformers into conservatives.[56]

The reformers continued their agitation throughout 1824 and 1825. In the process, *Mutual Rights* gained a far greater popularity than the *Wesleyan Repository* had ever enjoyed, and it became obvious that the reform movement was gaining strength nationwide.[57] In January 1826, the Baltimore Union Society selected seven men, including Jennings, McCaine, Williams, Starr, and Chappell, to consider calling a national convention to discuss possible responses to official recalcitrance. One month later, such a call went out, under the auspices of the Methodist Society of New York City. In five years, William Stilwell's splinter group had grown from three hundred original members to eight hundred in New York City and two thousand in surrounding areas. Their activities, including their recruitment of the eccentric but widely respected Lorenzo Dow as one of their "general missionaries" had by now attracted national attention from both sympathizers and opponents.[58] The growth of the Stilwellites frightened the Methodist

56. Drinkhouse, *History of Methodist Reform*, 2:134; *Wesleyan Repository* 2 (June 1822): 48; 3 (May 1823): 11; *Mutual Rights* 1 (Feb. 1825): 261. Complaints about low ministerial pay and annoyingly patronizing treatment of local preachers completed the picture. "Massachusettensis," in this regard, bitterly noted the "frigid" practice of the General Conference granting to economically distressed local preachers "what relief they [i.e., the conference] judge proper, after the allowance of the travelling preachers . . . are discharged." *Mutual Rights* 1 (Jan. 1825): 420–21. Aggravating this situation was the perceived lack of status for local preachers, many of whom had exhausted themselves physically and spiritually in their previous work as itinerants. *Mutual Rights* 1 (Jan. 1825): 232–33.

57. Drinkhouse, *History of Methodist Reform*, 2:76; George Brown, *Recollections of Itinerant Life: Including Early Reminiscences* (Cincinnati, 1866), 125.

58. *Friendly Visitor* 1 (Dec. 7, 1825): 390. On November 27, 1825, Dow was ordained a deacon and an elder, after which he made his way south and west on one of his many revival pilgrimages. *Friendly Visitor* 1 (Nov. 30, 1825): 383. For more on Dow's storied career and

Episcopal leadership and they were roundly denounced, in the revealing words of the archconservative bishop Joshua Soule, as "disastrous, . . . properly speaking, an ecclesiastical democracy, in the most extensive sense of the word."[59]

Recruiting Lorenzo Dow was highly significant because his revival successes, extreme disdain for respectability, reliance on charismatic gifts, thoroughgoing populism, and producerist sympathies had made him one of the most popular revivalists in America.[60] These traits, however, had also anathematized him to any Methodist with conservative tendencies. The official British Methodist refusal to countenance his peculiar form of revivalism was well known; it followed the publication of a highly publicized letter from none other than Nicholas Snethen, warning the British Methodists of Dow's baneful influence. "Crazy" Dow was a firebrand—a compatriot of Theophilus Gates of the *Reformer* and an outspoken defender of the British radical Kilhamite Methodists—and his utter contempt for the doctrine of submission to authority was legendary, as evidenced by his threatening hints regarding the process of regaining usurped power. "Power, even . . . in France and Denmark, was not relinquished but by *intimidation.* How much *less* is the *hope* for the relinquishment of clerical power, by a voluntary act of their own free will."[61] The addition of Dow to the Methodist Society, along with the bylaws granting women equal power in church matters and proscribing any connection with slave-holding, smuggling, and offensive war, bespoke the radical proclivities of that branch of Methodism.

As the Methodist Society thrived, William Stilwell and James Covel branched out into other radical organizations. As founding members of the New York Society for Promoting Communities (NYSPC) in 1823, their explicit anticapitalist critiques grounded in scriptural exegesis presented the most significant evangelical solution to capitalist accumulation. In its official

---

immense popularity, see Hatch, *Democratization of Christianity,* 36–40; Charles C. Sellers, *Lorenzo Dow: The Bearer of the Word* (New York, 1928). Thomas Stockton had recorded in 1822 the existence of four other independent Methodist Societies in unnamed locales. *Wesleyan Repository* 2 (July 1822): 106.

59. Horace M. DuBose, *Life of Joshua Soule* (Nashville, 1911), 161, cited in Bradley, *History of A. M. E. Zion Church,* 79.

60. "No man, doubtless, in the Union," according to the *Baltimore Saturday Visiter,* "is so familiar . . . with every portion of the republic." *Baltimore Saturday Visiter,* June 15, 1833. Dow's popularity was reflected in the unusual number of children named for him by Methodist parents. Hatch, *Democratization of Christianity,* 281–82, n27.

61. Lorenzo Dow, *History of Cosmopolite; or the Four Volumes of Lorenzo's Journal* (New York, 1814), 286, cited in Bucke, ed., *History of American Methodism,* 1:631.

publication *An Essay on Common Wealths*, written principally by Quaker radical Cornelius Blatchly, the NYSPC condemned in biblical terms usury, high interest rates, violations of the labor theory of value, and the exploitation of powerless workers. But members distinguished themselves among evangelical social critics by proposing an alternative socioeconomic system grounded in scriptural precedents and producerist consciousness. Among other things, the NYSPC proposed a system, based on the Pentateuchal Jubilee (Lev. 25:1–17), whereby all property sold due to economic distress would be returned to the original owner (but not the profit accrued from its use during that time) at fifty-year intervals.[62] Such a system would allow for individual initiative and limited upward mobility based on industry and frugality, while at the same time it would circumscribe the possibilities for abuses endemic to any permanent accumulation of wealth and power. Because the feudal traditions of primogeniture and entail had been outlawed in the new republic, the society's proposals would require government intervention, something usually held suspect by American republicans in either political or ecclesiastical structures. To address this objection, the NYSPC proposed establishing "an evangelical government" to enable such legislation to pass.[63] Without being consciously aware of it, the NYSPC had reached the same conclusion regarding the evils of capitalist accumulation as had Jonathan Edwards seventy-five years earlier.[64]

The radicalism of the NYSPC, then, was not unprecedented although the specificity of their proposals was unusual. But William Stilwell was equally interested in the evangelical program promoting revivalism, holy living, and

62. Cornelius Blatchly, *An Essay on Common Wealths* (New York, 1822), 22–23. For the centrality of the notion of the Jubilee to radical evangelicalism, see also Thomas Branagan's condemnation of the contemporaneous European celebrations of the Protestant Reformation (which they called "jubilee") because they were making a mockery of the genuine article. He questioned publicly whether such celebrations ("a burlesque on religion, an outrage on reason, an insult to common sense, and blasphemy against the truth, the justice, the benevolence of Heaven") would "force a curse of holiness itself, unless they imitate the Jewish Jubilee, by relieving the needy and letting the oppressed go free." Thomas Branagan, *A Glimpse of the Beauties of Eternal Truth* . . . (Philadelphia, 1817), 10, 15. For a contemporary example of activist artisan use of the Jubilee arguments, see Robert Townsend's speech to the Journeymen Carpenter's Society of New York City in 1834. *National Trades' Union*, Jan. 17, 1835. The longstanding attraction of the Jubilee for Anglo-American artisans is described in Linebaugh, "Jubilating," 143–80.

63. Blatchly, *Common Wealths*, 14, 40. There were limits to the interventions appropriate to this "evangelical government," however; in 1828, Blatchly produced a small tract opposing Sabbatarian attempts to halt the carrying of mail on Sundays." Idem, *Sunday Tract* (New York, 1828).

64. Valeri, "The Economic Thought of Jonathan Edwards," 37–54.

family and community harmony. In January 1825, he introduced a family-oriented weekly newspaper called the *Friendly Visitor*. For this endeavor, Stilwell toned down his radicalism; his desire to reach a broad Methodist audience was exhibited in both the masthead ("to err is human, to forgive divine") and the prospectus (his work was to be informed by "cheerfulness flowing from understanding by experience, that great truth 'we love him because he first loved us,' and that those who have this experience, will love their neighbour also . . . therefore controverted subjects of any kind will not be introduced"). Despite these caveats, the paper was staunchly populist and critical of the increasingly autocratic tendencies of the Methodist hierarchy, in particular, and of similar developments in the political and economic realms. One of the longest serial articles was a sympathetic treatment of the dissident English Methodist Alexander Kilham, and Irish Methodist attempts to establish lay representation were praised. Its antimodernist tendencies were expressed in articles denouncing current Methodist camp meeting practices (causing them to degenerate into holiday excursions at best) and in its criticism of liberal capitalism.[65] But its dedication to traditional producer-ism was at times moderated by its recognition of the hurdles faced by disestablished churches in their efforts to improve society along biblical lines. Stilwell's work on the *Friendly Visitor* limited the time he had for his other interests, and as a result, he reluctantly announced its suspension at the end of 1825.

Presumably, one of those distractions was his desire to promote the national organization of his Methodist Society. Many populist evangelicals were sympathetic to its fundamental concerns, but little came of the Stil-wellite invitation issued in February 1826, although the New York leaders did hold a convention in June to create a separate Methodist connection.[66] This

65. *Friendly Visitor* 1 (Jan. 1, 1825): 1; (June 3, 1825): 184. The serial article on Kilham appeared weekly from July 8 through August 5, 1825. Kilham has been described as an archetypical evangelical traditionalist; see David Hempton, *Methodism and Politics in British Society, 1750–1850* (Stanford: Stanford University Press, 1984), 66–72. *Friendly Visitor* 1 (Feb. 26, 1825): 72; (Aug. 12, 1825): 263.

66. *Journal of the M. P. Church* (1831), 4. The exact nature of this conference remains obscure. Drinkhouse maintained that he had available the minutes of the "Yearly Conference of the Methodist Society," but he made no comment on them. By 1826, Stilwell himself and his congregation had gone independent, and "it seems that he favored union with the 'Radicals' of Maryland and elsewhere." Apparently, the Methodist Society had established a branch in Baltimore, eventually claiming membership of 110 and publishing a short catechism for its members. In time, "nearly this whole organization . . . merged in the Methodist Protestant Church." Drinkhouse, *History of Methodist Reform*, 2:83n1; Bucke, ed., *History of American Methodism*, 1:647.

convention was apparently something of a disappointment because soon afterward the New York radicals began to drift apart. Stilwell, in the finest tradition of Protestant sectarianism, pursued an alternative, independent congregation rather than attempting to reform the increasingly resistant Methodist Episcopal Church, and although he led the congregation until his death in 1851, he soon disappeared from a position of wider influence. Stilwell's approach settled for the limited influence of a visionary congregation, rather than the continued pursuit of interjecting radical critiques into an established institution.

For reasons unrelated to the radicalism of the New York leaders, however, the Baltimoreans rejected the convention call, repeating their earlier claim that they had "no design to separate from the church, much less to divide it, but, on the contrary, we are laboring to prevent secessions and divisions . . . consequently any participation in the measures you propose would be inconsistent with our avowed intentions."[67] The refusal of the Baltimore reformers to join the Stilwellites was critical—from then on, Stilwellite radicalism was increasingly marginalized within the Methodist reform effort, although its contribution to the subsequent radicalism of Thomas Skidmore and the Workingmen's movement in the late 1820s in New York City was significant.[68]

In refusing to join the Stilwellites, the Baltimore reformers adopted a conciliatory tone that belied the increasing hostility between the reformers and spokesmen for the opposition. As evident in a published exchange between Alexander McCaine and James Smith, a Virginia Methodist who had espoused lay representation since 1810 but had switched sides after becoming disgusted with the polemical level of the debate, personal invective was rapidly superseding reasoned disagreement. Responding in the October 1825 issue of *Mutual Rights* to McCaine's contributions to the journal, Smith condemned McCaine for defaming Methodism, and then he printed a pamphlet in which he insisted that all reformers quit hiding behind pseudonyms. In

67. *Mutual Rights* 2 (Aug. 1825): 2; Bucke, ed., *History of American Methodism,* 1:647. As early as 1821, reformers refused to condemn the Stilwellite schism but acknowledged that such actions "are not always necessary to our happiness." *Wesleyan Repository* 1 (Dec. 20, 1821): 306. For another sympathetic comment on the Stilwellite separation, see Snethen's letter to James Williams, published in the *Wesleyan Repository* 2 (Nov. 1822): 241. In support of the Baltimore reformers' unwillingness to take the same step of schism, however, Shinn wrote, "Nor are we in favour of the sentiment adopted by our brethren who formed a church constitution in New-York—that private members have an indefeisible right, in all cases, to choose their minister." *Mutual Rights* 3 (Sept. 1827): 43. See also *Wesleyan Repository* 2 (Oct. 1822): 226.

68. Wilentz, *Chants Democratic,* 157–62, 183–89.

February 1826, McCaine responded. Ridiculing Smith's "obscurity of style" as a failed attempt to appear "vastly profound" and rejecting the alleged "impracticality" of reform, McCaine praised the decentralized nature of the early Christian church and claimed that nothing in modern times, given "the genius and character of the American people," was incapable of improvement. On the issue of pseudonymous authorship, McCaine again decried the illegitimate monopoly of power and discipline held by the bishops and suggested as an alternative to the method used by the Stilwellites and the American criminal court system, where equals determined guilt and innocence. Then, after expressing his suspicion that Smith had been paid off by the hierarchy, McCaine noted that he, too, had been offered a bribe—a supernumerary position that would have placed him within the ruling General Conference—but he had turned it down because the offer precluded the possibility of addressing the systemic injustice of Methodist practice. Appealing to the ultimate nonscriptural authority in his conclusion, McCaine cited the Scottish Common Sense writer Thomas Reid to clinch his argument favoring reform.[69]

Not surprisingly, McCaine's attack increased the level of personal invective at the expense of systemic criticisms and made McCaine something of a movement hatchet man—a position to which he seemed temperamentally well suited. In the aftermath of the McCaine-Smith pamphlet war, the Baltimore brethren issued a limited invitation for a General Convention of Reformers from the state of Maryland only, which met on November 1, 1826. Officiated over by Jennings, McCaine, Chappell, and Harrod, the ratio of representation was one preacher to two laymen, and it was determined to hold another convention the following year. In the meantime, *Mutual Rights* was to continue agitation; union societies sprang up in Cincinnati, Pittsburgh, and smaller cities in Ohio, North Carolina, Virginia, Alabama, and Vermont; and in Baltimore, a second union society was organized for the Fell's Point Methodists.[70] The die was cast for confrontation and the antireformers were to prove equal to the task.

In April 1827, at the Annual Conference, which met at Eutaw Street Church, the Baltimore antireformers finally instituted organized discipline. At Annual Conferences, itinerants under the direction of the presiding elder examined

69. Alexander McCaine, *An Appeal to the Public, from the Charges Contained in the "Reply of the Rev. James Smith, to the Strictures of the Rev. Alexander McCaine"; Accompanied with Remarks upon the Government of the Methodist Episcopal Church* (Baltimore, 1826), 3–5, 8–9, 13, 15, 19–23.

70. *Mutual Rights* 3 (Dec. 1826): 101–2, 105–6; (Apr. 1827): 235; (Feb. 1827): 175–76; *Journal of the M. P. Church* (1831), 8; Drinkhouse, *History of Methodist Reform*, 2:102.

each other for character or theological defects, and local officials along with presiding elders then made appointments for the coming year. The reactionary Joshua Soule was in charge of this particular conference. When the proposed appointment of Dennis Dorsey came up for discussion on April 12, his character was judged defective because he had "actively engaged in the circulation of an improper periodical work" (i.e., *Mutual Rights*); consequently, he was refused appointment as a result of his "contumacy in regard to the authority of the conference." Dorsey's specific transgression was sending a letter to Hugh Sharp recommending that he read *Mutual Rights*, and his "contumacy" was in his refusal to promise to desist.[71] The rejection of Dennis Dorsey moved the reform issue from discussion to action.

Dennis Dorsey was born in 1799 in Baltimore County and grew up in rural Virginia. At fifteen he was left as the sole support of his mother and three sisters, and he found work as a carpenter and farm laborer. Converted at a camp meeting in western Virginia at seventeen, he was self-educated and particularly attracted to John Locke and the Scottish Common Sense philosophers. Three years after his conversion, he was received into the Baltimore Conference and served in various administrative capacities. His finances, apparently, were always marginal, as was his health. Introduced to *Mutual Rights* in September 1824, he became an enthusiastic advocate of its views, distributing the periodical to friends and family. In 1827, his activities were reported to the Methodist authorities, and he found himself singled out for ecclesiastical martyrdom. He was equal to the occasion.[72]

Dorsey's defense of himself and the sympathetic reactions to his plight reflected the strong republican, populist, and class feelings among Methodists. Much was made, during and after his trial, of his vulnerability as a poor man. Writing to boost Dorsey's morale, Henry Bascom noted the problem: "I cannot pause . . . to write the many denunciations that common sense, throughout an outraged community, will pronounce upon this overbearing act of abandoned tyranny! But I . . . enquire why were you selected as the . . . sole victim, when it was in proof before them that others were in the same condemnation? . . . Was it because, like your master, you were poor, and with the humbler sharer of fortunes 'had scarcely where to lay your head?'" For

71. Jennings, *Exposition of the Late Controversy*, 198. Expulsions of reformers had already taken place in Tennessee and North Carolina. Ibid., 141–42. *Journal of the Baltimore Annual Conference* (Apr. 17–18, 1827), 201, cited in Bucke, ed., *History of American Methodism*, 1:653; Drinkhouse, *History of Methodist Reform*, 2:105–6; *Mutual Rights* 3 (Jan. 1828): 165, 168.

72. Colhouer, *Sketches of the Founders*, 153–57, 168; William G. Hawkins, *Life of John Hawkins*, 47.

his part, Dorsey's comments drew attention to the "monstrous anomaly in ecclesiastical government" represented by the conference's confusion over its executive and legislative roles; he pointed out that, according to received republican wisdom, it could not act simultaneously as both. As for his reading *Mutual Rights,* he said, "The bishops themselves read it, the preachers read it, . . . and will any one say, that the people have no right to read it?"[73]

Other reformers rushed to Dorsey's defense. Cornelius Springer, already in trouble with Methodist authorities, expressed sentiments similar to Bascom's: "The course I have pursued in relation to this controversy, I honestly and conscientiously think is right, consequently, shall continue to pursue it until I am otherwise convinced. And after I do what I think is right, the administration, can do in relation to me, what they think is right. As it regards consequences, I have long been indifferent; although I would not necessarily provoke persecution, yet I would not swerve an inch from the course of a manly independence, to prevent the worst that might ensue. I am, dear brother, yours in the kingdom and patience of Jesus Christ." Asa Shinn, wondering if all that were to be left to Methodists were "the consolations of passive obedience and non-resistance," declared himself a reformer publicly for the first time. Nicholas Snethen also dropped all his aliases and in a melodramatic "Address to the Friends of Reform" wrote that since "the fiery trial has come upon one who is, as the shadow of a man, a walking skeleton," he himself could no longer "desert the cause and be innocent before God or man." Henry Bascom summed up the reformers' reaction: "*We* have the Bible on our side; the practice of the primitive church sustains us; public opinion is our friend and ally; the civil institutions of our country lend us aid, and the *genius* of American freedom throws her protective shadow over every friend of equal representation and mutual rights. . . . We *resist* only when we are *oppressed.*"[74]

The outrage generated by the Dorsey case was not limited to scattered individual complaints: the union societies were quick to respond with generous financial and moral support. Dorsey publicly thanked them for

73. Colhouer, *Sketches of the Founders,* 164–65, 161–62, 160. This action, which aroused public sympathy, especially in the nonhierarchical evangelical denominations, was deemed sufficiently significant that it made the local secular newspapers. Drinkhouse, *History of Methodist Reform,* 2:107, 122.

74. James R. Williams, *History of the Methodist Protestant Church* (Baltimore, 1843), 165; Shinn, quoted in Bucke, ed., *History of American Methodism,* 1:653; Snethen, *On Lay Representation,* 346, 344–45; Bascom, quoted in Drinkhouse, *History of Methodist Reform,* 2:110.

"the hand of munificence, in imitation of Him who 'giveth to all men *liberally* and *upbraideth* not,'" in order "to demonstrate . . . that he who does 'what he *thinks*' is right, shall not be forsaken."[75] The reaction of the Baltimore Union Society casts interesting light on contemporary attitudes toward perceived oppression and appropriate resistance—beliefs accessible to Methodist common folk and particularly pertinent for evangelical artisans receptive to the arguments of both Methodist populists and trade unionists. The objections of the Baltimore Union Society were not, as one might expect, based on freedom of speech or the press, but rather "a subject of vital importance to . . . the community at large," that is, based on the older legacy of producerist morality. For the Methodist establishment had left "brother Dorsey . . . without a prospect of support for himself and family," a circumstance that "was oppressive in its character, and not warranted by the scriptures, nor the discipline of the church." The overriding concern for Dorsey's access to a competence was producerism at its purest, as was the importance of maintaining social harmony and avoiding class distinctions. In a discussion of Methodist polity that was in fact unintentionally analogous to the developing class system of industrialism, a union society author described the evil that might befall the mother church: "Two schools may thus be gradually formed; the one to learn domination, and the other mental and religious servility. The natural volitions and affections are thus transformed; society becomes almost wholly artificial, and is separated into castes, or separate orders take place."[76] The Baltimore Union Society, while refusing to back off from conflict, was clearly opposed to widening social class divisions. Rather than pitting one class of Methodists against another, it earnestly sought resolution, through sharing power, in order to safeguard community harmony.

In view of this continued agitation, the original rationales for forming the Baltimore Union Society are instructive, especially when compared to prevailing artisan attitudes. The union societies were not founded strictly on trade union principles, although central aspects were compatible with traditional protective notions of craft unions and guild policies. Snethen conceived of them as "a kind of patriotic societies" to further education and strengthen ties until the reform issue could be forced, and a later apologist compared them, somewhat grandiosely, to the revolutionary Sons of Liberty.

75. *Mutual Rights* 3 (Feb. 1828): 222–23.

76. *Mutual Rights* 3 (June 1827): 276, 278–79; *Mutual Rights and Methodist Protestant* 2 (Feb. 17, 1832): 52.

Still, it was recognized that they were uniting—reluctantly—as a "class" to protect their own particular interests.[77] What they shared with artisan trade unionists was an understanding of the efficacy of group solidarity and a willingness to join together to resist inequitable and illegitimate authority, the oppression of power associated against them, and the threats against their livelihoods and self-esteem. Pious docility and unquestioned submission to authority and power were simply not elements of their evangelical populism, but neither was a desire to embrace class conflict.

77. *Wesleyan Repository* 3 (Aug. 1823): 123; Colhouer, *Sketches of the Founders*, 130, 269. "As preachers, you have one set of interests, and we, as members of the church, have another," wrote one reformer. "What sympathy can . . . you . . . feel in our privation, when all the power you abstract from us, you add to yourselves?" *Wesleyan Repository* 1 (Nov. 8, 1821): 279. This understanding informed one of the antireform attacks; lay representation would acknowledge that there was "a distinction of interests between the itinerancy and the membership." *Mutual Rights* 1 (Sept. 1824): 46. Incipient "class" feeling between itinerants, on the one hand, and local preachers and lay Methodists, on the other, however, was a constant concern to those reformers for whom dreams of community harmony still resonated. For that reason, they chose the slogan "Mutual Rights." *Mutual Rights* 1 (Aug. 1824): 5.

Chapter Three

The Institutionalization of Methodist Protestantism 1827–1835

In May 1827, one month after Dennis Dorsey's expulsion, Alexander McCaine complied with the request of Baltimore Union Society members to publish a recently delivered address. The rhythmically entitled and incendiary work, *The History and Mystery of Methodist Episcopacy*, became an instant sensation.[1] McCaine's purpose was to encourage "the laity and local ministry . . . to persevere in demanding their rights," and his intent was to prove that the present American system of episcopacy was a monstrous

1. McCaine wrote that, after he presented his work to the Baltimore Union Society, he was "requested to print it for the information of his brethren." Alexander McCaine, *The History and Mystery of Methodist Episcopacy, or, A Glance at "The Institutions of the Church, As We Received Them from Our Fathers"* (Baltimore, 1827), iv. Daniel Reese was one of those accused of encouraging McCaine, but he denied it. Reese, *Protests, Arguments, and Address,* 10. Antireformers complained that the impression was thereby given that the entire Union Society supported McCaine's views, that an official authorization to publish was made, and that such an impression was deliberately misleading on McCaine's part. John Emory, *Defense of "Our Fathers," and of the Original Organization of the Methodist Episcopal Church, Against the Rev. Alexander McCaine and Others: With Historical and Critical Notices of Early American Methodism,* 5th ed. (New York, 1840), 147–49. Baker, ed., *Those Incredible Methodists,* 152–53.

mistake imposed on Americans by the conspiratorial operations of the English-born bishops, Francis Asbury and Thomas Coke (appointed by Wesley but entitled by themselves), and their minions. Supported by a mass of correspondence and undergirded by the rhetoric of classical republicanism, McCaine warned that "when the principles of a government are unjust or oppressive, it becomes necessary to keep them concealed from the eyes of the multitude; for the perpetuity of a government founded on such principles, must depend on the ignorance of the people, or on physical force. Hence the necessity of large standing armies in all monarchical and tyrannical governments to keep the people in awe." To bolster his argument, McCaine repeated the Wesley statement he had used in his reply to James Smith the year before, quoting from a letter written in 1790: "Men may call me a knave, or a fool, a rascal, a scoundrel, and I am content; but they shall never by my consent call me a bishop." Throughout *History and Mystery*, McCaine's tone was as usual polemical and accusatory, but his summation was decidedly less cantankerous: "Let the local ministers and the laity be represented in the legislative department of the church. On the other points which we have mentioned above, we place, comparatively, no stress." McCaine's conciliatory nod was understandable. The dissidents, including McCaine, were still deeply Methodist, and their participation in the Methodist communities formed their most significant social ties. They were, however, convinced that the conference had acted irresponsibly, and their response made it clear that they would submit only to legitimate authority. If there was any doubt about that stance, McCaine was happy to clear it up: "representation from the local ministry and laity, by the help of God, we will never relinquish."[2] The crux of the issue, then, remained lay representation even as the larger issues were being obscured by personal vindictiveness.

But the possibility of respectful discussion reconciling Baltimore Methodists had long since passed, and so McCaine's efforts, not surprisingly, went unappreciated by the conservatives. During summer 1827, the antireformers, led by Dr. Thomas Bond, John Emory (officials in the highly profitable Methodist Book Concern), William Wilkens (brush manufactory owner), Christian Keener (merchant and temperance organizer), and John Howland (later owner of the controversial steam-planing mill; see chapter 1), began first secretly, then (after a meeting of the male members of the Methodist Church in August) openly to discuss official expulsions. The reformers adamantly refused to withdraw from the Methodist connection. In September

2. McCaine, *History and Mystery*, 6, v, 71–72.

1827, leaders of the Baltimore Conference, with the support of wealthy and socially prominent laymen as well as James Hanson, the preacher in charge of the station, took action: eleven preachers and twenty-five laymen were expelled after refusing to bend to antireform pressure. Preachers thus honored included Jennings, McCaine, Reese, and Kesley, and notable laymen included the master cabinetmaker Lambert Thomas and journeyman hatter John H. W. Hawkins. The Baltimore Annual Conference City Minutes listed no explanation for the expulsions, but it was clear that the transgressions were threefold: membership in the Baltimore Union Society, support of *Mutual Rights*, and public approval of McCaine's *History and Mystery*. The rationale given later for the expulsions was that the reformers had gone beyond "the temperate expression of opinion" to "the severest invectives, and the most vehement railing," thereby dishonoring in the public eye traveling preachers and Methodism in general. The reformers, for their part, found equally outrageous Thomas Bond's use of scatological terminology to defend the actions of the antireformers: "The present storm may be necessary to defecate and purify the church from Laodicean lukewarm professors."[3]

Although the turmoil and reaction had been largely confined to Baltimore, Philadelphia reformers now rejoined the lists. Disturbed by the Dorsey case and the subsequent expulsions, Philadelphia's Methodists reminded lay leaders Wilkens and Howland that power "*ascends* from the people to their rulers," according not only to the New Testament but also to republican principles. They pointed out that the love of power was as pernicious as the love of money and concluded with a warning familiar to both primitive Methodists and proponents of producerism: "In vain are taken from our travelling preachers the temptations of high salaries and splendid equipages, if they be left exposed to still greater temptations in the possession of absolute authority. Inordinate wealth would not lead them further from the simplicity of the gospel than will inordinate power."[4]

3. McCaine, *Defence of the Truth*, v, vii; Jennings, *Exposition of the Late Controversy*, 85; Bucke, ed., *History of American Methodism*, 1:654. Those who took special umbrage to such labeling included Samuel Jennings, Daniel Reese, and his expelled nephew Levi Reese. Jennings, *Exposition of the Late Controversy*, 42; Reese, *Protests, Arguments, and Address*, iv; Levi R. Reese, *Levi R. Reese's Argument and Protests Against the Whole of the Proceedings of His Prosecutors, &c. by the Baltimore City Station, Who Have Combined to Prefer Charges Against Him and Others* (Baltimore, 1827), 13.

4. Thomas Dunn and William Whitesides, *A Reply to the Address of the Male Members of the Methodist Episcopal Church in Baltimore, Who Held a Meeting on the 7th of August, 1827* (Philadelphia, 1827), 8.

Despite such remonstrances, the Baltimore antireformers pushed ahead with trials of expulsion.

At the trial of Daniel Reese, a local preacher rejected by the Methodist hierarchy six years earlier, Baltimore merchant Alexander Yearley set forth the conservatives' case: "I have been a Methodist ever since the days of Wesley, and have lived happily under the Discipline which our brother has thought so despotic, until this political scheme of liberty (A liberty to do wrong, I suppose) was got up. . . . It is strange to me that brethren made such a hue and cry about right. They have as much right to take up arms against the state, and consider themselves good citizens, as to rise up against the Discipline . . . and call themselves good Methodists." Reese responded with an emotional statement, recalling his thirty-three years of service to the Methodist Church and expressing his continued affection for "our Zion," his outrage at the secret and high-handed initiation of expulsion activity by powerful lay members (including Yearley, Jacob Rogers, Samuel Harden, John W. Berry, and Fielder Israel, all wealthy merchants or manufacturers), his disgust with the temerity of those local preachers who found the reformers guilty of all charges, and his distress with the collapse of Methodist harmony. Appealing to the larger community as well as to neutral Methodists, he concluded, "I shall only add . . . the prayer of Jesus, suffering under a similar prosecution, gotten up by his . . . enemies; 'Father forgive them, for they know not what they do.'"[5] The conservatives, however, remained unimpressed by his arguments, and expulsions continued apace.

If, as Daniel Reese intimated, the Methodist hierarchy knew not what they were doing, those expelled were equally uninformed. A national convention of reformers met again in Baltimore on November 15, 1827,[6] at the end of which the reformers sent out "An Address to Members of the Methodist Episcopal Church throughout the United States." In this, they put forth their

5. Reese, *Protests, Arguments, and Address,* 16, iii, 7–8, iv. The odious nature of the political maneuverings in this process continued at the District Conference months later where the expulsions were upheld. Using the votes of local black preachers, who attended but had never before (nor did they ever again, until recent times) voted in District Conference matters, the antireformers barely sustained the expulsions and quickly adjourned. The black preachers stated that they had been so instructed by the presiding elder, but not all went along. Still, there were enough votes to uphold the suspensions. Drinkhouse, *History of Methodist Reform,* 2:144–45; Williams, *History of the Methodist Protestant Church,* 192–93.

6. Baker, ed., *Those Incredible Methodists,* 161; *Proceedings of the General Conference of Delegates from the Members and Local Preachers of the Methodist Episcopal Church, Friendly to Reform, Assembled in the First English Evangelical Lutheran Church, in the City of Baltimore, Nov., 15, 1827* (Baltimore, 1827), 8, 16–17.

arguments, couched in language familiar to their populist audience. "Opposition to all our efforts has advanced with incredible violence . . . , and, in the same proportion as the cause of Reform has advanced, . . . an extraordinary combination [has been] systematically organized, to break up the Union Society of the city of Baltimore . . . merely because they have advocated in *Mutual Rights*, a lay representation in the legislative department of the church." Objections to the union societies, in turn, were invalid because the societies had "been instituted for no other object but to embody our sentiments, and to act together advisedly. It is our duty to be united; and if our ingenious and politic opponents attempt to scatter us . . . , it is probable that these societies will save us eventually from ruin." Citing Wesley favorably (with the usual reservations), the reformers maintained that they could not accomplish all of God's purposes; thus, "the time has now come for the attention of the christian public to be called to the importance of liberal principles in church government." The reformers concluded their address with the egalitarian doctrine of Matt. 23:9–10: "*Call no man your father upon earth; for one is your father who is in heaven:—and be ye not called masters; for one is your Master, even Christ; all ye are brethren.*"[7]

The expulsions left the reformers with difficult choices, and they spent winter 1827–28 assessing their situation. On December 23, 1827, male lay reformers—Thomas, Hawkins, Starr, Chappell, Harrod and others—officially united together. Two weeks later the reformers were bolstered by what amounted to a sympathy walk-out, as forty-seven women, including the wives, mothers, sisters, and some class members of those expelled, sent letters of withdrawal to the Baltimore Conference, explaining that to "remain in the Church under the circumstances now existing, would be to evince a want of filial, connubial, and fraternal attachment to our persecuted friends and a want of self-respect." At the end of January, the suspended preachers, elders, and deacons, including Jennings, Williams, Reese, and Kesley, joined the laymen and laywomen, and on February 5, 1828, thirty-three more members of the Baltimore Union Society withdrew from the Methodist Episcopal Church to support those expelled. On April 1, this group designated themselves "Associated Methodist Reformers," announced that women members

7. Ibid., 24, 29, 25, 32. The antireformers responded to the dissidents in their own idiom. Because domestic comforts are few for itinerants, claimed Nathan Bangs, they deserve their power. If they "were really ambitious of worldly interest and . . . domestic comfort," they would accept reform and move toward the advantages of a settled ministry. If they were willing to bow to the "wealthy and liberal friends" of reform, however, they might easily "tend to increase our temporal comforts." Nathan Bangs, *A History of the Methodist Episcopal Church*, 4 vols. (New York, 1845), 3:417.

would vote on all church business, and prepared a temporary constitution based on Wesley's original rules, while they waited to "see whether the present abuses in the administration of the government will be corrected." At the General Conference a month later, the reformers' attempts to reconcile (which included offers to consider discontinuing *Mutual Rights* and disbanding union societies, as well as an impassioned speech by Asa Shinn) were rejected. As sympathizers, including Shinn and Snethen, withdrew, it became apparent that lay representation in the Methodist Episcopal Church was a dead issue.[8]

The General Conference of Methodist Reformers met November 12–20, 1828, at St. John's Church in Baltimore, formerly an Episcopal church and recently purchased by the reformers for their own congregation. One hundred ten delegates had been elected by union societies and ninety-five attended; thirty-nine were from Maryland, and union societies in eleven other states were represented. James Covel, an original Stilwellite and now a delegate "from the Methodist Society of New York," was among them. At last (although not in the manner they desired) the reformers could implement their reforms. Their ideological commitments remained the same; in the initial organizational meeting, they were encouraged to "remember the tenacious grasp with which power is held when once acquired. Its march is ever onward, and its tremendous tendency is to accumulation." On April 2, 1829, the local Annual Conference for Baltimore was organized, consisting of twenty-nine ministers (including Snethen, McCaine, Jennings, Williams, Dorsey, Reese, and Kesley) and twenty-five lay delegates (including Chappell, Starr, and Harrod). Two weeks later, the remaining members of Stilwell's Methodist Societies (but not Stilwell's congregation in New York) formed their own Annual Conferences, the New York and the Genessee. The Associated Reformers became Methodist Protestants in 1830, with equality between local preachers and itinerants, lay representation, and no bishops.[9]

With the adoption of a new constitution, the slight modification of the old Methodist *Discipline*, and the official transformation of the polemic periodical

8. Baker, ed. *Those Incredible Methodists*, 159; Drinkhouse, *History of Methodist Reform*, 2:148–51; *Instrument of Association, Together with the General Rules of Messrs. John and Charles Wesley, and the Additional Regulations Prepared by the Associated Methodist Reformers in Baltimore* (Baltimore, 1828), 3, 5, 7. Jennings, *Exposition of the Late Controversy*, 77–83. Class meetings were small, organized groups of Methodists who met together during the week for mutual support, discipline (if necessary), and prayer. Levi R. Reese, *Thoughts of an Itinerant* (Baltimore, 1847), 94–95.

9. Drinkhouse, *History of Methodist Reform*, 2:208, 214, 233–36; Williams, *History of the Methodist Protestant Church*, 271, 284–87.

Mutual Rights into the noncontroversial *Mutual Rights and Methodist Protestant* (later shortened to *Methodist Protestant*), Methodist Protestantism passed from agitation and self-definition to consolidation and institutionalization. Subsequent growth, especially in the Chesapeake and Ohio Valley regions, was phenomenal. At the General Conference of 1830, there were an estimated 500 members; four years later, the denomination reported 28,000 members, an increase of 600 percent with more than half of the new members in Maryland and Ohio. Two separate congregations were formed in Baltimore: Pitt Street and St. John's churches, with the latter reporting significant revivals in 1831 and 1834. With the exception of the specific reforms included within the rubric of "lay representation," the churches of the reformers, in theology, practice, and social make-up, were nearly identical to the old congregations. In fact, despite continual sniping from some quarters, by the early 1830s, Methodist Protestant and Methodist Episcopal itinerants were collaborating at camp meetings, and the new denomination had taken its place in the Baltimore evangelical community.[10] Although the initial stages of reform had been stormy, the final phase was remarkably calm.

Given that the social base for Methodist Protestantism remained in the middling classes and the doctrinal package was unaltered, what did the Methodist Protestant challenge to the notion of Christian submission to authority mean in terms of socioeconomic morality?[11] For the artisans, the more important question was: what effect did the institutionalization of Methodist Protestantism have on the tensions between producerist and

10. Drinkhouse, *History of Methodist Reform*, 2:296. Stephen Novak puts the 1834 number at 26,587, with Maryland at 4,200 members and Ohio at 10,500. The Maryland Annual Conference grew to 4,227 by 1834, dropped to 3,618 three years later, and then gradually increased to 9,522 by 1843. This was the high water mark for Maryland Methodist Protestantism; by 1850, the numbers had dropped to around 6,000. Novak, "Perils of Respectability," 11; Thomas H. Lewis, comp., *Historical Record of the Maryland Annual Conference of the Methodist Protestant Church* (Baltimore, Methodist Protestant Book Concern, 1918), 5. *Mutual Rights and Methodist Protestant* 3 (Aug. 2, 1833): 241.

11. Rick Nutt, in an excellent description of the political philosophy of the Methodist Protestant Reformers, portrays them as poor and rural and less middle class and less wealthy than the Methodist Episcopal mainstream. This neglects the class complexity present in both groups. The national leadership of professionals like Samuel Jennings and Nicholas Snethen, and the emerging leadership within the definitely urban setting of Baltimore, suggests rather the frustrations of rising, increasingly privileged individuals eager to match their ecclesiastical status with their social positions. Nevertheless, the presence of artisans like Lambert Thomas and John Hawkins among the initial leadership indicate the attraction of Methodist Protestantism for the laboring classes. Nutt, "'Advantages of Liberty,'" 16–25.

capitalist ethics? Two factors were critical in the determination of this course: (1) the ambivalence of changing Methodist socioeconomic traditions regarding capitalist innovations and (2) the problems related to the ability of disestablished, voluntaristic religious organizations to meet the demands of contracted clergy, community discipline, status concerns, and social melioration. Being accountable to congregational authority was now a realized goal, but this change inadvertently undermined the prophetic potential of paid preachers. Furthermore, even if Methodist Protestantism, following the lead of William Stilwell and James Covel, had desired to embrace producerist restrictions, the difficulty of enforcing any kind of discipline and the growing reliance of congregations on the whims of the wealthy would have made such a stance problematic. Yet producerist sentiments remained operative within both the Methodist Protestant and the Methodist Episcopal denominations.

The predominant issue for populist evangelicals was accessibility to power. When they were denied access to congregational control, political direction, cultural formation, or socioeconomic opportunity, they reacted strongly against what they perceived to be illegitimate authority. Once access to power structures had been guaranteed, however, the radical thrust of evangelical egalitarianism was blunted, and populist evangelicals turned their attention to making sure that structure was moral and more or less just. The determination of what constituted social justice was always conflicted, but invariably the evangelical preoccupation became one of maintaining the existing order, rather than following the more difficult path of continued social melioration. This did not necessarily mandate embracing inequalities inherent in those power structures (although possibilities for such were often evident), but it usually meant that the radically transforming thrust of evangelical social ethics was deflected. This pattern was obvious in the development of institutionalized Methodist Protestantism.

For many evangelical populists, including Methodist Protestants, the ambivalent legacy of John Wesley's socioeconomic ethics still loomed large.[12] Wesley's ability to take seriously the spiritual needs of common Englishmen empowered thousands, and he shared the disgust of both producers and liberals with monopolies, usury, and excessive rents as well as the former's distrust of wealth. Yet Wesley's ethics were those of a traditionalist Catholic,

12. As Thomas Madron notes, Wesley's view of economics "represented an ethical critique of problems rather than a theory of economic relations." Thomas W. Madron, "John Wesley on Economics," in Theodore Runyon, ed., *Sanctification and Liberation: Liberation Theologies in the Wesleyan Tradition* (Nashville: Abingdon Press, 1981), 102.

not an American populist; friends and foes alike often cited his assertion, "we are no republicans and never intend to be."[13] In many ways, moreover, Wesley, like his contemporary George Whitefield, challenged the boundaries of traditionalism, as the very essence of their revival tactics and publicity methods encouraged modernist tendencies and introduced market perspectives into the religious realm.[14] Using as his text the parable of the unrighteous steward (Luke 16:9), Wesley preached: "Gain all you can by honest industry . . . by using common sense, by using in your business all the understanding which God has given you. . . . It is amazing to observe, how few do this; how men run on in the same dull track with their forefathers. . . . It is a shame for a Christian not to improve upon them, in whatever he takes in hand." His embrace of the producerist ethic of limited improvement, however, delineated the boundaries of Wesley's willingness to accommodate liberalism; wealth was not for luxury, for massive inheritances, or for capitalist investment.[15]

Wesley's allegiance to traditional economic morality further limited his endorsement of liberal ethics, and he placed strict restrictions on commercial morality. Wesley asked merchants: "Are you not an extortioner? Do you not make a gain of any one's ignorance, or necessity? . . . Suppose you were engaged in trade: do you demand, do you receive, no more than the real value of what you sell?" Wesley's emphasis on the ethical implications of actions led him to oppose the buying, selling, and holding of slaves and the making and selling of liquor, on the grounds that one's economic advancement, in such cases, came at the clear expense of another's welfare. In a

13. Cameron, *Methodism and Society*, 45. John Walsh, according to David Hempton, has characterized Wesley as a "traditionalist Catholic" in direct contradistinction to an "individualist Protestant." Producerism, of course, had solid roots in medieval Catholic social morality. Hempton, *Methodism and Politics in British Society*, 233. Though Wesley was important, neither his word nor his character were sacrosanct to American Methodists; as Nicholas Snethen noted, "Constitutionally considered he [Wesley] forms no exception to the general characteristic of human nature." *Mutual Rights* 1 (Dec. 1824): 176, 184. In fact, "Mr. Locke understood the science of government much better than Mr. W[esley]." *Wesleyan Repository* 2 (Nov. 1822): 310.

14. This is Bernard Semmel's argument in *The Methodist Revolution* (New York: Basic Books, 1973), reinforced (for Whitefield) in Harry S. Stout, *The Divine Dramatist: George Whitefield and the Rise of Modern Evangelicalism* (Grand Rapids, Mich.: William Eerdmans, 1991), and Frank Lambert, *Pedlar in Divinity: George Whitefield and the Transatlantic Revivals, 1737–70* (Princeton: Princeton University Press, 1994).

15. Wesley, *Works*, 1:440, 444. Wesley also argued that a man cannot "properly be said to save any thing, if he only lays it up. You may as well throw your money into the sea, as bury it in the earth. And you may as well bury it in the earth, as in your chest, or in the bank of England." Ibid., 1:446.

similar vein, Wesley condemned profits accrued from interest, realizing that moneylenders often took advantage of adverse circumstances to gouge the needy. Wesley, when he set up a small loan fund for suffering Methodists, made no provision for extracting interest with the payment.[16]

Late in his life, Wesley realized that evangelical wealth was a growing reality, perhaps a menace: "religion must necessarily produce both industry and frugality; and these cannot but produce riches." Recognizing that excessive prosperity held both spiritual and material dangers, Wesley feared that wealth undermined the need for reliance on God and dependence on the community; "in sixty years," he noted, he "did not know six religious persons that were exalted temporally, but degenerated spiritually, and though they retained the shell, lost the kernel of religion." Equally problematic was the power of control available to the wealthy, leading Wesley to urge: "Let all Preaching-houses be built plain and decent, but not more expensively than is absolutely unavoidable. Otherwise, *the necessity of raising money will make rich men necessary to us; but, if so, we must be dependent on them; yea, and governed by them.* AND THEN FAREWELL TO THE METHODIST DISCIPLINE, IF NOT DOCTRINE, TOO."[17] In this, Wesley proved more than a little prophetic.

In assessing economic problems, Wesley offered no coherent program, but at times his suggestions neared radical positions. He realized, for instance, that the poor were often in straitened circumstances through no fault of their own and that poverty was more likely the result of environmental distresses than personal shortcomings.[18] Although he shared the populist suspicion of state intervention, even if it was effected philanthropically, Wesley did on occasion suggest governmental solutions to the problems of poverty, especially in espousing a return to mercantilist regulatory policies. His proposals to address the problem of scarce commodities, summed up by the phrase "restraining luxury," included legal prohibition of the distillation of spirits, taxation of the sale of every British horse to French buyers, taxation of every horse bought for the purpose of pulling carriages, and establishment of a ceiling on the size and profitability of enclosed farms. As

16. Wesley, *Works,* 1:229; Cameron, *Methodism and Society,* 51–55, 61.

17. Wesley, *Works,* 7:317; Wesley, quoted in Branagan, *Guardian Genius,* 76; *Methodist Protestant* 1 (Apr. 25, 1835): 376; cited also by Nicholas Snethen in *Essays on Lay Representation,* xxiv.

18. In a visit to an economically depressed area in 1753, Wesley wrote, "I found not one unemployed who was able to crawl around the room. So wickedly, devilishly false is that common objection, 'They are poor only because they are idle.'" Wesley cited in Cameron, *Methodism and Society,* 58. See also Runyon, ed., *Sanctification and Liberation,* 39, 11–12; Wesley, *Works,* 7:487.

he made these proposals, however, he revealed his lack of faith in their complete efficacy. "But will this ever be done? I fear not. . . . It seems as if God must shortly arise and maintain his own cause."[19]

To help maintain God's cause, Wesley's contributed his important doctrine of stewardship. Herein lay Wesley's understanding of the nonsacred nature of private property: owners were only stewards and if they used their property for evil purposes or to contravene the laws of God, they could be legitimately deprived of it. In answering how the increasingly wealthy Methodists could escape "the nethermost hell" reserved for those who abused the blessings of their prosperity, Wesley concluded there "is one way, . . . If those who 'gain all they can,' and 'save all they can,' will likewise 'give all they can'; then, the more they gain, the more they will gain in grace, and the more treasure they will lay up in heaven.[20] The serious ramifications of such reworked economic ethics for the Methodist community lay in Wesley's decision to support garnering wealth for paternalistic benevolence and for voluntarist reforms against an emphasis on systemic adjustments to limit accumulation and to share profits according to the dictates of social justice. This shift was significant: it transferred the ethical emphasis from the relations of production to relations of distribution. The distinction gave rich evangelicals in succeeding generations moral authority to control the distribution of profits according to their own standards. The result in many cases was the establishment of paternalistic work regimes to replace producerist mutuality—a change that was often welcomed by workers, as long as it was not overly intrusive.[21]

Evidence for the persistence of a moderated producerist economic morality can also be seen in the evolution of the Methodist *Discipline.*

19. Runyon, ed., *Sanctification and Liberation,* 17; Wesley, *Works,* 6:277–78.

20. "Suppose now the fulness of time to be come. . . . What a prospect is this! . . . Here is no oppression to 'make' even 'the wise man mad'; no extortion to 'grind the face of the poor'; no robbery or wrong; no rapine or injustice; for all are 'content with such things as they possess.' . . . 'Neither saith any of them, that aught of the things which he possesseth is his own.' There is none among them that lacketh; for every man loveth his neighbour as himself." Wesley, quoted in Runyon, ed., *Sanctification and Liberation,* 46. On at least one occasion, echoing arguments made by William Stilwell and Cornelius Blatchly in the New York Society for Promoting Commonwealths, Wesley spoke out in favor of land redistribution, the accomplishment of which would occur through the prohibition of any rent over one hundred pounds per year. Wesley also strongly disliked the undue influence and power afforded to those with inherited wealth. Ibid., 109, 112. Wesley, *Works,* 6:274, 276–77, 5:46; Cameron, *Methodism and Society,* 61.

21. Bill Harvey, "Hampden-Woodberry: Baltimore's Mill Villages," in Elizabeth Fee, Linda Shopes, and Linda Zeidman, eds., *The Baltimore Book: New Views of Local History* (Philadelphia: Temple University Press, 1991), 46, 49.

Partially due to their failure to effectively ban slavery[22] and partially due to the increasing popularity of economic liberalism, Methodists became leery of attempts to legislate economic morality. As a result, the foundations of many of Wesley's strictures were not built upon, although the Methodist *Discipline* did reflect attempts to instill a high standard of economic ethics. Indicative of the extent to which economic liberalism had permeated their outlooks, Methodists restricted their rules on economics to insisting that debts be paid and that resolution of economic disputes be handled within the Methodist community rather than in the courts. Excessive speculation was discouraged, as was bribery, buying or selling uncustomed goods, "treating" for votes, and smuggling. Particularly condemned was "the base practice of raising money by coining notes (commonly called the bill trade)."[23]

If the *Discipline* was vague on economic issues, a short catechism prepared by the Methodist Society was more forthright. In general tone, the catechism, designed presumably for the young and new initiates, emphasized spiritual attitudes over political pronouncements and socio-economic ethics. Lessons 20 through 23 and lesson 25 concerned the propriety of idleness, lawlessness, insubordination at work, and giving to the poor. New Methodists, according to scriptural injunctions in Gen. 3:19, 2 Thess. 3:10, Rom. 13: 1–2, Heb. 13:17, Eph. 6: 5–7, Matt. 5:42, Prov. 19:17, 21:13, Ps. 41:1–2, and 2 Cor. 9:6–7, were to work hard, to obey constituted authority, and to be "bountifully" charitable. There were, however, limits to expected obedience; since God was "no respecter of persons," masters were under divine judgment for their treatment of their workers (Eph. 6:9) and all Methodists were encouraged, in cases of sinful behavior, to "rebuke thy neighbor" in order to preserve communal harmony (Lev. 19:17). In the midst of these general instructions, the catechism, in lesson 24, specifically asked, "What is our duty in buying and selling with one another?" The answer, though typically spiritual, was amenable to producerist interpretation.

> A. Yes; as ye would that men should do to you, do ye also to them likewise, Luke 6:31.

22. Donald G. Mathews, *Slavery and Methodism* (Princeton: Princeton University Press, 1965); Richard Cameron, "The New Church Takes Root," in Bucke, ed., *History of American Methodism*, 1:251–56.

23. John Emory, *History of the Discipline of the Methodist Episcopal Church* (New York, 1844), 214–17, 38.

Q. Has St. Paul given us advice relative to the things of this world?

A. Yes, he saith, Godliness with contentment is great gain. For we brought nothing into this world, and it is certain we can carry nothing out. And having food and raiment, let us be forthwith content. 1 Tim. 6:6–8.[24]

Just as it informed Wesley's critiques, portions of the *Discipline*, and the short catechism, populist producerism, with its ethic of limits on individual ambition and its emphasis on traditional economic morality, was a vital element in many of the Methodist reformers' self-understanding. As an anonymous Methodist wrote, a producer "has a right to enjoy or dispose of the fruits of his labour. His property is his own." Asa Shinn set out a similar perspective: "We must not be influenced by the desire of wealth, ease, or accommodation. Our Saviour was poor; Paul's glory was, that he was 'in labours more abundant;' and Lazarus went from among the dogs into an eternal paradise. 'A competence, is vital to content.' And what is a competence? Answer, 'Having food and raiment, let us be therewith content.' 1 Tim. 6. 8 'Be content with such things as ye have.' Heb. 13. 5." In keeping with Shinn's presentation, one of the proposals in the reformers' program was a plank forbidding "that course of stratagem, or policy, which aims to conceal the truth from men by taking advantage of their ignorance, their passions, or their fears, which has in it the essence of lying, and ought to be discouraged among all people as having a pernicious influence upon the best interests of society." Similarly, the original Associated Reformers in Baltimore, when they adopted Wesley's General Rules in 1828, agreed to proscribe "the using many words in buying or selling," the "*giving* or *taking things on usury*; i.e., unlawful interest," the "*putting on of gold or costly apparel*," and, in general, echoing the summation of the Stilwellites in the original rules, "needless self-indulgence."[25]

Although they maintained much of the producerist concern with liberal economics, Methodist Protestants gradually moved away from directly addressing the proper relations between the products of labor and the distribution of profits. Instead, they concentrated on the detrimental effects

24. *A Short Scriptural Catechism Intended for the Use of the Methodist Society* (Baltimore, 1826).

25. *Mutual Rights* 1 (Aug. 1824): 14; 2 (Jan. 1826): 135; Stephens, *Defense of the Founders*, no. 1, 2; *Instrument of Association . . . the Associated Methodist Reformers*, 5. The General Rules also encouraged economic mutuality within the Methodist community by defining "doing good," in part, by "employing [Methodists] preferably to others, buying one of another, [and] helping each other in business" (p. 5).

of accumulating wealth and following fashion.[26] In "Truth Resides with the Common People," which appeared in *Mutual Rights*, a correspondent argued that all heretical perversions within Christianity, "adapted to subserve the purposes of avarice and ambition," came from "the higher classes, among men of pleasure and speculation."[27] The Hamiltonian maxim "power over a man's subsistence amounts to a power over his will" remained in the consciousness of Methodist Protestants, and the effects of wealth gained through unjust profit was viewed as antisocial. As Asa Shinn wondered: "Why does any man wish to be very rich? Plainly, that he may separate his interests from the interests of the community, and have a selfish happiness, independent of the public welfare. . . . But he cannot trust the community with his happiness . . . because he imagines all the members of it . . . generally and constantly sacrifice the social to the selfish principle, and care nothing about any indigent or helpless members, farther than self-love may chance to dictate." Gideon Davis echoed these sentiments. The rich, he wrote, "had much rather trust to their wealth and influence to screen them from their penalties, than to exonerate the poorer order from their obligations." Since "it is from the rich that the greatest temporal assistance is expected," there exists for the ministers so supported "a strong temptation to overlook transgressions, when an investigation would tend to the withdrawal of those temporal comforts from his family, which it had enjoyed."[28] The reformers' understanding of wealth then, even before the final phase of institutionalization, centered on its organizational impact rather than on the relations between producers and capitalists or consumers.[29]

Despite the striking increase in membership, the legacy of suspicion toward capitalist innovation, and the heroic efforts of lay organizers to supply

26. The antimodernist Thomas H. Stockton (son of William) chided "our members in Baltimore" for their "fashionable vanities among the young." *Methodist Protestant* 1 (July 9, 1834): 34; 2 (Aug. 19, 1835): 83.

27. *Mutual Rights and Methodist Protestant* 3 (Sept. 9, 1833): 312; 1 (Apr. 15, 1831): 115. Snethen presented a similar argument earlier; in "An Essay on 2 Tim. 1 Ch. 7 V." ("For God hath not given us the spirit of fear, but of power and of love, and of a sound mind."), he warned against, in the character of church leaders, the presence of indolence, avarice, and, especially, ambition. Snethen, *On Lay Representation*, 276, 279.

28. *Mutual Rights and Christian Intelligencer* 2 (June 5, 1830): 164; *Wesleyan Repository* 2 (July 1822): 90; *Mutual Rights* 1 (May 1825): 394; 2 (Jan. 1826): 135; (July 1826): 276–77; Drinkhouse, *History of American Methodism*, 2:218.

29. The editor of *Mutual Rights*, John Harrod, for instance, in taking issue with a publication equating republicanism with infidelity, completely ignored that part of the argument linking republicanism to "the prevalence of a peculiarly eager and uncorrected commercial temper." *Mutual Rights and Methodist Protestant* 1 (Mar. 4, 1831): 65, 67.

leadership to the nascent denomination, the radical promise of Methodist Protestantism was not to be fulfilled in the 1830s. This became particularly obvious in the publicized expressions of Methodist Protestantism: the new constitution, and the reorganized *Mutual Rights and Methodist Protestant*. The retreat from their initial radical egalitarianism became quickly evident: Methodist Protestant women were disenfranchised in the final consolidation of 1830; slave-holding (although most of the Baltimore contingent were at least moderate abolitionists) was explicitly protected; and only James Covel's Genessee Conference guaranteed suffrage equality to members of color.[30] A retreat from explicit producerism was also evident; instead, modernist trends toward individualized ethics, pretensions of respectability, increased concerns with anarchy instead of tyranny, and the realities of religious voluntarism, as well as a preoccupation with institutional harmony, pushed Methodist Protestants into new directions.

The emphasis on institutional harmony over producerist concerns and the fragile nature of the new denomination in a free market religious environment was evident in the final discussions of socioeconomic ethics during the organizational meetings. At the November 1830 convention in Baltimore, the first item on the agenda was discussion of proposed Elementary Principles (eleven of them). The third principle read: "Every person who loves the Lord Jesus Christ, and obeys the gospel of God our Savior is entitled to church membership." William Stockton moved for a substitution: "All who fear God and work righteousness are entitled to church membership." Eventually the motion was withdrawn, but the wording revealed critical nuances in the approach to social issues.[31] "Love" and "obey" implied an internal, devotional emphasis within personal religion, which undervalued attempts at ethical social interventions. "Fear" and "works," however, indicated the presence within personal religion of an outward ethic stressing the responsibility, not just to believe and act according to a circumscribed code of individual behavioral conduct, but also to intervene on the side of justice and mercy.

The tendency toward individualized ethics became more obvious on November 4 during a debate on the two conditions of membership. The first

30. Drinkhouse, *History of Methodist Reform*, 2:208, 214, 283; Williams, *History of the Methodist Protestant Church*, 271, 284–87.

31. Drinkhouse, *History of Methodist Reform*, 2:254, 258; "Proceedings of the General Convention of Delegates from the Ministers and Members of the Associated Methodist Churches Held in St. John's Church, Baltimore, Maryland, November 2–23, 1830," in *Journal of the M. P. Church* (1831), 9, 11.

suggestion merely repeated Wesley's criterion: "A desire to flee from the wrath to come," with an addition "and be saved by grace, through faith in the Lord Jesus Christ, and, an avowed determination to walk in all the commandments of God blameless." A proposed amendment to this motion further defined seven "fruits," following which would indicate the appropriate desire to "walk" blamelessly. One of the fruits was being "diligent in business, honest in dealing, frugal in the management of domestic concerns, patient under trials, and temperate in all things."[32] When the convention reconvened the next day, discussion of the expanded motion was renewed, and it was moved to strike the seven definitions of "fruit," leaving only the "desire to flee" clause and a watered-down rule on training children. The discussion was tabled, but the amended motion carried unanimously the next day, without the "fruits." The majority of Methodist Protestant leadership apparently wanted few restrictions on their activities and were willing to accept the new laissez-faire ideal of communal harmony through pursuit of self-interest.[33] The tone of this decision, which occurred at the beginning of official Methodist Protestantism, had profound implications for its development, especially in terms of the concerns of its traditionalist wing.

Besides this rapprochement with liberal culture, the Methodist Protestant leadership in 1830 made a momentous decision in regards to their official publication, the *Mutual Rights and Methodist Protestant.* Its predecessor had been open to all manner of political polemic and social critique, but the editorial board now deemed it expedient to present a dignified family newspaper, self-consciously rejecting the controversial nature of the earlier paper. At the urging of John J. Harrod, printer turned prosperous book merchant and longtime reformer, the *Mutual Rights and Methodist Protestant* was turned over to Gamaliel Bailey Jr., a friend of reformer Thomas Stockton and an educated young man who had just returned to the United States from a harrowing tour as a common seaman. It was expected that he would turn the journal into a literary success and avoid any discussion of domestic politics or other controversial topics. Temperamentally suited to conciliation and philosophically dedicated to liberal republican principles, Bailey championed unity among Methodists, evangelical accommodation to the market culture, and the agendas of elite-dominated reform organizations. His radical proclivities were limited to strong antislavery feelings—procolonization sentiments that he was prevented from expressing in the journal. Under his

32. Ibid., 11–12.
33. *Constitution and Discipline of Methodist Protestant Church* (Baltimore, 1830), 16.

direction, the *Mutual Rights and Methodist Protestant*, on the rare occasions it addressed issues of socioeconomic ethics, espoused positions that rarely challenged the emergent status quo.[34] The change in tone expressed and issues raised between the journal of the early 1820s and its successor a decade later could hardly have been more dramatic.

The increased preoccupation with respectability, as defined by social status, education, and prosperity, was a compelling issue for many Methodists, not just Methodist Protestants. Comments published in the *Catholic Sentinel* (and reprinted in the *Methodist Protestant*) that described Methodists in such generically pejorative terms as "*irreligious, fanatic, and ignorant*" because they had "no gentlemen of literary ability, of historical knowledge, or of expansive mind among them" and were "a living disgrace to the literature, liberality and intellect of the age" did not improve their collective self-esteem. But respectability, as opposed to simple respect, usually turned on wealth and refinement, through the early nineteenth century version of conspicuous consumption. And for those still rising socially, wealth was limited; if money was spent on unnecessary consumption, there would be little left for the obligations of Methodist stewardship. Addressing this concern in the new Methodist Protestant weekly, Judge Philemon Hopper encouraged readers to meet the demands of stewardship in ways that "*would not detract aught from our respectability as citizens, or as Christians.*"[35] The doctrine of stewardship itself was a step removed from producerist ethics, and so such advice had little in common with traditional morality.

The official drift away from producerism was matched by a turn toward social conservatism on the part of leaders like Thomas Stockton, Alexander McCaine, and James Covel. This change was reflected by shifts in emphasis between the polarities of classical republicanism. From the beginning of the reform agitation in 1820, reformers had stressed the dangers of tyranny—inordinate power in the hands of the few, oppression of the majoritarian powerless, and disregard for the commonweal. With the establishment of the Methodist Protestant denomination and the accompanying onset of Jacksonian social and political unsettledness, Methodist Protestant leaders saw more danger in anarchy. To be sure, according to Asa Shinn, tyranny and anarchy were still linked as two sides of the same undesirable coin; Shinn made this clear in 1832: "My opposition to anarchy arises from my detestation of

34. Stanley Harrold, *Gamaliel Bailey and Antislavery Union* (Kent: Kent State University Press, 1986), 4–9.

35. *Methodist Protestant* 2 (July 22, 1835): 55; *Mutual Rights and Methodist Protestant* 1 (Mar. 4, 1831): 67.

absolute despotism: for the former opens a wide door for the latter, and the world has had large experience and proof, that anarchy carries the worst elements of tyranny in its bosom. . . . We are as fond of law as our opponents are: the difference is, that our affection is given to the law of liberty, and their's to the law of mastery. . . . My plan then was to take a middle course between anarchy and despotism."[36]

Nicholas Snethen, under the pseudonym "Senex," reentered the discussion in 1833 by refurbishing traditionalist language opposed to both tyranny and anarchy: "obedience and submission in the ruled; and accountability in the rulers." For Methodist reformers, such a suggestion was a genuine innovation; only two years before they were still ridiculing the conservatives for their devotion to "passive obedience and non-resistance." Equally reactionary was Snethen's conclusion: "Anarchy! shall this most fatal of all diseases become epidemic, among a people just struggling for a responsible ministry? . . . Save us brethren, O! save us from the irredeemable and eternal curse of anarchy. You can do so only by obeying accountable guides. Rise, then, unite, and resolve, as one man, to place sufficient power in the hands of your rulers to govern; and let the conviction sink deep in every heart, that no evil can befal [*sic*] us, or prove more ruinous to our character than disobedience and insubordination." Asa Shinn supported Snethen, asserting "that the love of power is the common disease of human nature, and that the people are as fond of assuming an authority which does not belong to them, as any priest-hood in the universe."[37]

These were not just the sentiments of disillusioned old radicals; these perspectives were becoming widespread. In rationalizing the drift toward conservatism inherent in antianarchy rhetoric, an anonymous author described the proper process of dynamic social change: "The social principle must be first expanded and then concentrated, in order to give the greatest effect to social action. . . . [In] any disengagement from such . . . government, the social principle may expand, and then the difficulty is to concentrate its action. The French revolution furnishes one of the clearest examples of this kind. The downfall of the monarchy and the hierarchy which had become

36. *Mutual Rights and Methodist Protestant* 2 (Nov. 9, 1832): 354.

37. *Mutual Rights and Methodist Protestant* 1 (Sept. 2, 1831): 274; 3 (Oct. 11, 1833): 323; (Oct. 25, 1833): 338; (Nov. 15, 1833): 366. In this process, Shinn resurrected the old straw man, Thomas Paine, but rejected him, not for his infidelity but for his ultrademocracy. "We hear . . . about the *people, the people!* but who are they? Are they an order of *holy angels,* without any deficiency of nature whatever?" *Mutual Rights and Methodist Protestant* 3 (Aug. 9, 1833): 250. For similar sentiments, see Nicholas Snethen, *The Identifier of the Ministers and Members of the Methodist Protestant Church* (Philadelphia, 1839), 45.

extremely oppressive, was followed by a reaction . . . ; but when this force of the social principle began to expand itself . . . , the action diverged and destroyed itself for the want of concentration."[38] It is hard to imagine sentiments further removed from the populism that originally fueled the Methodist Protestant movement.

Finally, the ecclesiastical realities of disestablishment and voluntarism, coupled with the liberal relaxation of traditional proscriptions against accumulations of wealth and power, led some reformers to advocate ethics that were formerly anathema. Although the producerist tradition continued to equate wealth with greed and antisocial behavior, the official Methodist Protestant line, as reflected in *Mutual Rights and Methodist Protestant,* defined wealth as idolatry and spiritualized the sinfulness of its hold over people. There was even praise for the motivations of the ambitious. This transformation reached full flower when Methodist Protestants began to salute genius and industry as the key to "wealth and esteem" and to replace the ideal of a competence with sentiments advocating "becoming independent and respectable, and perhaps rich." The indicators of godliness became industry ("time and skill are your capital"), thrift ("whatever it be live within your income"), financial prudence ("buy not what you can do without"), resoluteness ("let your economy be always to day, not to-morrow"), and thankfulness, with no mention of fair dealing or meaningful work.[39] An anonymous Methodist Protestant, citing Lk. 12:15 and defining covetousness as "the love of money for its own sake—in distinction from the love of money on account of those things which it may procure, which is not covetousness," claimed that Jesus declined to arbitrate the legal ownership of property because his mission was strictly soteriological; to establish economic justice "formed no part of his mission to mankind."[40] Such a narrowed Christology was a necessary (but contested) part of the intellectual transformation of Jesus from the vigorous and militant carpenter of artisan perception (who threw the economic blasphemers out of the temple) to the meek and mild

38. *Methodist Protestant* 1 (Sept. 17, 1834): 117.

39. *Mutual Rights and Methodist Protestant* 1 (Apr. 15, 1831): 115; 3 (Feb. 8, 1832): 47; *Methodist Protestant* 1 (June 25, 1834): 19; 2 (June 10, 1835): 7.

40. *Mutual Rights and Methodist Protestant* 1 (Dec. 9, 1831): 386. The traditional view, in contrast, held that "truth is more valuable than gold: therefore for any man to give it up or to give up his right to pursue and sustain it, through considerations of temporal interest, is a species of that *covetousness which is idolatry.*" Stephens, *Defense of Our Fathers,* no. 1, 10. This perspective informed the youthful Levi Reese's populist defense against his expulsion; "a man's reputation is his all on earth and in sustaining it against any attack, he is obliged to contemplate all men, whether old or young, bond or free, high or low, as his equals." Reese, *Argument and Protests,* 12.

comforter of the emerging middle class (who wiped away the tears of those suffering from economic misfortune).

For many American evangelicals steeped in Calvinist traditions, to imagine that the love of money was no longer idolatrous proved powerfully seductive. The notion that wealth used for benevolent purposes was sanctified wealth, regardless of its procurement, however, was not immediately acceptable, nor were the producerist prohibitions that ran contrary to such logic easily abandoned. Yet even the anticapitalist stalwart William Stilwell could entertain suggestions that compelling social needs might outweigh traditional artisan practices and economic morality, as long as such practices were clearly immoral. In 1825, just three months after Stilwell had published "Crito's" ringing condemnation of capitalist innovation, the *Friendly Visitor* carried an anonymous article entitled "An Address to Master Mechanics, Whom It May Concern" that addressed the problem of intemperance among working men. After labeling the drinker as neither "a fit husband, a good parent, nor a true friend," the author disabused his readers of the "general opinion that a man needs liquor who labours hard . . . to recruit and animate his spirits." He suggest replacing the deadly daily grog ration with "a small luncheon twice a day." This would go far to guarantee a healthy, industrious work force, and he defended the innovation in typical republican language.[41]

This author's solutions, however, exposed a different sort of "republicanism," one in which individual self-determination was replaced by externally enforced ideals. After proposing the morality (not just the expediency) of hiring those "who labour for those families, instead of those who spend all their earnings, for that which destroys both soul and body, and who never take any thing home to their families but poverty," the author asked, "Which has the greatest appearance of Tyranny, for one man to bend the minds of a hundred men to the welfare of their families and society, or for a hundred men to impoverish their families, by spending all their earnings for that which cannot benefit themselves or families." He concluded with an appeal that would be irresistible to evangelicals: "So the gain will be the wages of five men, besides a quiet mind, the answer of a good conscience, and to be said in the end, well done good and faithful servant, enter thou into the joy of the Lord."[42] Such paternalism, to be sure, was actually refurbished tradition-

41. *Friendly Visitor* 1 (May 21, 1825): 164–65.

42. *Friendly Visitor* 1 (May 28, 1825): 173. Interestingly enough, the description of the evils of intemperance did not include its ability to inculcate unprofitable work habits—a common interpretation of evangelical temperance presentations. For an excellent discussion of this tendency, see Wilentz, *Chants Democratic*, 148–49.

alism and was not an automatic apologetic for capitalist-controlled workplaces. But it was clearly amenable to industrial capitalist morality in allowing accumulators of wealth to maintain their evangelical standing if their profits promoted evangelical ends and in its willingness to suspend judgment regarding the accumulation of those means.

This appreciation of the positive possibilities of wealth fit well with the realities of establishing new denominations: financial resources would enable the new Methodist Protestant leadership to donate time for such activities as leading class meetings, holding individual religious conversations, attending conferences, and it would allow them to make meaningful monetary contributions. Such arguments were also compelling to Methodist refugees struggling to raise funds for itinerants, build or buy new meetinghouses, and provide support services for located preachers. In this light, Stilwell had published a plea from the British Wesleyan Richard Reece for the efficacy of rented pews. Reece admitted that the "fear of introducing Aristocracy into the Church" was "salutary," but making "the rich pay for their superior accommodations . . . enables us to build chapels for the benefit of the poor, where we could not otherwise raise them."[43] In a similarly curious vein, Nicholas Snethen proposed that wealth be embraced as an opportunity for lay Methodists to keep the power of the itinerants in line. "The old Methodist precautions against rich men . . . were only one eyed." Instead, "we will neither preach nor write against money, but try to teach the people how to make it minister to their own liberty, while it feeds and clothes those who labour for them in the gospel." In arguing for the propriety of lay wealth as a check on clerical power, he added, "if you are afraid [preachers] will get too much power, then make your money operate as a balancing power."[44]

The perspectives offered by Stilwell and Snethen made perfect sense as answers to the respective problems of social justice and ecclesiastical democracy faced by each. But just as the evangelical habit of channeling the psychic energy of conversion into self-discipline inadvertently made Methodists

43. *Friendly Visitor* 1 (May 28, 1825): 173.

44. *Mutual Rights and Christian Intelligencer* 1 (Jan. 20, 1829): 38. Similarly, the proper response to the negative model of the avaricious, the ambitious, and the libertine, was to emulate their methods and attitudes in the service of the church. *Mutual Rights and Methodist Protestant* 1 (Apr. 15, 1831): 115. Snethen later made a more generalized statement of this mainstreaming trend: "As a people we must readily and speedily give up all our old peculiar Methodist prejudices. . . . Gentleness and courtesy have now become essentially parts of our religion. The old boast, viz. I am a plain spoken man, must no longer be indulged in." *Methodist Protestant* (Apr. 1, 1835), cited in Stephens, *Defense of Our Fathers*, no. 1, 22.

amenable to the exigencies of an open and industrializing society,[45] the new criteria for judging the morality of wealth accumulation also had unintended results: either the clergy lost their prophetic voice, at least concerning the systemic sins of capitalist development, or their audiences desired less challenging sermons, or both. This change eventuated in the market-oriented understanding that their polity must fit "the *humour* and *character* of the people." The new process of selecting ministers reflected this transformation. Whereas Methodist ministers had been selected by authoritarian means, which meant popular pressures were relatively insignificant, preachers now became another commodity in the market economy. The moderate antireformer Henry Slicer (whose populist credentials were impeccable) noted this with a caustic comment: "Their itinerancy has degenerated into a local system and their preachers are in the market for hire." Samuel Jennings concluded approvingly that market competition would force preachers to be harder working and more effective.[46] While such may have indeed been the case, the causes of economic justice could easily be reduced from moral to practical issues.

Although Methodist Protestantism evolved toward an accommodation with liberal culture in the 1830s, it did not lose its counterhegemonic capabilities. Moreover, the refusal of Methodist Protestantism to realize its producerist promise—to challenge the capitalist causes of artisan dislocation as a moral issue—did not mark the end of Methodist ability to sympathize with the concerns of disgruntled producers. Neither did it indicate that either branch of Methodism (Methodist Episcopal or Methodist Protestant) had abandoned traditional economic morality, as Methodist critics continued to make the connections between biblical definitions of oppression and economic realities. The activities and popularity of Baltimore-area Methodist leaders Daniel Reese and John Hersey are indicative of a broader consensus within Methodist communities in regard to the moral superiority of producerist ethics.

The case of Daniel Reese is suggestive, although difficult to reconstruct and interpret. Circumstantial evidence, based on Thomas Branagan's praise

45. It is, however, by no means clear that individuals became Methodists "to assume positions of prominence and prestige"; more accurately, as populist evangelicals, they joined to celebrate and strengthen their enhanced self-images as saved, affirmed individuals. Steffen, *Mechanics of Baltimore*, 260. See also Sutton, "Tied to the Whipping Post," 267–68.

46. *Wesleyan Repository*, 2 (June 1822): 56; Murray and Lewis, *Historical Sketches*, 17; Jennings, *Exposition of the Late Controversy*, 109. For more on Slicer, see chapter 6.

of Reese as "the patriotic and intelligent principal of a large and popular seminary in Old Town, Baltimore," implies that Reese's countercultural proclivities were not limited to advocating lay representation. Branagan, like William Stilwell, was outspoken in his rejection of capitalist ethics (a notion he considered oxymoronic) and included as an appendix in his *The Pleasures of Contemplation* Cornelius Blatchly's *Some Causes of Popular Poverty*. Branagan also supported legally capping individual income as the best means of discouraging maldistribution of income and concomitant social evils.[47] Although there is no direct evidence that Reese taught a similar ethic, Branagan's explicit acknowledgement of the Baltimore lay preacher suggests a common suspicion of capitalist transformation.

Further complicating an accurate positioning of Reese is his later rejection of Methodist Protestantism, which is particularly surprising given Reese's longstanding commitment to Methodist reform. Back in 1821, Reese, along with William Kesley, was the first to run afoul of the reactionary bishops, and when he was expelled six years later, he published an impassioned defense of his dedication to Methodist principles. From 1827 into the early 1830s Reese remained important to the movement. Elected president pro tem of the General Convention of Reformers in 1828, he was one of the first Methodist Protestant itinerants and organized congregations in the areas around Baltimore, including the Methodist congregation in Uniontown, Maryland, which under his influence defected en masse to the Methodist Protestants. But in 1833, Reese inexplicably returned to the Methodist Episcopal Church, where he spent his remaining years as an itinerant. Edward Drinkhouse, a late-nineteenth-century Methodist Protestant historian has conjectured that Reese, as an old man, sought the financial and emotional security offered by the more established community.[48] It is equally possible and more in keeping with Reese's radical sensibilities, however, to suppose that he recognized the limited acceptance of radical evangelical positions within mature Methodist Protestantism and decided that its official accommodation to liberal sensibilities would be of minimal benefit.

47. Branagan, *Pleasures of Contemplation*, 222; Cornelius Blatchly, *Some Causes of Popular Poverty, Derived from the Enriching Nature of Interests, Rents, Duties, Inheritances, and Church Establishments, Investigated in Their Principles and Consequences, and Agreement with Scripture* (New York, 1817), in Branagan, *Pleasures of Contemplation*, 195–220.

48. J. T. Murray and T. H. Lewis, *Historical Sketch of the Maryland Annual Conference of the Methodist Protestant Church*, 5th rev. ed. (Baltimore, 1939), 11, 14; Drinkhouse, *History of Methodist Reform*, 2:172. Significantly enough, despite his high visibility early on in the turmoil, Daniel Reese does not appear in Colhouer's *Sketches of the Founders*, although his three nephews (including one who was his namesake) do.

There is little mystery regarding the career of John Hersey. Hersey was well known throughout the Baltimore evangelical community as a vocal proponent of primitive Methodism, and he was heavily involved in a wide array of Methodist reform efforts. Highly critical of liberal culture, he was neither the philosophical nor organizational radical that William Stilwell was; his refusal to embrace Methodist Protestant reform was a conscious acknowledgment of divine order in ecclesiastical authority, and he approached social problems through moral suasion and personal example. With the exception of his intensely perfectionistic individualism, Hersey was easily the most consistent antiliberal among the contemporary Methodist authors in Jacksonian Baltimore, and the five manuals on Christian living and socioeconomic ethics that he published in Baltimore between 1833 and 1841 were widely popular.[49] He was outspokenly abolitionist in an area dependent on slave labor, he was explicitly producerist in a time open to capitalist innovation, and he tied these two together in his books in an explication of economic ethics that singled out for judgment any form of oppression or exploitation.[50] He eked out an existence as a traveling local preacher and the first home missionary to Baltimore's growing ranks of poor, and his vigorous and prophetic condemnation of growing Methodist wealth and respectability was silenced only with his death in 1862. Lacking personal charisma and warmth, "Father Hersey," as he was respectfully known throughout the 1830s, ministered to the spiritual and temporal needs of Baltimore's common folk,

49. The common people were his audience of choice; he believed that the "most honorable and independent employment on earth, is the cultivation of the ground; next to this stands *plain,* useful mechanism." Hersey, *Advice to Christian Parents,* 113. For fuller explorations into Hersey's career, see Fletcher E. Marine, *Sketch of Rev. John Hersey, Minister of the Gospel of the M. E. Church* (Baltimore, 1879); John B. Boles, "John Hersey: Dissenting Theologian of Abolitionism, Perfectionism, and Millennialism, *Methodist History* 14 (July 1976): 215–34; and Sutton, "To Extract Poison."

50. Hersey's abolitionism was as scriptural as it was producerist; in his mind there was no distinction. Emphasizing the biblical dichotomy between the powerful (usually perceived as unrighteous) and the powerless (usually presented as faithful) Hersey condemned the exploitation inherent in slavery. Quoting from Exod. 22:21; Deut. 24:14, 15; Ps. 9:9 and 72:4; Prov. 22: 22–23; Isa. 58:6; and Jas. 5:5, Hersey reminded readers that "Thou shalt not oppress a hired servant that is poor and needy" because "The Lord . . . SHALL BREAK IN PIECES THE OPPRESSOR." Hersey followed this warning with one that reflected the producerist suspicion that exploitation and injustice usually accompanied the accumulation of wealth. "*Go to now* [sic], *ye rich men, weep and howl for your miseries that shall come upon you. . . . Behold, the hire of the labourers which have reaped down your fields, which is of you kept back by fraud, crieth; and the cries of them that have reaped are entered into the ears of the Lord of Sabaoth.*" Hersey, *Appeal on Slavery,* 121–22. While such argumentation was offered in condemnation of the slave-holding prevalent in the areas of Virginia and Maryland where he preached, Hersey also used those perspectives to criticize economic liberalism.

and as a self-conscious populist, he loved, in the fond memory of one of his fellow workers, "to pepper the rich."[51]

Hersey's straightforward insistence on the religious duty to ignore worldly social distinctions was legendary. In the early 1830s, Hersey was summoned to the palatial Baltimore home of Moses Sheppard to be offered a position as the American Colonization Society's assistant agent for the newly established colony of Liberia. With Sheppard was Benjamin Latrobe, also a member of the Baltimore elite, and Hersey knew their philanthropy was largely responsible for the project. But Hersey also knew that the job was difficult and believed that success would be assured only if divine blessing was sought by all involved. Accordingly, Hersey, dressed in his usual coarse linsey-woolsey suit, insisted that his well-dressed benefactors kneel with him to pray.[52] Obviously annoyed at Hersey's presumption and lack of deference, Sheppard and Latrobe nonetheless complied. Soon thereafter Hersey sailed for Liberia in the employ of the American Colonization Society.[53]

In Hersey's universal condemnation of modern liberal economics, he saved his particular disgust for those dismantling the just price ideal and the labor theory of value. "Do not qualify [your children] for the bar, if you wish for them to live in heaven," he warned parents. "Neither can we recommend, but utterly condemn, merchandising. There are more snares and dangers connected to the mercantile business, than any other; therefore 'lead them not into temptation.'" He also cautioned his audience against dependence on credit and warned them to forbear accumulation.[54] In the section entitled

51. C. E. Weirich to John Hersey, personal correspondence, Feb. 28, 1861, Fletcher Marine Papers, MS 1016.3, Maryland Historical Society, Baltimore. In 1822, Hersey abandoned the merchant trade forever and became a local preacher, traveling throughout Virginia and Maryland. He eschewed official itinerancy because he did not want people to think he was dodging the debts outstanding from his last commercial fiasco. As a government factor for the United States Trade Agency in Cawahba, Alabama, his religious fervor and eccentricities—particularly his emphasis on plain dress and his habit of incessant praying—caused the Choctaws to refer to him as "the Man that talks to the Clouds." Marine, *Sketch of Hersey*, 5–16, 25, 94; Boles, "John Hersey," 215–16."

52. *History of Baltimore, Maryland* (Baltimore: S. B. Nelson, 1898), 88. For a similar, apocryphal episode involving Hersey and Andrew Jackson, see Armstrong, *History of the Old Baltimore Conference*, 191–92. For a discussion of the subversive potential in such acts, see Joyce Appleby, James Jacob, and Margaret Jacob, "Introduction," in Jacob and Jacob, eds., *Origin of Anglo-American Radicalism*, 7. For Hersey's biblically oriented antielitism, see Hersey, *Importance of Small Things*, 158, 189.

53. Hersey stayed in Liberia for only a short time because the conduct of his immediate superior in the colony did not meet his rigorous standards of godliness. Boles, "John Hersey," 217.

54. Hersey, *Importance of Small Things*, 206. "*Don't save and then suffer it to accumulate on your hands*, or it will be like the excess of manna which the covetous Israelites gathered and laid up for future use; *it bred worms and stank.*" Ibid., 291.

"Justice" in *Advice to Parents*, Hersey wrote: "Show them that a desire to get more for any article they may have to sell, than its real value, or to purchase any thing for less than its worth, discovers an unjust and dishonorable principle in the sight of God their heavenly Father. Suffer them never to higgle, nor use many words in their transactions one with another. Let them know that to ask any honourable man to take less than the price he asks for any article they may wish to purchase of him, should be considered a direct insult, and a dark reflection upon his character."[55] The central producerist tenet of the labor theory of value, therefore, was of critical importance in the establishment of justice. If there was any question concerning this matter, Hersey was more explicit. "If we withhold from others that which they are justly entitled to, and which belongs of right to them, we are as certainly *unjust* as if we had stolen or taken their property by force or fraud."[56]

Although traditional producers would fully agree with these sentiments, the rigid consistency of Hersey's critique could prove problematic for them as well. Hersey, for instance, consistently decried the negative effects of the burgeoning productive capacity of the American economy, while many artisans, radicals included, believed that industrial innovation, if managed correctly, could redound to their favor.[57] Contemporary commercial practices were inherently unrighteous because the consumer was encouraged to purchase at the cheapest price possible, regardless of any concern for "the immediate or remote benefit of the vendor, or the maker of the article" even though it remained incumbent on employers and masters to "render JUSTICE" unto every worker, "i.e., give them the full value of their labour."[58] Covering the full range of obligations in the market nexus, Hersey defended the rights of producers in an explicitly religious idiom. Although his writings reflected the perspective of a frustrated professional minister, home missionary, and humanitarian benefactor of the poor, such powerful anticapitalist commentary was not likely to be lost on the evangelical artisans in his audience.

55. Hersey, *Advice to Parents*, 81.

56. Ibid., 113; idem, *Importance of Small Things*, 45. For interpretations of Hersey's perspective on producerism, see Laurie, *Working People of Philadelphia*, 140, and Sutton, "Tied to the Whipping Post," 271–72.

57. In rebuking fashion and luxury, Hersey appealed to Isa. 3:16–25, part of the section condemning those who "grind the faces of the poor." Hersey, *Advice to Parents*, 94–95; idem, *Importance of Small Things*, 274.

58. Hersey, *Importance of Small Things*, 276; idem, *Appeal on Slavery*, 63. Hersey's disgust with economic liberalism led him to an apocalyptic metaphor: "Is the reign of the Beast already so universal, and so powerful that none are permitted to buy and sell, or manufacture, unless they receive his mark either on their foreheads or in their hands?" Hersey, *Importance of Small Things*, 73.

As Baltimore Methodists moved into the mid-1830s, they seemed relieved to have the painful Methodist Protestantism schism behind them; now it was time for reconciliation in order to move on to achieve the millennial promises driving the second phase of the Second Great Awakening. Hard feelings remained in some quarters, but for the most part both groups could concentrate on common perspectives: concern for the salvation of sinners lost in their personal unrighteousness coupled with cautious optimism toward a future that seemed to be multiplying prosperity and consumer comforts as well as evangelical influence. Yet the Jacksonian era, especially in the urban industrializing centers, was increasingly tumultuous, and social problems persisted. Evangelicals, however, remained hopeful that education efforts and reform societies could solve intemperance, slavery, socio-economic barriers, and other social ills. Exemplifying this trend, veteran Baltimore populists William Kesley, Asa Shinn, John Chappell, and Levi Reese discussed plans to create a manual labor school for the express purpose of serving as "a class leveler" to wipe out malignant distinctions between rich and poor.[59]

The question of class differentiation and conflict remained problematic for Baltimore evangelicals well into the 1840s. Accordingly, the *Baltimore Saturday Visiter* republished an article entitled "Distinctions in Society" that first appeared in the *Methodist Protestant.* The article focused on the role of "*self-love*" in encouraging upwardly mobile common Americans "when they take a rise in the world, to forget their once impoverished condition, and to feel that they are of better, and nobler blood, than those through whose instrumentality, their riches have been obtained." The author contrasted this tendency with the scriptural reminder that God "is no respecter of persons" and wondered why any "would wish to exalt themselves above those whom God hath created their equals?" The author continued by reiterating the traditional ideal of the harmony of productive interests.

> Why is it that he who toils day and night for the honest maintenance of himself and family, is considered as one of the lower classes of society? . . . Is it not because this native principle, *self-love,* has taken such deep root in the human breast? It is, and we fear if it is not exposed and guarded against, by those who are just stepping upon the threshold of mankind, it may yet be the means of exciting feelings of indignation and rebellion that may be subversive of the interest of

59. *Methodist Protestant* 2 (Mar. 18, 1835); Bucke, ed., *History of American Methodism,* 1:668.

> the whole community, for what can one portion of the community do without the other? Nothing, the mechanic is dependent on the tradesman, and the wealthy portion of the community, and they in turn, are as much indebted to him. Why then should men seek to make distinctions by calling one class or profession higher than another, when it can be productive of no real good, but may tend to very great injury?

The article, in an interesting switch, intimated that class consciousness, perceived as an antisocial phenomenon of the rich, was to be rejected and it prophetically warned that the only alternative might be violent crowd action.[60]

As Methodist Protestants successfully negotiated the issues of Christian submission to authority and restated their allegiance to producerist mutuality, their fellow evangelicals—Baptists, New School Presbyterians, Congregationalists, low church Episcopalians, and others—were beginning to explore new political opportunities in their quest for social justice. Methodists and other populist evangelicals were also busy establishing their own congregations as alternative havens wherein John Wesley's central assertion of Christianity as an essentially "social religion" could be realized.[61] Evangelical churches had a dual mission: first, to offer sanctuary from both the turmoil of urban social relations and from the temptations offered by unrestrained economic opportunity and, second, to moderate the pressures threatening to create antagonistic class divisions and social strife.[62] As they gradually, if hesitantly, came to grips with liberal culture, the residual ethic of producerism, as evident in the writings of John Hersey and the practices of conscientious consumers and masters, remained viable for many Baltimore Methodists. For artisans who shared the evangelical ethos of the Methodist denominations, the activist lessons and producerist legacies of the Methodist dissidents of the 1820s and early 1830s would be put to good use as artisan resistance to capitalist dislocation reached new heights.

60. *Baltimore Saturday Visiter,* Oct. 18, 1834.

61. Runyon, ed., *Sanctification and Liberation,* 41–42; Fowler, *Unconventional Partners,* 4.

62. Ronald Schultz, "Alternative Communities: American Artisans and the Evangelical Appeal, 1780–1830," in Rock, Gilje, and Asher, eds., *American Artisans,* 73–75.

Artisan Labor Militancy 1833–1837

Chapter Four

Trade Unions Take Hold in Baltimore

The Methodist Protestant schism was not the only social upheaval Baltimore experienced in the mid-1830s. In early July 1833, both the journeymen hatters and journeymen tobacconists were making public their respective grievances toward certain innovative employers. On July 6, the tobacconists announced, in resolutions printed in the *Workingmen's Advocate* and reprinted verbatim in the *Baltimore Saturday Visiter*, their intention to organize in order to protest the growing practice at local cigar manufactories of employing "Boys and Coloured persons who have not served in regular apprenticeship." The tobacconists' complaint was simple—such "destructive" practices, if continued, would result "in the depreciation of our wages," as was the case with "the introduction of Coloured people into the factories of Virginia." The meeting was called to establish a constitution for a new journeyman's society and a list of prices "for the purpose of devising some means that may be most conducive to our own welfare and also that of our employers,"[1] As the tobacconists promised to organize, the similarly disgruntled hatters went on strike. Their specific grievance was that an association of master hatters

1. *Baltimore Saturday Visiter*, July 6, 1833.

had unilaterally reduced the wages of their journeymen by 25 percent in late June, claiming that this brought wages in line with those paid in other eastern hatting centers.[2] The hatters' strike in particular galvanized unprecedented producerist opposition to capitalist innovation throughout the next few years.

As a direct result of this agitation, a vibrant labor movement, similar in many ways to those in Philadelphia, New York, and smaller urban centers, was taking shape.[3] In the previous decade, Baltimore had entered a transitional economic phase, characterized by both expanding opportunities (construction workers, machinists, and other workers were in great demand due to technological innovations and growing population) and occupational constriction (workers in consumer finishing trades and ship-building industries). There was, in addition, a growing tendency among master craftsmen to identify themselves as manufacturers and to reduce their journeymen and apprentices to the status of wage laborers, no longer accorded the consideration traditionally extended to them as fellow craftsmen.[4] The labor movement of the 1830s reflected this transitional ambiguity: a phenomenon similar to the ambivalence toward liberal culture characteristic of populist evangelicalism. Baltimore workers, including union activists, were torn between the traditional republican emphases on protection of artisan autonomy and maintenance of personalized socioeconomic ethics, on the one hand, and the modern liberal stress on increased profits through capitalist organization and the sacralization of restrictive and disciplined social attitudes, on the other hand. Modernization in the Jacksonian era was a double-edged sword as opportunities for personal freedom and mobility for white males clashed with the inherent breakdown of the traditional order

2. *Republican*, July 17; July 30, 1833.

3. Save for Anita Gorochow's 1949 master's thesis ("Baltimore Labor in the Age of Jackson"), which examined the abortive effort to establish a separate Workingman's Party in 1833, there has been no sustained research done on Baltimore labor during this critical period, despite the fact that Baltimore artisan militancy "compares favorably with trade union activity in Philadelphia and New York during the same period." Richard E. Morris, "Labor Militancy in the Old South," *Labor and Nation* 4 (May-June 1948) 32. For trade unionism in New York and Philadelphia, see Wilentz, *Chants Democratic*, 219–96; Laurie, *Working People of Philadelphia*, 85–104; and Louis H. Arky, "The Mechanics' Union of Trade Associations and the Formation of the Philadelphia Working-men's Movement," *Pennsylvania Magazine of History and Biography* 76 (1952): 142–76. By 1836, at least thirteen general trades unions had been established throughout the United States, with Baltimore's organized second. Hattam, *Labor Visions*, 82.

4. Charles G. Steffen, "Changes in the Organization of Artisan Production in Baltimore, 1790–1820," *William and Mary Quarterly*, 3d ser., 36 (1979): 101–17; Browne, *Baltimore in the Nation*, 69–158, esp. 96–98.

due to urbanization, industrialization, and depersonalized social relations. Large-scale organization occurred for the first time in the 1830s, and Baltimore's artisans played an important role in the development of a national labor movement.[5]

The familiar producerist arguments of traditional economic morality and the labor theory of value were used by participants in Baltimore's labor movement to condemn what they perceived as unjust practices: below-subsistence wage rates replacing livable "just price" scales; mechanical innovations in the workplace replacing skill, pride, identity, and self-imposed discipline; and personal aggrandizement replacing concern for public welfare. A growing recognition of their own interests, defined in contradistinction to the capitalist power relations in which they found themselves increasingly enmeshed, led artisans to explore separate class consciousness and organization, yet such considerations were always subordinate to their allegiance to corporatist and producerist ethics, and they continued to support identities constructed as a "middling" option in opposition to both the indolent poor and the parasitic wealthy. And even then, not all activity was oppositional. Their increasing access to wealth engendered new possibilities for upwardly mobile artisans for personal security, social readjustments, and philanthropic benevolence. In addition, the organizational efforts of artisans, which emphasized punctuality, discipline, industry, and regulation, demanded as well as reflected the same personality traits, survival skills, and cultural innovations as the industrial morality of liberal capitalism that they were resisting.

These countervailing impulses (both backward and forward looking) were reshaping artisan culture. Devotion to an old corporatist ideal of a harmony of interests persisted even as the attraction to the new individualistic ethos of unrestrained personal opportunity increased. Taken together, these cultural influences tended to avert, without eliminating them altogether, the potential for class conflict. Appealing to and depending on the sympathy and support of the community (as opposed to contending directly with rising capitalists for power and control), the trade union effort in Baltimore was more concerned with reestablishing a just socioeconomic order than with developing an inclusive sense of worker identity or engaging in class struggle. These American workers, according to their own self-perceptions, were primarily producers, not proletarians.[6]

5. Christopher Tomlins, *Law, Labor, and Ideology in the Early Republic* (Cambridge: Cambridge University Press, 1993), 152–60.

6. Gray, "Languages of Factory Reform in Britain," in Joyce, ed., *Historical Meanings of Work*, 143. Sean Wilentz claims that by 1850 in New York City, the historical "fact" of class

Historians have asserted that the economic dislocations of the panic of 1837 devastated the Jacksonian trade union movements.[7] It is certainly true that from 1837 to 1843 (the years of the most severe economic decline) there was little evidence of trade union militancy, as artisan activists developed alternative strategies to deal with such effects of capitalist dislocation as poverty and dependency among those unaccustomed to neither, tensions over immigrant competition for work, and increased alcoholic dysfunctions within the artisan community. This, however, should not diminish the fact that the successes of the Baltimore labor movement were dramatic and its legacy powerful. In reality, the movement was disintegrating before the full effects of the panic were felt. For the labor movement had already run afoul of the socioeconomic temptations inherent in liberal capitalist development, by celebrating the economic achievements of individual initiative, by embracing socioeconomic opportunity outside of skilled labor itself, and by advocating consumer habits that emphasized cheap prices over all other considerations. Nevertheless, as American culture moved steadily toward capitalism, artisan producerism remained operative in Jacksonian Baltimore.

At the beginning of the nineteenth century, Baltimore was the third largest city in the United States, although it was a newer urban center than its competitors, New York and Philadelphia. Situated at the confluence of the Patapsco River and the northern reaches of Chesapeake Bay, and on the border between free and slave societies, this distinctive city grew rapidly after the American Revolution. It was the American port closest to the West Indies and South America and the most accessible market and supplier for the expanding agriculture of southern Pennsylvania and western Maryland. The town had grown slowly after its founding in 1729, extending out from major turnpike routes and along the streams (Gwynn's Falls, Jones's Falls, Herring Run, and Little Gunpowder Falls) that emptied into the Baltimore harbor, with subsequent growth gradually filling in the gaps. Baltimore was also characterized by a succession of hills separating the stream valleys from each

formation, manifested in class conflict, had been achieved, which, in turn, necessitated the existence of differentiated class consciousness(es). Wilentz, *Chants Democratic*, 386–89. See also Wilentz, "Rise of the American Working Class" in *Perspectives on American Labor History*, 83–151. Nick Salvatore has disputed this interpretation, positing instead a hypothesis of conflict within consensus. Salvatore, "Response," 25–30. Salvatore's interpretation is particularly helpful in understanding the trade union movement in Jacksonian Baltimore. In this light, Victoria Hattam asserts that the primary focus of the Jacksonian labor movement was to force capitalist behavior to fit producerist morality. Hattam, *Labor Visions*, 76–111.

7. Laurie, *Artisans into Workers*, 214–15; Browne, *Baltimore in the Nation*, 130–36.

other, thereby making high ground intermittently available; the wealthy in each area built on the hills and major streets, and the poorer folk occupied the lowlands and alleys.[8]

Jacksonian Baltimore consisted of three distinctive areas—the wharf area of Fell's Point on the Baltimore harbor, the original downtown district centered along Baltimore Street just west of Jones's Falls, and Oldtown (grafted onto Baltimore Town in 1745) on the east side of the stream. Merchants dominated the downtown district; ship builders, carpenters, mariners, and dockworkers were concentrated on Fell's Point; and Oldtown was the hub of various artisan activities, with "mechanics" making up 60 percent of its population. Butchers set up their shops along the turnpikes at the west edge of town leading into the central market district, printers worked in the downtown district, brickmakers and potters utilized the clay deposits in the western areas of town, leather crafts were concentrated at the convergence of Oldtown and Fell's Point, garment workers scattered throughout the area where Fell's Point met original Baltimore, and practitioners of other trades were distributed throughout the city. Politically, the town was split into twelve wards, with workers predominating in the First, Second, Third, Fourth, and Twelfth and forming strong constituencies in the Sixth, Tenth, and Eleventh Wards, not coincidentally also centers of Methodist strength (especially the Second, Sixth, and Eleventh Wards). But Baltimore's hilly geography guaranteed a certain social heterogeneity so that, in both political wards and neighborhood congregations, common and elite Baltimoreans shared social spaces, although by the 1830s a trend toward the creation of exclusive neighborhoods was visible.[9]

Continuous migration into Baltimore from Europe and from outlying rural areas swelled the population of the city in the early decades of the nineteenth century. Until the dramatic influx of Irish and German immigrants in the 1840s, however, Baltimore's white population was relatively demographically homogeneous, as most newcomers were of nonconforming British or German Lutheran descent. This situation reinforced the geographic tendency toward socioeconomic integration, with social class

8. Sherry Olson, *Baltimore* (Cambridge, Mass.: Ballinger, 1976), 71; Browne, *Baltimore in the Nation*, 3–4; Rhoda M. Dorsey, "Comment" in David T. Gilchrist, ed., *The Growth of Seaport Cities, 1790–1825* (Charlottesville: University Press of Virginia, 1967), 62; Robert J. Brugger, *Maryland: A Middle Temperament* (Baltimore: Johns Hopkins University Press, 1988), 151–52, 196–206, 216–21; Steffen, *Mechanics of Baltimore*, 18–20; Gorochow, "Baltimore Labor," 8–13.

9. Richard M. Bernard, "A Portrait of Baltimore in 1800: Economic and Occupational Patterns in an Early American City," *Maryland Historical Magazine* 69 (winter 1974): 352–53, 358; Bilhartz, *Urban Religion*, 19–27.

divisions further moderated by ethnic and religious loyalties.[10] Baltimore's exceptionality also included a tradition of religious diversity and sectarian struggle, as seen in the Methodist Protestant conflict, with an unusual degree of influence enjoyed by populist evangelical sects, which were deeply concerned with issues of power, authority, dependency, social justice, and communal harmony. Throughout the Revolutionary period and during Federalist-Republican political conflict, Baltimore witnessed militant crowd activity among competing groups.[11] Thus in the first two decades of the nineteenth century, Baltimore was still predominantly a traditional pre-industrial society with strong potential for egalitarian dissent in keeping with eighteenth-century republican norms.

Baltimore was also the scene of a thriving African-American community, which contained almost a quarter of Baltimore's population after 1800 and consisted of a rapidly growing percentage of free blacks (78 percent of the black total) as well as a shrinking number of urban slaves. Occupational segregation was apparent early on; during the British attack on Baltimore in 1814, for instance, slave carpenters were enlisted to help in the defense of the city when it became obvious that the number of white carpenters would not be sufficient. When cigar manufacturers employed white boys and African-Americans to drive down their costs and journeymen's wages, the white journeymen tobacconists organized to exclude black workers. Because of such job competition and the endemic racism of the larger culture, and despite the presence of African-American artisans in the brickmaking, shoemaking, and tailoring trades (including masters in the last case), Baltimore's blacks increasingly filled the semiskilled and unskilled occupations, such as sawyers, porters, carters, caulkers, laundresses, domestic servants, and day laborers—jobs that by the 1830s were largely controlled by the free black population and as yet uncontested by European immigrants. Baltimore's most famous black worker was Frederick Douglass, who worked as a caulker at a Fell's Point shipyard for a time before his escape in 1838; his autobiography richly detailed his difficult life as an artisan slave.[12]

10. Steffen, *Mechanics of Baltimore*, 4–6; Bilhartz, *Urban Religion*, 12–13. Only 2.8 percent of the population in 1820 was listed as foreign-born. Christopher W. Phillips, "'Negroes and Other Slaves': The African American Community of Baltimore, 1790–1860," (PhD. diss., University of Georgia, 1992), 156.

11. Bilhartz, *Urban Religion*, 19–25; Steffen, *Mechanics of Baltimore*, 253–58, 267; Andrews, "Popular Religion in the Middle Atlantic Ports"; Mathews, "Methodist Ideology," in Richey and Rowe, eds., *Rethinking Methodist History*, 91.

12. D. Randall Beirne, "The Impact of Black Labor on European Immigration into Baltimore's Oldtown, 1790–1910," *Maryland Historical Society* 83 (winter 1988), 335–36; William D.

Yet, if many occupations were segregated, the dockyards were not, and a modicum of interracial unity in the Jacksonian ten-hour movement became evident in August 1833. At that time, representatives of seventeen separate trades, including shipwrights, involved in shipbuilding joined together to demand a ten-hour workday. The predominantly black caulkers organized their own journeymen's society and announced that "we . . . pledge our word and honor that we will go heart and hand to support the Journeymen Shipwrights in their noble and glorious Turn-Out for the [Ten-Hour] System." Moreover, the caulkers resolved that "we do not adhere to anything our Boss Carpenters shall say, unless they shall sign these resolutions for the Ten Hour System." In addition they respectfully asked that "we will be permitted to walk in the rear [of a civic parade] on the 12th of September, which we think nothing but a reasonable request." Such deference should not obscure the obvious effort on the part of these caulkers to support the otherwise white trade's union movement and the publication of this notice in the mainstream press suggests the possibility of public appreciation. Life for Jacksonian African-Americans was typically characterized by discrimination and restricted opportunities, but Baltimore's people of color were usually spared the worst of the depredations experienced by blacks in other cities.[13]

The factor of race had a dual impact on Baltimore's emerging labor consciousness in the 1830s. White racism, coupled with African-American determination to create semiautonomous spaces within the Baltimore community, meant that Baltimore blacks rarely participated in broader labor organizations, although by the 1850s, they were able to create an Association of Black Caulkers. Besides limiting African-American opportunities, the

Hoyt Jr., "Civilian Defense in Baltimore, 1814–15," *Maryland Historical Society* 39 (Dec. 1944): 295; Linda Shopes, "Fells Point: Community and Conflict in a Working-Class Neighborhood," in Fee et al., eds., *Baltimore Book*, 125; Frederick Douglass, *Narrative of the Life of Frederick Douglass, an American Slave, Written by Himself* (New York: Signet Books, 1968), 99–104; *Baltimore Literary and Religious Magazine* 4 (Apr. 1838): 174. The journeymen brickmakers were segregated at least by the early 1840s. *Sun*, March 13, 1843.

13. *Baltimore Saturday Visiter*, Aug. 24, 1833. Whether or not the caulkers were allowed to participate in the September parade remains unclear. The shipwrights marched, but there was no mention of a separate caulkers' group. *Baltimore Saturday Visiter*, Sept. 7, 1833. Randall Beirne has stressed the importance of racism in forestalling tensions within the ranks of the unskilled labor (on Fell's Point as well as in Oldtown), which until the Irish influx in the 1840s had been controlled by Baltimore's sizable number of free blacks. Discussion with Randall Beirne, May 16, 1991. The political rioting that rocked Baltimore in summer 1812, when a mob destroyed two houses owned by James Briscoe, a free black and outspoken opponent of racial discrimination, was an exception. Paul A. Gilje, "The Baltimore Riots of 1812 and the Breakdown of the Anglo-American Mob Tradition," *Journal of Social History* 13 (summer 1980), 551.

racial configuration of Baltimore's work force dramatically limited the number of unskilled white laborers, which meant that the domination of the movement by respectable skilled white workers was largely unchallenged by the unskilled, possibly rowdier element.[14] Eventually, under the leadership of Isaac Myers, a caulker and stalwart in Baltimore's African Methodist congregations, Baltimore's black shipyard workers formed the influential Colored National Labor Union and led the fight for the inclusion of Baltimore workers in largely white unions during Reconstruction. Myers's contributions were remarkable: in 1865 he and fourteen other blacks organized the highly successful Chesapeake Marine Rail Way and Dry Dock Company, with Samuel Dorrity (one of the caulkers striking in 1833 in support of the shipwrights' ten-hour efforts) as superintendent and Joseph Thomas (another of the 1833 strikers) as treasurer. During the Jacksonian period, however, Baltimore's black workers were for the most part bypassed by the trade union movement.[15]

With its excellent harbor, its proximity to thriving agriculture, its abundance of streams suitable for generating mill power, its nearness to such resources as iron and coal, and its burgeoning population, Baltimore provided many opportunities for artisans and hopeful entrepreneurs, as well as for its established elites. The end of the wars of the French Revolution in 1815 and the panic of 1819 introduced a series of far-reaching economic readjustments that encouraged this growth and accompanying structural changes. One such change related to banking practices, where bank notes replaced the informal agreements characteristic of prewar credit arrangements, where traditional paternalism was conformed to investment innovations, and where the hope of modest accumulation for retirement or investment was extended to workers. Founded by leading Quaker industrialists like Isaac Tyson, Evan Ellicott, and Moses Sheppard, as well as by commoners like Methodist bookseller Isaac Cook, large and small savings institutions permitted deposits as low as a dollar a week and distributed interest directly to the small-scale depositors at an overall average of 6 percent with discounts offered for transactions on Saturday, the normal payday for many workers.[16] These new

14. Steffen, *Mechanics of Baltimore,* 5–6; Gorochow, "Baltimore Labor," 5; Phillips, "'Negroes and Other Slaves,'" 6–7, 151, 156.

15. Shopes, "Fell's Point," in Fee et al., eds., *Baltimore Book,* 125–29; *Baltimore Saturday Visiter,* Aug. 24, 1833.

16. Olson, *Baltimore,* 64. The Savings Bank, founded in 1818 and granting interest without charging commission rates, was tremendously popular; within three years, more than $80,000 had been deposited. Dennis R. Clark, "Baltimore, 1729–1829: The Genesis of a Community" (Ph.D. diss., Catholic University of America, 1976), 317.

banks promised greater possibilities for achieving competences, and many from Baltimore's artisan community were quick to capitalize.

The prosperity of Baltimore's elites had historically been tied to its growth as a seaport city, but dependence on maritime trade caused serious problems after Jefferson's embargo in 1807 and ultimately devastated Baltimore's commercial economy when, after the peace, European goods glutted American markets and European competitors in the carrying trades were freed. Exacerbating the negative effect of international competition, overspeculation in Baltimore's leading banks helped cause a financial panic in May 1819.[17] The subsequent postpanic depression and continued European competition was part of a nationwide downturn from 1819 to 1823, which led, in Baltimore, to serious laboring-class dislocation; as Baltimore's potters pointed out in their 1820 plea to Congress, Baltimore artisans needed government protection and help in healing "the injury we the Manufacturers of Earthenware sustain owing to the vast influx of [English] Queensware."[18] In the late 1820s, Baltimore's artisan communities were in as much trouble as its established mercantile sector, where many of the older established elites began to disappear from prominence.

The resulting socioeconomic and political vacuum led to the rise of new and capable entrepreneurs (many of whom were skilled workers themselves).[19]

17. Tina H. Sheller, "Artisans, Manufacturing, and the Rise of a Manufacturing Interest in Revolutionary Baltimore Town," *Maryland Historical Magazine* 83 (spring 1988): 12; Browne, *Baltimore in the Nation*, 69, 88; idem, "Baltimore and the Panic of 1819," in Aubrey C. Land, Lois Green Carr, and Edward C. Papenfuse, eds., *Law, Society, and Politics in Early Maryland* (Baltimore: Johns Hopkins University Press, 1977), 223. For studies of Baltimore workers in the War of 1812 era, see Steffen, *Mechanics of Baltimore*, 171–252, and Theodore Glocker, *Trade Unionism in Baltimore Before the War of 1812* (Baltimore, 1907).

18. Steffen, *Mechanics of Baltimore*, 9; Gorochow, "Baltimore Labor," 18–19; John N. Pearce, "The Early Baltimore Potters and Their Wares, 1763–1850," (master's thesis, University of Delaware, 1959), 131.

19. George Rogers Taylor, *The Transformation Revolution: 1815–1860* (New York: Rinehart, 1951), 1–14, 207–28; Browne, *Baltimore in the Nation*, 52. For more on this economic change, see Cochran, *Frontiers of Change*; Douglas C. North, *The Economic Growth of the United States: 1790–1860* (Englewood Cliffs, N.J.: Prentice-Hall, 1961); Stuart W. Bruchey, *The Roots of American Economic Growth: 1607–1861* (New York: Harper and Row, 1968); and Robert L. Heilbroner, *The Economic Transformation of America* (New York: Harcourt, Brace, Jovanovich, 1977); Walter Licht, *Industrializing America: The Nineteenth Century* (Baltimore, 1995). For its political impact in Baltimore, see Whitman H. Ridgway, "Community Leadership: Baltimore During the First and Second Party Systems," *Maryland Historical Magazine* 71 (1976): 348. Ridgway mentions that the percentage of skilled workers who moved into the decisional elite in Baltimore from the First Party System to the Second rose from three to eighteen. By the 1820s, the leadership of Baltimore was thoroughly penetrated by a heterogeneous group of newcomers, including Mayor Jesse Hunt, who was a saddler by trade. See Whitman H. Ridgway,

The major foci of industrialization in the Baltimore area were in the surrounding mill villages, incorporated into the city well after the Jacksonian period. As a result, manufacturing employees made up only 8 percent of Baltimore's workers. The first significant industrial manufacturing effort in Baltimore was the Baltimore City Cotton Factory, established in 1829 by Charles Crook Jr. and Robert Buchanan and employing two hundred operatives. Following closely behind this effort was Howland's and Woollen's steam-powered flooring factory, built in 1832 and a year later expanded into the steam-driven sawmill that attracted the opposition of Baltimore carpenters (see chapter 1). The most important clothing manufacturing factory was that belonging to Robert Walker, opening in 1838.[20] Thus, even though the postwar Baltimore economy was weak, under the protection of tariff legislation promoted by hometown political economists Daniel Raymond and Hezekiah Niles (but opposed by the local party in power), Baltimore did began to support a small-scale manufacturing base by the late 1830s.[21] The positions proposed by the proto-Whigs, Niles and Raymond, in fact led many Baltimore artisans to support the National Republicanism of Henry Clay (with no prescience of the antiworker directions that later manifestations of Whig political economy were to take), while other workers were attracted to Jacksonian democracy.[22] In fact, artisan accessibility to both parties in the 1830s was sufficient to effect a situation in 1837 whereby both candidates (Francis Gallagher, Democratic cordwainer, and Philip Adams, Whig hatter) running for the state legislature from Baltimore were also trade union leaders and compatriots in Baltimore's Jacksonian labor movement.

Indicative of this pattern of economic and public opportunity was Jacob Daley (or Daily), a moderately successful chairmaker and Methodist layman who was active in civic and laborite activity in the 1830s. The son of a master chairmaker, Daley worked his way through the craft traditions and was quite likely among the first to pioneer the mass production of chairs for broadened markets. He took his Methodist obligations sufficiently seriously to encourage

---

"A Social Analysis of Maryland Community Elites, 1827–1836: A Study of the Distribution of Power in Baltimore City, Frederick County, and Talbot County" (Ph.D. diss., University of Pennsylvania, 1973). See also Sherry H. Olson, *Baltimore: The Building of an American City* (Baltimore: Johns Hopkins University Press, 1980), 41–48, and Browne, *Baltimore in the Nation*, 85.

20. Gorochow, "Baltimore Labor," 4; Laurie, *Artisans into Workers*, 28; Browne, *Baltimore in the Nation*, 86, 146; Fee et al., eds., *Baltimore Book*, 81.

21. Browne, *Baltimore in the Nation*, 70; Joseph Garonzik, "The Racial and Ethnic Make-up of Baltimore Neighborhoods, 1850–70," *Maryland Historical Magazine* 71 (fall 1976): 392; Olson, *Baltimore*, 83. For Raymond's input and influence, see Freyer, *Producers Versus Capitalists*, 6.

22. Gorochow, "Baltimore Labor," 15–22.

two of his apprentices, Daniel Evans Reese and Henry Slicer, to abandon the craft for which he had trained them to pursue what turned out to be very successful preaching careers. Daley's career spanned the years of this book; in 1827 Daily took out a patent on his new chair-making techniques, and as late as 1841 he was chosen to supply presumably plain chairs to the Baltimore city schools. In 1833, Daley established a bazaar—selling hardware, crockery, jewelry, tobacco, and cutlery—at Harrison and Baltimore at the conjunction of Oldtown and the downtown district. Adjoining the bazaar and crossing Jones's Falls, Daley built a bridge, which featured a lamp-holding statue to light the way for night travelers. The improvements, beneficial to both entrepreneur and public, apparently cost him $25,000 and also housed a separate steam-powered glass-cutting factory. Men like Daley were characteristic of the small entrepreneurial masters who linked civic improvement and private gain in the wide-open economic environment of the 1820s. Yet Daley was hardly the epitome of the capitalist master on the make; he also made his bazaar open to various trade union groups and served as a secretary and treasurer for Baltimore's organized seamstresses.[23]

By 1835, the national economy had improved dramatically, with Baltimore sharing in that general prosperity. At the same time, Baltimore's population grew from 62,000 in 1820 to 102,000 by 1840. The growth of population was matched by significant social change, yet hidden economic tensions for artisans persisted. Profits began to increase, at times astronomically, and foreign (mostly English) investment in America proliferated, aided by and strengthening the growth of capitalist banking and credit systems. Foreign visitors often commented on the relatively high standard of living enjoyed by Baltimore artisans; one visitor judged them "more industrious and in better circumstances than the same class in England."[24] With the postwar collapse of

23. Files accumulated by Michael Franch for his dissertation work, which he graciously made available to me (hereafter cited as Franch cards); Jack Larkin, *The Reshaping of Everyday Life, 1790–1840* (New York: Harper and Row, 1988), from illustrations between 174 and 175; G. Terry Sharrer, "Patents by Marylanders, 1790–1830," *Maryland Historical Society* 71 (spring 1976): 52; Michael A. Grimes, "More Baltimore Cabinet-Makers and Allied Tradesmen, 1800–1845," *Maryland Historical Society* 83 (fall 1988): 245; Varle, *View of Baltimore*, 37–8, 85. Daley's ecumenical spirit was evident in the fact that Daniel Evans Reese left Episcopal Methodism for Methodist Protestantism with Daley's blessing. *Baltimore Saturday Visiter*, Dec. 17, 1842. This Reese is not to be confused with his uncle Daniel Reese, who was disciplined by the Methodist establishment in the 1820s.

24. James Buckingham, *America, Historical, Statistic and Descriptive*, 3 vols. (London, 1841), 3:455; Clark, "Baltimore, 1729–1829," 193. In 1835, British politician Richard Cobden commented that he had seen no beggars in Baltimore. Raphael Semmes, *Baltimore As Seen by Visitors, 1783–1860* (Baltimore: Maryland Historical Society, 1953), 128–29.

the Baltimore elite, politics became as open as economics, and Baltimore created a new municipal government modeled on the Constitution with universal suffrage for white adult Marylanders. With a legacy of militant, sometimes violent political disagreements that earned Baltimore the sobriquet "Mobtown,"[25] and with a history of animosity toward the dominance of Annapolis, local and national politics attracted the attention of many within the artisan community. Economic prosperity and political opportunity, however, did not domesticate all Baltimore's artisans, as evidenced by the continued practice of riotous politics, favorite forms of rough entertainment, and, at times, crude disdain for the rich and powerful.[26] Nor, as evidenced by the uprisings of the coopers and hatters in 1833–34, were they always willing to accept capitalist transformation. As it turned out, many of those most suspicious of capitalist transformation had enjoyed a previous measure of success and social status.

In the mid-1820s, carpenters, hatters, coopers, blacksmiths, and sailmakers in Baltimore earned between $1.25 and $2.00 a day, with unskilled laborers making $1.00 a day, working as long as sixteen hours a day in winter and fourteen in the heat of summer. But the volume of work was rarely constant or satisfactory.[27] The skilled trades in Baltimore had long attempted to deal with the vagaries of employment and wage rates through the creation of craft societies. The older guild associations resembled those found in other

25. Gilje, "Baltimore Riots of 1812," 547–64.

26. Baltimore was apparently the last urban center where spittoons were introduced into the church sanctuaries to discourage promiscuous spitting during the worship services. See also Joseph Pickering's description of contemporary Baltimore life, cited in Semmes, *Baltimore As Seen by Visitors*, 74–75, and Patricia C. Click, *The Spirit of the Times: Amusements in Nineteenth-Century Baltimore, Norfolk, and Richmond* (Charlottesville: University of Virginia Press, 1989). When Charles Carroll of Carrollton died in the early 1830s, the funeral crowd was almost festive, "showing no reverence and some even laughing." Others went so far as to "touch the lifeless body." C. D. Arfwedson, *The United States and Canada in 1832, 1833, and 1834* (London, 1834) cited in Semmes, *Baltimore As Seen by Visitors*, 114.

27. Brigham, *Baltimore Hats*, 57–59; Olson, *Baltimore*, 85; Browne, *Baltimore in the Nation*, 97–98; *Republican*, July 30, 1833; *American*, May 23, 1825. These rates fluctuated seasonally and reflected the relative health of the overall economy. In 1812 at the Kemp shipyard on Fell's Point, foremen received $2.00 a day; ship carpenters, $1.75 (down $.25 from 1806); caulkers, $1.50; and pitch boilers and laborers, $1.25. Kemp Family Papers MS 2335, reel 3, Maryland Historical Society, Baltimore. In 1811, Baltimore cordwainers complained about working fourteen-hour days. David R. Roediger and Philip S. Foner, *Our Own Time: A History of American Labor and the Working Day* (New York: Greenwood Press, 1989), 10. When John Hawkins was reduced to unskilled bakery labor in 1836, he was paid $1.00 for sixteen hours. William G. Hawkins, *Life of Hawkins*, 59.

American seaports, with the usual internal tensions that had by the 1790s led journeymen cordwainers, tailors, and hatters to break from their masters to establish their own associations or to engage in coordinated oppositional activity. Carpenters and printers also formed inclusive societies in which employers and employed were encouraged to maintain unity within their craft, and after 1793, the Baltimore Mechanical Society fostered a collective sense of identity for all Baltimore artisans. Early in the nineteenth century, some of these societies established the closed shop. For example, the journeymen cabinetmakers and chairmakers insisted that any practitioner of the craft, within six weeks of his arrival in Baltimore, join the United Society of Journeymen Cabinet and Chair-Makers or pay a fine. Besides controlling employment, these organizations set prices for work performed, established welfare benefits for members, and suggested the appropriate length of the work day. They disciplined as well as supported their members and, when necessary (as was the case for Baltimore cordwainers in 1809), authorized strikes.[28]

The Fourth of July parade in 1828, where groundbreaking for the Baltimore and Ohio railroad was celebrated, marked a highpoint for the trade societies. With Charles Carroll, the last surviving signer of the Declaration of Independence, officiating, the parade was "a unique display of the mechanic arts." A large number of trades marched carrying craft slogans, biblical motifs, and Democratic-Republican credos. While parading, Baltimore's hatters were making a hat to be presented to Carroll, a cabinetmaker and carver were building a cradle, and coopersmiths were tossing engraved tumblers to the happy crowd. The printers and shipwrights put on the most impressive performances, with the former employing a fully operational press to print and distribute copies of the Declaration of Independence and the latter navigating a full-rigged ship (on wheels, presumably) through the streets. Leaders of the trade societies who later played major roles in labor activity included the cedar cooper Samuel Mass and the Universalist cordwainer Richard Marley. Many societies invited employers to participate; Hezekiah

28. Gorochow, "Baltimore Labor," 33–35; Clark, "Baltimore, 1729–1829," 218; Charles F. Montgomery, *American Furniture: The Federal Period* (New York: Viking Press, 1966), 21–22; Tomlins, *Law, Labor, and Ideology*, 141n37; Steffen, *Mechanics of Baltimore*, 109–220; John R. Commons et al., *A Documentary History of American Industrial Society*, 10 vols. (Cleveland: Arthur H. Clark, 1910), 3:249. Evidence that the hatters' organization was still operational in 1818 is found in William G. Hawkins, *Life of Hawkins*, 20. For examples of price books for cabinetmakers and printers, see Montgomery, *American Furniture*, 19–26, and *Constitution and By-Laws of the Baltimore Typographical Society, Adopted June 2, 1832; To Which Is Added, the List of Prices* (Baltimore, 1832), 15–17.

Niles headed the printers' delegation. Some observers saw this cooperation as evidence of the assimilation of entrepreneurial goals into artisan culture.[29]

The alleged acceptance of entrepreneurial attitudes was severely challenged less than a year later. On March 5, 1829, a group of 227 journeymen weavers, after a public meeting with friendly master weavers (led by the Methodist Protestant layman William Knox), refused to work for Richard Whiteworth, who had reduced wages and fired those who objected. Whiteworth took the workers to court for creating an unlawful combination, but the journeymen, defended by John Van Lear McMahon, a rising political star who became a mainstay in the Maryland Whig Party in the 1830s, and supported by the other master weavers in Baltimore, were acquitted. The case, significant in itself because of the respect and solidarity expressed between the determined journeymen and the sympathetic masters, reflected the important relationship between artisans and the larger community. In the first place, the striking workers agreed to call off their strike if all the masters decided to pay Whiteworth's reduced wages. Second, the journeymen and masters united to oppose Whiteworth's attempt to unilaterally shatter trade wage agreements. Finally, the jury took the law into its hands by ruling in favor of the journeymen before the state had a chance to plead its case.[30] The case exhibited the power of unified artisans and the limits to entrepreneurial aggrandizement in the face of opposition from the community. It also presaged the militancy of the 1830s.

The early 1830s in Baltimore were marked by economic prosperity and little labor strife. Despite this apparent tranquility, Baltimore artisans continued to organize into craft societies. One of the most important was the reinvigorated Baltimore Typographical Society (BTS), the most recent manifestation of a Baltimore printers' union that was first organized around

29. John H. Hewitt, *Shadows on the Wall, or Glimpses of the Past* (Baltimore, 1877), 133; James D. Dilts, *The Great Road: The Building of the Baltimore and Ohio, the Nation's First Railroad, 1828–1853* (Stanford: Stanford University Press, 1993), 7–10. One recent interpretation of this parade asserts that it "showed a turn toward a different participation of the masses, reminiscent of the mechanics' politics of 1809 but now harmonized with the goals of the entrepreneurs." Olson, *Baltimore*, 89. Olsen offers as compelling evidence the fact that invitations of some of the crafts (e.g., the chairmakers) "particularly requested" both employers and journeymen to participate. *American*, June 19, 1828. But it would be wrong to conclude that, by 1828, the artisan masses were completely in harmony with entrepreneurial capitalism.

30. *Banner of the Constitution*, Dec. 5, 1829, 1:7. The central role of William Knox is reflected in Whiteworth's stated purpose of breaking down "what he termed William Knox's Store Pay." Commons et al., *Documentary History*, 4:271. For McMahon's subsequent political meanderings and successes, see Mark H. Haller, "The Rise of the Jackson Party in Maryland, 1820–29," *Journal of Southern History* 28 (Aug. 1962): 319, 325.

the turn of the century and was reestablished on November 26, 1831. The printers were widely recognized as one of the best organized and most activist trade societies in the early republic. Easy access to a wide range of social criticism coupled with the precarious nature of the craft given the technological advances and entrepreneurial reorganization and the relatively high numbers of journeymen compared to masters made militancy in the face of dislocation almost a given for printers.[31] In 1802, the original Baltimore Typographical Society (including booksellers, bookbinders, papermakers, and stationers) had asked Congress to resist increasing tariff duties on print type; had discussed with New York, Philadelphia, and Boston printers plans for suggesting increased duties on book imports; and a year later, had been steadfast in their support of striking and suffering printers in other cities. During 1809 and 1810, "generous and friendly" Baltimore printers agreed to cooperate with their Philadelphia brethren in setting and then altering bookselling prices.[32] In subsequent years, the Baltimore Typographical Society reflected the instability characteristic of industrializing crafts, disappearing sometime around the war years, reorganizing in 1815, and dissolving again in 1826. According to its constitution and by-laws, the 1830s incarnation of printer solidarity combined mechanic solidarity with producerist desire to maintain craft unity and social harmony.[33]

31. Browne, *Baltimore in the Nation*, 114; *Baltimore Saturday Visiter*, Sept. 29, 1832; Scharf, *Chronicles of Baltimore*, 624; Laurie, *Artisans into Workers*, 38–39; Commons et al., *History of Labour*, 1:419, 359, 375; Gorochow, "Baltimore Labor," 19. Steffen cites both 1800 and 1803 as times of similar organizational efforts while Rollo Silver claims 1802. Rollo G. Silver, *The Baltimore Book Trade, 1800–1825* (New York: New York Public Library, 1953), 9; Steffen, *Mechanics of Baltimore*, 210. The November date is based on the dates of initiation given in the constitution and in an obituary of Edmund Bull, one of the founding members. *Constitution of the Baltimore Typographical Society*, 18; *Sun*, Dec. 22, 1875; Gorochow, "Baltimore Labor," 35. The percentage of journeymen printers to masters, according to Charles Sellers, was one in eleven, while in other crafts it was one in three. Sellers, *Market Revolution*, 25. A similar renaissance of artisan consciousness is reflected in the trade societies that were organized to participate in such civic celebrations as the one honoring the French Revolution of 1830. The Baltimore Typographical Society was prominent in this effort. Scharf, *Chronicles of Baltimore*, 456. For a contemporary celebration of the journeyman printer, see *Baltimore Saturday Visiter*, Sept. 14, 1833.

32. Silver, *Baltimore Book Trade*, 9. Notices of BTS cooperation with other printer unions appear in *Baltimore Telegraph*, Oct. 18, 1803; *Baltimore Evening Post*, Jan. 7, 1809; *Baltimore Federal Gazette*, Jan. 9, 1809; *American*, Jan. 9, 1809; *Evening Post*, May 9, 1810, cited in Silver, *Baltimore Book Trade*, 15, 25, 27.

33. There was also an organization called the Typographical Association operating just during the war years. Scharf, *Chronicles of Baltimore*, 456; Silver, *Baltimore Book Trade*, 15; *American*, Oct. 18, 1830. Silver maintains that the BTS was the third such printer society formed in the United States, with New York and Philadelphia branches preceding it. Silver, *Baltimore Book Trade*, 9.

Qualifications for membership listed in the society's constitution included "a good moral character, industrious habits, and a practical knowledge of the art and mystery of letter-press printing." All members were required to "discountenance all vice and immorality" and to cultivate "a spirit of industry and fidelity." The society promised to police its own members: "Frequent intoxication, gross immorality, needless and frequent neglect of business, so that his employer is seriously injured, or the member's family thereby reduced to a state of suffering, shall, upon information and conviction by the Society, be punished with suspension or deprivation of membership." Moreover, both undercutting the list of prices and injuring "the interests of his employers by revealing the secrets of the office" were prohibited. Members' benefits included $2.50 per week for sick relief while the fund remained solvent, provided "sickness does not arise from immoral conduct." Finally, three pages of price lists were included, as well as the injunction that "ten hours shall be considered a day's work in book and job offices." The constitution was signed by more than a score of Baltimore's printers; among those agreeing to its conditions were a disproportionate number of leaders of the trade union movement that flourished in the 1830s, including Alexander I. W. Jackson (identified as "one of the oldest journeymen of the profession"), Edmund Bull, William Tuttle, Robert Ricketts, John Millington, Joshua Jones, and Josiah Bailey.[34] The document was a clear indication that preindustrial arrangements, with power balanced between masters and journeymen, continued to resonate within the printer community. Producerist limitations on personal aggrandizement and insistence on worker autonomy were central to the printers' arguments, but so were traditional restrictions regarding socially regressive and nonproductive behavior and celebrations of "industrial morality" normally attributed to the machinations of grasping entrepreneurs.[35]

Members of the BTS characteristically supported harmony between employer and employee, but there were ominous portents for the future of labor relations in the sentiments expressed at its anniversary supper on January 26, 1833. The gathering was held at the establishment of Josiah Bailey, a former printer who had traded the art and mysteries of the craft for the financial security of operating a tavern but who had lost none of his sense of artisan militancy. Hezekiah Niles, editor of the nationally prominent *Niles' Weekly Register*, and Jesse Hunt, former saddler and now mayor of

34. *Constitution of the Baltimore Typographical Society*, 6, 8, 10, 16–19.

35. For industrial morality, see Faler, "Cultural Aspects of the Industrial Revolution," 357–94; and Steffen *Mechanics of Baltimore*, 215.

Baltimore, were guests of honor. Other guests included John D. Toy, former publisher of the dissident Methodist periodical, *Mutual Rights*; Samuel Harker, Jacksonian editor of the *Baltimore Republican*; Samuel Sands, a publisher who as a fourteen-year-old apprentice had first set Francis Scott Key's "The Star-Spangled Banner" in print and a leading Baptist layman; and John H. Hewitt, editor of the weekly *Baltimore Saturday Visiter*, reputed to be "one of the *largest* and *cheapest* [weekly] papers in the Union." Harker and Hewitt were openly sympathetic to trade union activism in the years to follow, and their publications consistently reflected the tenets of producerism.[36]

The anniversary supper was followed by the customary round of toasts. President A. I. W. Jackson toasted Niles as well as "employers and employed": "The success of the one is dependant [*sic*] on the exertions of the other. They will always find mutual advantage in mutual good will." Niles then addressed the audience, declaring that "the employers and the employed had corresponding duties—and both parties were deeply interested in a faithful and kind performance of them. He offered a cheerful testimony in favor of the general good conduct of the journeymen printers of Baltimore and exhorted them to perseverance in well doing." He concluded, "Accursed be that policy which takes 'from the mouth of labor the bread it has earned,' or sends the working man supperless to bed." Following Niles's lead, Jackson tellingly qualified his endorsement of the employers:

> Success to all that have a fair *title* to our regard—to all others.
> *Battered type* and *empty cases,*
> Presses *broke* and *rueful faces.*[37]

36. The *Proceedings of the Baltimore Typographical Society at Their Anniversary Supper* (Baltimore, 1833), 3–4; Ridgway, "Community Leadership," 346; Scharf, *Chronicles of Baltimore,* 616. According to Michael Franch, Harker by the 1840s at least was a prominent member of the Madison Street Baptist Church and active in their Sabbatarian efforts. Franch cards. Samuel Sands, also a Baptist layman, later allied himself politically with such Whig trade unionists as cordwainer William McCauley and hatter Philip Adams and went on to edit in 1837 *The Sunday School and Family Gazette. American,* Sept. 6, 1834; Scharf, *Chronicles of Baltimore,* 559. Sands's connection to "The Star-Spangled Banner" is chronicled in Silver, *Baltimore Book Trade,* 9. For the *Baltimore Saturday Visiter* claim, see its masthead anytime in the early 1830s.

37. *Proceedings of the Baltimore Typographical Society,* 5–8. Niles was supportive of artisan efforts to organize for political purposes. In response to the appearance of the Working Man's Party in New York in 1830, he wrote, "The 'working people' have always constituted the body of the solid, true and faithful democratic party—and, though we like not divisions of citizens into particular sects, . . . we are not sorry that the free laboring classes are rallying themselves, to resist oppression. The power is in them—and they have only to use it, in self-defence." *Niles' Weekly Register,* May 22, 1830, quoted in Norval N. Luxon, *Niles' Weekly Register: News Magazine of the Nineteenth Century* (Baton Rouge: Louisiana State University Press, 1947), 145.

Later in the evening, J. H. Hewitt was prevailed upon to sing his sarcastic spoof, "The Rat-ified Printer," in which a maiden scorns an overly ambitious journeyman printer, leading to his suicide, because:

> She hated the man who would injure his trade,
> For her lover was only a "*Rat.*"[38]

For the rest of the evening, enjoying muscatel-induced conviviality, the printers entertained themselves. Despite the remarks about unfair employers and "rats," their robust celebration seemed to indicate harmonious relations on the Baltimore labor front.

By early summer 1833, this peace was growing more fragile, and the Baltimore press was not oblivious to the plight of displaced artisans. In March, J. H. Hewitt commented on the diminished status of artisans—their contributions were often underappreciated and they were "excluded from privileges which were emphatically their own"—but he optimistically concluded that circumstances were bound to improve if the mechanics worked hard to change them. Then in July, the *Baltimore Saturday Visiter*, recognizable by its literary contents and contributors as a middle-class organ, announced the appearance of Baltimore's own *Workingmen's Advocate*, published by John F. Weishampel, an itinerant Baptist minister and producer-oriented activist. "Perhaps it is not very generally known that there is a weekly paper bearing the above title [*Workingmen's Advocate*] published in Baltimore at the very low rate of $1 a year. It bravely supports the interest of mechanic's, and by them should be encouraged—for, it seems, it is only through such organs as these that they can speak. To the laboring class generally it will be found fully worth the trifling sum of yearly subscription." This column was indicative of the Baltimore papers' (with the notable exception of the *Baltimore Patriot*) consistent support of the city's workers. Such backing was a significant element in the broader producerist consensus of the 1830s.[39]

At this time, the major concern of the artisan societies was the "great lukewarmness" of contemporary patriotism, as evidenced by lack of public

38. *Proceedings of the Baltimore Typographical Society*, 12–13; *Baltimore Saturday Visiter*, Apr. 5, 1834.

39. *Baltimore Saturday Visiter*, July 13, 1833. When the journeymen shipwrights and ten-hour association organized during the following month, their resolutions explicitly excluded the *Patriot. Baltimore Saturday Visiter*, Aug. 17, 1833. Weishampel's itinerancy is mentioned in Rosalind Robinson Levering, *Baltimore Baptists, 1773–1973: A History of the Baptist Work in Baltimore During 200 Years* (Lutherville, Md.: Baltimore Baptist Association; 1974), 200.

planning for the Fourth of July. To remedy this disrespect and to celebrate "their unshaken confidence in . . . republican institutions," the Baltimore Typographical Society and the cordwainers' society, led by Universalist Richard Marley and his eighteen-year-old protégé (and future labor activist and state legislator) Francis Gallagher, urged all mechanics' societies to make appropriate plans. But no coordinated celebration materialized, and the cordwainers marked the occasion by taking the newly built B & O Railroad to the Carrollton Viaduct where they frolicked and drank toasts all day. A particularly demonstrative group, they toasted "A good Boss, plenty of work, and money Saturday night," and, prophetically as it turned out, warned "the aristocracy that there is virtue in a sound drubbing."[40]

Two days later, the illusory nature of that harmony became apparent as the journeymen tobacconists and hatters exhibited their discontent with the innovations of various masters. The cigarmakers' call for organization, reflective of the ideal of the harmony of productive interests, was quickly overshadowed by the more militant attitude of the hatters. By mid-July, the hatters' strike had blossomed into a major controversy, with Baltimore employers taking up various positions. The master hatters' association involved a number of newly prominent hat manufacturers, such as William P. Cole, Peter Leary, and absentee owner Thomas Sappington. Baltimore's most prominent master hatter—Jacob Rogers—apparently steered clear of the fray, and other hatting establishments stood by the set prices. Led by William Hopewell and Charles Pratt and quickly joined by George Uhler, Jacob Boston, George K. Quail, John Warner Niles (the son of Hezekiah), James Thomas, and others, these producerist masters received public thanks from the journeymen hatters and approbation from other artisans, especially the printers, who were supportive of the journeymen.[41] Before long, this support became communitywide: the press reported favorably on the strike's progress, and newly organized trade unions and other sympathizers sent money. The public discussion of this strike indicated a broad-based

40. *Baltimore Saturday Visiter*, Mar. 2, 1833; *American*, July 2, 7, 1833; *Republican* June 12, 13, 1833; *Baltimore Saturday Visiter*, June 15, 1833.

41. *Republican*, July 6, July 22, July 30, 1833; *American*, July 6, 1833. The BTS originally made public the names of the supportive masters. Three Baltimore papers reported favorably on the strike: the *American* was a Whig paper, the *Republican* was Democratic, and the *Saturday Visiter* was avowedly nonsectarian and nonpartisan. When the journeymen cordwainers of the ladies branch published their praise of the journeymen and sympathetic master hatters, they also thanked these Baltimore editors for having "gratuitously published the notices . . . of the several meetings, of this and other bodies of mechanics on this occasion." *Baltimore Saturday Visiter*, Aug. 3, 1833.

producerist consciousness antagonistic to what was perceived as monopolistic innovations.[42]

A letter signed "No Hatter" in the July 17 *Republican* is representative of this public support. Defining the masters' action as an attempt "to oppress . . . respectable and industrious citizens . . . for the sole purpose of putting so much more of the hard-earnings of the Journeymen into their own pockets," "No Hatter" called on the public to rally against the masters in order "to turn back . . . this mighty tide of wealth and influence." Finally, he urged all trades to follow the lead of the printers and shoemakers, who had already held meetings to support the hatters, and especially recommended the example of the printers, who had contributed forty dollars to the hatters "to aid the weak to repulse the assaults of the strong."[43] Continuing to manifest this solidarity among Baltimore artisans, journeymen coopers announced a meeting to address the issues mentioned by "No Hatter" on July 18, and two days later the Typographical Society met for a second time to further consider the plight of the hatters. A. I. W. Jackson and four others were selected to present appropriate resolutions, indicative, at least on the surface, of an embryonic sense of artisan class consciousness. Yet their sense of class identity was circumscribed by their traditional allegiance to just employers. The printers began by condemning "all combinations of employers, which tend to aggrandize themselves at the cost of employed." They claimed that the cause of the hatters was identical to that of other trades because "the success of the present oppressors will but serve to whet the appetite of the avaricious of other professions." Echoing "No Hatter," they urged other trades to organize, "as the only sure means of defence from that spirit of innovation which has presented itself, and which threatens to degrade the condition of journeymen, in order that the employer may fatten on their labor." The printers decided to distribute ten thousand copies of the hatters' appeal to the public (which had not yet appeared in the public press), and a

42. The following notice a month into the strike was typical: "Since the *turning out* of this useful class of mechanics for higher wages—they have been generously aided by the Typographical Society, the Cordwainers, the Carpenters, the Cabinet Makers and the Coopers. It is expected that almost every branch of mechanics will, through public meetings, express themselves favorable to the course pursued by the Hatters, and tender them all the aid in their power." *Baltimore Saturday Visiter*, July 27, 1833. The hatters were not the only ones complaining about the market innovations of economic liberalism. That same month, the corders of wood claimed that most of the wood coming into Baltimore had been "an object of general speculation and purchase for re-sale," therefore acquitting themselves for the responsibility of the higher prices. The inspectors responded by promising to "require the legal compensation." *American*, July 15, 1833. See also Hattam, *Labor Visions*, 101.

43. *Republican*, July 17, 1833.

copy of their resolutions was sent to the striking hatters to boost their morale.[44]

The plea to organize in support of the hatters did not go unanswered: new societies of journeymen tailors, cordwainers, bootmakers, and house carpenters offered aid, both financial and moral. Drawing on the producerist doctrine of the labor theory of value, they urged readers to use their power as consumers to patronize only the masters paying the higher wages. "Crispianus" lauded the hatters who were "resisting the high handed measures of those Bosses, who have grown fat on their labor" and wondered sarcastically if those employers "actually believe that the working men should be fully content with the glorious privilege of breathing." Crispianus concluded cryptically, "Shall it be said . . . that the mechanics of Baltimore stood meekly by and saw those petty monopolists, in their thrust for filthy lucre, drive the poor man and his family supperless to bed, forbid it philanthropy [*sic*]."[45] And "Mechanics of All Denominations" met on July 25 to denounce the masters' action as "subversive of the dearest principles for which our forefathers bled."[46]

The masters, "finding themselves publicly and violently assailed, in the most strange and virulent manner," finally defended themselves in print. Their response, tellingly entitled "To the Public," began by turning one of the strikers' argument on its head: if journeymen could associate to regulate wages for the trade, masters had every right to do the same. Basing their argument on the alleged natural enmity between employer and employee, they did not pretend "to claim exemption from that frailty which makes man so often the dupe of his interest." Resorting to republican ideology, they asserted that conflicts between master and journeyman were positive, comparing them to checks and balances in government, "both being essential to restrain man in his proneness to abuse power when stimulated by interest." The association also disputed the issue of wages, claiming that even with the 25 percent reduction hatters were still making more money than other

44. *Republican*, July 18, 22, 1833.

45. *Republican*, July 3, 24, 27, 1833; *American*, July 25, 1833; *Baltimore Saturday Visiter*, July 27, Aug. 3, 1833. The bootmakers, under the leadership of George King and John Rodgers, announced a gift of $50.00 with a promise of $50.00 more if necessary. Within the year, both King and Rodgers had become masters, paying the society wages. *Republican*, Oct. 10, 1833. Not all labor supporters were so fortunate. In an ominous precedent, Silas Tucker, who had publicly announced in September that he was paying his cordwainers the society wages, was forced into insolvency. *American*, Sept. 14, 1833; *Baltimore Saturday Visiter*, Oct. 16, 1833; *Republican*, Nov. 18, 1833. Tucker's plight was symptomatic of the difficulties faced by producerist masters. Tucker regained his financial standing, only to fall back into insolvency in 1843. *Baltimore Saturday Visiter*, June 10, 1843.

46. *American*, July 23, 1833; *Republican*, July 23, 27, 1833.

artisans and laborers in Baltimore. Having sufficiently justified their pursuit of personal aggrandizement, however, they quickly abandoned those sentiments; competition from other cities, not greed, had necessitated their reductions and if the masters were not obeyed, the hatting trade in Baltimore might be destroyed. Finally, the masters appealed to public opinion: they hoped that the public would reject "the unnatural excitement which has been so mysteriously conjured up."[47] In an ironic twist, it was the masters not the journeymen who introduced the alleged inevitability of class conflict into the public conversation.

On July 30, a general meeting of the Baltimore citizenry responded to the masters. Chaired by John F. Hoss, a carpenter and local officeholder, the assembly declared a boycott and established ward committees to solicit contributions from citizens to help the journeymen "make a successful resistance against the aggression of their would-be Lords, who would fain obliterate the truth, that the laborer is worthy of his hire."[48] Accompanying this activity was the reply drawn up by John H. W. Hawkins and two other journeymen hatters. Hawkins, as we have seen, was no stranger to struggle; he had previously been active in efforts to bring democracy to the Methodist polity in Baltimore. Just as the printers had done, Hawkins drew attention to the fact that the journeymen had not profited from the wealth generated by their labor because wages had not changed in eleven years, and his arguments exemplified the producerist ethics of respectable artisans.[49] Support continued to pour in for the striking hatters, and they published their official thanks, especially to the printers, tailors, cabinetmakers, coopers, carpenters, and cordwainers for their "very liberal donations." Throughout August, the hatters persisted and the offending combination finally collapsed; after a two-month strike, the journeymen returned to work at their previous wages.[50]

47. *Republican*, July 29, 1833. The communication was signed by Thomas Sappington, William P. Cole, and Peter Leary. Sappington was a politician and chair of the state reform convention who lived in Frederick, Maryland. Cole was soon joined by the Universalist master Thaddeus Craft in his growing manufactory, and his successful career extended into the 1870s. Brigham, *Baltimore Hats*, 48, 84, and Franch cards. Ironically, the arguments of the masters later proved prophetic: "Clinging tenaciously to old ways, [Baltimore's master hatters] incurred unnecessary labor costs. By 1850, Baltimore had lost the bulk of the market to progressive New England manufacturers." Kahn, *Stitch in Time*, 37; Brigham, *Baltimore Hats*, 82.

48. *Baltimore Saturday Visiter*, Aug. 26, 1843; *Republican*, July, 29, 1833. The list of participants was long, including many of those later active in the trades' union movement.

49. Ibid. See chap. 1 for a summary of Hawkins's arguments in this piece.

50. *Baltimore Saturday Visiter*, July 27, 1833; *Republican*, July 31, Aug. 1, 2, 1833; *American*, Aug. 5, 1833; *Republican*, Aug. 2, 1833; Gorochow, "Baltimore Labor," 47, citing *American*, Aug. 27, 1833.

Although it was by no means a final victory, the triumph of the journeymen hatters was significant, and the lessons learned were not lost on Baltimore's increasingly beleaguered artisan community.

The hatters' strike marked the beginning of a summer of unprecedented labor strife in Baltimore. In the midst of the uproar over the hatters' situation, Baltimore witnessed another expression of labor agitation that quickly became popular among artisans and extended the discussion from wages to working conditions. Shipyard workers and others met at Fell's Point on July 27 to devise measures "to establish the Ten Hour System, in this city, among all those mechanics who work by the week or the day." Jacob Dunham, a ship carpenter, chaired the meeting, James Heath presented the major address, and John F. Weishampel, publisher of Baltimore's own *Workingmen's Advocate*, was called as secretary (a service which earned for him the gratitude of those assembled as well as their promise to subscribe to his paper). The dockyards trades dominated this agitation at first, but other crafts quickly picked up their arguments. At the initial meeting representatives of the ship joiners, shipwrights, house carpenters, riggers, sailmakers, house and ship painters, blacksmiths, blockmakers, tailors, bricklayers, ropemakers, boat builders, coopers, cabinetmakers, plumbers, shoemakers, and wheelwrights agreed to ascertain the masters' sentiments toward the proposed regulation. A list of masters' responses followed: the ship joiners, house carpenters, painters, blockmakers, boat builders, stone masons and stone cutters all reported unanimous consent, while the shipwrights, riggers, blacksmiths, tailors, coopers, and cabinetmakers reported general agreement on the part of the masters.[51]

Before their next meeting, the ten-hour men issued a statement explaining the systemic nature of the injustices effected by the innovations of industrial capitalism. They defined competitive capitalist workplaces as inherently exploitative, "without careing [*sic*] whether the oppression proceeds immediately from the Master Workmen, or is the indirect result of an illiberal and exacting spirit on the part of the merchant, the contracting agent or the purchasers among the public at large." In accordance with the producerist assertion of the mutual responsibilities operative in all economic transactions,

51. *Republican*, Aug. 2, 7, 8, 10, 20, 1833. At a meeting at Whitehall Gardens on August 8, the journeymen reiterated their determination to work no more than ten hours and announced that they would erect a large bell, at their own expense, on Market Space, which would "regulate the time" for breakfast and dinner. *American*, Aug. 9, 1833. The ten-hour movement was also advertised in the *Baltimore Saturday Visiter*, Aug. 17, 1833.

they listed among the oppressors consumers whose decisions were based on cheapest prices without regard for the just price ideal. In support of their demands for a more humane work schedule, they noted that "long continued labor" was both socially and physically detrimental because it induced "the improper use of ardent spirits to support the strength under long and laborious exertion."[52] In the course of this argument, the producerist critique came to describe an intrinsically immoral system, not just a random collection of unjust individuals.

The initial ten-hour meetings bore immediate results. The blacksmiths, engineers, and machinists were the first to report responses from the masters, and 154 of them announced their intention to work no more than ten hours a day. The specialized nature of their work and the fact that their organization was not restricted to journeymen may have been responsible for the relative harmony within this group. Whatever the cause, at an August 16 meeting, the bosses present were reported to be "generally in favor of the system." The journeymen gave the other bosses until Monday to respond favorably and "expected that every man who considers himself a Mechanic, or a Freemen . . . be requested to sign his name to our protest" to establish a principle "the justness of which, cannot be questioned." The bricklayers, who bemoaned the fact that fifteen hours labor in the hot sun made a bricklayer "worried and dejected" and "his spirits . . . oppressed by fatigue" so that "he feels no relish for society or improvement" and who desired to refrain from "materially injuring" their bosses or the public, also promised to strike until employers agreed to these regulations.[53]

Both groups were at least partially successful: the journeymen blacksmiths, engineers, and machinists instructed members who had been working at ten-hour shops to return to work immediately. The journeymen also denied that they had encouraged apprentices to ignore the instructions and rules of their masters and publicly advised the apprentices to attend to their masters' instructions. On August 26 it became apparent that their generosity to their fellow artisans earlier in the summer was now being repaid; they acknowledged "the liberal donation" of the journeymen hatters, whose successful effort could now result in beneficence to others.[54] Other journeymen's groups met to endorse the ten-hour system. The house carpenters, plasterers, coachmakers, painters, metal turners, pattern makers, brass and iron

52. *American*, Aug. 13, 15, 1833; *Republican*, Aug. 16, 1833; *Baltimore Saturday Visiter*, Aug. 17, 1833.

53. *American*, Aug. 20, 1833; *Republican*, Aug. 19, 1833.

54. *Republican*, Aug. 20, 24, 27, 29, 1833.

founders, and millwrights all called on their masters for response, and the journeymen coachmakers quickly announced that twenty masters, including John Curlett, the "practical" coachmaker of chapter 1, were agreeable to their demands. The societies of the metal trades also sought the opinions of local officials. One of these, James Mowton, the manager of the Baltimore Gas Company and a master himself, offered a lukewarm endorsement: a ten-hour system had "been in operation for several years in a shop under my superintendence, and that I have not perceived any ill consequences resulting from it." To further buttress the argument, the *Baltimore Saturday Visiter* noted approvingly that, according to the *Washington, D.C., Mechanic,* carpenters there had established the ten-hour day.[55]

During this time, Baltimore's artisans were also struggling to define the parameters of class solidarity within a producerist context. The journeymen cordwainers of the ladies' branch, under the leadership of Richard Marley, expressed, somewhat ambiguously, both their harmonious intent and the need for class solidarity. Complaining about reduced wages, desiring the specifically delineated "advancement of our interests," and believing that no melioration would be possible "unless by the united exertion of all," they organized "for the purpose of promoting Union and Harmony among ourselves, and regularity in our wages." Full-blown class conflict was well beyond their purview as the cordwainers explicitly disclaimed "all intention to do any to the detriment of the employers, believing that a co-operation with us will be an advantage to all."[56]

On September 12, the artisans of Baltimore used a traditional patriotic parade (celebrating the successful defense against the British invasion nineteen years earlier) to further display worker solidarity. The printer A. I. W. Jackson was grand marshall, journeyman hatter John H. W. Hawkins was appointed one of six regular marshalls, and fellow hatter Joshua Vansant gave the main address.[57] Groups representing blacksmiths, coopers, tailors, hatters, chair-

55. *Baltimore Saturday Visiter,* Aug. 24, 1833; *Republican,* Aug. 20, 21, 27, 1833. The replies of Mayor Jesse Hunt (a former saddler) and Charles and Philip Endicott (Quaker owners of Baltimore-area cotton factories) were masterpieces of fence-straddling, with the Endicotts asserting that "every man has a right to stipulate the terms on which he will work." *Republican,* Aug. 24, 1833; *American,* Aug. 27, 1833; *Baltimore Saturday Visiter,* Aug. 24, 1833.

56. During this time, the cordwainers of the men's' branch and the combmakers also met, with the latter opposing piece rates replacing already insufficient daily wages. *Republican,* Aug. 21, 24, 1833. For discussion of these ambiguities regarding "class," see Hattam, *Labor Visions,* 204–8.

57. *Republican,* Aug. 24, 1833. Vansant opened his own manufactory in 1836. William G. Hawkins, *Life of Hawkins,* 44–45; *Baltimore Trades' Union,* May 28, 1836. A lifelong Democrat, he

makers, printers, sailmakers, and copper, tin plate, and sheet iron workers, and others marched through the streets of Baltimore with great ceremony. Not listed but possibly attending was the association of African-American journeymen caulkers, which had asked to "be permitted to walk in their rear on the 12th of September, which we think nothing but a reasonable request."[58] Joshua Vansant's address followed the parade. Couching his arguments in republican rhetoric, he reminded his audience of "the ancient lawgiver" who defined perfect government as one "where to wrong the humblest individual would be to insult the entire community." Vansant framed this in terms of producerism: history revealed that "the productive classes of society" had never "oppressed or prostrated the rights of the other portions of society. . . . But history is pregnant with circumstances whereby the operatives have been oppressed," turning them inevitably into "willing and ready instruments to overthrow government." In conclusion, he condemned those modernists "of selfish interest" who "have asserted that it does not require united exertions of men to sustain a just value for labor, or to resist the inroads which may be attempted upon their rights." *Niles' Weekly Register* reported that the entire affair "was proposed and managed exclusively by the workingmen and all things were done in a workman-like manner."[59]

The parade marked an effort by Baltimore artisans to expand the scope of their vision and operations. Just a week before, on September 4, 1833, Baltimore's disgruntled journeymen created a citywide organization of workers, the Union Trade Society, later known as the Working Men's Trades' Union (WMTU). The formation of this general trades' union followed a similar effort in New York City and preceded by two months the central unions organized in Philadelphia and Washington, D.C. Richard Marley was appointed chair of the Union Trade Society; William L. McCauley, vice president; Robert Ricketts, publisher of the recently established *Mechanic's Banner and Workingmen's Shield*, secretary. Trades represented included cord-

was active politically and missed being elected state representative by one (or three) vote(s) in 1846. He was elected mayor in 1870. His Democratic convictions did not, however, preclude his support for internal improvements. *Republican*, March 11, 1835; Scharf, *Chronicles of Baltimore*, 123; Archibald Hawkins, *The Life and Times of Hon. Elijah Stansbury, an "Old Defender" and Ex-Mayor of Baltimore; Together with Early Reminiscences, Dating from 1662, and Embracing a Period of 212 Years* (Baltimore, 1874), 83, 124, 215. By the mid-1870s Vansant was widely recognized and respected as one of Baltimore's elder statesmen. *Sun*, Dec. 21, 1875.

58. *Republican*, Aug. 29, Sept. 5, 1833; *American*, Aug. 29, 1833; *Baltimore Saturday Visiter*, Aug. 24, Sept. 7, 1833.

59. *American*, Sept. 17, 1833; *Niles' Weekly Register*, Sept. 14, 1833.

wainers (ladies' and men's branches); coachmakers; cabinetmakers; hatters; copper, tin plate, and sheet iron workers; tobacconists; tailors; coopers; blacksmiths, engineers, and machinists; marble stone cutters; house carpenters; printers; chairmakers and ornamental painters; and painters.[60] An "Address to the Operative Mechanics of the City of Baltimore," prepared by cordwainer Thomas Stanford and four others, appeared on September 10, calling for artisan solidarity and assigning to the union an unusual degree of centralized power, with the right to make final decisions "on all questions and objects which require, for their successful accomplishment, the united action of mechanics." The union's goal was to arrest the spread, already apparent nationally, of a "spirit unfriendly to the standing and pursuits of mechanics." Condemning the current trend toward the accumulation of wealth, the address concluded: "It will be the earnest . . . desire of the Union Society to advance the intellectual character of mechanics—and by encouraging everything calculated to better their condition, awaken a confidence in each other, which by judicious application of their united efforts will tend to place the working class in the scale of human society, to which by their industry and usefulness, they are justly entitled."[61]

As the Union Trade Society was being formed, however, the Baltimore workingmen's movement was engulfed in the murky waters of local party politics. This situation was exacerbated by conditions in both state and national politics in the wake of the collapse of the First Party System and the reordering of party affiliations. As national parties reformed around Henry Clay and John Quincy Adams, on the one hand, and Andrew Jackson, Martin Van Buren, and John C. Calhoun, on the other, and as the importance of party patronage and organization replaced the primacy of political principle, it became increasingly difficult for Baltimore's artisans to extract any substance from the political rhetoric of various party candidates who claimed to represent workingmen's interests. Throughout September and October 1833, both Clay and Jackson forces bid for artisan political support. At the same time, artisans were trying to woo workingmen away from their traditional ethnocultural allegiances and establishing workingmen's political

60. *Republican*, Aug. 24, Sept. 6, 1833; *Baltimore Saturday Visiter*, Sept. 7, 1833; Commons et al., *History of Labour*, 1:358; Hattam, *Labor Visions*, 82. Unfortunately, there appear to be no extant copies of the paper. Ricketts, a Jacksonian partisan, was later active in Washington, D.C., and apparently a Methodist. His correspondence with "Brother [Henry] Slicer" is a fascinating discussion of attempts to further Democratic political concerns among the Methodists as well as the larger society. Robert Ricketts to Henry Slicer, Aug. 15, 1840, Henry Slicer Papers, Lovely Lane Museum, Baltimore.

61. *Republican*, Sept. 12, 1833; *Baltimore Saturday Visiter*, Sept. 7, 1833.

organizations to protect their interests. The result was utter confusion, even as individual artisan political representatives enjoyed success.[62]

The political imbroglio began less than a week after the Union Trade Society was created. On September 9, a communication in the *Republican* announced a meeting "to form a Mechanical ticket," on which none but mechanics would be nominated, to contest the upcoming state and local elections. Chairing this meeting were Francis Burke of the Typographical Society and Robert Ricketts, publisher of *Mechanic's Banner.* Complaining about being "overlooked" by both parties in Maryland, the artisans at the meeting chose two delegates ("no other than a Mechanic") to run for the state legislature on their populist platform: abolition of convict labor; reform of the Maryland Constitution to give the City of Baltimore representation commensurate with its burgeoning population; and an end to all "monopoly of privilege," including but not exclusive to that enjoyed by the national bank. Ward meetings were called, and Joshua Vansant and Elijah Stansbury, both Jeffersonian Democrats with strong artisan ties, were unanimously nominated.[63] When both declined, Joshua Jones and Charles Peregoy were chosen.[64]

The so-called Workingmen's Party was a hodgepodge of political affiliations. Among those involved in the nominating process were printers Francis

62. *American*, Sept. 18, 1833; Haller, "Rise of the Jackson Party in Maryland," 307–66; Browne, *Baltimore in the Nation*, 103.

63. Abolition of convict labor was a genuine concern; by 1834 Baltimore artisans were competing with 134 convict weavers, 75 granite stone workers, 13 combmakers, 13 cordwainers, and 11 bakers. Stansbury's candidacy had been promoted in an article that first appeared in the *Workingmen's Advocate* (reprinted in the *Baltimore Saturday Visiter*), presented by "A Third Ward Working Man," a pro-Jackson opponent of the "monied Lords" and "the caucus system." *Baltimore Saturday Visiter*, Aug 24, 1833. Stansbury was formerly a bricklayer who had used his competence to establish himself in lime merchandising and peddling Thompsonian medicine. His Thompsonian involvement was equally interesting in light of the subsequent populist resistance to the scientific medical establishment's efforts to regulate medicine by outlawing herbal treatments. "Will the mechanics and labouring people of the city of Baltimore submit to have crammed down their throats the horrible mineral poisons of the learned faculty, or seek from the vegetable kingdom those inoffensive herbs which can alone give them health and longevity." *Republican*, Jan. 31, 1835. Archibald Hawkins, *Life of Stansbury*, 54–55, 297–98. While Stansbury was not centrally involved in the trade union movement, Vansant certainly was.

64. Peregoy's connection to the workingmen remains unclear; he had not been mentioned in any leadership role to this point. Jones was a member of the Typographical Society, but less than a year later his anti-Jackson proclivities emerged, as he was one of those (along with J. V. L. McMahon, the lawyer for the striking weavers in 1829) instrumental in forming the Maryland Whig Party. Scharf, *Chronicles of Baltimore*, 120. Vansant, apparently very popular that year, refused the Jackson Party's offer as well, but he did endorse Jones and Peregoy. Gorochow, "Baltimore Labor," 24; *American*, Sept. 26, 1833.

Burke and John Millington, hatter John H. W. Hawkins, cordwainers William McCauley and John Wright, cooper Samuel Mass, and painter and druggist John Seidenstricker. Some had Clayite ties, but most were disgruntled Jacksonians, unwilling to be represented by the aristocratic Charles Carroll Harper, their party's nominee for the Maryland general assembly. Others, obviously suspicious of those now claiming to represent workingmen remained independent, and some were simply confused.[65] Equally uncertain was a common understanding of what constituted the "mechanical interest." The internal squabbling that resulted revealed ambivalence toward using "class" as a determinant for political affiliation. On September 23, a meeting of the workingmen's partisans, chaired by the sailmaker and ten-hour advocate Thomas Bruff, resolved that a five-man committee be appointed "from the laboring class exclusively" to "increase their body as they may deem expedient to forward their undertakings." This exclusivity sparked furious discussion among workingmen's partisans. In a letter to the *Republican*, "No Monopoly," expressed his displeasure with the workingmen's announcement that it would nominate none but mechanics and complained, "Was that not monopolizing?" Instead of voting on "the old Jeffersonian" principles, "nothing is to rule now but class." Moreover, he complained, if "the question be 'Is he honest?' the answer must be, 'he earns his bread by the sweat of his brow.'" The author concluded by asking: "Is it true that the Mechanics of Baltimore have clothed themselves with the cast off follies, worn thread-bare by the frantic followers of the infamous Fanny Wright, in another state?"[66] Claiming that artisans had long wielded political power in Baltimore, he reminded his audience that "it is not the Jackson party who have made the Granite monopoly which we have such just cause to complain at."[67]

This last dig was aimed at Colonel William Steuart, builder, state legislator from Baltimore County, and owner of a large granite works employing

65. *Republican*, Sept. 9, 18, 1833; *American*, Sept. 12, 18, 1833. Whitman H. Ridgway, "McCulloch vs. the Jacksonians: Patronage and Politics in Maryland," *Maryland Historical Magazine* 70 (winter 1975): 360. The political confusion was reflected in the affiliations of the two leaders of the meeting: Ricketts was a Jacksonian Democrat and Burke was a Clayite Whig. Hawkins, in contrast, was not otherwise politically active or identifiable; Mass, in the next few years, was, at different times, allied with both the Whigs and Democrats. *American*, Jan. 17, 1834.

66. *Republican*, Sept. 26, 28, 1833. The editor, J. H. Hewitt, commented about Wright's fleeting popularity and definite antireligious sentiments in Baltimore. He attributed the relative success of her lecture tour to the attraction of her novel views as curiosities and claimed that her extended influence in Baltimore was negligible. Hewitt, *Shadows on the Wall*, 45. Compare this perception to the importance accorded to Wright's influence among New York City's workingmen in Wilentz, *Chants Democratic*, 176–83.

67. *Republican*, Sept. 26, 1833.

convict labor. Some of the Clayite leaders supported Steuart as well as the candidates of the Workingmen's Party. Writing in the *Republican*, "A Mechanic" brought this discrepancy to light. Again decrying class as the determinant in voting behavior, he pointed out that the support of some of the Workingmen's leaders for Colonel Steuart (elected with the votes of mechanics but supporting practices designed to "aggrandize the would-be Aristocracy") exposed their underlying motives. In urging workingmen to maintain their allegiance to the Jacksonians, "A Mechanic" argued that in an agriculturally dominated slave state like Maryland, the workingmen, by themselves, would never garner enough votes to gain power; therefore, they must make their presence felt within the Jackson Party, where egalitarianism allegedly reigned. The reason for this, however, was not to deal specifically with artisan issues, but rather to effect reform in the state constitution: equal votes in the house of delegates, direct election of state senators and the governor, and abolition of the appointive executive council. Finally, the author appealed for rejection of "the power of sycophancy and a feverish ambition" and reconciliation of prodigal artisans to the Jackson program: "Let us kill the fatted calf and receive them back again, 'more in sorrow than in anger,' when they have found the error of their way."[68]

When the elections were held on October 7, the Workingmen discovered, not "the error of their way," but that they had triumphed. Even in the pro-Jackson Eighth Ward, they had fared well, and on the strength of workers in the First, Second, Third, Fourth, and Twelfth Wards, Jones and Peregoy had won easily. So had James Heath, who although he had addressed one of the earliest meetings of the supporters of the ten-hour system, had not sought the endorsement of the Workingmen's Party, asking instead for the support of both Clay and Jackson men in his race for Congress. Not all went as the Workingmen's political leaders had hoped, however; the other elected congressman was Quaker manufacturer and Jacksonian Isaac McKim, who handily defeated their candidate, Colonel Steuart. The pro-Jackson editor, Samuel Harker, admitted that the Jackson Party had been soundly drubbed, but he claimed that all those elected stood staunchly for Jackson principles, so that, in the end, he had no quarrel with the results. Later, Harker gloried in the epithet, "workies," being applied to the victors by the rival *Baltimore*

68. Gorochow, "Baltimore Labor," 25–26; *Republican*, Oct. 1, 1833; Browne, *Baltimore in the Nation*, 103–4; A. Clarke Hagensick, "Revolution or Reform in 1836: Maryland's Preface to the Dorr Rebellion," *Maryland Historical Magazine* 57 (Dec. 1962): 346–66. By 1834, Samuel Harker, the editor of the Jacksonian *Republican*, agreed that the schism had been healed. See *Republican*, April 25, 1834, cited in Ridgway, "McCulloch vs. the Jacksonians," 360n25.

Chronicle.[69] The results of the election were again ambiguous; the "mechanical interest" had prevailed but their candidates proved worthless to them. Months after the victory of the Workingmen's slate, "Franklin," citing the Clayite support for "our candidates" with the promise of patronage, none of which, he complained, had been forthcoming, insisted that the Clayites fulfill their bargain with "the producing classes of the community."[70] Baltimore workingmen's initial foray into organized political activity indicated the potential for the fragmentation of artisan unity in the political arena.

Meanwhile, artisan dissatisfaction surfaced in new areas, most significantly among the Baltimore seamstresses. Clothing production in Baltimore was widespread with at least forty-seven separate establishments, mostly situated in the central district but increasingly dependent on outwork sent into artisan neighborhoods. Cloth manufacturing was slowly developing in the 1830s, but competition from other eastern cities put pressure on master tailors to reduce labor costs. Baltimore's seamstresses were determined that such changes not come at their expense. Discouraged by their low wages and "the insupportable oppression resulting therefrom," the seamstresses called "a large meeting of the WORKINGWOMEN of Fells Point" on September 14, during which they established a wage list that would remunerate them appropriately and, until such a time as proper rates were established, they promptly went on strike.[71]

Soon after the meeting, Susan (or Susannah) L. Stansbury issued "An Appeal to Tailoresses and Seamstresses in General" to support the women's efforts to organize. Her activist message combined militancy with sentimentality. Knowing "of no method so likely to procure us relief, as that which

69. *Republican*, Sept. 26, Oct. 1, 8, 10, 1833. Subsequent political activities by various factions of Baltimore's "workingmen" indicate the abounding confusion as well as the preoccupation with state and national issues. Later in October, during preparation for the local elections, the Workingmen's Party offered no slate. A later, widely publicized meeting degenerated into mass confusion. *American*, Oct. 30, 1833; *Republican*, Oct. 30, 1833; *Baltimore Saturday Visiter*, Nov. 2, 1833. In retrospect, Samuel Harker acknowledged that he had never been able to determine who had called the latter meeting or what their purposes were. *Republican*, Nov. 21, 1833; Ridgway, "McCulloch vs. the Jacksonians," 360.

70. *Republican*, Jan. 14, 1834.

71. Muller and Groves, "Changing Location of the Clothing Industry," 405; *Republican*, Sept. 14, 1833. For women and work in the early republic, see Thomas Dublin, *Women at Work: The Transformation of Work and Community in Lowell, Massachusetts, 1826–1860* (New York: Columbia University Press, 1979); Christine Stansell, *City of Women: Sex and Class in New York, 1789–1860* (New York: Oxford University Press, 1986); Mary H. Blewett, *Men, Women, and Work: Class, Gender, and Protest in the New England Shoe Industry, 1790–1910* (Urbana: University of Illinois Press, 1988).

has of late been successfully practised by the mechanics of this city," she encouraged "women of the needle" to unite in their efforts to raise wages (apparently recently reduced) to a reasonable rate. Citing the problems of widows with children, she argued that a working mother would be forced to "disperse her sons and daughters over the city," to the detriment of society because these children would grow up, "torn from the maternal embrace and virtuous counsel" of their mothers. These circumstances were particularly problematic for girls, whose "opening charms and virtuous promise" were often lost in "disgrace and ruin." She ended with a plea for public funds for widows and orphans: "we hope to be sustained by that merciful and beneficent Being, who has promised to support the weak and feeble, who will call his name, and to be a father to the widow and orphan." This address was followed by a statement from citizens from the First and Second Wards in support of the seamstresses, because "philanthropy, as well as gallantry, calls on each and all." In a striking example of artisan solidarity across gender lines, journeymen tailors supported the women.[72]

To enlist public support for the seamstresses, the *American* printed Mathew Carey's "Appeal to the Wealthy of the Land," which it advertised as "especially deserving the attention of philanthropists—of all who are opposed to 'grinding the faces of the poor.'"[73] Drawing on statistics of stark poverty among female handicraft workers, Carey called for the establishment of manufactories where living wages would be paid.[74] On September 30, the Female Union Society of Tailoresses and Seamstresses met to decide when to join their striking sisters from Fell's Point. They elected Susannah L. Stansbury president, Hannah Moran secretary, and Jacob Daley (master chairmaker, Methodist layman, and proprietor of the popular bazaar between Oldtown and the central business district) permanent treasurer of the society, to receive donations from the public to support the seamstresses. They thanked John F. Hoss and Josiah Bailey, both leaders in the public support for the striking hatters, for preparing the room where they had

72. *Republican*, Sept. 14, 20, 26, Oct. 2, 1833; *American*, Sept. 20, 1833.

73. *American*, Aug. 9, 1833. Carey was a patron of the radical evangelical Thomas Branagan, who printed another of Carey's treatments of the plight of exploited seamstresses in *Beauties of Philanthropy*, 275–82. Carey was recognized by artisan activists as a hero of sorts; his background as a penniless immigrant journeyman printer was emphasized, as was his philanthropic generosity toward female operatives. *American*, Dec. 25, 1833; *National Trades' Union*, July 4, 1835. His critique was not without precedent; a New York author made a similar argument in behalf of seamstresses. *Saturday Evening Post*, Apr. 30, 1831. I am indebted to Tim Rowell for the last citation.

74. *American*, Sept. 7, 11, 16, 1833.

met.[75] The women had tapped deep reservoirs of discontent and solidarity, and their union meetings, held at the Pitt Street Methodist Protestant Church, met regularly for years. In addition, their strike was successful: their new rate of twelve and one-half cents per shirt was, according to Mathew Carey's statistics, equal to the highest rates in the nation.[76] Their victory marked the first phase of an ongoing struggle for Baltimore's organized seamstresses.

The blacksmiths at the Savage Factory, owned by the S. M. Cobb Company, were also dissatisfied, and they met to discuss their "rather too oppressive labour, during the winter season." The Savage Factory was turning out iron tracks, railings, and chairs for the fledgling Baltimore and Ohio Railroad and was therefore in the forefront of industrial modernization, but the blacksmiths were not impressed. Complaining that working from sunup to 7:30 at night left "not any time for the improvement of our mental faculties"; claiming that such labor, after a few years, tended to "incapacitate and render [them] unfit, or incapable of providing for a family"; and insisting that the difficulty of their work precluded the competent performance of it by lamp light, the blacksmiths addressed the company agent: "we . . . condescendingly request, relying upon your generosity," that night work be prohibited, with the promise that they would "attend to the duties of our several avocations, with the greatest possible alacrity and assiduity."[77] Noting that its absentee proprietors insisted on running the Savage Factory on the Waltham plan, agent and B & O official Amos Williams asserted simply that "it is not in my power, to meet your wishes in this respect." He went on, however, to claim that the Waltham plan had "probably done more toward dignifying and exalting" mechanical pursuits "than any other establishment in our country," so that "until we see a change of measure with them . . . this Company will feel it to be its duty to continue to follow strictly an example so every way worthy its imitation [*sic*]."[78]

75. *Republican*, Sept. 30, Oct. 3, 5, 1833; Varle, *Complete View of Baltimore*, 159; *American*, Oct. 3, 1833.

76. *American*, Sept. 23, Oct. 22, 1833; *Republican*, Oct. 23, 1833. However, their erstwhile ally, Samuel Armor, had a less sanguine opinion of the whole affair; he claimed evidence that those who assented to the price list had no intention of paying the prices for long, just until the public furor died down. *American*, Oct. 26, 1833. Nevertheless, for a time the women had gained a 25 percent wage increase and an unprecedented victory. Organizational efforts among women workers were not restricted to seamstresses; on Oct. 12, women engaged in the caning trade called a meeting at Jacob Daley's bazaar to organize.

77. *Republican*, Oct. 1, 1833; Dilts, *Great Road*, 168, 207.

78. Ibid. The Waltham plan, for its time, was among the most innovative attempts to integrate and centralize all work procedures in a single area, as well as to control the personal

The blacksmiths repeated their resolve to do no more night work, to forbid apprentices to do any, and to refuse to "suffer any reduction in our wages, in consequence of our determination against night work." If anyone was fired for holding to these resolutions, all would walk out. They promised to contribute to each other's need, if necessary, and asked fellow mechanics for aid.[79] The plight of the blacksmiths illustrates the conflict endemic to both industrializing and nation-building: the producerist ethos of local communities was threatened not only by domestic capitalist development but also by extralocal competition. The issues raised had as much to do with quality of life as they did with standard of living. The artisans' recognition that they must maintain solidarity within their trades was matched by their desire to attract the support of the community at large as well as that of their fellow workers.

Throughout fall 1833, labor activity diminished but did not cease. Uncertain party politics had deflected attention from workingmen's issues, and this had apparently taken its toll on John Weishampel and his *Workingmen's Advocate.* In an advertisement in early October Weishampel informed the public that his six hundred subscribers were "not sufficient to carry him through square with world [*sic*]," and he sought an increase. He reminded potential subscribers that he had been the first to have "'caused a shaking of the dry bones' or, in other words, aroused a great number of them to wield the sword of justice and resoluton [*sic*] against the oppression, monopoly and aristocracy of this city" and noted that his efforts had earned for him "the frowns and displeasure of those who would rob labor of its reward." But he promised "to persevere in strenuously advocating equal rights, universal education, abolition of all chartered monopolies, the promotion of morality, & every other just measure that may have the tendency to elevate the producers of all the wealth of the country to that standing in society which they so duly merit over those who live in idleness and splendour, only consuming what is produced by the industrious" as long as he was able.[80]

As winter approached, saddlers and harnessmakers, carters, and cordwainers organized and agitated for higher wages. And on November 13, the journeymen copper, tin plate, and sheet iron workers struck to maintain

habits of the workers. Laurie, *Artisans into Workers*, 31–33. Howard M. Gitelman, *Workingmen of Waltham: Mobility in American Urban Industrial Development, 1850–1890* (Baltimore: Johns Hopkins University Press, 1974), 1–22.

79. *Republican*, Oct. 1, 1833.

80. *Baltimore Saturday Visiter*, Oct. 5, 1833.

their wage structure. Their wages had been gradually shrinking for a decade; they had made approximately 10 percent more in 1824 and now demanded an increase of 15 percent.[81] To rally public support and to deflect the suspicion that their activity was due only to the recent "excitement which has existed amongst the mechanical portion of the community," the journeymen explained that price maintenance "prevents unfair competition" among the masters themselves, which inevitably allowed the avaricious to "undersell those whose sense of justice deters them from a similar course." Although the masters had promised to discuss the matter, it had become apparent to the workers that negotiations were a stalling tactic until winter set in and the workers were at the mercy of their masters for work. The strike notice explicitly acknowledged that traditional economic morality was influencing sympathetic masters, and it included a short list of those who were paying appropriate wages. As had become the norm, other journeymen rushed to the support of the strikers, with the oak coopers making a generous donation to those "who are deprived of work by our intriguing employers." The eventual outcome of this strike is not clear, but it was apparently a long one; two months later, the journeymen, at their monthly meeting, urged all coopers not yet actively involved and willing to support them in their "stand against unprincipled changelings," to join them.[82]

As the metal workers' strike began, the journeymen carpenters met to express their continuing objection to the new steam planing mill. This mill had recently burned to the ground, and the carpenters assured the public that they had had nothing to do with the fire, but they also made clear their hope that the mill would not be rebuilt. They presented three arguments against mill production of planks, especially flooring boards: the rollers in the machinery failed to adequately compensate for soft spots, knots, and other anomalies; the untrustworthiness of the ends of floor boards meant that the resulting waste would negate any potential savings; and, finally, using such boards eliminated winter work for carpenters. The elimination of winter employment would necessitate higher wages for summer work to keep solvent "a large number of persons with families, all of which subsists upon the labour of the workingman" who otherwise would be forced "to ask charity of their fellow-man or else obtrude themselves upon other branches

81. *Republican*, Oct. 28, 1833; Nov. 25, 1833. Two years later, unskilled haulers still opposed the continued extension of the railroad, with 2,000 carters and draymen signing petitions, but their efforts at both times were apparently unsuccessful. *American*, Nov. 11, 1833; *Republican*, Dec. 6, 1833; Olson, *Baltimore*, 76.

82. *American*, Nov. 11, 1833; *Republican*, Dec. 3, 1833; Jan. 7, 1834.

of mechanicism [*sic*]." The carpenters concluded with a plea for a communitywide boycott of the mill.[83]

Summer 1833 marked a watershed in Baltimore's post-Revolutionary labor relations. Militant leaders successfully appealed to the sensibilities of producerist solidarity within the artisan workforce. This labor opposition was invariably driven by traditional expressions of a harmony of productive interests that condemned the disruptive innovations of industrialization in the language of artisan republicanism and traditional Protestant economic morality. Artisans established numerous journeymen's societies and a citywide union to coordinate protective activity and, in one instance, extended that support to women workers. They waged successful strikes and established a ten-hour workday in many trades, and they enlisted sufficient public support to insure the success of the journeymen hatters and others. Their achievements were significant.

83. *Baltimore Saturday Visiter*, Oct. 19, 1833.

Chapter Five

The Flowering and Decline of Artisan Activism in Baltimore

The turbulent year of 1833 ended with another Baltimore Typographical Society anniversary supper, an event that manifested the wide range of ideological and political presentiments among the artisans. A. I. W. Jackson, Francis Burke, and Edmund Bull, all now connected to the Union Trade Society, continued as officers. Hezekiah Niles and Mayor Jesse Hunt were again guests of honor, as were a number of prominent Baltimoreans, including Methodist publisher John D. Toy, Samuel Harker of the *Republican*, and Joshua Jones (introduced as "the Workey's member"). Some nationally prominent figures were invited, including Davy Crockett (who attended and was toasted as "a granite specimen of a Western workey") and Henry Clay (who apologetically did not). Also sending regrets was John Harrod, editor of the *Methodist Protestant*, because he was unavoidably detained by a promise to attend a protracted revival meeting in his church. The meeting included the usual round of toasts, celebrating opportunity, condemning "rats" and enemies of the BTS, extolling unity between employers and employed as long as justice prevailed, and praising Niles, Jackson, Harker, Jones, and others for their leadership. Also feted were "the Working Men of Baltimore,"

who were celebrated as "real workmen in the day of trial." Yet, as would become evident in succeeding years, this was not a simple celebration of an American working class self-consciously opposed to the new social relations that accompanied emergent capitalism. Too many opportunities—political and religious as well as social and economic—continued to present themselves to Baltimore artisans to warrant such a reaction. Instead, the workers maintained their allegiance to the producerist ideals of artisan skill and mutuality, as characterized by a George W. Bailey toast offered in honor of "the *Printers of Baltimore*—May fellowship and harmony be manifested between the *employer* and the *employed* in all their transactions." But if capitalist innovation (or "foul offices" in J. H. Hewitt's earthy terminology) threatened that harmony, resistance was still mandated.[1]

The hatters' strike in June 1833 inaugurated the initial phase of trade unionism in Baltimore, which lasted for a little more than two years. In July 1835, general socioeconomic tensions, catalyzed by public outrage at the collapse of a local bank and its directors' failure to return the deposits to small investors, exploded in a four-day riot. This outburst was followed by a public backlash against any crowd actions perceived as anarchy. This marked the beginning of the second phase of Jacksonian trade unionism, which extended well into 1837 but was increasingly fragmented by internal tensions and growing public disregard. When the full effects of the panic of 1837 appeared, the already weakened artisan societies collapsed. The first phase of artisan activism saw the creation of worker organizations and militant opposition to capitalist innovation, coupled with a preoccupation with public approval based on producerist ethics. After the 1835 riots, however, the artisans operated in an uncertain social atmosphere. The Baltimore trade union leadership concentrated on forming national organizations, but in terms of politics, they restricted themselves to the local arena, while various journeymen's unions worked to achieve a range of reforms, including ten-hour workdays, closed shops, and cooperative ventures. In addition, tensions surfaced within the artisan movement itself: ideological conflicts over differing needs among producers, middlemen, and consumers; difficulties in maintaining public attention to trade union goals; and resentment on the part of some workers toward the leaders of the central trades' union, many

1. Davy Crockett responded to Hewitt's toast by offering one of his own: "A pair of cobweb breeches, a porcupine saddle, and a hard trotting horse, to all the enemies of the Baltimore Typographical Society, and when they get down may they have their toes chopt off so as to be known by their tracks." *Baltimore Saturday Visiter*, Dec. 12, 1833; *American*, Dec. 12, 1833; *Republican*, Dec. 21, 1833.

of whom were no longer practicing their crafts. By 1837 (even before the full effect of the panic was felt), trade union activity and artisan unity in Baltimore had lessened significantly, although suspicions of capitalist innovation persisted.

There was continued union activity during 1834 (though on a lesser scale than in the preceding year) and several significant displays of artisan solidarity. Almost as if to establish the fact that the militancy of the previous summer had been no fluke, the coopers went on strike in January (see chapter 1). The journeymen coopers had originally organized the previous summer and had been prominent in their support of the striking hatters. Now, fearing that recently imposed unilateral wage cuts would permanently impoverish them, the journeymen coopers, quoting from Isaiah on grinding the faces of the poor, appealed to the citizens of Baltimore to help assuage their fear of being sent "supperless to bed."[2]

The final resolution of the journeymen coopers' strike, like so many contemporary turnouts, remains unclear, but six months later the strikers felt sufficiently comfortable with the master coopers to march with them as a craft unit in a parade honoring the memory of Lafayette, suggesting that the journeymen may have won some concessions. This parade is revealing about the state of trade unionism in Baltimore in 1834. The central Working Men's and Trades' Union (formerly the United Trade Society, now the WMTU or, more simply, the Trade's Union) took the lead in organizing the event and named A. I. W. Jackson as chief marshall. In a powerful transposition of authority, Jackson invited all employers to participate either with their journeymen or, in a place assigned them by a Trades' Union committee, and he urged unorganized workers to join as well. The parade was well attended and manifested again the producerist unity underlying Baltimore trade unionism. Particularly interesting was the fact that the hatters marched as a craft unit, with friendly masters, journeymen, and apprentices all represented. With clergymen Robert Breckinridge (Presbyterian) and J. P. K. Henshaw (Episcopalian) offering prayer, the parade ended in Howard Park. By all accounts it was community success, manifesting again Baltimore artisans' dual attraction to the potentially contradictory ideals of producerist harmony and laboring-class identity.[3]

2. *Baltimore Saturday Visiter*, Aug. 17, 1833; *Republican*, Jan. 13, 15, 17, 24, 1834. One of the signers of the original communication, Levi Rathell (Rattle), was also a leader in the ten-hour movement. *Baltimore Saturday Visiter*, Aug. 3, 1833.

3. *Republican*, July 4, 7, 9, 10, 12, 1834; *American*, July 9, 12, 1834.

The year 1834 was marked by a temporary depression and "great pressure in the commercial cities,"[4] and so it is not surprising that the coopers' strike was apparently the only major turnout in Baltimore. But an awareness of the plight of operatives in an expanding industrial society did not diminish, nor did the public memory of the militancy of the previous summer. In an article praising the resistance to wage reductions by factory girls in Dover, New Hampshire, for instance, the *Republican* remarked: "Our mechanics who resisted the attempts which were made last summer, to reduce their wages, will, no doubt, admire the spirited measure of these Yankee girls." Similar notice was taken of the strike of female operatives in Lowell, Massachusetts, wherein the women issued their noted "union is power" manifesto.[5] The WMTU, reorganized in January 1834, continued to consolidate its organizational gains, and its meetings were regularly advertised in the Baltimore press. In summer 1834, the WMTU announced the completion of its hall, to be marked by a celebration to which members of the various union societies were invited, as well as the local clergy and newspaper editors. Joshua Vansant of the journeymen hatters and Democratic Mayor Jesse Hunt, formerly a master saddler, presented the addresses at this gathering.[6]

In an attempt to maintain solidarity, political divisions were glossed over. Thus, when the WMTU celebrated its first anniversary on January 1, 1835, Hezekiah Niles and Mayor Hunt were the guests of honor. The toasts reflected the intention of softening political conflicts and exhibiting toleration: the Whig hatter Philip Adams toasted the Democratic politician Richard M. Johnson of Kentucky for his antisabbatarianism and his opposition to imprisonment for debt; the Democratic printer A. I. W. Jackson feted Henry Clay for his protection of American manufacturers; and the Democratic cordwainer Francis Gallagher commended the local Whig politician Joseph Cushing for his upright character. Other toasts included those from the hatter Joshua Vansant in honor of Mathew Carey, already complimented by

4. Commons et al., *History of Labour*, 1:375; *Mutual Rights and Methodist Protestant* 4 (Jan. 24, 1834): 32.

5. *Republican*, Mar. 11, 1834; *Baltimore Saturday Visiter*, Mar. 1, 1834. For more on the Lowell turnout, see Dublin, *Women at Work*, 89–98. The *Baltimore Saturday Visiter* also reprinted at this time a more class-conscious manifesto from the Philadelphia Trades Union, entitled "An Address to the Mechanics and Workingmen, by the Trades Union, for the City and County of Philadelphia" and signed by William Dorres and William English. *Baltimore Saturday Visiter*, Feb. 8, 1834. For mention of this organization, see Laurie, *Working People of Philadelphia*, 86–89.

6. *Republican*, Apr. 30, 1834. The erection of the Trades' Union Hall in Baltimore predated by at least one year the construction of a similar edifice in New York. Wilentz, *Chants Democratic*, 234.

Niles, for his "benevolent efforts to palliate the condition of the poor, and especially the female portion"; the hatter William Wright in honor of Ely Moore, New York legislator and president of the National Trades' Union; and the master hatter John Warner Niles (son of Hezekiah) in honor of the association of journeymen hatters of Baltimore. Sending their regrets were Henry Clay and Reverdy Johnson, a city lawyer for the B & O and renegade Jackson Democrat recently turned Whig.[7]

The printers' festivity and qualified openness to employers exhibited in both the Lafayette memorial parade and the anniversary supper of the Trades' Union did not indicate any lack of vigilance or lessened militancy. In September 1834, the printers of Baltimore learned of a threat to their collective well-being—an attempt by Duff Green, the Washington, D.C., printer and publisher of congressional materials, to establish "Washington Institutes." These proposed manual labor schools, were portrayed by Green as a brilliant educational innovation but perceived by the printers as a thinly disguised attempt to undermine the traditional apprentice system. At a meeting to address this problem, the Baltimore printers had argued that the supply of journeymen printers was hardly ever less than the demand, and even with full employment "none (even the most industrious and skilful among them) earn more than a competence." Green's efforts would, in effect, glut the market with young printers who had not served apprenticeships while making Green wealthy. The Baltimore printers, therefore, had determined to support the Columbia Typographical Society (as did the New York Typographical Society) and petitioned Congress to stop sending Green work. This represented a new direction for trade unionists; a willingness to ask Congress for help was contrary to the republican proclivity to avoid seeking government intervention, set a precedent for later efforts to petition Congress to establish the ten-hour day, and recognized the potential importance of state protection of artisan interests. The quick demise of Green's plan indicated the success of the printers' efforts.[8]

7. *National Trades' Union*, July 25, 1835; Brooks and Rockel, *History of Baltimore County*, 125. J. W. Niles was one of the masters who refused to reduce the journeymen's wages in summer 1833. *Republican*, July 30, 1833. For Ely Moore's checkered career as a workingman's politician, see Wilentz, *Chants Democratic*, 238–41.

8. *Republican*, Sept. 4, 9, 1834; *National Trades' Union*, Nov. 1, 1834; Laurie, *Artisans into Workers*, 47–52, 85; Hattam, *Labor Visions*, 83. After Congress rebuffed their advances, the National Trades' Union petitioned the president for help in the ten-hour struggle. Commons et al., *Documentary History*, 6:274; Morris, "Labor Militancy in the Old South," 35. This conflict reflects the journeymen's recognition of the possible inadequacy of their voluntarist approach in the face of "the common law tradition's increasingly hegemonic interpretation of liberty

Apparent prosperity, manifested in an inflationary boom, begot economic optimism in 1835–36, but wage-earners continued to experience declining real wages. It was widely perceived that this problem was compounded by constrictive federal banking policies, with the result that wages remained constant while the rents and the price of goods increased. Thus, agitation, turnouts, and other organized efforts to secure acceptable wages, prevent reductions, or improve conditions continued.[9] In January 1835, the Fell's Point seamstresses, who originally organized in October 1833 and emphasized family values as a deterrent to socioeconomic dislocation, reorganized as the United Working Men's and Women's Trading Society (UWMWTS). They established their cooperative trading society under the inspiration in part of Mathew Carey, and they benefited from the tireless promotion of the radical Baptist and now former editor of the *Workingmen's Advocate*, John F. Weishampel. Their goal was to offer livable wages for unemployed or underemployed women heading households in the hope of making "the oppressed and depressed women . . . one independent family." Dependent on the generosity of the public, Weishampel and the female leadership of the UWMWTS set up a profit-sharing and dues-paying system specifically designed to keep profits out of the hands of capitalists and stockholders. By October 1835, with the support of local clergy and politicians and a benefit at the Front Street Theater, the society was solvent.[10]

Throughout summer 1835, Baltimore witnessed further consolidation of the central union as well as a single wave of strike activity. In late spring, the central union reported that, despite problems with employment caused by the "past inclement season," fifteen associations had made their regular contributions and the union was thriving. Reflecting the essentially conservative nature of the union as one concentrating on "protective power," the

and individual freedom of contract." Christopher L. Tomlins, *The State and the Unions: Labor Relations, Law, and the Organized Labor Movement in America, 1880–1960* (Cambridge: Cambridge University Press, 1985), 43.

9. Browne, *Baltimore in the Nation*, 129–30; Wilentz, *Chants Democratic*, 220. According to "A Working-Man," he was receiving "no more now for my labor than I did seven years since, while the prices of provisions have advanced at least one-third, and my landlord has raised his rent for a small, though comfortable two-story house, twenty-four dollars per annum!" *Republican*, June 20, 1836.

10. *Republican*, Jan. 3, 6; June 8, 1835. Weishampel's earlier requests for sufficient subscription rates among Baltimore workers had apparently proved fruitless and he was forced to apply for protection under insolvency laws in March 1834. This disappointment obviously did not dampen his enthusiasm for anticapitalist organizational activities. *Baltimore Saturday Visiter*, Oct. 5, 1833; Mar. 8, 1834.

committee proudly repeated its claim that the "institution . . . mutually assists the employer and employed, in maintaining a steady tariff of wages," with no "self-aggrandizement" or extortion of "an undue remuneration for our services" on the part of the artisans.[11]

Although some trades had gained the ten-hour day by the end of 1833, others had not; in June 1835 carpenters, bricklayers, millwrights, and plasterers resumed drives to improve their work conditions, with the plasterers being immediately successful. At the end of the month, the carpenters and bricklayers declared their intention to work only for masters who agreed to the ten-hour system and went on strike against all others. The strike announcement was accompanied by an address from "St. Clements" that appealed to traditional themes of traditional economic morality, artisan republicanism, and producerism: "You ask that you may be allowed a short respite from labour, in order that your physical system may become invigorated to renew the toil of each returning day. And is it possible that in this Christian land, men are to be found, avowing the doctrine of a benign Saviour, and yet be so lost to every feeling of humanity as to withhold from you even this poor request? The Arab listens to the cries of the o'erloaded Camel, and lightens his burden . . . yet, strange to tell, the grasping hand of avarice has made man feel less commiseration for the natural wants of his fellow man, than for those of the brute creation."[12] After recounting the toll that dawn-to-dusk labor demanded from the family, St. Clements cited computations showing that seven hours' labor per day was sufficient to satisfy the needs of the family and society, leaving three hours, "the fruits of which the producing and operative classes have never received, but which goes to build up princely fortunes for those who speculate upon honest industry, and to satiate the profligacy of the idle." The plea concluded, "Remember, that 'IN UNION THERE IS STRENGTH!' . . . Emulate the example of your brothers of Philadelphia! . . . And the praises of toiling generations will rest upon your names."[13]

11. *National Trades' Union*, May 9, 1835; *Republican*, May 30, 1835.

12. *Republican*, June 23, 24, 26, 1835; Commons et al., *History of Labour*, 1:480.

13. *Republican*, June 24, 1835. Boston carpenters and bricklayers had made similar arguments a month earlier: "One of the greatest objections to the present system is its tendency to keep the laboring man in a state of mental imbecility. . . . Thou shalt not muzzle the ox that treadeth out the corn, spake the law of Moses." *National Trades' Union*, May 9, 1835. Refuting this line of reasoning and claiming such actions would threaten the "sudden prosperity" enjoyed by Baltimoreans, an anonymous author argued that united efforts would "force" out of the individual mechanic's control "the business which properly belongs" to him. *Republican*, June 25, 1835. The Philadelphia general ten-hour strike is discussed in Laurie, *Working People of Philadelphia*, 90–91.

At the same time, the millwrights, equally determined to gain a ten-hour day, also demanded a minimum wage of $1.75 per day and pledged to refuse to allow any unemployed carpenters to work with them. These counter-arguments (particularly the millwrights' avowed hostility to sharing their work with other skilled workers) held significant implications for the future of trade union solidarity, but at this point they caused little stir. The militant printers of the Baltimore Typographical Society pronounced the millwrights' strike "just and necessary" and maintained that a ten-hour workday would "be in no ways injurious to [employers'] interests." And the journeymen hatters represented by William E. Wright and Joshua Vansant, in another demonstration of the continued unity among artisan producers, provided "unsolicited aid," for which the house carpenters were appreciative. Carpenter leader Philip Kehoe reiterated the journeymen's position: "We have commenced the work, with a determination never to yield until we have . . . time to cultivate social friendship and moral virtues."[14]

Three articles by "Working-Man" published in the *Republican* in early July reflected the tenets of the small producer tradition combined with artisan domesticity. In support of the bricklayers' push for the ten-hour day, "Working-Man" pointed out that such a system "will give the labouring man time for relaxation, and . . . time to call his little family around him to offer up the thanks which are due to the Great Creator," so that "he can proceed to his work invigorated, and will . . . do his work . . . consequently with greater advantage to the employer and capitalist." In answering the question of what prevents the worker from enjoying his "domestic duties," the author replied, "the avarice of the employer, and his constant hankering after paltry lucre. . . . For by [the artisan's] labour, and his labour alone, is produced the 'creation of value.'" By the time of the final article, the granite workers had also struck, and "Working-Man" commended them for their militancy. He declared that the existing monopolistic system would force a granite worker to "send his family supperless to bed," as well as drive him from his livelihood. His broadly based populist and producerist solution was for the yeomanry and the mechanics to unite and elect legislators willing to abolish the convict labor system; "let the Farmer remember that on the prosperity of the Mechanics depends theirs."[15]

The resolution of these strikes was not reported in the papers, but in October it was announced (with no statistical evidence) that "the ten hour

14. *Republican* June 26, 27, 1835; July 1, 2, 3, 24, 1835.
15. *Republican*, July 1, 11, 25, 1835.

system is generally adopted" in Baltimore.[16] In the meantime, other events, indirectly connected to the activity of the unionists but by no means unrelated to their overarching concerns, distracted attention from the labor agitation. Most notable was the final explosion of public outrage, from August 5 through August 10, against those held responsible for the collapse of the Bank of Maryland a year and a half earlier. This was exacerbated by the realization that most of the bank's directors and their lawyers were involved in an effective legal scheme to shift responsibility onto the bank's president, Evan Poultney, whose published defenses of his actions in the local papers in March had garnered public sympathy. In a larger context, the Bank of Maryland had collapsed during the period of widespread opposition to the Bank of the United States, which was controlled by Andrew Jackson's opponents.[17]

The preoccupation with banking issues revealed anew the ambivalence toward economic modernization and the international capitalist economy. The period from 1834 to 1836 was one of relative, though uneven, prosperity for Baltimore; more important, economic optimism, whether valid or not, prevailed. The major factor in this confidence was the infusion of British and other foreign capital into internal improvements in the United States, with railroad building emanating from Baltimore a major beneficiary. Without understanding the implications of international investment, many working Baltimoreans were induced to invest in various state-chartered banks

16. *National Trades' Union*, Oct. 17, 1835. Although the evidence is sketchy, contemporary reports seem to contradict the claim that "Baltimore workers agitated the [ten-hour] cause in 1833 without much success." Laurie, *Artisans into Workers*, 85. Comments made during the trial of Peter Harmon for his actions in the Baltimore Bank Riot of August 1835 imply that the ten-hour system had been established by that point. *Baltimore Gazette*, Dec. 29, 1835, cited in David Grimsted, "Democratic Rioting: A Case Study of the Baltimore Bank Mob of 1835" in William L. O'Neill, ed., *Insights and Parallels: Problems and Issues of American Social History* (Minneapolis: Burgess, 1973), 172, 181. For conclusions also contradicting Laurie's, see John Mitchell, *Organized Labor, Its Problems, Purposes, and Ideals, and the Present and Future of American Wage Earners* (Philadelphia: American Book and Bible House, 1903), 70; Roediger and Foner, *Our Own Time*, 34; Gorochow, "Baltimore Labor," 46–47. At the National Trades' Union meeting in 1836, it was suggested that the activity of the WMTU was responsible for the government's support of the ten-hour day. Commons et al., *Documentary History*, 6:301–2. Whatever the case, the depression following the panic of 1837 wiped out all gains, but the agitation persisted for decades. See *Address of the Maryland Ten Hour Association to the Working Men of the State* (Ellicott Mills, Md., 1850).

17. The *Republican* printed the resolutions of a meeting of Philadelphia cordwainers, headed by William English, in which they refuted the claim of rising unemployment and reiterated their stand against all forms of monopoly, including the hated bank. To this end, "Crispianus" extolled the workingmen to "rise from your slumber/And tell these gold dealers, in language that's frank/That mechanics are freemen, not slaves to the bank." *Republican*, Jan. 28, Mar. 11, July 10, 1834.

established in Baltimore for the purpose of financing these improvements. They realized, with constant reminders from pro-Jackson politicians and press, that control of the state banks lay in the hands of the national bank, and they were encouraged to resist all attempts by the latter to curb the proliferation of the former. The availability of unregulated banks, coupled with the acceptance of investment as an ethical option toward achieving a competence, was particularly significant, especially in light of the fact that traditional economic morality had long proscribed such "speculation." As capitalism transformed the workplace, workers' sense of acceptable investment practices was changing, in keeping with liberal financial schemes.[18]

Concerns over banking policy had heated up in early 1834 as Jackson's antibank policies began to take effect. The particular focus in Baltimore was the Bank of Maryland, which in winter 1831–32 initiated the practice of paying interest on all deposits. This made it the favorite of small investors who could not afford to invest in larger schemes. The bank's directors were privy to inside information concerning Jackson's prospective financial policies, which enabled them to speculate heavily. By issuing almost seven times more notes than their specie reserves justified, and by investing the reserves in stock in the Union Bank of Maryland (which they knew would be the "pet bank" in Maryland once Jackson had dismantled the national bank), the directors and their secret partners became dangerously overextended. When their scheme, dependent on an expected rise in value of Union Bank stock, failed to materialize, the Bank of Maryland notes began to lose value. After a short run by worried depositors, the Bank of Maryland closed on March 22, 1834, leaving its small-scale, often laboring-class (black and white) investors with threatened life savings.[19] A potential panic was averted only because the Union Bank was sufficiently solvent to restore confidence. The

18. Browne, *Baltimore in the Nation,* 126; *Republican,* Aug. 21, 1835. The ongoing concern with the immorality of speculation was reflected in a new round of resistance to lotteries as acceptable modes of fund-raising or gaining financial independence. They were condemned in light of their "direct tendency to encourage idleness, improvidence, and profligacy because, in order to raise a certain amount of revenue, at least ten times that amount is wrung from those who pay it; and because the burthen falls chiefly on the poor, the idle and improvident, who are least able to bear it." *American.* Dec. 12, 1834.

19. Peter Lester Payne and Lance Edwin Davis, *The Savings Bank of Baltimore, 1818–1866; A Historical and Analytical Study* (New York: Arno Press, 1976), 82–85. For excellent descriptions of the machinations of the Bank of Maryland directors, see Grimsted, "Democratic Rioting," 139–40; and Dilts, *Great Road,* 171–75. Grimsted's insightful treatment of the subsequent situation in this chapter in an earlier article (David Grimsted, "Rioting in Its Jacksonian Setting" *American Historical Review* 77 [Apr. 1972]: 361–97) provides the framework for the following.

discontent of those suffering losses was widespread, although it was moderated for a time by assurances from the wealthy directors that they could raise the money to repay the bank's obligations.[20] The collapse of the Bank of Maryland revived producerist denunciations of speculative financial practices and threw Baltimore into an uproar.

Vague promises of retribution began to appear in the Baltimore press, offered by writers who drew on Scripture to excoriate the morally and socially suspect actions of the state bank's directors. Samuel Harker of the *Republican*, for instance, sharing the concerns of the defrauded depositors and seeking to tie the collapse to general Democratic opposition to the national bank, published a number of editorials on the subject. In one such article, Harker condemned the directors by citing Prov. 18:11–12: "The rich man's wealth is his strong city, and as a high wall in his own conceit. Before destruction the heart of man is haughty." Alluding to the biblical story of Esther in another editorial, Harker compared Andrew Jackson to the biblical hero Mordecai, who "sitting at the King's gate, was never more offensive to the proud and cruel Homan [*sic*], than is the Hero of New Orleans to the purse proud Aristocrats," that is, "Nicholas Biddle and his satellites." Harker also rejected the trickle down theories of the bank supporters, who suggested "that 'the poor will discover that the wealth of the rich is the support of the poor.'" He warned readers that to support such doctrines would only place the laborer more fully under the thumb of "aristocratic monopolies," in other words, masters who allegedly fired workers opposed to current bank practices. Harker was supported by "A thinking, working Lancaster County Farmer, who has always earned his bread by the sweat of his brow." Turning the scriptural admonition to obey rulers against those who ordinarily found it useful to forestall popular uprisings, the farmer admonished the anti-Jackson forces, "Stick to the truth and you will obey the Good Book, which says, 'Revile not the rulers of the land.'"[21] In these articles, concern with the specific immorality of the Bank of Maryland was linked to general distrust of the national bank, in the context of biblical ethics.

This renewed concern with economic morality was more than a smoke screen for Jacksonian politics, at least among the population at large. During July, the *American* published a conversation, obviously framed within the context of the collapse of the Bank of Maryland, concerned with economic morality. The question, proposed as an indication of "the low standard of

20. *Baltimore Saturday Visiter*, Mar. 29, 1834; *Lutheran Observer*, Apr. 2, 1834.
21. *Republican*, Mar. 27, Apr. 30, May 31, 1834.

morals in our community," was: "Is there moral guilt involved in paying a just debt to a moneyed institution, which has suspended payment, by purchasing the depreciated currency of that institution for that purpose?" The original respondent said no, criticizing the "scrupulosity" of the question and implying that, because such action was protected by law, it was therefore necessarily moral. The idea that legality defined morality did not go unchallenged. "A Subscriber" took umbrage at the tone of the first response and objected specifically to the idea that "law is necessarily moral." Reaffirming the Golden Rule ("do unto others, as you would be done by"), he mentioned a number of legal but shady bankruptcy practices that covered the ill-gotten gains of government-protected speculators. Although it was not always the case, legality should reflect morality, the author concluded, so that economic man could avoid appearing "presumptuous before . . . God."[22]

The contest between authority based on traditional views of community morality and authority grounded in modern perceptions of legal proscriptions was characteristic of the Jacksonian era. In the *American*, "Truth" complained that the very existence of such a discussion was evidence that "the moral sensibilities of the community have become blunted almost to extinction." Particularly bothered by the elevated social status of the transgressors, he announced:

> The time must come when, in the march of morality and Gospel truth, every individual found guilty of fraud, will be held up to public execration with the public frown upon him, until he shall furnish evidence of his conversion to the just and true principles, otherwise the object of society is nullified. . . . It is true we are on the verge of a vortex which may and will draw us in if every moral energy is not exerted; but I trust the spirit of God has not yet forsaken us as a community, and affixed its seal upon our future destiny. May it not be said in language of Inspiration of us, "The whole head is sick, the whole heart faint, and from the crown of the head to the sole of the foot, we are nothing but wounds, bruises and putrifying [*sic*] sores."[23]

Even more blunt was the response of "Honesty" in his prophetic articulation of the sensibilities of those whose anger would continue to simmer: "The

22. *American*, July 1, 14, 25, 1834. In this context, William Birch, paper hanger and Methodist class leader, announced that he would accept Bank of Maryland notes "at a moderate discount." *American*, Sept. 5, 1834.

23. *American*, July 25, 1834. The biblical reference is Isa. 1:6.

writer . . . would call upon his fellow citizens to demonstrate, by some public act, that they will no more permit imposture and ruinous speculation upon their means, to stalk like pestilence, through their streets."[24]

The unresolved financial mess dragged on well into the next year, with no indication of closure. During summer 1835, the interminable legal maneuverings of those responsible for the collapse of the Bank of Maryland had become especially galling to small depositors, often skilled workers, who depended on their minimal interest to fund competences or supply retirements. Adding to that discontent was the public admission of bank director Evan Poultney that the bank had sufficient assets to pay its depositors at least ninety cents on the dollar. Yet general tranquility prevailed in Baltimore in the early summer months. Watching Baltimoreans admiring a visiting Boston military company on June 18, a Cuban visitor, Don Ramon de la Sagra, remarked (oblivious to the pending irony of his observations) that "the Americans act like children watching the soldiers. . . . How fortunate they are not to need arms to maintain public order!"[25] Less than two months later, the public mood had soured, further agitated at the end of July by accounts of the alleged seduction of a young Washington woman by Joseph Bossier, an educated and wealthy Baltimore gentleman. Bossier was subsequently beaten severely by the woman's guardian and then brought to trial, both of which demonstrated his guilt to the public. Bossier was in no way connected to the Bank of Maryland, but he seemed rather to serve as a focus of working- and middling-class resentment of the presumptions of the wealthy—feelings that were soon to spill into the streets.[26]

A new phenomenon—the circulation of inflammatory handbills—increased the volatility of the bank situation in early August. One such

24. Browne, *Baltimore in the Nation,* 122. Scharf, *Chronicles of Baltimore,* 784. That real suffering resulted from the collapse was evident in an open letter from Thomas Williams to bank director Evan Poultney in which Williams cited the loss of his retirement nest egg, his inability to help a neighbor widow, and the imminent loss of his home to creditors: "In a moment, I was reduced from competence to wretchedness and poverty." *Republican,* Mar. 11, 1836, cited in Grimsted, "Democratic Rioting," 173. Although Baltimoreans bore the bank failures "with astonishing meekness" at the time, their forbearance was not limitless. *Republican,* June 25, 1834.

25. Douglas Carroll, "A Botanist's Visit to Baltimore in 1835," *Maryland State Medical Journal* 23 (Apr. 1974): 52.

26. Grimsted, "Democratic Rioting," 130; Hewitt, *Shadows on the Wall,* 147; Grimsted, "Rioting," 382; Archhibald Hawkins, *Life of Stansbury,* 90–91. Archibald Hawkins was the younger brother of trade unionist and Methodist reformer John H. W. Hawkins; his account was taken almost verbatim from a contemporary pamphlet, *A Full and Authentic Account of the Rise and Progress of the Late Mob, in the City of Baltimore* (Baltimore, 1835) by Thomas Beach, a publishing associate of John Weishampel.

circular presented the cause of the unrest in classic populist terminology; incorporating republicanism, producerism, and traditional economic morality with older traditions of crowd action, the anonymous author called on his audience "to rally around . . . judge Lynch" with "the people en masse" as "the members of the Bar . . . to . . . redress their own grievances." These grievances encompassed "designing lawyers and lazy, greedy peculators," who were "linked in a combination together . . . to swindle and rob the industrious and poor part of the community" and then "laughing to scorn the people they have just robbed." The victims included widows, orphans, and daughters of "hard working mechanics," who were unprotected from the alleged propensity of the wealthy to "polute [*sic*] and prostitute" them. "Gracious God!" the writer of the handbill exploded, "is this our far famed Baltimore—is our moral city come to this." The suggested remedies were again those of Judge Lynch: "Tar and Feathers, effigys, gallows, and extermination," and the specified objects of this attention were Reverdy Johnson, John B. Morris, John Glenn, Evan Ellicott, and Hugh McElderry—all members of the new Baltimore elite and participants in the shady dealings of the bank—as well as the unfortunate scapegoat, "that dirty fellow Bossier."[27]

Trouble began on Wednesday evening, August 5, when a small public meeting held at Monument Square to denounce the speculators developed into a scattered round of rock-throwing at the nearby mansion of the bank's lawyer, Reverdy Johnson. On Thursday, as news of the events of the previous evening circulated, Mayor Jesse Hunt addressed the issue at another outdoor meeting, held at the courthouse, which was close to Monument Square and Johnson's mansion. This crowd was less compliant and expressed anger toward Hunt as well, who was seen by many as a symbol of violated public trust. Soon Hunt's pleas for order could scarcely be heard above the tinkling sound of Johnson's windows breaking. This minor vandalism seemed to satiate the crowd, and no further damage was reported that evening.[28]

At a public meeting on Friday, held, fortunately for Johnson, nowhere near his home, Mayor Hunt, Dr. Thomas Bond (the bane of Methodist

27. Grimsted, "Rioting," 380–81; idem, "Democratic Rioting," 155–56.

28. *Republican*, Aug. 8, 1835. Johnson epitomized the upward mobility available to the ambitious, as well as the ambiguity toward mobility and ambition within artisan culture. As an Episcopalian and a lawyer, he seemed the antithesis of the populism of the labor movement, yet seven months earlier he had been one of the featured guests at the anniversary supper of the BTS. *National Trades' Union*, July 25, 1835. Archibald Hawkins, *Life of Stansbury*, 92. Hunt's rumored connection to the Bank of Maryland and its lost deposits was a political liability; before the mayoral election earlier that summer, he issued a denial of any gain from the transactions. *American*, Oct. 20, 1834; Grimsted, "Democratic Rioting," 133.

reformers in previous years), and other prominent citizens representing the forces of order, drafted a set of resolutions. Acknowledging that "popular excesses are, under despotic governments, sometimes justified" but "inexcusable in free states," they decried "the spirit of violence exhibited of late in different parts of the United States." This reference was to the antigambling, antiabolitionist, nativist, and racist riots in Vicksburg, New York, Boston, and Philadelphia, respectively, the reports of which had filled the Baltimore papers during the previous year.[29] The committee's solutions included rewards for information identifying those "who may be guilty of disseminating papers instigating the rash and the unthinking," and instructions to parents to keep their children away from public meetings. Almost as an afterthought, the committee added a resolution calling on the trustees of the bank to hand over to creditors the bank's books.[30]

The aggrieved were not impressed with these toothless resolutions. As the town meeting ended, another boisterous crowd gathered near the courthouse and engaged in verbal sparring with various citizens. Stone-throwing once again ensued, giving Reverdy Johnson ample cause to rue the day he built on Monument Square. Mayor Hunt and others, arriving from the recently adjourned town meeting, attempted to halt the vandalism by positioning themselves on Johnson's portico, an act of bravery which only served to make them appealing targets in lieu of the rapidly diminishing supply of unbroken windows. For a time it appeared that Hunt was in danger, but the city watchmen, led by WMTU official A. I. W. Jackson, in his newly appointed capacity as captain of the Night Watch of the Middle District, rescued the mayor. Attempts to arrest the participants proved fruitless, with the crowd freeing almost everyone captured, but late in the night the fighting finally subsided. The next day an anonymous handbill appeared, celebrating the activities of the rioters the previous night ("We have nobly shown what robbers are to expect at the hands of Baltimoreans") and calling

29. Ironically, the previous year Hunt had been presented to the electorate as one who, by appealing to reason, would help Baltimore avoid the rioting that had racked other major urban centers in 1834. *American*, Oct. 15, 1834. For other Jacksonian riots, see Carl E. Prince, "The Great 'Riot Year': Jacksonian Democracy and Patterns of Violence in 1834," *Journal of the Early Republic* 5 (spring 1985): 2; Grimsted, "Rioting," 362. Dr. Bond was later called upon to lend his reputation to the forces of order and was successful in dispersing a part of the crowd without recourse to weapons. *Republican*, Aug. 11, 1835. Longtime Maryland politician, now Secretary of the Treasury Roger Taney suggested after the fact that full police force would have been appropriate at the initial outbreak of destruction. Roger B. Taney to James M. Campbell, Aug. 19, 1835, cited in Grimsted, "Democratic Rioting," 168.

30. Archibald Hawkins, *Life of Stansbury*, 93–95.

for yet another public meeting to determine justice to "afford, in mercy to the guilty, once more a chance to turn from the evil of their ways. It would be doing as we would be done by." Hunt responded by deputizing five hundred citizens to be armed only with sticks, an action later derisively referred to as organizing "the rolling pin brigade."[31]

The dawn's early light on Saturday morning found Reverdy Johnson safely ensconced in Fort McHenry in south Baltimore, where legendary resistance to British avengers twenty-one years earlier had been immortalized by Francis Scott Key, but no such heroism was forthcoming from the Johnson camp this day. Instead, life in Baltimore proceeded as usual, but since Saturday was also payday and workers often celebrated by drinking and carousing, the evening proved to be unusually lively. A large crowd, mostly curious, yet sympathetic to the concerns of the angry, made the mixture particularly unstable as they once again gathered at Johnson's mansion. The mounted charges of Jackson and his men managed to keep the crowd away from what was left of the house, but, unknown to the watchmen, another crowd was gathering near John Glenn's house on North Charles Street. There the obligatory rock throwing commenced about nine o'clock, followed by a charge on the barricaded house and the stoning of the police when they arrived. For the first time in these disturbances, blood was shed by gunfire when Samuel Baker, a guard, wounded himself in the hip trying to pull his pistol. This singular act of ineptitude seemed to escalate the level of confusion. Some of Baker's fellows, proving more skilled with firearms, fired on the crowd, killing two people. At that point, fearing the further escalation of violence, the volunteer police then left Charles Street to return to Monument Square.[32]

With the withdrawal of the watchmen, the crowd—shaken but more furiously intent on destruction than ever—entered the Glenn house. They broke down the doors, emptied the wine cellar, tossed the expensive furniture into the street, and made a huge bonfire out of the wreckage. Meanwhile, back at the square, the embattled watchmen were more successful in protecting Johnson's shell of a mansion, and although more blood was shed, no one died. By midnight, the action was limited to a small group at Glenn's

31. Jackson was one of six such emergency officials throughout Baltimore, responsible for protecting order during fires, disturbances, or any other unusual circumstances; these officials were not a professional police force. One of the other captains was Daniel Perigo, a leader of the journeymen shipjoiners and an active Methodist Protestant layman. *Baltimore Saturday Visiter*, Mar. 8, 1834. Archibald Hawkins, *Life of Stansbury*, 96–98; Grimsted, "Democratic Rioting," 134, 157; Frank A. Cassell, *Merchant Congressman in the Young Republic: Samuel Smith of Maryland, 1752–1839* (Madison: University of Wisconsin Press, 1971), 258.

32. Scharf, *Chronicles of Baltimore*, 479; Archibald Hawkins, *Life of Stansbury*, 101–2.

house who were reveling in the liberation of his supply of imported wines. When the police arrested ten revelers, the remnant of the crowd attacked. Their patience exhausted, the watchmen fired indiscriminately into the crowd and at least three (unofficial estimates reached twenty-two) died. This last exercise of force was highly resented by the crowd who judged the police action murder and singled out various officers of the watch for subsequent punishment. By dawn, a tension-filled sense of quiet reigned.[33]

Sunday morning brought no relief. A rally called to organize opposition to the rioters went unattended, church services throughout the city were canceled, and the antibank crowd, enjoying the implicit sympathy of most onlookers, was eager for more vengeance. Mayor Hunt issued a statement absolving himself from all responsibility for the police-inflicted fatalities. Most of the voluntary watchmen, because of their concern over threats, their disgust with Hunt's disavowal, and their general weariness, joined Johnson in exile, leaving the city with no official forces for restraint. Starting as early as 10:00 A.M., the crowd began to dismantle Glenn's mansion and when they realized that the volunteer police force had abandoned the city, they determined to punish others equally responsible for the suffering of the Bank of Maryland depositors. As night fell, the unopposed crowd (including a fair number of women), rather leisurely completed the destruction of the Glenn and Johnson mansions, emptying Johnson's law library and burning it in the street.[34] They were led by "Red Jacket," who was really Samuel Mass, a past president of the journeymen cedar coopers society (although by 1832 he was listed as a master), a former member of the Maryland executive council, and, at various times, both a Whig and a Democratic politico. Newspapers later identified Mass "with remarks calculated to reflect" on him that August morning, but he denied guilt and in the end was charged with nothing.[35]

33. Archibald Hawkins, *Life of Stansbury*, 102–5. According to the *Baltimore Patriot*, eight to ten were "killed or dangerously wounded," *Patriot*, Aug. 10, 1835. Although his chronology of events is inaccurate (he claims the deaths occurred Sunday night), Frank Cassell asserts that "at least ten but probably dozens more were killed." Cassell, *Merchant Congressman*, 258.

34. Dilts, *Great Road*, 182. David Grimsted offers an interesting explanation of the festive nature of the proceedings as a sort of "Saturnalia" celebration. Somewhere between fifty and two hundred performed the actual demolition while thousands watched approvingly. Grimsted, "Democratic Rioting," 141, 135; Beach, *Rise and Progress of the Late Mob*, 17–19.

35. *Patriot*, Aug. 10, 1835; Archibald Hawkins, *Life of Stansbury*, 107–10; Scharf, *Chronicles of Baltimore*, 477; Grimsted, "Rioting," 388. For an eyewitness account from the perspective of one of the ward military organizations, see Hewitt, *Shadows on the Wall*, 150–51. If indeed there was only one Baltimore activist by this name, Mass was a unique specimen. Grimsted (following Roger Taney) identifies him as one of the leaders of the "plebeian wing of the Jacksonians," but his political career was actually more convoluted. Grimsted, "Rioting," 388.

The rampage continued well into the night, as the homes of bank director John B. Morris and Mayor Hunt were destroyed and that of secret bank partner Hugh McElderry was spared only because of the frantic pleas of its builder, who had not yet been paid and stood to absorb the loss. The crowd threatened three homes belonging to the forces of order, but left them alone either because of the pleas of women living in them or because of ownership questions. Finally the crowd arrived at Evan Poultney's house. Poultney, president of the Bank of Maryland, had been involved in its speculative activity from the beginning. But because Reverdy Johnson (his former attorney), Hugh McElderry (head of a recent grand jury probe considering the primary role of Poultney in the confusion), and others had been trying to lay the blame solely on Poultney and because Poultney had gone public in exposing the bank's lawyers and their continued complicity in refusing to return the deposits, the crowd was ambivalent regarding the extent of Poultney's guilt.[36]

Poultney met the crowd at his front porch. In keeping with his Quaker background, Poultney assured the crowd they would meet no resistance at his house. A contemporary noted that because Poultney had "confessed his sins," the crowd decided that "they would not hurt him or his house, they would only punish those who sought to justify themselves"; thus the crowd moved on, its collective rage finally spent.[37] By the afternoon of Monday, August 10,

An early Jackson supporter, by 1834 he supported Whig candidates. *American*, Apr. 24, 1834; Oct. 3, 15, 1834. By this time he had also moved away from his journeymen roots. Charles Varle listed him as one of only ten master cedar coopers in 1833; by 1834 he was advertising for house builders and carpenters to buy lots in a neighborhood of increasing property values, and two years later he was signing himself as "Samuel Mass, Esq." Varle, *Complete View of Baltimore*, 160; *American*, Nov. 8, 1834; *Republican*, Aug. 23, 1836. His general contracting activity is probably the source of his identification by one riot observer as "the stupid Dutch paver." Grimsted, "Democratic Rioting," 172. In 1835, however, he was a Tenth Ward Democratic Republican again, and by 1836 he was a Baltimore delegate to the Democratic State Convention. *Republican*, July 23, 1835, May 20, 1836. He apparently participated personally in the destruction of Johnson's house, and he was arrested two days after the riot for chairing a meeting of Tenth Ward citizens who had passed resolutions condemning the anarchy but warning Johnson never to return to the city of Baltimore under the threat of lynching. Grimsted, "Rioting," 388; *Republican*, Aug. 13, 1835. Mass had been involved with the trades' union movement from its inception, although he was not a member of the central leadership.

36. Archibald Hawkins, *Life of Stansbury*, 114; *Niles' Weekly Register* 48 (Aug. 15, 1835); Grimsted, "Democratic Rioting," 139, 152–53. For mention of McElderry's involvement in Jackson Party politics and Bank of Maryland speculation, see Tina H. Sheller, "The Origins of Public Education in Baltimore, 1825–1829," *History of Education Quarterly* 22 (spring 1982), 32; Browne, *Baltimore in the Nation*, 112; and Grimsted, "Democratic Rioting," 139.

37. *Maryland Gazette*, Aug. 27, 1835; Archibald Hawkins, *Life of Stansbury*, 114. Poultney continued to enjoy public support as the affair dragged on. *Republican*, Feb. 4, Mar. 23, 1836. "Junius," whose articles on the Bank of Maryland collapse were the most detailed, concluded

the crowd had dispersed and civilian militia troops under the elderly Baltimore politician and general Samuel Smith took control of a quiet city. The Baltimore Bank Riot was over, except for the trials of those few arrested during the earlier confrontations, in which twelve were convicted and ten acquitted.[38] As one observer concluded: "No body knew where the mob was on Monday morning—in fact it had vanished.—It is true it had left behind, as terrible things commonly do, a good deal of alarm,—and Rumor as usual was amusing herself with the fears of the timid—but the mob—the genuine mob was defunct.—Public opinion which had breathed into its nostrils the breath of life, had withdrawn its vitality, and the mob was no more."[39]

A classic example of the spontaneous defense of the corporatist "moral economy" of Baltimore society, the crowd action was, for the most part, a rational expression of what Paul Gilje has called "traditional Anglo-American mob behavior." As David Grimsted points out, however, it was highly unusual in the Jacksonian milieu that the objects of the crowd's wrath were persons enjoying elevated socioeconomic status.[40] The importance of traditional economic morality to the public conscience was obvious; its tenets were employed to stimulate public opinion and to sanctify the crowd activity. In defending the crowd, "Junius," for instance, suggested that when fraud was law, mob action was order; the people were operating "upon the republican maxim 'resistance to tyrants is obedience to God.'"[41] The participants were self-controlled and cognizant that undesirable consequences might result from their activity. The crowd discussed the pros and cons of burning Hugh McElderry's boatyard, finally deciding against such action by a one-vote majority because they feared the fire would spread. When one of their

---

that Poultney was responsible for speculative excesses but for very little of the actual financial losses, which occurred when the other directors and their lawyers hid the deposits. *Republican*, Aug. 23, 1836. Scarf, *Chronicles of Baltimore*, 497; Grimsted, "Rioting," 387–88.

38. Grimsted gives totals of twenty-three accused and eight convicted, with all the convicted pardoned in June 1836 after continual public outcry in Baltimore. Grimsted, "Democratic Rioting," 138.

39. *Republican*, Mar. 5, 1836, cited in Grimsted, "Democratic Rioting," 187. Even in attributing Smith's heroics to ending the riot, Frank Cassell acknowledges, "Either because they had achieved their goals or feared the show of force, the rioters had fled, and no resistance was met." Cassell, *Merchant Congressman*, 259.

40. Gilje, "Baltimore Riots of 1812," 557; Grimsted, "Rioting," 374.

41. The symbolic importance of the republican tradition was evidenced by the crowd's careful removal of a statue of an eagle from above Reverdy Johnson's front door (in the midst of the destruction) and its placement above the door on the nearby Battle Monument. Archibald Hawkins, *Life of Stansbury*, 108; *Republican*, Aug. 12, 1835.

number disregarded the wishes of the majority and proceeded with his personal arson agenda, the crowd forcibly restrained him. In a similar situation, when a rioter was found stealing from the house of bank director Evan Ellicott, the crowd threatened to tar and feather him. And when the fire at Johnson's house on Sunday showed signs of spreading to the Mechanic's Bank, the crowd successfully organized and contained the flames. Finally, on the Monday morning after the rioting had ended, some members of the crowd returned to wash Evan Poultney's steps and to replace mistakenly broken windows in the house next to Ellicott's.[42] The patterns of destruction, circumscribed and purposive as they were, served to humiliate the objects of the crowd's wrath, whose combination of social mobility, corruption, and disregard for public welfare earned them the hostility of many. Moreover, their choice of objects for bonfires—expensive and probably imported furniture and law books—reflected populist disgust with foreign imports and elite education.[43]

The festive nature of the crowd was also significant: despite the very real danger of armed police, large numbers of Baltimoreans turned out to watch and to participate, and their hilarity, at times at the expense of their fellow rioters, was part of the attraction.[44] Reverdy Johnson, rather understandably, referred to them as the "dregs of society," but his judgment of their social status was no more acute than his banking ethics.[45] Although most of those ultimately arrested were young with ties to the increasingly rowdy fire companies and had presumably been drinking heavily, they invariably had artisan roots and were skilled and property-holding; "Junius" referred to them as "upright, industrious mechanics." Fully half of those tried were

42. Grimsted, "Democratic Rioting," 137; idem, "Rioting," 381; Archibald Hawkins, *Life of Stansbury*, 108, 114. Another rioter was rebuked by a bystander for trying to steal coffee from John Morris's house. *Maryland Gazette*, Dec. 14, 1835, cited in Grimsted, "Democratic Rioting," 176. One who did steal (three or four bedsheets from Evan Ellicott's house) announced that it was a fair trade for the fifty dollars he had lost. Ibid., 180. See also *Maryland Gazette*, Jan. 6, Jan. 7, 1836.

43. The desire for public humiliation of those held responsible was exhibited in one of the handbills printed in the week before the riot. It read, "Tar & feathers will forever disgrace them. Let it be done," and was signed "Ruined Widows & Orphans." Grimsted, "Rioting," 383.

44. Hijinxs abounded as the demolition continued; one man threw a keg into the fire at Johnson's house and shouted "Gunpowder!" to the consternation of those nearby and to the amusement of those more safely situated. At other times, the crowd heckled some of its own members. Archibald Hawkins, *Life of Stansbury*, 108–9.

45. A French visitor, Michel Chevalier, agreed with Johnson's assessment; he ascribed the crowd's activity to "a handful of drunkards and depraved boys." Michel Chevalier, *Society, Manners, and Politics in the United States, Being a Series of Letters on North America*, cited in Grimsted, "Democratic Rioting," 188–89.

carpenters. Butchers were also well represented, and unlike riots in other urban centers, few Irish immigrants were involved. Benjamin Latrobe Jr. cited "20 or 30 individuals in the middling classes, principally butchers who had sustained losses of varying extent, by the breakup of the bank," and butcher Leon Dyer was one of the handful of leaders mentioned. There was no indication that the crowd was being manipulated behind the scenes by disgruntled elites, and there was a high probability that those involved were established in the community. Trade union leaders (e.g., A. I. W. Jackson and Samuel Mass) appeared on both sides of the activity, but no evidence suggests a purposeful trade unionist presence, and no official pronouncements regarding the riot emanated from the city's central union. The *National Trades' Union*, however, was not so circumspect; referring to "the most disgraceful riots" that had recently ravaged "this fine and flourishing city," it quoted the *Republican*, which assured all that, despite the violence, the only property damaged belonged to bank officials or those in the city guard who "had given particular umbrage" to the crowd.[46]

Like the local unions, the local religious press was silent, expressing distress only with the breakdown of social harmony. The influence of the clergy, however, had been sought by William Preston, one of the bank's lawyers, who had urged Mayor Hunt to "have notice sent to the several ministers of this City let them address their congregations in the open sts. [*sic*] and explain to them the inestimable blessings of social life and civil rule." No such effort materialized; perhaps the Baltimore clergy were more concerned with righteous retribution according to popular understandings

46. *Republican*, Feb. 26, 1836; Grimsted, "Democratic Rioting," 144, 171; Archibald Hawkins, *Life of Stansbury*, 96; Grimsted, "Rioting," 385. For Johnson's self-serving public reaction to the destruction of his mansion, see *Republican*, Aug. 22, 1835 and Reverdy Johnson, *The Memorial of Reverdy Johnson to the Legislature of Maryland, Praying Indemnity for the Destruction of His Property in the City of Baltimore by a Mob in August, 1835* (Annapolis, 1836). Presumably, Jackson joined the watchmen's "turnout" during the riot, but he continued in his position as captain of the Night Watch for the Middle District. Leon Dyer was a Jewish butcher and, like Samuel Mass, a political contortionist; identified by Grimsted (and Roger Taney) as prominent in the affairs of the plebeian Jacksonians, he was less than a year before the riot a Whig. Grimsted, "Rioting," 388; *American*, Oct. 2, 1834. Taney's comments are cited in Frank Otto Gatell, ed., "Roger B. Taney, the Bank of Maryland Rioters, and a Whiff of Grapeshot," *Maryland Historical Magazine* 59 (Sept. 1964): 266. Dyer, too, escaped criminal charges, presumably because he helped dissuade the crowd from burning McElderry's boatyard, as attested to publicly and in subsequent trials by six individuals present. Grimsted, "Rioting," 387–88; *Republican*, Aug. 12, 1835; Grimsted, "Democratic Rioting," 153–54, 177–78. When a movement arose later to reduce the penalties of the convicted, no trade unionists headed the ward committees, although the effort was chaired by Marcus Wolf, a victualer and prominent leader of the butchers' association. *Republican*, May 12, 1836. *National Trades' Union*, Aug. 15, 1835.

of economic morality than with the sacralization of social order. This was the interpretation of Benjamin Latrobe, certainly no friend to the crowd; he recognized "a sentiment of sympathy with the mob against the Bank of Maryland" which "paralyzed the peaceable portion of the community and the work of destruction was suffered to proceed unchecked."[47]

This sympathy with the mob reflected the ambivalence evangelicals felt toward state coercion and popular enforcement of community mores. Well after the fact, in 1840, in an oblique reference to the morality of the crowd action in an article on temperance, Baltimore Presbyterian minister Robert Breckinridge compared the antisocial actions of the bank directors to the rationalizations of liquor manufacturers. "You say, 'It is the means by which we obtain bread for our families—If we do not do it others will—We do not compel people to buy and drink the liquor.' Now if these are good and sufficient reasons for carrying on your business, would they not be equally good for the following of some other trades, licensed or connived at by law? Let us examine: A company of individuals obtain a charter for carrying on banking operations, and open an office of deposit of the savings of the industrious. After a while the bank fails—the vaults are empty, and the books show that the directors and their friends ******. Well, who finds fault?" Breckinridge was also an outspoken opponent of papists, and his remarks relative to anti-Catholic riots indicates the confusion felt by evangelicals toward crowd actions. In 1835, in regard to a report of screams coming from the Carmelite convent on Aisquith Street, Breckinridge encouraged civil investigation of alleged abuses in the nunnery but warned: "*Let no man violate any law, even bad ones. Let the persons, property and rights of all be held sacred. We are no Jesuits; we know that no end can justify any improper means.* But . . . the laws ought to be so made that the poor victims can get out." Four years later in response to another alleged crisis at the convent, however, Breckinridge had modified his views: if the civil authorities failed in their responsibilities to investigate convent abuses, "society *en masse* is divinely commissioned to rise and correct them. The right of revolution itself is a sacred and an inalienable right; much more the right, to protect the weak, the oppressed, the suffering,—when in God's name they demand it at our hands."[48]

47. Grimsted, "Democratic Rioting," 170–71. In the mayoral election to follow, however, such socially prominent Methodists as Thomas Kelso and Christian Keener supported Samuel Smith, the candidate of law and order. Keener went out of his way to acknowledge that such backing was in no way a personal rejection of soon-to-resign Mayor Jesse Hunt. *Republican,* Sept. 5, 1835.

48. *Baltimore Literary and Religious Magazine* 6 (Nov. 1840): 515–16; Robert J. Breckinridge, *Tracts to Vindicate Religion and Liberty. No. 1. Containing the Review of the Case of Olevia Neal, the*

In the end, however, the riot was undoubtedly counterproductive in its effect on Baltimoreans distrustful of liberalized business ethics and their impact on the community. With the crowd's rage and desire for the public humiliation of the offenders sated, no further legal action was taken against Johnson and company, who quickly began to agitate for legislation requiring local communities to reimburse individuals whose property suffered damage. The reimbursement proposition was endorsed by the commercial-oriented Baltimore *Patriot* (the only local paper earlier condemned by trade unionists) and drew various responses from the Baltimore populace.[49] "Justice" allowed that those discomforted by the riot should be reimbursed from statewide taxation, adding that those who had lost savings should be compensated as well. "A Tax Payer," expressing himself in scientific idiom, maintained that there are no effects like riots without causes and the cause was most certainly the carelessness and dishonesty of those attacked. "Junius" agreed: "It is said—'Thou shalt not do evil that good may come,' and this, as a prohibitory command is certainly correct; but after the act is done, and the supreme power is about to determine on the punishment . . . , the motive of the criminal and the manner of the deed, are both to be taken into consideration." In a similar argument, "A Friend to Justice" took "Order" to task for suggesting that he favored law "so long as it is administered with an eye to Justice" and that citizens have the right to "exercise . . . their liberties."[50] Nevertheless, the collective release of emotion seemed to blunt the impetus toward redressing the possibility of similar corruptions in the future.

The aftershocks of the bank riot continued to reverberate into the fall, influencing the local elections and, on a broader scale, informing public conceptions of the proper expression of opposition to corruption or violations of economic morality. It was in this respect that the crowd action of August had its greatest impact on Baltimore society. This generation of Baltimoreans had never witnessed such social upheaval and when the now-resigned Jesse Hunt refused to run for mayor, Jacksonians and Whigs fell all

---

Carmelite Nun, and the Review of the Correspondence Between the Archbishop and Mayor of Baltimore. With Important Additional Matter to Both Reviews (Baltimore, 1839), 12, 4.

49. *Baltimore Saturday Visiter*, Aug. 17, 1833. At first, the *Patriot* blamed the rioting on the Jacksonians, but it later backed away from that stance, asserting that nothing positive would result from trying to connect the riots to political parties. Harker gleefully pointed out this switch as a tacit acknowledgement of major Whig participation, which was equally likely. *Republican*, Aug. 23, 1835. This attempt, however, was coupled with nascent nativism and continued into the state elections two months later, to the discomfort of the Jacksonians, who were called "Unnatural Foreigners," "Workies," and "Mobites." *Republican*, Oct. 3, 1835.

50. *Republican*, Aug. 21, 1835; Mar. 9, 1836; Sept. 2, 1835.

over each other in their support for General Samuel Smith, the law-and-order candidate.[51] His opponent, Moses Davis, was a carpenter, a "very spirited man," and a political neophyte who presented himself as one who had no party to support him, had "no great Lineage to boast of," and had "rendered no service to the republic, but Industry and hard Labour for the support of a helpless family." His populist appeal was genuine, but it spoke to postriot exigencies. His qualifications were that he had "lived long enough . . . to know the wiles of the crafty and the snares of the politician . . . to know who deserves a Fish, and who a Stone," and he pledged "to hold the Scales of Justice fairly, neither to bow to wealth nor to deride the poor—see that the laws are fairly and impartially executed," and to "afford ample protection to all by a well regulated police" to avoid "the mania that unhappily rages throughout our beloved country."[52]

Davis's candidacy and the support of Smith by both parties made the election results particularly interesting. Davis received 25 percent of the vote, a significant number for such an unorganized campaign and an indication of the ongoing resonance of populist producerism. Such qualifications, to be sure, were increasingly suspect in this era, leading one Baltimorean to complain: "THEY [opponents of General Smith] HAD NO MAN TO VOTE FOR. For the honor of their city they would not vote for the NOMINAL opponent of Gen. Smith, for fear he might be elected; and therefore did not vote at all." The total vote had indeed fallen off by 33 percent from the previous election, but Davis's showing and the refusal of some to embrace the law-and-order candidacy of Smith indicated the continued public disgust with the violation of community welfare and socioeconomic ethics manifested by the Bank of Maryland fiasco.[53]

This anger surfaced six months later when the Baltimore City Council adopted resolutions offered by Samuel Harker of the *Republican* regarding the final settlement of riot damages. Harker's resolutions were designed to muster opposition to the request made by Johnson, Glenn, and others for

51. In the trial of Samuel Farr, lawyer William H. Norris interceded to support the prosecution. Citing the widespread occurrence of rioting throughout the United States in 1834, Norris called on the jury to convict in order to preserve "the existence of our Republican Institutions." Without leaving the jury box, they agreed. *Gazette,* Dec. 15, 1835, cited in Grimsted, "Democratic Rioting," 178.

52. Grimsted refers to Davis as "a town drunk, presumably," because of the reference to his "*spirited*" demeanor. Grimsted, "Rioting," 389. His public statement, however, was a coherent exposition of the mechanic ethos and his strong showing may have reflected the continued popularity of that tradition rather than a politically ineffective protest vote. *Republican,* Sept. 5, 1835.

53. *Republican,* Sept. 5, 9, 1835; Grimsted, "Rioting," 389.

remuneration from the Maryland legislature. The highly publicized and emotionally charged indemnification bill was supported by Secretary of Treasury Roger Taney and President Andrew Jackson and presented by prominent Baltimore politician John Van Lear McMahon, but both Baltimore Democratic delegates—Beale Richardson (also a Methodist Protestant lay leader) and Cornelius McLean Jr.—voted against the measure. Nevertheless, the bill passed, awarding damages of $102,552.82, with Johnson receiving roughly $41,000 and Glenn $37,000. As Harker acidly summarized this process, "The passage of [this bill] affords an evidence of the fact that in this land of liberty, the power of wealth and influence controls the actions of those who make the laws." Although their social rehabilitation was contested, Johnson, Glenn, Ellicott, and McElderry eventually regained the social prestige to match their generous indemnifications; Johnson, in fact, became a United States senator and served as attorney general under Zachary Taylor.[54] Yet even in defeat Harker had the last word: "If the sufferers by the riots are to be indemnified, why should not also the sufferers by the failure of the Bank of Maryland?" In 1838, the Bank of Maryland settled its accounts by paying its debts in full with a 10 percent dividend. But by then, in the aftermath of the depression that began in late 1837, most of the common investors had sold their credits for next to nothing to well-heeled speculators.[55]

54. Gatell, ed., "Roger Taney and the Bank of Maryland Rioters," 266n11, 267; John Thomson Mason, *Life of John Van Lear McMahon* (Baltimore, 1879), 62–66; *Republican*, Mar. 25, 1836, cited in Ridgway, "McCulloch vs. the Jacksonians," 361n40. John V. L. McMahon in 1829 had successfully represented the journeymen weavers in their important court case. Damage awards are cited in J. Thomas Scharf, *History of Baltimore City and County from the Earliest Period to the Present Day* (Philadelphia, 1881), 786n1. In 1855, Reverdy Johnson, by now a leading American lawyer, was retained by the Cyrus McCormick Company to sue a rival reaper manufacturer, and the trial was to be held in federal court in Springfield, Illinois. In order to gain some local leverage, defense attorneys George Harding and Edwin Stanton hired a Springfield lawyer named Abraham Lincoln. Lincoln worked for months on the case, but when the venue was changed to Cincinnati, Lincoln's value to the defense disappeared. He came to Cincinnati anyway, with, according to another member of the defense team, "the fond hope for making fame in a forensic contest with Reverdy Johnson." Stanton (later to be Lincoln's secretary of war), however, refused to have anything to do with "such a damned, gawky, long-armed ape" as Lincoln, and Lincoln returned to Springfield frustrated and humiliated, never to face Reverdy Johnson in court. Sarah-Eva Carlson, "Lincoln and the McCormick-Manny Case," *Illinois History* 48 (Feb. 1995): 30–31.

55. *Republican*, Aug. 20, 21, Sept. 2, 1835; Mar. 9, 24, 1836, with the Harker quote cited in Gatell, ed., "Roger Taney and the Bank of Maryland Rioters," 267n14; Ridgway, "McCulloch vs. the Jacksonians," 361. For more on this subject from "Junius," see *Republican*, Oct. 19, 26, 1835; Feb. 4, Mar. 31, 1836; Grimsted, "Rioting," 389. The concern of the depositors did not disappear; calling for "an act of justice due from you," "A Suffering Creditor" asked Evan Poultney to publish in the press the amounts each of the directors owed when the Bank of

The small depositors of the Bank of Maryland received little more than the ephemeral satisfaction of seeing their perceived tormentors humiliated in the Baltimore Bank Riot of 1835.

The riot and the local elections may have attracted the most attention in the early fall, but they were not the only expressions of opposition to economic innovations: Baltimore trade unionists continued to fight capitalist exploitation, as evidenced by their unified reaction against the Thompsonville Carpet Weavers Corporation of Connecticut in October 1835. This corporation had attempted to form a national combination in summer 1833 to reduce the wages of journeymen carpet weavers (the owners of the Baltimore firm that the Connecticut capitalists approached refused to join) and had instituted criminal charges against workers who organized to resist wage cuts. In a large public meeting, called by Baltimore's Working Men's Trades' Union, chaired by Richard Marley and addressed by New England labor activist Seth Luther, resolutions were passed condemning the "rich and powerful corporation" that had exhibited "extraordinary tyranny and oppression . . . whereby a portion of their hands were deprived of liberty, and cast into a loathsome cell, merely for refusing to labor for them at their own prices." This action was characterized as an effort to "rob honest labor of its just reward, and send not only the poor man, but his wife and helpless infants supperless to bed." A committee, including Samuel Mass, John Seidenstricker, and Joshua Vansant, was appointed to raise funds to support the weavers, whose bond had been set at an exorbitant $15,000 each, and the resolutions, along with Luther's address, were sent to the *National Trades' Union* for publication.[56]

Maryland collapsed. *Republican*, Dec. 12, 1835. Claiming he had no legal obligation to do so, Poultney acknowledged his moral responsibility and agreed to furnish the information. *Republican*, Dec. 17, 1835.

56. *Republican*, Oct. 3, 1835; *National Trades' Union*, Nov. 14, 1835. For Seth Luther, see Louis Hartz, "Seth Luther: The Story of a Working-Class Rebel," *New England Quarterly* 13 (Sept. 1940): 401–18; *National Trades' Union*, Nov. 21, 1835; *Republican*, Nov. 17, 1835. Indicative of populist evangelical willingness to contest the social meanings of the faith with elite coreligionists was Luther's public controversy with Dr. Jonathan Wainwright, Episcopal rector of Boston's Trinity Church. Wainwright maintained that poverty existed by divine providence to provide motivation for the masses and he celebrated economic inequality. Luther responded, "A man who tells you that the Great Author of our existence designed that the *many* should be poor and miserable, in order that the few may roll and riot in splendid luxury, would pick your pocket if he had a good opportunity, let him profess what he may. He may even profess to be a minister of him who had not where to lay his head, and hypocritically pretend to great regard for his fellow creatures, but he is not worthy of his profession and does not fulfill the duties of his 'high calling.'" Seth Luther, *Address Delivered Before the Mechanics and the Workingmen of the City of Brooklyn* (Brooklyn, 1836), 12. The ninth resolution

The central union was strengthen by the establishment, in early 1836, of its own newspaper, the *Baltimore Trades' Union,* under the editorship of Edmund Bull and William Tuttle. Its prospectus reflected a determination to avoid dissension as the editors forbade discussion of sectarian religious or political issues and promised intransigence in the face of industrial innovations threatening their artisanal way of life.[57] Bull, in particular, had long been active in BTS activity and WMTU militancy, and in February 1836, the WMTU delegates voted to support Bull's and Tuttle's new publishing effort in order to fulfill the obligations of the "aggrieved" portion of the community "to frustrate the designs of those who, for self-aggrandizement, would thus subvert the first principles of government." Unfortunately, only one copy of this newspaper, that of May 28, 1836, has survived. This edition included a suggestive story about a revolutionary patriot captured in Poland, his trial ("Prince, . . . there is a point at which resistance becomes a virtue, and silence a crime."), and subsequent execution by agents of the Russian czar. When his mother prophesied doom, both eternal and imminent, for the perpetrators, she was also arrested, but this proved to be too much for the citizens of Warsaw, who "fulfilled the prophecy" by killing their masters.[58]

The *Baltimore Trades' Union* printed notices relevant to the organizational activities of Baltimore artisans and listed the titles and officers of various journeymen's organizations. In addition, the paper carried critiques of industrial capitalism. An anonymous and perceptive letter addressed to workingmen decried the continual extension of "aristocracy," wherein the "liberty" offered artisans was "to work as hard and as long as you please for their maintenance and support" and "to grumble as much as you please, provided you pay up," while "equality" meant that "they are obliged to flatter, beguile, and deceive you out of their votes." The writer's concept of class

---

adopted by the Baltimore meeting indicated, once again, the preoccupation of the central union with organizing those trades that had not yet formed associations. *Republican,* Nov. 17, 1835. The drive to support the Thompsonville weavers extended into December, as the "Mechanics and Working Men of Baltimore" authorized a committee consisting of Francis Gallagher and others to receive gifts from those societies who had not yet contributed. *Republican,* Dec. 7, 1835. The bricklayers offered their public support, both moral and financial, to the weavers at the end of November. *Republican,* Nov. 25, 1835; David Montgomery, "The Working Classes of the Pre-Industrial American City, 1780–1830," *Labor History* 9 (winter 1968): 10. Such aid was not offered in vain; eventually, the weavers were acquitted. Tomlins, *Law, Labor, and Ideology,* 128n1.

57. *Baltimore Trades' Union,* May 28, 1836. An earlier attempt, Robert Ricketts's the *Mechanic's Banner,* had, like John Weishampel's *Workingmen's Advocate,* apparently folded by this time, after which Ricketts had moved to Washington, D.C.

58. *National Trades' Union,* Feb. 20, 1836; *Baltimore Trades' Union,* May 28, 1836.

consciousness, however, was as much political as economic: the "diversity of interest" which eventuated in constant conflict and "unredressed grievances" was that between "the governing and the governed," not between employer and employee. Linking producerism and artisan republicanism, the author ridiculed the popular argument that America's "productive classes are favored. . . . Republicans enjoy rights, not favors, and it is their right to enjoy the fruits of their own industry, without being compelled to share them with the idle and the domineering." Moreover, it was the right of republican artisans "to abolish that monopoly of wealth which compels the laboring man to place the fruits of his toil at the absolute disposal of the greedy capitalists, and to receive from his hands, as their value, the least share he is willing to leave them." The solution was "to reform, to alter and amend" those "constitutions, or laws, or customs" which were to blame for these inequities.[59]

Articles in the *Baltimore Trades' Union* also described local participation in the National Trades' Union and ongoing efforts to nationalize labor activism.[60] On the national level, Baltimore artisans, including Francis Gallagher, John Dohm, William McCauley, and Richard Marley (cordwainers), Philip Kehoe (carpenter), Daniel Piper, and William Roberts, were active in the creation of the National Trades' Union, and, in 1837, A. I. W. Jackson was elected president of the National Typographical Society.[61] Francis Gallagher's

59. Journeymen's societies listed were printers, cabinetmakers, bricklayers, marble workers, carpet weavers, tin plate and sheet iron workers, cordwainers (both men's and ladies' branches), shipwrights, smiths and machinists, combmakers, tailors, tobacconists, hatters, house carpenters, and cedar coopers. In addition, Joshua Vansant advertised his new hat manufactory, and Stephen Abbot, claiming that he could not find a job at journeymen's wages and asking for the patronage of mechanics, announced the opening of his shoemaking business. *Baltimore Trades' Union*, May 28, 1836. Vansant's hat manufactory was open as early as fall, 1835, and it thrived. *Republican*, Sept. 9, 1835; *Baltimore Saturday Visiter*, 1843. Abbot's venture was not as immediately fortunate; he sought insolvency protection a year and a half later, but by the 1840s he, too, was successful. *Republican*, Dec. 26, 1836.

60. When the National Trades' Union was organized in New York in June 1834, it was estimated that there were 3,500 trade unionists in Baltimore. In comparison, Commons estimated that New York had 11,500 trade unionists; Philadelphia, 6,000; Boston, 4,000; and Washington, D.C., 500. Commons et al., *Documentary History*, 6:191. For a discussion of the approximate number of Jacksonian trade unionists, see Maurice F. Neufeld, "The Size of the Jacksonian Labor Movement: A Cautionary Account," *Labor History* (fall 1982): 599–607. The influence of Baltimore artisans, however, was felt; the National Trades' Union looked, among other things, at the plight of women workers, instigated by the seamstresses strike in Baltimore. Stansell, *City of Women*, 133.

61. John Dohm joined other nationally known cordwainers in a lecture tour of New England in 1835, and William McCauley was present at the last meeting of the national

emergence as a local and national leader during this period was striking. As an eighteen-year-old, Gallagher helped organize the cordwainers during summer 1833 but otherwise was not noticeable in local trade union affairs, perhaps because he was studying law on his own at the time. He had avoided the political confusions of the state elections in 1833 but emerged in late 1835 to serve as a Jacksonian Democrat ward worker. He had also become active in nationwide trade union activities as a founding member of the national cordwainers society, but in 1835 and was prevented from attending their 1836 convention only because Baltimore harbor was closed by ice and overland travel was too expensive. He chaired the meeting of Baltimore artisans when Seth Luther spoke against the Thompsonville Carpet Manufactory and, in his capacity as one of Baltimore's delegates to the national convention, helped write the constitution for the National Trades' Union. In 1837, he assumed editorship of the *Baltimore Trades' Union* from Bull and Tuttle and then ran successfully for the state legislature in October.[62]

Gallagher's increased participation coincided with national efforts to examine the systemic implications of industrial capitalism and to suggest producerist alternatives. As part of his duties for the National Trades' Union, Gallagher, along with Daniel Piper of Baltimore and printer Thomas Hogan of Philadelphia, coauthored an anticapitalist position paper defining the use of paper money and the function of petty bourgeois middlemen in the dilution of producers' profits as examples of "speculation" and rejecting the ethics of accumulation without labor. "Another thing which encourages speculation," they explained, "is the division of the workingmen into employers and journeymen, a system which places the actual operative in a situation that effectually debars him from having a control over his labor,

---

cordwainers' society in 1837. While Philip Kehoe was not explicitly mentioned, Baltimore carpenters sent a delegate to the national organization of carpenters, which met in Philadelphia in October 1836. Another carpenters' convention was to meet in Baltimore in April 1837, but apparently, as a result of the disintegration of the movement in 1837, never did. Commons et al., *Documentary History*, 6:340.

62. Commons et al., *Documentary History*, 6:311–12, 263; *National Trades' Union*, Apr. 16, Oct. 10, Nov. 14, Nov. 21, 1835; *Republican*, Oct. 17, 1835; Scharf, *Chronicles of Baltimore*, 624. When Gallagher went to Annapolis he returned the paper to its previous editors, assuring his readership that Bull and Tuttle were "eminently qualified to make the Trades' Union what it ever should be, the 'TYRANT'S FOE, THE PEOPLE'S FRIEND.'" *Republican*, Nov. 16, 1837. As representative, he worked hard for the abolition of imprisonment for debt; later he participated in the Washingtonian temperance movement, antinativist efforts, the legal defense of the abolitionist Charles Torrey, and as a Union captain, in the Civil War. After the war he became an inspector of customs, never returning to his cordwainer roots. *Sun*, Dec. 11, 1866; Francis Gallagher Papers, MS 2147, Maryland Historical Society, Baltimore.

and gives him no voice in its disposal." They proposed a "Co-operative Trade Associations"; if "the mechanics sold their labor directly to the consumer, speculation would cease, and they would receive a full reward for their labor."[63] This was pure and simple producerism, but not without innovative implications; cooperationism undercut the traditional goal of becoming a master by attaining a competence and denied the ideal of collaboration between artisans and well-intentioned middlemen.

Heeding the call of Gallagher and their own collectivist proclivities,[64] Baltimore's journeymen cabinetmakers opened their own warehouse at the end of May 1837. In doing so, they explained that one year earlier, after long negotiations with employers, the journeymen had reduced their prices on some items by 10 percent and eliminated others altogether. A new price book was then adopted by both parties. In early May, however, employers demanded an immediate 12.5 percent reduction, an action especially galling to journeymen who had given employers weeks to consider their proposals offered in 1836. Not only were these new prices deemed unfair, but they also threatened to impoverish cabinetmakers' wives and children. "We therefore have come to the determination," concluded the journeymen, "to sustain ourselves independently of the employers." Their work, "made of the best materials and workmanship unsurpassed" able to be sold "at reduced prices," proved quite acceptable. The cooperative impulse was not restricted to cabinetmakers, although few of their fellows followed their lead at this time. The journeymen tobacconists solved the problems that had led to public complaints about African-American and nonapprentice labor back in 1833 and their own strike eight months earlier by establishing "The Journeymen Co-operative Tobacco and Segar Factory," which opened in June. And Baltimore's butchers had a long tradition of cooperative efforts. Cooperationism in Baltimore continued to thrive into the 1840s and became one of the producerist hallmarks of nineteenth century labor culture.[65]

63. Gallagher and his friends defined paper money as "the mere representative of the products of labor" and condemned its fluctuations as opportunities for "capitalists" to defraud the worker of "the reward of his industry," thereby opening "a field . . . for speculation." *National Labourer,* Nov. 19, 1836, cited in Commons et al., *Documentary History* 6:291–93; Laurie, *Artisans into Workers,* 89–90. For Thomas Hogan, see Laurie, *Working People of Philadelphia,* 94.

64. The cooperative ideal among Baltimore artisans was in evidence in the example of the United Trade Society of seamstresses in 1834 and was reflected in a report from Lyon, France, where journeymen tailors had united to form "associations in shares" to "thus work on their own account." *Republican,* Jan. 11, 1834.

65. Commons et al., *History of Labour,* 1:483, citing *National Trades' Union,* Apr. 16, 1836; *Republican,* Apr. 21, 1836; May 26, July 8, 1837. The cabinetmakers had also apparently been

Efforts to organize nationally were evident in two strikes in winter 1835–36, one by marble workers and one by carpet weavers. At the end of 1835, marble workers, with the support of the Trades' Union, resisted attempts to reduce their wages. By the end of January 1836, they had been out for several weeks, and a notice appeared in the *National Trades' Union* commending the Baltimore unionists as well as unionized marble workers in Raleigh, North Carolina, who had sent $150 for their support: "we have reason to hope the Journeymen will be sustained, and rescued from the oppression, with which the bosses are attempting to grind them to dust." By February, the Typographical Society was recommending double monthly dues from members of the central union to cover the expenses of the marble workers and, at the next meeting of the WMTU, tobacconists, carpet weavers, printers, cordwainers, and tailors all agreed. At the same time, the carpet weavers turned out; by the end of February they were resisting wage reductions and condemning a recent advertisement for new hands to be hired as scabs at the Baltimore Carpet Factory, the same establishment that had earlier rejected the overtures of the Thompsonville Carpet Company.[66]

The year 1836 was a difficult one for artisan solidarity and producerist unity as Baltimore trade unionists were forced to take steps (such as closing their crafts to outsiders) that tended to alienate public opinion. This was exacerbated by internal dissension within the trade union movement, as some members began to resent WMTU leadership and journeymen began to quarrel among themselves over work. Nevertheless, by April and May, workers in ten trades, including such disparate groups as cordwainers, handloom weavers, bricklayers, blacksmiths, carpenters, and stone masons, struck or threatened to do so, marking the greatest outburst of artisan militancy since summer 1833. Their demands were varied and sometimes

---

threatened by the introduction of unskilled, female labor in an archetypical example of the bastardization of craft; their advertisement announced that work was to be "manufactured by men only." Almost a year after they began their cooperative and reflecting the mutuality of Jacksonian trade unionism, the Society of Journeymen Cabinet Makers, through their agent, William Blass, expressed their thanks for the public's "liberal patronage" of their enterprise, which "far exceeded their most sanguine expectations." *Republican*, Apr. 16, 1838. Matchett's directory for 1840–41 included the location of their warehouse at 10 Gay Street. *Republican*, May 26, June 17, 1837. For a discussion of the butchers' activities, see chap. 6, and for the continued success of cooperationism in the late nineteenth century, see Fones-Wolf, *Trade Union Gospel: Christianity and Labor in Industrial Philadelphia, 1865–1915* (Philadelphia, Temple University Press, 1989), 33 and Laurie, *Artisans into Workers*, 89–90.

66. *National Trades' Union*, Jan. 30, Feb. 6, 20, 1836; *Republican*, Feb. 3, 13, 26, 1836; Gorochow, "Baltimore Labor," 50.

overlapping, with higher wages, ten-hour workdays, and closed shops being paramount. Rationales remained rooted in producerism, and artisans continued to appeal to the public to ostracize scabs, to boycott exploitative masters or capitalists, to contribute to their societies, and to patronize businesses friendly to workers. When the handloom weavers turned out for higher wages, for instance, they assigned for public humiliation a list of "scabby members . . . rotten to the core," including their former president, Gregory Barrett. Even the semiskilled were touched by artisan activism; the wood sawyers announced their demand for higher wages and threatened expulsion for members engaged in underselling the list prices.[67]

In a typical appeal, the blacksmiths cited "the expenses attending the reasonable comforts of a family" as justification for their demand for an increase in wages. Again seeking contributions from the public and appealing to "the bond of Union which ought at all times to exist between the employer and the employed," the aggrieved artisans indicated the extent to which they had embraced the sentiment of deferred gratification so essential to the expansion of a capitalist economy: "those of us that are married are making sure of supporting our families in comfort, and those who are single can with acting prudently save something for the time of marriage, old age, or a sick bed." The carpenters summed up many of these arguments in defending their own strike. Hoping that "the public will give us a hearing; as we are of the positive opinion that they have been influenced by wrong statements of our affairs," the carpenters resorted to the usual explanations of inflation, rising costs, and family responsibilities. Cognizant that they were being "daily assailed as being guilty of injustice towards the employers," they asserted their willingness to negotiate and questioned the relative social value of their employers. "By our labour we live, not on the charity of those monopolizers of labour which (by the bye) do not work one day in a year. . . . They have grown fat on our labour, and now they cry out because they are not stall fed any longer."[68]

In the meantime, the cordwainers, after providing statistics on rises in the cost of living, announced that their wages must also be increased. According to their president Richard Marley, because of "the ready acquiescence of the

67. *National Trades' Union*, Feb., 20, 1837; *Republican*, Feb. 24, Mar. 4, 24, Apr. 2, 21, 25, 26, 28, June 26, 1836. But two months later, when Philadelphia cordwainers struck and the employers asked for cooperation from the Baltimore employers, they were rejected. Commons et al., *Documentary History*, 5:361–67, citing *National Labourer*, June 11, 1836; *Republican*, May 2, 9, 1836.

68. *Republican*, Apr. 28, May 2, 9, 1836.

public," the employers were agreeable to the changes, but soon thereafter many employers began laying off their employees and reducing wages. In order to offset this "determination to still further oppress and grind the already poverty-stricken and over-worked Journeymen," the cordwainers resolved to publish the names of those respecting the new wage rates so that "the public may distinguish between those who wish to 'live and let live' and those who live by entailing a living death on others."[69] This announcement was followed by a list of thirty-seven such producer-oriented employers.

Protecting the ten-hour workday and establishing a closed shop now became primary goals for many Baltimore artisans. In the latter case, maintaining power over membership was not an innovation; Baltimore cabinetmakers and chairmakers in the early nineteenth century demanded that any journeymen new to the city join their society or face sanctions.[70] But the closed shop, as necessary as it might have been to control trades, splintered producerist unity within the artisan community. The inherent restrictiveness of the practice seemed to violate contemporary notions of liberty by refusing opportunities to artisan permanently displaced or temporarily unemployed in related trades. Despite such misgivings, the push for the closed shop reemerged in 1836, starting with the stone masons. By the end of 1835, the stone masons had generally succeeded in establishing the ten-hour day, and they now resisted their masters' attempt to extend working hours. They resolved not to work with any boss or journeymen who did not follow the ten-hour restriction. In this they imitated the bricklayers (who had discussed the idea that none of them would work with any who had not joined their society) and the millwrights (who had refused to work with carpenters in areas they considered their own). Appealing for public support, the stone masons presented their arguments in April 1836 in the *Republican*. The journeymen noted the difficulties in preserving pride in craft and supporting their families in the face of rising inflation, and they complained about the innovations of subcontracting, which permitted wages below the list and allowed incompetent workmen access to the trade at the same time that it "defrauded the employer." They therefore established a closed shop for members, with the proviso that "any old and respectable member of the craft" could work for wages he deemed proper. Along the same lines,

69. *Republican*, Apr. 16, 21, 1836.

70. The WMTU in February 1836 adopted a motion to memorialize Congress in support of the ten-hour day and appointed a committee, including Francis Gallagher, to publish one hundred copies of their ten-hour resolutions. *Republican*, Feb. 29, 1836. For the cabinetmakers, see Tomlins, *Law, Labor, and Ideology*, 141n37.

journeymen bricklayers felt compelled to deny the "rumour in circulation" that they were striking for higher wages and a closed shop for all the building trades. Instead, they asserted, their drive for the closed shop extended only to bricklaying; it was necessary because employers were attempting to crush their union and because many of their fellows were being forced to leave Baltimore and find work elsewhere.[71]

The renewed advocacy for the closed shop did not pass unnoticed in Baltimore. Samuel Harker of the *Republican* expressed his ideas about the appropriate limits to trade union activism, particularly in light of union attempts to establish closed shops and to enforce regulations on their members or fellow workmen. Harker had long been one of the artisan's strongest nonlaboring supporters, and his sympathy for the bank rioters, though understated, was obvious, especially in his publication of the "Junius" letters, yet his allegiance to restrictive union methods had its limits. Affirming the propriety of striking for higher wages to maintain an appropriate standard of living, Harker interpreted the harmony-of-interests ideal in a light favorable to the artisans, calling contrary arguments "perfectly absurd and ridiculous." Enforcing union solidarity and the closed shop were, however, different issues, and Harker rejected such compulsion as "impudent and improper," without offering constructive alternatives to intracraft coercion to prevent the proliferation of "ratting." That nonartisans were less willing to back steps deemed necessary by trade unionists was evident in the claim that mechanics would have to resort to class-inclusive actions to halt further deterioration. Soon thereafter, "A Workingman," who wrote the *Republican* in disgust over the proliferation of "soulless corporations" that made the rich richer and the poor poorer, presented the converse of Harker's qualifications. Citing the difficulties being caused by inflation, he declared that "it will shortly become necessary for the entire body of mechanics and working-men . . . to exert all their power . . . to prevent their sinking into that depth of dependance and servility, which is the fate of . . . operatives in England."[72]

As if the shifting tides of ever-fickle but all-important public opinion were not sufficiently problematic for trade unionists, dissension arose between some journeymen and the trade union leadership in summer 1836. The

71. *Republican*, Feb. 24; Apr. 28, 1836.

72. *Republican*, Feb. 29, Mar. 3, 10, 1836. Harker was responding to a New York *Journal of Commerce* article condemning the strike activities of riggers and stevedores. See Wilentz, *Chants Democratic*, 288. Commons mistakenly attributes this strike to Baltimore ship laborers, probably because of Harker's public discussion of it in the *Republican*. Commons et al., *History of Labour*, 1:483.

cedar coopers were in the midst of a dispute over whether journeymen should be considered "as Rats, real Simon Pure, singed Rats" if they worked for someone not considered "a practical [i.e., practicing] cooper." Their conclusion was to condemn the nonpractical coopers and their "avaricious desires" to "slink into our business" to violate the wage agreements and to dilute the purity of the craft. The editors of the *Baltimore Trades' Union*, in contrast, reflecting the opinions of the central leadership, came down on the side of the nonpractical owners, offering the expedient if ideologically suspect argument that employers unacquainted with the mysteries of the craft necessarily had to hire more journeymen. The journeymen responded with intense irritation. Appealing to "ancient custom," they maintained that they were perfectly capable of determining the parameters of membership for their organization "without the interference of any one, much less the employers at the head of a public journal." This last was a telling shot; increasingly trade union officials were pursuing occupational directions away from their artisanal origins and were therefore, the coopers implied, incapable of relating to journeymen's concerns. And they prefaced their remarks with a significant apology: "to be brief, we are aware that the public in general are nearly tired of so many of our Mechanical controversies."[73] In this last statement, the cedar coopers hit a sensitive nerve even as they revealed a potential weakness within Jacksonian trade unionism: so many appeals had been geared to gain public support, without which producerist militancy would be in trouble.

The public might be tiring of artisan militancy, but there were also hints that Baltimore's artisans were themselves wearying of the struggles of the previous three years. The strikes of summer 1836 were to be the last in Baltimore for years. To be sure, artisan concern over living wages, political representation, and maintenance of producerist ethics manifested itself in a number of other distinctive expressions. But for the trade union movement as a whole, internal conflicts and identity shifts continued to undermine both its militancy and its unity. Evidence of this deterioration emerged during a ship joiners strike that broke out in July. The ship joiners' demands were familiar ones, but they also addressed a new threat. Some desperate house carpenters, presumably still on strike themselves, had accepted employment as strikebreakers.

73. *Baltimore Trades' Union*, May 28, 1836; *Republican*, June 6, July 20, 1836. Examples of the "nonpractical" coopers included those grain millers against whom the journeymen coopers struck in January 1834. The importance of being a "practical" worker was evident in John Curlett's advertisement for his coachmaking establishment (see chap. 1). *Republican*, Oct. 12, 1835.

Such a significant violation of trade union loyalty was no doubt the result of severe economic pressures, but it was also an indication of crumbling unity.[74]

The willingness to abandon essential trade union principles was equally apparent in the reaction (or lack thereof) to the contemporaneous and highly important New York City tailors' strike and the subsequent conspiracy trial in June 1836. Although some (most notably Samuel Harker) advocated the cause of the tailors, Baltimore trade unionists were strangely silent. The trial was followed closely in Baltimore. Harker reported that Judge Ogden Edwards, in his opening charge to the jury, exposed his sympathies by referring to unions as "illegal combinations." Following a quick guilty verdict and the levying of heavy fines, anonymous handbills appeared in New York, which began, "The Rich against the Poor! Judge Edwards, the tool of the Aristocracy, against the People!" and ended sarcastically, "But remember, offer no violence to Judge Edwards! Bend meekly, and receive the chains wherewith you are bound! Keep the peace! Above all things, keep the peace!"[75] Edwards's verdict was significant in its extension of the legal precedents, recently established in trials in Philadelphia and New York, outlawing trade unions as "conspiracies," and it prompted Harker to write: "It is astonishing to what a degree of boldness the petty aristocracy of this country have arrived," but "what is most astonishing is, that the members of the Trades Union in that city should passively look on, and see those rights thus openly trampled upon." Condemning the judge's legal opinions as doctrines that "could be controverted by the merest school boy," Harker continued, "if Judge Edwards imagines the workingmen of this country, to be such ignorant asses as his charge would seem to indicate, he will find himself egregiously mistaken"; any alternative interpretation would necessitate the conclusions "those who have heretofore considered themselves freemen, are nothing but abject slaves." His concluding statement clearly reflected the shifting currents of public opinion and cultural hegemony: "It is surprising that his honor should . . . have imagined that any man could be found sufficiently wanting in common sense to harbor such a doctrine;—yet . . . there is a number."[76]

74. The only strike in the fall was carried out by the journeymen tobacconists. *Republican*, Sept. 14, 1836.

75. *Republican*, June 10, July 20, 1836; *Union*, June 1, 1836, cited in Wilentz, *Chants Democratic*, 291.

76. Tomlins, *State and the Unions*, 36–39; Hattam, *Labor Visions*, 15; *Republican*, June 14, 1836. Harker's uncomplimentary reference to the General Trades' Union of New York City should probably be taken at face value, although there existed within that body a number of Whig partisans, which might have had something to do with Harker's negative presentation of them.

Subsequent articles revealed more about the case and the public's response. Quoting from the *New York Evening Post*, Harker's second editorial on the subject supported the producerist understanding of artisan labor as property ("the only thing which is our own, the cunning of our hands") and the artisans' right to unite as "true brothers" to protect it. The piece, however, also stated the limits of his support of trade union possibilities and reiterated Harker's opposition to the closed shop. Harker's third editorial, "Infallibility of Courts," pointed out the social dangers of legal partiality toward the wealthy. Most of this article was devoted to Jacksonian populist rhetoric, and, in conclusion, he addressed the penultimate adjudicator: "There is a higher tribunal to which all must bend; and that tribunal is the cool and deliberate exercise of public opinion among an intelligent and free people," the decisions of which "must ultimately be obeyed."[77]

Interestingly enough, Harker's was the only public voice in Baltimore to back the New York tailors. In contrast to the supportive reaction of the WMTU to the Thompsonville Carpet Weavers less than a year earlier, the central trade union did not address the implications of this verdict. Instead, on the day that Harker's editorial condemning Judge Edwards's antiunionism appeared, WMTU leaders—Francis Gallagher, Richard Marley, Philip Adams, and others—issued a notice entitled "Knowledge Is Power" announcing the establishment of "a society for the diffusion of useful knowledge." The juxtaposition of these events may have been purely coincidental.[78] In light of the internal tensions between the trade union leadership and some of the journeymen, as expressed by the cedar coopers, and in conjunction with subsequent developments, a trend within the trade union leadership toward educated respectability and away from the producerist concerns of journeymen can be discerned. For years the Baltimore Lyceum had discussed issues relevant to an informed small producer audience including: "Are storekeepers justified in asking a higher wage for their goods than the lowest they intend asking?" "Is it expedient that an Assize of bread should be established by law in our city?" "Does law operate as powerfully as the fear of punishment in a future state in deterring men from the commission of a crime?" "Ought

77. *Republican*, June 17, 18, 1836. Harker's sarcasm toward the decision did not quickly die. When the local auctioneers "combined" to withdraw advertisements from the *Republican* and other Baltimore papers for some perceived slight, Harker suggested invoking Judge Edwards's law to restore his lost advertising income. *Republican*, July 2, 1836.

78. Lacking the appropriate issues of the *Baltimore Trades' Union*, there is no way to know the trade unionists' response to the conspiracy decision. Philadelphia trade unionists, on the other hand, went on public record to denounce Judge Edwards and his decision. Hattam, *Labor Visions*, 61–62, 90–91.

Temperance Societies to discourage the use of fermented as well as distilled liquors?" and "Ought the present banking system be suffered to continue?"[79] Locally controlled, voluntarist lyceums played a key role in the transmission of modern, scientifically informed popular culture for the comfortable middling classes.[80]

The new Society for the Diffusion of Useful Knowledge (SDUK) in Baltimore seemed designed to resemble more closely the calm discussion and hyperrational ambiance of the lyceum than the high energy and moral outrage of the union organizational meetings of 1833. Bruce Laurie has described Philadelphia's similar Society for the Diffusion of Useful Knowledge as "the major educative auxiliary" of the General Trades' Union and interprets them as evidence of "self-improvement, radical style."[81] In Baltimore, however, the founding group—despite the presence of Francis Gallagher, Richard Marley, and Philip Adams—included a high percentage of men who had not been previously identified with the trade union movement. Nowhere was this embrace of respectability more clear than in the announcements a few months after the establishment of the SDUK for the "Grand Mechanical Fancy Ball," sponsored by almost every prominent member of the WMTU, including Gallagher, Jackson, Bull, Tuttle, Mass, Vansant, Marley, Piper, and more than one hundred "managers." The purpose was to raise money for the Institution for the Diffusion of Useful Knowledge among the Working Classes, tickets were $2.00 (two days' pay for many workers), and an "efficient police" was guaranteed. Close to two thousand attended, and the evening was judged to be "of universal splendour and of rare enjoyment."[82] But the affair was a far cry from the craft-oriented parades and artisan celebrations of the previous decade.

79. *Republican*, Mar. 2, 30, Apr. 7, 27, June 30, 1837.

80. Russell B. Nye, *Society and Culture in America, 1830–1860* (New York: Harper and Row, 1974), 246, 360–61; Donald M. Scott, "The Popular Lecture and the Creation of a Public in Mid-Nineteenth-Century America," *Journal of American History* 66 (1980): 801, 809.

81. Laurie, *Working People of Philadelphia*, 100–101.

82. *Republican*, Feb. 4, 18, 22, 1837. This type of phenomenon among American trade unionists was noted sixty years later by Friedrich Engels: "It is remarkable, but quite natural, how firmly rooted are bourgeois prejudices even in the working class in such a young country which has never known feudalism and have grown up on a bourgeois basis from the beginning." Engels quoted in DeLeon, *American As Anarchist*, 103. Among artisans and their sympathizers, the precedent for the Grand Fancy Mechanical Ball had been set by a similar benefit held by the paternalists supportive of the United Seamstresses Society. *Republican*, Jan. 27, 1836. The drift away from journeymen-focused trade unionism was also evident in the memorial parade honoring recently deceased former president James Madison on August 22, 1836, organized by union leaders A. I. W. Jackson, Samuel Mass, and John Warner Niles;

The difficulties of the trade union movement in the face of increasingly ambivalent public support, weakening devotion to rank-and-file militancy, and the allure of respectability among the leadership was accompanied by renewed artisan political activity. After the debacle of "workingmen's" candidacies in fall 1833, Baltimore's artisans had eschewed overt political participation in order to preserve the unity of the trade union cause.[83] But in fall 1836, the journeymen and master weavers of Baltimore began to reconsider the efficacy of political solutions to their continued opposition to penitentiary labor. In the customary explanation of their underlying motives, the weavers, "oppressed and injured by the grievances which they long patiently have borne . . . in duty to themselves and their families," desired "to lay their cause of complaint before the public." They explained how prices charged by penitentiary officials for their convict-produced goods undercut their livelihoods and degraded the status of their occupation.[84] Their protectionism, however, had limits. The weavers embraced competition with "honest men"; if such "can undersell us we have no objections; fair play is bonny play." In a sarcastic digression reflecting populist disdain for professionals, the weavers pointed out that the practice was not only unfair, but also discriminatory: "we can see no reason why reformed forgers, robbers, or murderers should not be transformed into lawyers and doctors as well as into shoemakers and weavers." More seriously, the respondents promised "to agitate this subject in a lawful manner until every voter in the state becomes thoroughly acquainted with it." Most remarkably, the communication was signed by Richard Whiteworth Jr., son of the master weaver whose unilateral

Jacksonian politicians; and leaders in the Society for the Diffusion of Useful Knowledge and addressed by Methodist Protestant (now chaplain of the United States Senate) Thomas Stockton. *Republican,* July 4, 7, Aug. 11, 23, 1836.

83. Commons et al., *Documentary History,* 5:213. Baltimore's workingmen were fully cognizant of their precarious political situation and the limits to which their concerns were to be addressed in the state legislature. Thus, the granite stone cutters and masons, in condemning the employment of convicts from the Maryland penitentiary in their trade, had earlier resolved, "That the fruitless attempts before the Legislature of Maryland to procure the abolition of the 'system' gives little cause to hope for a favourable issue before that body,—coming as the major part do, from sections of the state, where the voice of the Mechanic is faint, and little heeded," because of the predominance of agricultural interests. *Republican,* July 24, 1835.

84. *Republican,* Oct. 29, 1836. The Cuban visitor Don Ramon de la Sagra described this allegedly profitable operation in June 1835. "In Baltimore, the prisoners work in large groups but there are rules of silence. There are large workshops under the surveillance of employees and directed by construction workers. . . . Each prisoner is assigned to a particular job. If he finishes his assigned duty, he may work for wages of three cents per yard of woven material. Working hours are from dawn to sunset." Carroll, "Botanist's Visit to Baltimore," 53–54.

wage reductions sparked the weavers' strike in 1829, and James McElroy and Samuel Miles, two of the journeymen arrested and acquitted in the court case stemming from that strike.[85]

Resort to political solutions was by no means restricted to artisan issues; the most compelling issue in October 1836 was the proposed reform of the Maryland constitution to more accurately represent population distribution in the state. Ironically, this activity was an initial point of unification for Baltimore politicos regardless of party affiliation, since Baltimore's 80,000 white residents had only two representatives while Calvert County's 8,000 had four. The Maryland Whigs were in control and opposed reform, so Democrats had a tailor-made issue. At "the largest meeting of the Mechanics and Workingmen ever convened in the City of Baltimore," called by ornamental painter and druggist John Seidenstricker in late September 1836, a group of journeymen leaders and friendly masters urged workingmen to suspend normal work in order to vote for reform candidates in the upcoming election.[86]

The published resolutions of this meeting explained the antidemocratic nature of Maryland's political structure. Much attention was also paid to the opposition's attempt to brand the Reformers as politically radical ("Jacobins") and socially dangerous ("Destructives"), the specific argument being that reform sympathizers were known "to excite discord in the relations of employer and employed." Claiming that "peace, order, and general prosperity are as desirable to us as to any other class of citizens," the mechanics' representatives added: "We solemnly disclaim having ever been moved to make the relation of the employer and the employed a source of social strife."[87] The trade unionists realized their dilemma: in order to maintain public support for trade unionism and to achieve their union-oriented political goals, they would have to publicly disavow working-class exclusivity and any form of militancy that might lead to violence. Without hesitation, the trade union leadership made that step.

The implications of this decision were not immediately apparent; in fact, the political fortunes of the workingmen seemed to be improving. With their help, the reform candidate triumphed in October 1836, and the next year

85. *Republican*, Oct. 29, 1836.

86. *Republican*, Oct. 1, 1836. Leaders of this meeting included (again) master hatter John Warner Niles, master tin plate worker John Potter Jr., and veteran trade unionists Francis Gallagher, Richard Marley, A. I. W. Jackson, J. J. Johnson, and Philip Kehoe, as well as a number of newcomers to the cause.

87. *Republican*, Oct. 1, 1836.

activist artisans were guaranteed representation, as union regular Francis Gallagher (a cordwainer and Democrat) was running against fellow union leader Philip Adams (a hatter and Whig) for the Baltimore seat in the state legislature. Gallagher enjoyed the support of A. I. W. Jackson and other WMTU leaders, as well as state representative Beale Richardson (local merchant, Methodist Protestant layman, and leader of the anti-indemnification efforts in the wake of the bank riot) who, in concert with Gallagher, organized and presided over a massive public meeting condemning the suspension of specie payments by local banks and backing "hard money." Adams, in contrast, was supported by John Millington, a Baltimore Typographical Society stalwart and WMTU leader and other union supporters of Clay's American System. The race was tight, with Gallagher prevailing 5,497 to 5,374.[88] Baltimore artisans finally had their representative in the state legislature.

The nature of that victory and its ideological implications for Baltimore trade unionism were made clear in Francis Gallagher's victory speech. He opened with a denial of the inherent necessity of class conflict: "It is not by keeping up an eternal war between employers and journeymen that our condition is to be bettered. If any man believes that all the evils which the workingmen suffer are heaped upon them by their employers, he is egregiously deceived. . . . True there may be many employers . . . who have rendered themselves obnoxious by their tyranical [*sic*] conduct to men in their employ, and by repeated and successful attempts to reduce the wages of their hands." Gallagher's solution, however, differed from what he and others had espoused in the recent past: "If the workingmen desire to ameliorate their condition, . . . they should look well into the principles of those into whose hands they intrust [*sic*] the power of making laws for the nation." The problem was that the government had hitherto been under control "of those 'drones of society,' who monopolize and fatten upon the products of honest industry." Until trade unionists succeeded in throwing off such monopolists, "the producing classes will struggle in vain for that station in society to which the 'laws of nature and of nature's God entitle them.'" But when friends of the workingman become legislators and overthrow by legislation "the moneyed aristocracy," the goals of the trades' union would be realizable. In commenting favorably on Gallagher's speech, the *National Labourer*, (the organ of Philadelphia's trade union movement) concluded that when "the laws are in fault . . . the radical remedy must come through

88. *Republican*, May 31, Oct. 2, 1837; *Sun*, May 30, 1837; *Republican*, Oct. 5, 1837.

our Legislative Halls."[89] By late 1837, at least for trade union leaders like Gallagher, artisan militancy and public allegiance to producerist tenets were no longer espoused as solutions to capitalist dislocation. Even trade unionism itself was seemingly passe. The American political system was now seen to provide the means to protect and favor the respectable artisan element.[90]

Historians of Jacksonian labor movements have long maintained that the panic of 1837 and subsequent economic depression effectively extinguished the vitality of trade unionism just as it was on the brink of significant success.[91] They have also asserted that social realities accompanying the depression disrupted a powerful sense of class consciousness and militancy among American artisans. The Baltimore experience, however, suggests some important modifications of this picture. Baltimore's working men and women in the years 1833 through 1837, to be sure, relied on strikes and organizational solidarity in collective opposition to their increasingly degraded socioeconomic circumstances resulting from industrialization and capitalism. In spite of the fact that they early on recognized the structured inequality inherent in capitalist relations, only on isolated occasions did they identify themselves as a class with distinctive productive characteristics and interests. More often, they tried to maintain their allegiance to populist producerism, centered on the corporatist ideal of a harmony of class interests.[92] As a result, they depended heavily on the moral and economic support of favorably intentioned masters and employers, whose financial expectations were grounded in an ethic of limited accumulation and on the ethically informed consumer decisions of the public, which made sense in the face-to-face context of traditional community experience. But this mode of exchange was seriously threatened by urban and industrial developments in Jacksonian America. This process of modernization may have been slower in Baltimore than in New York or Philadelphia, but by the late 1830s it had definitely matured.

If public opinion was a key to artisan success, so were the assumptions sustaining it. As the culture shifted ideologically from classical republicanism

89. *National Labourer*, Oct. 28, 1837; *Republican*, Nov. 16, 1837.

90. Hattam, *Labor Visions*, 106–10.

91. See, e.g., Laurie, *Artisans into Workers*, 91, 214–15.

92. Although Christopher Tomlins asserts that this producerist consciousness did not arise until the middle of the nineteenth century, it seems well established in the Baltimore Jacksonian labor movement. Tomlins, *Law, Labor, and Ideology*, 9.

to liberalism, as industrial capitalism expanded, as urban exigencies depersonalized social relations, and as consumer demands for the lowest prices replaced concern for the livelihoods of artisans, the efficacy of appeals to producerism waned in key areas. Nor was this the only challenge to artisan producerism and militancy. The increased fear of social anarchy, especially as unleashed in 1834,[93] made the public more suspicious of readjustments from the bottom up and more amenable to centralized authority and social control by the powerful. In Baltimore this shift was almost imperceptible, yet dramatic—the strikes of 1836, despite repeated appeals and explanations, received significantly less public support than those of 1833, as the public's fear, in the aftermath of the bank riot and years of trade union tension, shifted from tyranny to anarchy. Equally important in the demise of trade union solidarity was the exaltation of individual opportunity over communal welfare, a part of the liberal ethos. Thus, public suspicion of the ten-hour day, the closed shop, and cooperationism should be interpreted as responses protective of the sanctity of individual rights. The sentiment expressed by Jesse Hunt in August 1833 in response to the initial ten-hour movement—"it is . . . the undoubted right of every individual to determine the number of hours which shall constitute his day's labour"—was gaining wider acceptance.[94]

This emerging crisis of confidence in the efficacy of labor confrontations—based on producerist commonality between employers and employees—was compounded by dissensions within the trade union movement. The gulf between trade union leadership and the journeymen was widening, as evidenced by the conflict between the cedar coopers and the editors of the *Baltimore Trades' Union.* By 1837, most of those activists who had remained

93. Thomas Branagan made note of the phenomenon of urban atomization, developing along socioeconomic lines and preceding suburbanization separation. "It often happens that next door neighbors in this city are such strangers to social intercourse, as not to speak to one another for years, especially if one is rich and the other poor." Branagan, *Serious Remonstrances,* 98. For discussions of the anxieties making riots and other social disruptions understandable, see Edward Pessen, "We Are All Jeffersonians, We Are All Jacksonians: or A Pox on Stultifying Periodizations," *Journal of the Early American Republic* 1 (spring 1981): 1–26; Prince, "Great 'Riot Year,'" 1–19. The tendency for this upheaval to generate appeals to restrictive solutions was reflected in the fears of Hezekiah Niles, a supporter of laborite activity in the early 1830s. "Does it not appear that the character of our people has suffered a considerable change for the worse? . . . We fear that the moral sense of right and wrong has been rendered less sensitive than it was." *Niles' Weekly Register,* Aug. 23, 1834, quoted in Prince, "Great 'Riot Year,'" 3–4.

94. *Republican,* Aug. 21, 1833. For similar (though often indecipherable) sentiments, see J. J. Roach's advertisement whereby, under the slogan "Free Trade and Sailors Rights," he presented "his claims . . . in free competition for the superior execution of House, Sign, Transparent, and Ornamental PAINTING, at the cheapest rates for CASH." *Sun,* Aug. 17, 1843.

journeymen had disappeared from leadership positions and most union officials were no longer actively engaged in artisan work. Francis Gallagher had become a lawyer and politician; Edmund Bull, an editor; John Seidenstricker, a druggist and city councilman; and Samuel Mass, a real estate agent. Among the hatters, Joshua Vansant had become a master hatter, soon-to-be postmaster, and successful politician, and Philip Adams had likewise embraced politics, while John H. W. Hawkins had not only dropped out of trade union leadership but had also been forced into bankruptcy, as had the unsuccessful mayoral candidate Moses Davis. In addition, technological innovations and shrinking economic opportunities turned some artisans against others, as evidenced by the tension between the ship joiners and house carpenters in 1836. By late 1836, the usual announcements of union contributions to other unions on strike, so prevalent in response to earlier turnouts, had disappeared. Even the labor press was under pressure, about to be dislocated by competition from the penny press, which appealed to the workers both in price and in perspective.[95]

By the end of 1837—a year when the only associated efforts to resist decreased opportunities to attain competences came from nascent restaurateurs and when the defenders of the hard-fisted mechanics regaled themselves at a "grand fancy ball"—the possibilities of militant, producerist correctives to economic abuses seemed far removed from the heady days of summer 1833, when the master hatters had been forced, through the combination of artisan solidarity and public support, to back down from their reduction of journeymen's wages. Although the economic disaster following the panic of 1837 made the continuation of trade union success less than likely, trade union leadership had already begun to retreat from the implications of class struggle inherent in the system of industrial capitalism. This is not to say that their efforts had been in vain. In refusing to participate in the sanctification of acquisitive accumulation that was to mark the expansion of capitalism, they maintained the moral oppositionalism of producerism. Thus, while

95. *Republican,* July 20, 1835. *Republican,* Sept. 9, 1836. The appearance of the *Sun,* a penny daily, in Baltimore in May 1837, proved to undercut the popularity and influence of the workers' press. Avowedly apolitical and opposed to religious controversy, the *Sun* proposed to foster "the moral and intellectual improvement of the labouring classes." It maintained sympathies with artisan concerns and continued to employ republican rhetoric to critique conditions but took few controversial stands and contributed to the creation of an amorphous popular culture rejecting class consciousness and promoting the viability of industrial innovations. Harold A. Williams, *The Baltimore Sun: 1837–1987* (Baltimore: Johns Hopkins Press, 1987), 6, 13, 16; Frank Luther Mott, *American Journalism: A History of Newspapers in the United States Through 260 Years, 1690 to 1950* (New York: MacMillan, 1950), 240–43.

their movement temporarily disintegrated, they provided the grounds for later labor critiques as well as a legacy of worker militancy. In the late 1830s, Baltimore's artisans turned their attention and energies to survival in the wake of the expansion of industrial capitalism; when economic conditions improved in 1843, they proved quite capable of reasserting themselves in opposition. By then, however, their socioeconomic circumstances had dramatically changed and so had the culture they were helping to negotiate.

The Legacy of Evangelical Artisan Culture in the 1840s

Chapter Six

Evangelical Involvement in Trade Unionism and Factory Preaching in Baltimore

At the height of WMTU organizing in 1834, the local organ of evangelical Lutheranism published an article taken from the *Trades' Union* entitled "Trade Societies." The article published in the *Lutheran Observer* began with an explanation of the ethical necessity of union formation and discipline: "Justice between man and man requires that every trade should have a society for the support of prices. In all trades, whether they have such societies or not, every man who works for less than the usual prices is sure to incur disgrace; and any person who happens to lose his situation, after having worked under price, finds it a difficult matter to procure another, as his offended fellow workingmen use every effort to keep such a dangerous person out of the shop in which they work." Recognizing the difficulty this placed on bread-winners responsible for their families' well-being, the author of the article asked, "Why not form societies to sustain the prices and to raise funds to support those who have to stand out for that purpose?" The article continued, "Unions of the members of a trade, and Union of Trades, is the only means by which an adequate compensation can be secured. When the members of any trade are disunited, each man must depend upon his own resources, and contend single handed against wealth and power, and will be in almost every case defeated." It concluded, "As trades societies and trades unions are intended to secure to the working classes an adequate compensation for their labor, . . . [the] only way that these institutions can be injured is by neglect; therefore the workingman who refuses to join is virtually their enemy."[1]

In spite of modern assertions to the contrary, this straightforward evangelical support for trade unionism should come as no surprise. The involvement of editor and minister Benjamin Kurtz in support of Baltimore's organizing artisans is particularly instructive. Kurtz's evangelical Lutheran congregation met on Sunday mornings in Trades' Union Hall, and pews were free to encourage social leveling within the congregation. In addition, his paper enjoyed the endorsement of Baltimore's labor press, with the *Mechanic's Banner* commenting favorably on the affordability of the *Lutheran Observer.* The prolabor *Baltimore Saturday Visiter* and the *Methodist Protestant* were equally supportive of the religious newspaper.[2] But as significant as this mutual support between evangelicals and trade unionists was, what the article lacked—theological critiques of the capitalist practices necessitating protective unionism and demands for a more righteous system protecting the producerist prerogatives of artisans—was equally important in the subsequent evolution of populist evangelical response to capitalist transformation in Baltimore.

The competition between producerist tradition and capitalist innovation during the years from 1833 to 1837, when the Working Men's Trades' Union flourished and faded in Baltimore, was emblematic of the volatility of American society in the Jacksonian period. Besides the protective efforts of trade unionists in the face of industrial capitalist encroachments, other work-related issues emerged: organized opposition to slavery, immigrant competition for semiskilled and unskilled jobs, and political disagreements over legislation regarding alcohol consumption and Sabbath-breaking. These tensions were part of the ongoing negotiation of a liberal republican culture in America that sought to balance individual freedom and non-dependency with communal welfare, and they eventually disrupted the most prominent American bonds of union in the mid-nineteenth century: religious denominations first and then political parties. These disagreements were more pronounced because evangelicals believed, on the one hand, that they had been empowered partly in order to hold American society morally accountable but they realized, on the other, that the separation of

1. *Lutheran Observer,* Apr. 4, 1834.
2. *Republican,* Apr. 30, 1834; *Lutheran Observer,* Apr. 11, 1834.

church and state had limited their access to control. Evangelicals had to reconcile the tenacious legacy of Calvinist hegemony with the fragmenting realities of disestablishment.

But the political powerlessness of disestablished American churches coupled with evangelical determination to remain a privileged arbiter of public values was only part of the problem; equally difficult was the evangelical commitment to reach consensus on disruptive socioeconomic issues. As some Protestants condemned as sinful the tyranny of slavery, the potential licentiousness of individualism, and the dependency compelled by capitalist accumulation of power, others constructed biblical rationales for paternalistic slave-holding ethics, philanthropic organizations to achieve social control, and industrious entrepreneurial efforts. For Baltimore artisans, these contradictions were most evident in the coopers' strike of January 1834, when militant journeymen constructed their appeal for community support in the strict and judgmental language of an Old Testament prophet and ambitious masters answered with the loose and creative interpretation of a New Testament parable. In often unsuccessful attempts to forestall schism and maintain influence, both national denominations and local congregations often tried to preserve their fragile unities by glossing over the causes and circumstances of economic exploitation and by preoccupying themselves with spiritual issues of conversion and individual holiness. Yet centrifugal forces persisted. In addition, and despite the danger such turmoil presented to Protestant unity, the spiritual energy of evangelical conversion continued to manifest itself in a broad range of activist politics and reform efforts, from the potentially revolutionary (the American Antislavery Society) to the possibly ludicrous (the National Truss Society for the Relief of the Ruptured Poor).[3] Such activism precipitated a Presbyterian split in 1837 over Arminianized revivalism and slavery and caused the Methodists and Baptists to follow suit in 1844 over the latter issue alone. It should come as no surprise that revivalist empowerment—the very antithesis of the quiescent and piously docile attitudes that have been attributed to evangelical workers by modern historians—continued to inform evangelical artisan opposition to capitalist social relations.[4] But if populist evangelicalism was not the collective embodiment of pious docility, neither was it always working-class radicalism

3. Carwardine, *Evangelicals and Politics,* 14–29; Marsden, *Evangelical Mind,* 17–21; Howe, "Evangelical Movement," 1222–23.

4. The unfortunate term "pious docility" comes from Johnson, *Shopkeeper's Millennium,* 120; see Sutton, "Tied to the Whipping Post," 261–65. Bruce Laurie recognizes the limits of this assumption by the 1840s and 1850s. Laurie, *Working People of Philadelphia,* 168–87.

unleashed. A third and middle way was equally available: evangelical activism was capable of generating bottom-up reforms aimed at abuses accompanying modernization. Although these populist alternatives were less oppositional than evangelical producerist militancy, they should not be seen as outright accommodation to capitalist culture and liberal hegemony.[5] They were instead the results of the creative collective agency of populist evangelicals intent on carving out viable social spaces for themselves.

Evangelicals could as easily engage the world to transform it as they could withdraw from the world to escape it, and in the Jacksonian period, they were more likely to choose the latter. The essence of revival conversion was the sublimation of the individual self to the presence and authority of a personal God who promised temporal as well as eternal blessing and demanded holy action. In the process of this liminal event, cultural rules and expectations that had determined individual and social perceptions of reality were shattered. Divine affirmation brought spiritual consolations and otherworldly transcendence to bear on difficult life situations, to be sure, but spiritual anarchy, of course, was not the desired result. Neither was resignation to the evils of a fallen world; in fact, such quietism was antithetical to the evangelical preoccupation with social reform. In the early nineteenth century, disciplined resistance to ungodly authority and the creation of alternative communities to meliorate unjust social conditions were more prevalent than passive acceptance of injustice as part of God's inscrutable will.[6] Like artisans confronted with capitalist transformation, evangelical converts seeking to engage disestablishment realities encountered a contested range of moral possibilities. The similar responses of both groups indicated areas of compatibility between trade union and congregation-building experience.

At a primary level, the success of both trade unions and disestablished congregations necessitated voluntary subordination of the individual to the whole, a premise that pervaded republican rhetoric, producerist tradition, and conversion experience. In fact, the very values central to evangelical congregational growth—self-discipline, character-building, deferred gratification, ethical economic behavior, and consideration of the larger good—proved necessary to the rise and continuation of the trade union movement in the

5. Harry G. Lefever, "The Religion of the Poor: Escape or Creative Force?" *Journal for the Scientific Study of Religion* 16 (1977): 225–36.

6. Christopher Lasch, in his excellent discussion of William James's seminal *Varieties of Religious Experience*, explores these conversion themes. Lasch, *True and Only Heaven*, 282–95, esp. 291–92.

1830s. The fluid nature of American social philosophy in this period also revealed elements of producerist culture common to emergent middling-class values. The emphasis on frugality, industry, and punctuality—so often described as "industrial morality" imposed from above—was endemic not only to the trade union movement but to much of the "respectable" artisan culture itself.[7] In essence, such habits were necessary for survival in an open and unregulated economic system. As Thomas Laqueur has noted in his study of British working-class Sunday Schools in the nineteenth century, these values, while helpful in the rise of factory exploitation, were understandable apart from that phenomenon and, as survival skills, were almost necessary reactions to the larger historical process of modernization.[8] Thus, the trade unions and evangelical congregations were both shaped by the voluntaristic nature of American institution formation, which necessitated a high level of self-discipline and group consciousness. Although the salvation of individuals dominated the revivalist agenda, the goals of traditional economic morality and the perspectives of populist producerism remained open possibilities for the social agenda.[9] As such, even as easy accessibility to power and respectability in the Jacksonian period helped reduce the potential for radical evangelical antagonism to liberal culture, evangelical artisans experienced no dissonance when joining craft organizations and trade unions in order to maintain producerist morality and to resist the dislocations of industrial capitalism.[10]

7. In this light, Baltimore printers insisted that their members "discountenance all vice and immorality" and exhibit "a spirit of industry and fidelity." *Constitution of the Baltimore Typographical Society*, 6. Similarly, Philadelphia journeymen carpenters declared, "Temperance and moderation are true requisites for carrying into effect any design or plan which may be contemplated." *Constitution and By-Laws of the Journeymen House Carpenters Association of the City and County of Philadelphia* (Philadelphia, 1837), 3. For the contemporary trade unionist affinity for elements of "industrial morality" and "radical rectitude," see "The Importance of Punctuality," *National Trades' Union*, Oct. 11, 1834.

8. In discussing working-class Sunday schools, Thomas Laqueur writes, "If there was a certain mechanistic quality about their discipline and an aggressive commitment to the puritan virtues, it was not because of the school's specific relationship with factory owners or other managers of large-scale enterprise. It was because both the school and the factory were part of the same stage of historical development in which it was, and is, more difficult to maintain humanistic values." Laqueur, *Religion and Respectability*, 227.

9. Mathews, "Methodist Ideology," in Richey and Rowe, eds., *Rethinking Methodist History*, 94–95; Howe, "Evangelical Movement," 1235–39. The problematic relation between evangelicalism and the "core values" of the new republic are discussed in Hanley, *Beyond a Christian Commonwealth*, and Dee Andrews, "The People and the Preachers at St. George's: An Anatomy of a Methodist Schism," in Richey and Rowe, eds., *Rethinking Methodist History*, 131.

10. The general friendliness of the labor press from 1834 to 1836 to populist evangelicalism was evident in the pages of the *National Trades' Union*. The paper regularly reported on religious news related to trade unionism, employed biblical themes in their puns, printed

Evangelical artisans defined themselves according to two compatible but separate identities. They were proud producers in the purest sense, and perfectly capable of identifying and resisting exploitation at points of production, but they were also committed to spiritual experience deeper than market-driven economics. In addition, the evangelical movement's ambivalence toward the socioeconomic values of liberal capitalism coupled with its reliance on the hefty financial support of those who benefited from capitalist innovations helped minimize the potential within populist evangelical circles for class-inclusive perceptions. And while conflict related to capitalist development was a constant possibility, conceptualizations of a distinctive working-class consciousness (at this point embryonic at best) were unnecessary, especially for those, like evangelical artisans, with dual identities.[11] Rather than developing into full-blown class-defined antagonism, the oppositional impulse for evangelical producers often became the creation of alternative, godly structures for converted individuals within secular society, in keeping with the age-old evangelical insistence on being "in the world but not of it." The establishment of artisan-dominated congregations became a focal point of this impulse in Jacksonian Baltimore. Two equally significant paradigms of congregation formation existed: one stemmed from the indigenous revivalism generated by evangelical artisans within their own localities, and the other emanated from external missionary outreach into worker neighborhoods and outlying factory areas.[12] In both cases, artisans exercised individual and collective agency in determining the nature of these institutions and in developing populist-oriented responses to the emerging society. Evangelical artisans, in short, developed programs—neither quiescent nor revolutionary—to address and fulfill their own class-inclusive agendas.

Nowhere were these ambiguities more obvious than in Baltimore Methodism. Charles Steffen has suggested that many Methodisms existed in early

---

evangelical-informed critiques of capitalism, and advertised works of John Calvin as well as radical producerist writings like William Cobbett's *Twelve Sermons* and Jesse Torrey's *The Moral Instructor. National Trades' Union*, July 5, Aug. 30, Oct. 4, 1834; Jan. 3, Feb. 21, July 11, Nov. 1, 1835; Jan. 30, 1836. Torrey's work, which included within its pages Cotton Mather's "Essay to Do Good," elicited widespread endorsements, with one reader commenting, "I find nothing in it to offend the strictest sectarian in religion or politics." *National Trades' Union*, Feb. 28, 1835.

11. John Ashworth, *Slavery, Capitalism, and Politics in the Antebellum Republic* (New York: Cambridge University Press, 1995), 13.

12. For a helpful discussion of the influence and formation of American congregations in the nineteenth century, see Holifield, "Toward a History of American Congregations," in Wind and Lewis, eds., *American Congregations*, 2:23–53.

national Baltimore, and in the sense that a variety of contradictory social and religious impulses coexisted within Methodism, he is on target.[13] More accurately for Baltimore Methodists, however, was the collective conviction there was to be only one Methodism, in order to maintain the integrity and viability of their revered institution. Thus, they necessarily rejected any socially exclusivist impulse, including working-class consciousness. As an anonymous contributor to *Mutual Rights and Methodist Protestant* suggested: "to promote . . . the gospel of peace," all evangelicals, "where circumstances will possibly admit," should "adjust and settle any difficulties which may occur in the transaction of business by a fair and mutual arbitration" without recourse to lawyers [he could have as easily said "labor militancy"] which tends "to spoil the quiet and comfort of society as well as religious life."[14] These realities, however, did not mean that social class conflict among evangelicals disappeared; although the Methodist Protestant schism was primarily a contest over power among rising but still middling-class groups, "class" tensions were clearly evident, both in the populist uprising itself and in subsequent discussions establishing the new denomination.

Such tensions within Baltimore Methodism were also apparent in the formation and development of the Columbia Avenue Methodist Episcopal Church in the early 1840s. The members of this congregation came from an area in west Baltimore bounded by Columbia, Paca, Cove, and Pratt streets. Part of the middling-class Eleventh Ward, the neighborhood was a mix of residential dwellings, small shops, a new chemical works, brickyards, and slaughtering grounds. Except for a church, all elements of artisan culture were present in the area, including the tavern, "the Beehive," whose sign proudly advertised:

In this hive we're all alive
And whiskey makes us merry.

The Fayette Street Church was the closest Methodist congregation, but it was relatively distant and preoccupied with internal matters. Thus, Methodists living near Columbia Avenue decided to petition the local Methodist

13. Steffen, *Mechanics of Baltimore,* 253. In covering the broad spectrum of Methodist responses to metropolitan industrialization, Steffen assumes that Methodism attracted masters because of "its condemnation of such social discord as striking and labor militancy." Ibid., 253. Yet Steffen cites (and I have found) no evidence to corroborate that claim.

14. *Mutual Rights and Methodist Protestant* 1 (Jan. 14, 1831): 9; Lazerow, "Spokesmen for the Working Class," 352–53.

hierarchy for the establishment of a new congregation. Initially they were rebuffed by the Baltimore City Station, but the laboring-class Methodists were not to be denied. By 1840, congregants had built a meeting room and a Sunday School building, and soon the City Station was supplying the new congregation, as a mission, with a steady stream of local itinerants.[15]

The new congregation thrived, but its members chafed under their subordinate status as a mission and finally withdrew from the City Station to be supplied by the larger District Conference. The conference sent the Reverend John Guyer (a vigorous revivalist who apparently emphasized "the wrath to come" over the joys of salvation) with less than stellar results. While Guyer was absent for a time, however, members instigated a "notable revival," which lasted throughout winter 1841–42. Among those leading the revival were Conduce Gatch (the B & O's master carpenter and Methodist class leader), Lewis Kalbfus (morocco dresser), Daniel M. Reese, (revivalist, local small officeholder, and Jacksonian ward leader), and Columbus J. Stewart (blacksmith). Stewart, characterized in reminiscences as loving the Bible and "being plain of speech and not offended by it," was a significant participant. A few years earlier he had been one of the blacksmiths and machinists who had publicly refused to work more than ten hours daily.[16]

The Columbia Street revival was typical of populist evangelicalism in the Second Great Awakening. Night after night, according to contemporary accounts, "the cry of the penitent was commingled with the shout of the new-born soul," so that many an individual in the neighborhood began to feel "for the first time that his Father's heavens were smiling lovingly upon him." This change was not merely internal; converts consequently "came out of the world and were separate," and changes in their lives were "most marked." One liquor trafficker was converted on a Sunday night and by Monday morning had consigned his entire stock of alcohol to a nearby gutter. The revivals provided a growing membership, which meant that a genuine church building was needed to replace the old meeting house. The new edifice, near the intersection of Columbia and Cove streets, was largely built and financed by the membership, with the unskilled and poor contributing as they could, cleaning old bricks and providing other necessary labor. At the

15. Gorochow, "Baltimore Labor," 15; "History of Columbia Avenue Methodist Church," 19–21, M1475, Maryland Hall of Records, Annapolis.

16. "History of Columbia Avenue Methodist Church," 28–30; Dilts, *Great Road,* 148; *American,* Aug. 20, 1833; *Republican,* July 24, 1833. Daniel M. Reese is not to be confused with Daniel E. Reese, a leader of the Methodist Protestant reform agitation. For mention of Stewart's smithing expertise, see Gobright, *City Rambles,* 83.

dedication on February 11, 1844, Bishop Evelyn Waugh and the Reverends Henry Slicer and Robert Emory preached, stressing the grace of God and the communal nature of Methodist religious experience.[17] In four years, Methodists of the Columbia Avenue neighborhood had bucked official lethargy and interference, empowering new converts to build positive self-identities as evangelicals and to create their own alternative community. Such efforts to assert control of their collective life were by no means unusual for Baltimore's evangelical artisans. More significant, such activism could easily spill over into their secular lives.[18]

Evangelicalism converged with populist producerism in Jacksonian Baltimore in three expressions of artisan militancy. The first was the broad participation of evangelical journeymen in trade union and local workingmen's political activity between 1833 and 1837. The second included examples of continued small master allegiance to the producerist ethic of limited accumulation in dealing with journeymen and in resisting exploitative practices. The third involved the use of biblical insights to support resistance to capitalist transformations, as evidenced in anticapitalist alternatives presented by the Female Union Society of seamstresses and in producerist rationalizations offered for the popular unrest following the collapse of the Bank of Maryland. Because of the fragmentary nature of the records and the difficulties presented by multiple name listings in the directories, accurate statistical assessments are impossible, but the identifiable contributions of evangelical artisans to producerist

17. Frederick Simmont left a record of his conversion. He originally dismissed of the entire affair as "fanaticism," but curiosity led him to observe the proceedings through a window. The preaching affected him and a few nights later he woke up in the night with an urge to pray. He was rewarded with a quintessential conversion experience; "the Lord poured light into my soul and so filled me with His love, that I threw up the window and shouted glory, glory, though it was midnight in the depths of winter." "History of Columbia Avenue Methodist Church," 22–25. The dedication was reported in the *Sun*, which noted that 80 percent of the cost of the $5,000 building had already been raised by "the disinterested exertions of the people." *Sun*, Feb. 9, 15, 1844.

18. This was not the only evidence of class tensions within Baltimore Methodism. The "transient settlers" of the Republican Street area also rejected the domination of the "respectable" Fayette Street Church, and their Sunday School mission refused to give money collected in offerings to the founding congregation because "the Republican Street Sunday School only wanted to manage their own governing rules." F. Y. Jaggers, "History of Fayette Street Methodist Episcopal Church," in *The Story of My Life: Fayette-Bennett Methodist Episcopal Church* (Baltimore, 1933), 5. Nor was it the only instance of Methodist artisans pulling together to create community institutions. After existing as a mission for years, the Fell's Point Chapel was established in 1842 under the leadership of Methodist artisans and small masters. William A. Haggerty, *150th Anniversary of the East Baltimore Station, Methodist Episcopal Church, 1773–1923* (Baltimore, 1923), 13; Isaac Cook Papers, Lovely Lane Museum, Baltimore.

activism is significant.[19] Although some evangelicals could presumably find reason to embrace economic liberalism, others found it both natural and moral to aggressively resist the deteriorating circumstances of artisans.

Collaborative efforts between populist evangelicals and labor activists in Baltimore went back as far as 1793 to the creation of the Baltimore Mechanical Society, an association of masters and journeymen led mostly by the former. The initial meetings were held at the "Rights of Man," a tavern owned by Nathan Griffin, a Baptist activist and prominent abolitionist, and the election of officers was held at the Lovely Lane Methodist meetinghouse. Adam Fonerden, blacksmith and Methodist local preacher, was made president;[20] other officers included master hatter, David Shields, founder of the Baptist Church in Baltimore, Baptist layman John McClellan, and German Reformed layman Christopher Raborg. This association, which disregarded the regulation of prices and hours, reflected an early awareness of the deterioration of artisan circumstances by establishing a welfare insurance system for skilled workers and their widows and orphans. By neglecting to distinguish between masters and journeymen, the organization maintained the populist producerist allegiance to craft harmony.[21]

Populist evangelical contributions to organized artisan activism continued throughout the first three decades of the nineteenth century. Traditional economic morality underscored the militancy of the mid-1830s, and it was particularly evident in the rhetoric and actions of the coopers, hatters, butchers, and printers. The coopers cited the Book of Isaiah in support of their cause and, based on their familiarity with New Testament teachings, contested the questionable exegesis of the masters.[22] The hatters appealed for public support for their 1833 strike in a similar communication, authored by John H. W. Hawkins and two others. The career of Hawkins is instructive in terms of both evangelical sources of artisan militancy and religious experience in the face of economic deterioration.

19. Sutton, "Tied to the Whipping Post," 254n8.

20. Fonerden was also an abolitionist and a popular health commissioner. Leroy Graham, *Baltimore, the Nineteenth Century Black Capital* (Washington, D.C.: University Press of America, 1982), 19–20; Armstrong, Old Baltimore Conference, 31.

21. Steffen, *Mechanics of Baltimore*, 109, 113.

22. As the journeymen no doubt recognized, the point of the parable of the laborers in the vineyard (Matt. 20:1–16) was that an all-sovereign master could be as generous as he wanted, provided that he lived up to wage agreements previously (and mutually) established. The masters qualified on neither count; they were not all-sovereign nor were they living up to the previously established agreement. The latter, in fact, was at the heart of the journeymen's complaint. The parable ended with a familiar statement that surely resonated with the journeymen—"Thus the last shall be first, and the first last."

Hawkins's roots in artisan culture ran deep and his conversion to Methodism as a young man was profound. But holy living, as Methodists understood the term, was not easy for Hawkins; the economic dislocations of modernization eventually bankrupted him. Hawkins's early education in activism was provided by Alexander McCaine, a fiery evangelical republican and one of the leaders of the Methodist Protestant uprising. Hawkins participated in the defense of Baltimore in 1814, and after his conversion he became one of Baltimore's earliest Sabbath School teachers, overcoming the ridicule of his fellow apprentice hatters. He was an active member in the dissident Baltimore Union Society and was among the first to leave official Methodism during the schism of the late 1820s. Having successfully defied the worldly authority of the Methodist hierarchy without endangering spiritual consolations, Hawkins was not likely to knuckle under to the master hatters, either from a sense of submission to authority or from a proclivity toward pious docility. Moreover, Hawkins's lack of deference toward his employers was evident in the sarcastic conclusion of the hatters' appeal of 1833: "We are pleased that [the employers] will be enabled to bequeath their children a heritage which will place them far above the ground upon which we stand." The most powerful factor in this appeal, however, was the use of traditional economic morality to illustrate and condemn the "avarice and cupidity" evident in the masters' combination.[23]

Although the record of his experience has survived more intact than that of any other evangelical journeyman, Hawkins was by no means the only evangelical Baltimore militant. Hawkins was the single identifiably evangelical journeyman among the handful of hatter leaders in 1833, but evangelicals (as well as other producerist activists) were prominent among the leadership of organized butchers, perhaps the most successful of all Baltimore workers at controlling their trade. As early as 1832, the "Baltimore Hide and Tallow Association" was formed, as well as the "Butcher's Association of Baltimore" to protect the hundred-odd butchers from the encroachments of outside competition. Chief manager of the butchers' group was Lewis Turner, a former apprentice shoemaker and product of a Methodist Sabbath School education who had become an active Methodist layman. Under Turner's leadership, the butchers were one of the most militant defenders of producerist economic morality and were singled out as leaders in the 1835 bank riot.[24]

23. *Republican*, July 30, 1833.

24. Varle, *Complete View of Baltimore*, 164. Benjamin Latrobe Jr. diary, Mrs. Gamble Latrobe Collection, MS 168, Maryland Historical Society , cited in Grimsted, "Democratic Rioting," in O'Neill, ed., *Insights and Parallels*, 171. The document mentions no butchers by name.

Conflict in regard to market competition among butchers came to a head in May 1837 when the butchers denounced "a few wealthy monopolizers" living far from Baltimore who, "to satisfy the worst of all evils, ambition for great wealth," were buying large amounts of beef at artificially high prices to sell profitably in foreign markets, thereby pricing the local butchers out of business because Baltimoreans would not pay such high prices for beef. Butchers proposed to lower the cost of beef by joining with their Philadelphia and New York brethren to regulate the price of cattle, "based on that moral principle which is termed live and let live." Thirty-seven "beef victualers" signed the resolutions. They were headed by John Pentz and included his brother and fellow Methodist class leader, Daniel; Lewis Turner; Leon Dyer, widely recognized as a leader in the Bank of Maryland riot; and Marcus Wolf, chair of the meeting proposing reduced sentences for those convicted in the bank riot. They persisted in these efforts for two years, and in 1839, the butchers succeeded in putting a ceiling on charges by threatening to walk off the job if speculators tried to undersell them. Their efforts—the actions of artisans resolved to protect their labor-as-property and of traditional middlemen bent on interjecting producerist ethics into dealings with large-scale capitalists—were well appreciated by the community.[25]

Evangelicals were also prominent among Baltimore's printers, arguably the most important single group in spearheading artisan militancy in the 1830s. Although positive identification of its members' simultaneous involvement in trade union militancy and evangelicalism is difficult, the Baltimore Typographical Society included evangelicals like Methodist Protestants John Harrod and John Millington, Baptists Edmund Bull and Samuel Sands, and Methodists William Johnston and Francis Burke. Harrod was the publisher of the dissident Methodist paper, *Mutual Rights*, during the Methodist Protestant schism but was apparently not active in trade union activities. Millington, a

25. *Republican*, May 26, June 5, 1837; Grimsted, "Rioting," 388; Isaac Cook Papers, Lovely Lane Museum, Baltimore. Again led by John Pentz, the butchers' determination to oppose abuses unleashed by laissez-faire economics was reflected in their 1842 resolution to forswear the use of unstable and inflationary "shinplasters." Scharf, *Chronicles of Baltimore*, 380–81. See also *Sun*, June 21, 1841; July 2, 1841; Oct. 29, 1841; Nov. 15, 1841. Interestingly enough, the butchers were one group whose work had not yet been dramatically disrupted by the innovations of industrialism. Wilentz, *Chants Democratic*, 407. The Pentz family was well represented in the butchers' association; in addition to John J. and Daniel, Henry, J. W., Samuel, William, and Charles were active. Jacob Hoff, a manager (like Lewis Turner) of the Butchers' Hide and Tallow Association and a member of the West Baltimore Station, was also active. Miscellaneous papers, 1818–1903, in Furlong-Baldwin Papers, MS#193, Maryland Historical Society, Baltimore; Methodist Class Meeting Records, MF#699, Maryland Historical Society, Baltimore; Scharf, *History of Baltimore City and County*, 381–82.

longstanding member of the West Baltimore Station Methodist Protestant Church, however, was very active in secular affairs. His presence in local politics in the 1830s was ubiquitous; he was, for instance, a leader in the workingmen's political activity following the heady summer of 1833. Millington eventually emerged as a leader of the Workingmen's-Whig faction and was a prominent backer of hatter Philip Adams's unsuccessful bid for state legislator in 1837.[26] Edmund Bull's involvement was also particularly significant; he was editor of the movement's newspaper, *Baltimore Trades' Union,* a leader of the Working Men's Trades' Union, and constantly active in the support of various journeymen's strikes and organizational efforts. It is, however, unclear when Bull's close association with the Reverend Richard Fuller and the First Baptist Church of Baltimore began. Among the Methodists, William Johnston was an official in both the BTS and the WMTU and a longstanding communicant, according to his obituary.[27] Burke was also heavily involved with the Working Men's Trades' Union, but his connection with the Monument Street Methodist Church can be positively documented only from 1844. And, although he did not stay in Baltimore long and never joined the Typographical Society, Robert Ricketts, editor of the early artisan paper the *Mechanic's Banner,* was a Methodist layman. Finally, the broad-based contributions of printer and Baptist lay preacher John Weishampel, publisher of the *Workingmen's Advocate* and designated leader of the seamstresses' organization, were biblically inspired.

Populist evangelical participation in producer-oriented protective activity was not limited to hatters, butchers, and printers. By 1836, a number of populist evangelicals had surfaced in leadership roles within the journeyman's movement across a broad spectrum of crafts. This should come as no surprise, given the Methodist propensity for activism and economic justice. Many of the trade unionists simultaneously carried on leadership roles within the Methodist community. Charles Towson, a Methodist prominent in the establishment of the plebeian Howard Street Chapel (later Strawbridge Methodist Church), was president of the journeymen hatters' society; Philip Sherwood, another Methodist Sabbath School teacher and organizer of the Emory Grove Camp Meetings, was president of the journeymen shipwrights' society; Methodist layman John Tuder was treasurer of the journeymen house carpenters' society and vice president of the Baltimore Carpenters' Humane Society; and Richard Donahue, a Methodist class leader, was

26. West Baltimore Station Methodist Protestant Church Records, M#1472, Maryland Hall of Records, Annapolis; *American,* Oct. 19, 1833; *Republican,* Oct. 2, 1837.

27. *Sun,* Dec. 24, 1875; *Baltimore Trades' Union,* May 28, 1836; *Sun,* Feb. 15, 1843.

president of the journeymen tailors. In addition, journeymen potters had sent David Parr, a Methodist Protestant class leader, as their delegate to the organizational meeting of the WMTU in 1833, and the president of the journeymen shipjoiners' society was Daniel Perigo (or Perigoy), the leader of their 1836 strike at the same time that he was serving as a trustee of the Aisquith Methodist Protestant Church (the church which had welcomed the militant seamstresses in 1833).[28] These individuals are positively identifiable as being simultaneously militants and Methodists;[29] other evidence suggests a larger number of such persons.[30]

28. Towson was not long for the journeyman's world; he opened his own shop at some point in the 1830s and by mid-century was prospering. Isaac Cook Papers, Lovely Lane Museum, Baltimore; *Baltimore Trades' Union*, May 28, 1836; Brigham, *Baltimore Hats*, 53. Sherwood was apparently involved in the Sabbath Schools in east Baltimore from the 1820s. Because these schools were as concerned with literacy as religious instruction, there was no inherent conflict between such efforts and journeymen's general concerns with educational opportunities. *Baltimore Trades' Union*, May 28, 1836; [Isaac P. Cook], *Early History of Methodist Sabbath Schools, in Baltimore City and Vicinity; and Other Interesting Facts Connected Therewith* (Baltimore, 1877), 40. Tuder was not the only evangelical prominent in the Baltimore Carpenters' Humane Society; Adam Denmead, Methodist lay leader, was secretary, and Lewis Audoun was elected manager at the same time. Audoun was listed in *Matchett's Directory* (1833) as a cabinetmaker; like Sherwood, he was early involved in the Sabbath School instruction and was later (in 1848) an unsuccessful Whig candidate for the city council. Another manager was William Altvator, a carpenter and member of the English Lutheran Church. These last three, however, were probably no longer journeymen. *Baltimore Trades' Union*, May 28, 1836; Methodist Episcopal Church Class Registers, 1825–33, Lovely Lane Museum, Baltimore; *Republican*, Mar. 14, 1834; *Minutes of the Convention of the Friends of the Lord's-Day, from Maryland, Delaware and the District of Columbia, Held in Light-street Church, Baltimore, January 10th and 11th, 1844* (Baltimore, 1844), 12. Mention of Parr appears in the *Republican*, July 1, 1833; *Baltimore Saturday Visiter*, Feb. 15, 1834; Records of the East Baltimore Methodist Protestant Church, 1833–47, Lovely Lane Museum, Baltimore, and Archibald Hawkins, *Life of Stansbury*, 158.

29. The vagaries of documentation are frustrating. John F. Fisher, for instance, was the president of the journeymen tailors in 1833, a John Fisher was an importer of hides and skins in *Matchett's Directory* (1833), a John E. Fisher was listed as a tailor in 1829, and a John Fisher was a Methodist class leader from at least 1825 to 1833. It is obviously impossible to draw any certain conclusions from such evidence. Similarly, from 1829 to 1833 there appeared in *Matchett's Directory* three men named George Evans—one a cabinetmaker, one a shoemaker, one a cooper. One of these was undoubtedly George Evans, the Methodist reform sympathizer and shop owner who lost his class for publicly questioning the fairness of the trial held to expel the members of the Baltimore Union Society from the Methodist Church. *Mutual Rights* 3 (Jan. 1828): 165, 168. Another (or the same) George Evans attended the BTS anniversary supper in 1835, toasting public schools and a system of national education. *National Trades' Union*, Dec. 5, 1835.

30. The conversion dates for the following cannot be positively determined, yet anyone rising to evangelical leadership had presumably undergone years of training and experience. Arthur Mitchell was a Methodist class leader who chaired the Fourth Ward's delegation to the 1833 convention of mechanics and working men. Two officials in the cabinetmakers' association in 1836 were populist evangelicals: Henry Shryock appears in the Baptist records

Evangelical artisans also participated in Baltimore's confused political arena. Popular misgivings and suspicions concerning the propriety of mixing religion and politics notwithstanding, populist evangelicals supported the abortive Workingman's Party in 1833 and provided leadership for both Whig and Democratic parties in subsequent elections. Despite the longstanding assumption that evangelicals eschewed secular political participation because of devotion to otherworldly quietism, questions concerning the source and distribution of power were as close to the heart of populist evangelicalism as matters of theology. Still, evangelical contributions to secular politics remained problematic for both evangelicals and the general population concerned with the separation of church and state. Politics were suspect for a number of reasons: doubts about the moral efficacy of politics itself, fears that political involvement would distract believers from more significant spiritual concerns, worries that political success would lead to pride and abuse of power, and concerns that political attachments would endanger evangelical unity.[31] Although popular and religious sentiment did demand

by 1837 and John B. Brashears is listed as a Methodist Protestant by 1845. Less certain is the evidence concerning Jesse Beauchamp, a trustee of the United Society of Journeymen Cordwainers (men's branch) who, by 1844, had risen to the level of Methodist class leader. Similarly, the shipjoiner William Stroble and the house and sign painter Alfred Armstrong both participated in the original ten-hour agitation and were, at least by 1845, identifiable as Methodist lay leaders. Edwin Caldwell, a delegate of the Plane Makers Society when that organization was reinstated into the WMTU upon payment of back dues in 1834; Caldwell was listed as a Methodist class leader by 1844. An organization of carters, who protested the extension of the Baltimore and Ohio Railroad, were also represented by Methodists Thomas Pindell and John Danaker. For Arthur Mitchell, see *American*, Sept. 18, 1833; Aug. 30, 1834. For Henry Shryock, see *Republican*, July 16, 1833; *The Member's Manual of the First Baptist Church in Baltimore* (Baltimore, 1836). Brashears, Stroble, and Armstrong appear in Franch cards. See also *Convention of the Friends of the Lord's-Day*, 14. Caldwell appears in the *Convention of the Friends of the Lord's-Day* (p. 12) and in the notice printed in the *National Trades' Union*, Feb. 20, 1836. Exhibiting the Methodist propensity for upward mobility, Pindell was listed as a carter in the directory of 1829 and a wood merchant by 1833. Pindell and Danaker (whose name is variously spelled throughout his career) are mentioned in the *Republican*, Nov. 11, 1833, and "Members Admitted to Classes," Baltimore City Station, 1822–33, Lovely Lane Museum, Baltimore. Danaker, apparently a bootmaker originally and the longtime keeper of the Methodist cemetery, became a minor Baltimore officeholder in later years. *Republican*, Oct. 14, 1833; Methodist Class Meeting Records, MF#699, Maryland Historical Society, Baltimore.

31. Donald G. Mathews, *Religion in the Old South* (Chicago: University of Chicago Press, 1977), 33–34; Paul Goodman, *Towards a Christian Republic: Antimasonry and the Great Transition in New England, 1826–1836* (New York: Oxford University Press, 1988), 186; Carwardine, "Methodist Ministers," in Richey and Rowe, eds., *Rethinking Methodist History*, 138. Henry Slicer, in 1833, proclaimed, "Various means have been employed by *Politicians, Philosophers, Moralists* and others to better [man's] condition. But they have all been inefficient because they could not affect the heart and thereby radically change the springs of action." Slicer,

that political activity be undertaken without the sanction of any specific denomination, evangelical artisans and their sympathizers in Baltimore were active in local and state politics.

Perhaps the most significant participant in this respect was Universalist Richard Marley, a high profile WMTU official, president of the journeymen cordwainers union and leader of their strike in 1836, organizer of support for the Connecticut weavers arrested for striking against the Thompsonville Carpet Weavers Corporation, and regular participant in the National Trades' Union meetings in New York. Marley was the only Baltimore trade unionist identified with Universalism, but assessing the impact of his commitment to Universalism is difficult because the only record of his religious involvement comes from 1844. Equally problematic was the evolving nature of Universalism itself—a hybrid theology that shared the Arminianism of various populist evangelicals and filtered Protestant traditions through rationalist sensibilities to posit that the grace of God through Christ was accessible to all, not just to the elect. In time, many Universalists moved toward the ultraliberalism of elite Unitarians and modified their initial message suggesting that all could be saved to one asserting that all would be saved—an optimistic doctrine glossing over the inherent human tendency toward selfishness and greed that less sanguine evangelical producers identified as the immoral force driving capitalist innovation. Yet, to the extent that Universalists like Marley clung to the traditional economic morality of the Calvinist heritage they were otherwise rejecting, they could and did embrace producerist ethics.[32] Such

Journal, 1:66. Back in 1801, United Brethren itinerant Henry Boehm complained of the congregational disruptions emanating from the "great political excitement" between the Adams and Jefferson parties. He warned that "our different political sentiments should never effect our Christian fellowship and affections." Henry Boehm, *Reminiscences, Historical and Biographical, of Sixty-four Years in the Ministry* (New York, 1866), 65. These concerns were shared by those with different allegiances, including trade unionists; thus, the motto of the *National Trades' Union*: "Party politics, and religious, or irreligious discussions, will be excluded from our columns." The *Republican* was just as forthright: "the impropriety and dangerous tendency" of ministerial participation "in the violent party struggles of the day" should be "so obvious that every reflecting mind must condemn it." *Republican*, Mar. 13, 1834. In case such a proposition was not immediately obvious, the paper later explained that "advocating political views" on the part of clergy "will give offense and lessen the influence of gospel ministers." *Republican*, Jan. 30, 1838.

32. Previous studies have exalted Universalism as the quintessential expression of "rationalist radicalism": deistic impulses or "free thinking" that promised to liberate the masses from the supposed lobotomizing effects of evangelicalism. For artisans and Universalism, see Laurie, *Working People of Philadelphia*, 68–72; Wallace, *Rockdale*, 243–95, esp. 289–92; and Schultz, "God and Workingmen," in Hoffman and Albert, eds. *Religion in a Revolutionary Age*, 148–55. For a discussion of free thinking influence on New York workingmen, see Wilentz,

perspectives motivated Marley's participation in the Workingman's Party of 1833 and his leadership role in the successful candidacy of fellow cordwainer activist and Democrat, Francis Gallagher.

The political activities of John B. Seidenstricker closely resembled those of Richard Marley. Seidenstricker, a house and ornamental sign painter, was president of the journeymen sign painters' society in 1835, even though he had opened a drug and paint store four years earlier. First a Methodist Protestant, then a Methodist, and long an admirer of Andrew Jackson's adherence "to the domination of the people," Seidenstricker surfaced politically as a delegate—along with Marley, John H. W. Hawkins, John Millington, and Methodist cooper Arthur Mitchell—to the convention of workingmen nominating candidates for the state legislature in 1833. Like Marley, he was also a leader in the WMTU support for the Thompsonville weavers in November 1835, and in September 1836, he originated the "largest meeting of the Mechanics and Workingmen ever convened" in Baltimore to support political reapportionment in the state legislature to adequately represent the city's burgeoning population. From 1835 to 1838 he was a Democratic member of the Baltimore City Council. His voting record there indicated ambivalence toward economic innovation; he distrusted laissez-faire economics, as evidenced by his vote against repealing regulations licensing pawnbrokers, but he also welcomed extension of the railroads into the city. During the commercial distress following the panic of 1837, he devised a plan for the city to issue small currency notes, a financially sound solution which apparently worked well for all. He also pushed legislation for education and was largely responsible for the establishment of Baltimore's first public high school. He was the elected to the state legislature in 1839 and 1840 and was subsequently a tax collector, assessor, and penal official. Eventually he became president of the National Fire Insurance Company, noted for its "sound, honest, conservative management" with a record of always paying off its

Chants Democratic, 153–57, 176–88, 224–26. But many nineteenth-century Universalists, particularly those outside educated circles of the elite, had more in common with anti-Calvinist and nondoctrinal populist evangelicals like Methodists than with their eventual ultraliberal partners, the Unitarians. In fact, the works of Universalists like Theophilus Gates, Jesse Torrey Jr., and William Heighton found ready acceptance among a broad range of populist evangelicals. Hatch, *Democratization of Christianity*, 40–42, 170–72; Philip S. Foner, *William Heighton: Pioneer Labor Leader of Jacksonian Philadelphia* (New York, International Publishers, 1991), 80–81. But like Methodists, Universalists lined up on both sides of the capitalist-producerist divide; Universalist Thaddeus Craft of Craft, Cole, and Co. was one of those cited disapprovingly by journeymen hatters for refusing to honor mutually established wages in 1844. *Sun*, Feb. 10, 1844; Franch cards.

claims.[33] Throughout his long career of public service, producerist integrity and evangelical economic morality informed his actions.

Methodist Protestant dry goods merchant Beale Richardson was equally prominent in Maryland state politics. Richardson's father, Benjamin, was one of the original Methodist Protestant reformers, and the son followed in his father's religious footsteps, becoming in 1831 a member of St. John's, the more respectable Methodist Protestant congregation in Baltimore. But Richardson's upward mobility and economic success did not proceed without self-imposed limits; in the midst of the capitalist opportunities available in the 1830s, he insisted on selling his "plaids, domestics, and checks" at "the old prices" established with the appropriate artisans. A lifelong Democrat, Richardson's first foray into politics came in the aftermath of the 1835 bank riot when he ran for the state legislature as a supporter of "the people's president." During the campaign, Richardson's membership in a temperance society proved to be a liability for a Democrat, but an anonymous defender publicly reminded the electorate of Richardson's "unflinching Jacksonism" during the bank war, "when so many of the same line of business as he, were willing to surrender their liberties for Bank accommodation." With the backing of the plebeian wing of the Democratic Party, including *Republican* editor Samuel Harker and WMTU leader A. I. W. Jackson, he won handily. Two years later, in 1837, he ran with Francis Gallagher as a backer of hard money (a staple of producerist morality) and both men won. In time, Richardson became one of the government-appointed directors of the Baltimore and Ohio Railroad and in 1846 took over proprietorship of the *Republican*, which he turned into a states' rights paper. Throughout his long political career, Richardson remained both an involved Democrat and an active Methodist Protestant lay leader.[34]

33. Scharf, *Chronicles of Baltimore*, 485–87; *Republican*, Feb. 7, 1835, Oct. 1, 1836; J. H. Hollander, *The Financial History of Baltimore* (Baltimore, 1899), 178–83; [no author], *Industries of Maryland: A Descriptive Review of the Manufacturing and Mercantile Industries of the City of Baltimore* (New York, 1882), 189.

34. Colhouer, *Sketches of the Founders*, 337–39. *Republican*, May 26, 1837; Sept. 22, 24, 25, 1835. Like Richardson, Robert W. Varden was both a Methodist Protestant class leader and the official "Fourth Vice President" of the Young Man's Democratic Republican Convention in 1837. *Republican*, June 14, 1837; manuscript records of Leaders' Meetings, 1833–47, Lovely Lane Museum, Baltimore. Not all evangelicals with Jeffersonian roots remained in the Democracy; in fact most (like printer John Millington) gradually moved into the Whig camp. Carwardine "Methodist Ministers" in Richey and Rowe, eds., *Rethinking Methodist History*, 139–44. The gradual shift of Methodism toward Whiggery was reflected in the number of Methodists running for local office as Whigs in the 1840s. Archibald Hawkins, *Life of Stansbury*, 126–28.

Despite the producerist ideal of cooperative mutuality, harmonious relations between masters and journeymen were by no means the norm, and capitalist transformations only exacerbated the potential for conflict. According to the assumption that equates capitalism and evangelicalism, one would expect to find evangelical masters among those most resistant to journeymen's concerns and organization. Indeed, when journeymen hatters threatened to strike in 1794 for higher wages, Baptist layman David Shields (like Methodist master cooper Joshua Stinchcomb almost forty years later) led the masters in their attempts to control wages and workplaces.[35] Much has been made in this respect of Methodist representation among the United Master Shoemakers who associated in 1810 to oppose the journeymen cordwainers' attempt to increase wages. At the inception of the association, according to Charles Steffen, seven of the thirteen masters who were also Methodist class leaders were part of the association, while six were not.[36] This group pioneered strike-breaking techniques, using blacklists and advertising for scabs, but their unity was short-lived; less than a year later fully one-third had defected. Although a tradition of antipathy toward journeymen's organizing certainly existed among one faction of Methodist masters, it remains unclear how representative that group was and how dedicated Methodist masters as a whole were to modern understandings of labor relations and practices.

If this pattern of antijourneymen militancy had held true during the hatters' strike of 1833, one would have expected evangelical entrepreneurs to have been prominent in the masters' combination. Yet none of the three mentioned as leaders can be identified as an evangelical and it appears from the comments of John H. W. Hawkins that Jacob Rogers, owner of the largest hat manufactory in Baltimore and a leading Methodist layman, was not involved in the effort to trim wages.[37] A well-publicized interaction between producerist and capitalist masters in the hatters' strike casts further doubt on

35. Steffen, *Mechanics of Baltimore*, 110–11, 113–14, 119.

36. Ibid., 224–25. This evidence convinces Steffen that "the Methodist Church condemned the social discord that journeymen committed through their strikes and boycotts." Steffen dismisses, with no evidence cited, the six Methodist masters who refused to join the shoemakers' association as among those who "had undoubtedly moved from Baltimore by the time the employers' organization was formed." Ibid., 266–67. The other six, however, may have been, because of producerist Methodist principles, quite willing to grant the higher wages. This was certainly the case by the 1830s. Steffen also mentions that the shoemakers' association suffered massive defections but does not identify those who left, reasons for leaving, or religious affiliations, if any.

37. *Republican*, July 30, 1833; *American*, July 9, 1833. John Hawkins had no reason to protect Jacob Rogers's reputation since Rogers had voted to expel Hawkins and other Methodist Protestants in 1828.

the assumption that a natural conjunction between evangelicalism and capitalist exploitation existed. On July 6, 1833, Charles Pratt and William Hopewell advertised their hat manufactory in both the *Republican* and the *American*. Here, they mentioned their intention to maintain the wages of their journeymen and to resist the reductions of the combination of master hatters. Three days later an anonymous threat appeared in response to their notice:

> To Hopewell & Pratt
>
> You d_____d infernal scoundrels—henceforth look out; we now give you fair warning; take our advice and have your *stock* and your *lives* insured immediately; so sure as you are now living you may calculate before long, your store in flames, and feel balls in your bodies. As stated above, we give you fair warning; we will most certainly make examples of both of you, for those who may hereafter have the presumption to set up their contemptible plans against the arrangement of respectable men.—The only way you can possibly escape the danger you are now in, is to come into the late arrangements immediately.
>
> We only add BEWARE.

If this note was indeed written by a representative of the master hatters' association to intimidate small masters, it was remarkably ineffective. Hopewell and Pratt quickly expressed outrage at such attempts and asserted that they "fear not the threats." They left the threatening note, along with a promise of a fifty-dollar reward for the identification of its author, in the mayor's office in the hope that the handwriting could be recognized, but the reward was apparently never claimed.[38] The rough (to evangelicals, almost blasphemous) language of the threat seems particularly surprising in view of the stereotype of entrepreneurs on the make as steeped in proto-Victorian (and probably evangelical) gentility, and it makes their claim to respectability ironic. The tension apparently proved too much for the Hopewell and Pratt partnership. On July 23, at the height of the strike, another ad appeared, taken out by Pratt alone, expressing his desire in the producerist vernacular "'to live and let live'" and announcing his willingness to "continue to pay the wages."[39]

Hopewell and Pratt were not alone in resisting the masters' combination. On June 12, well before the offending note appeared, the hat manufactory

38. *Republican*, July 6, 1833; *American*, July 6, 9, 1833.

39. *American*, Aug. 1, 1833.

of Elder and Boston announced their determination to meet the society's wages. And on July 30, twelve small masters—among them Jacob Boston (Methodist Protestant layman), George Quail (Methodist leader), George Uhler (Presbyterian elder), and John Warner Niles (son of the nationally known editor, Hezekiah)—announced that they would honor the agreement with the journeymen. Having proven their solidarity with the journeymen hatters, these masters were publicly commended for their determination to stand with Pratt and to maintain the agreed-upon wages.[40]

The decision of these hatters to support the journeymen was presumably not easy, but neither was it unique. As evident in the advertisement taken out by Methodist master tailor George Holtzman (who promised his potential customers goods "as cheap as it can be had of the same quality elsewhere" but at the same time reminded them that "the best work cannot be had without the best prices" being to paid his skilled workers), small masters sympathetic to the journeymen were faced with a serious dilemma in the 1830s—how to meet consumer demands without sacrificing fair wages or acceptable profits. Yet, throughout the Jacksonian trade union movement in Baltimore, many small masters refused to capitulate to competition, and a significant number of them were evangelicals. This was apparent from the beginning of labor activism in Baltimore; in the initial journeymen weavers' action against Richard Whiteworth's attempt to cut their wages in 1828, Methodist (later Methodist Protestant) master weaver William Knox led the small masters' support of the journeymen and testified in court in their behalf. Similarly, Thomas Maybury, a Baptist and master mason, and John Curlett, a low-church Episcopalian and master coachmaker, were among those agreeing to the ten-hour demands of their respective journeymen in 1833. And when the journeymen plasterers two years later presented their "principal employers" with the same demand, Methodist class leader Jesse Zumwalt (or Sumwalt), was among those readily agreeable.[41]

40. *Republican*, July 23, 1833; July 30, 1833; Franch cards. Pratt's troubles continued; on December 29, 1833, his store burned to the ground. *Republican*, Dec. 30, 1833. Despite the congruity between this fire and the earlier threat, the official explanation was that the fire started from a stove. Whatever the cause, Pratt apparently took his insurance money and went elsewhere; his name no longer appeared in the Baltimore directories. Neither did Hopewell's after the partnership dissolved. John Warner Niles's allegiance to producerist ethics continued; two years later, he publicly announced that he "would not consent to patronize any man who would attempt to cut down the wages of the Journeymen." *Republican*, Dec. 22, 1835.

41. *Republican*, April 17, 1837; *Minutes*, Maryland Baptist Union Association, 1836; *American*, Aug. 20, 1833; *Constitution and By-Laws of Masons and Bricklayers Beneficial Society of Baltimore City and Precincts* (Baltimore, 1822), 11; *Republican*, Aug. 21, 1833; *Republican*, June 26, 1835.

Interestingly enough, the pattern of masters accommodating the demands of journeymen in the 1830s emerged most strikingly in the same shoemaking trades that had spawned the antijourneymen actions of the United Master Shoemakers. When the journeymen cordwainers in fall 1833 announced their resolve to resist reductions, they listed those who were worthy of public patronage because they had met their wages, including Methodist class leaders Columbus Leaman (or Laman), Luke League, and George Deems; Methodist laymen George C. Addison and James Hagerty; and Methodist Protestant layman George No[r]therman. This was not a unique expression of craft solidarity; three years later, the journeymen cordwainers of the ladies' branch expressed their gratitude to friendly masters, including Leaman, Notherman, Hagerty, and Methodist class leaders Elisha Carback and Edmund Loane, for meeting their wage structure. By 1836 masters both identifiably Methodist and willing to grant the journeymen's wages were at least 11 percent of the total. The decisions of these men, simultaneously active in efforts to effect evangelical growth, call into question the accuracy of interpreting evangelicalism as either a source of artisan passivity or a bedrock of capitalist change.[42]

The actions of these masters, along with the trade union activism of evangelical journeymen, provide ample evidence of the populist evangelical concern for economic justice and the producerist harmony of interests. The creation and development of the Female Union Society and its successor, the United Working Men's and Women's Trading Society, marked another convergence of evangelical anticapitalism and artisan organization. John

42. *Republican*, April 26, 1836. In the 1810 figures for the antijourneymen master shoemakers' association cited by Charles Steffen, 15 percent of the total were Methodists. Steffen, *Mechanics of Baltimore*, 267. In 1828, George Notherman was one of the associated Methodist reformers. Records of the East Baltimore Methodist Protestant Leaders' Meetings, 1833–47, Lovely Lane Museum, Baltimore; *Instrument of Association of John and Charles Wesley*, 8; Commons et al., *Documentary History*, 4:271. John Morrow also supported the journeymen. This name appears in the Methodist class leaders records, but it is not clear if the Methodist was also the cordwainer because the directory lists three such names. *American*, Sept. 27, 1833; *Republican*, Sept. 28, 1833; Apr. 26, 1836; Methodist Class Records, 1825–1847, MF#699, Maryland Historical Society, Baltimore; *Matchett's Baltimore Directory*. The master cabinetmaker, local officeholder, and former Methodist Protestant exhorter (expelled for intemperance in 1834) Lambert Thomas was also among those supporting the journeymen hatters in 1833. *Republican*, July 29, 1833, Jan. 13, 1834. For the fall of Lambert Thomas, see the records of East Baltimore Methodist Protestant Leaders' Meetings, 1833–47, Lovely Lane Museum, Baltimore. This broad devotion to the concerns of economic morality did not readily disappear. As late as 1846 the master sailmakers, including Methodist leader Joseph Loane, set their prices with penalties assigned for any members underselling the list prices. Kahn, *Stitch in Time*, 17.

Weishampel, who merged producerism with paternalism in his critique of capitalist development, is representative of this effort.[43] Weishampel was an itinerant Baptist minister and Fell's Point printer as well as the publisher of Baltimore's original producerist paper, the *Workingmen's Advocate.* That he was a well-respected member of the artisan community is evidenced by this testimonial at an early ten-hours meeting:

SUPPORT A UNION
Support the Working Men's Advocate by
John F. Weishampel.
Meddle not with Politics but support your
rights by voting for who you please
and be not corrupted.
Look to the Bill of Rights and take no steps
that might have a tendency to violate the Civil Law.
Support Character, Firmness and Moderation.
Union between Town and Point, no Jealousy to exist.

Weishampel was involved in various phases of the labor movement, but his major contribution came in his efforts to provide alternative occupational opportunities for exploited seamstresses, even as he was experiencing extreme financial difficulties himself.[44]

Weishampel's initial efforts aimed at rallying public support for the establishment of a publicly financed cooperative shirt manufactory, which would provide employment for distressed seamstresses. The plan was based on Mathew Carey's "Appeal to the Wealthy of the Land."[45] In this work, Carey had

43. Concerning the trend toward labor-oriented paternalistic antidotes to the dislocations of capitalism, Sean Wilentz notes that "some unionists proclaimed a plebeian cult of domesticity—a cult quite unlike its emerging middle-class counterpart, one based not on a feminized evangelicalism, but on older notions of the primacy of male authority and duty." Wilentz, *Chants Democratic,* 249. This "plebeian cult of domesticity," however, was grounded in populist evangelicalism, as well as in popular beliefs concerning inherent gender differences and reflected the longstanding Methodist tradition of empowering women.

44. *Baltimore Saturday Visiter,* Oct. 5, 1833. Weishampel eventually abandoned Baltimore to itinerate in Pennsylvania, but it is not clear when he left. His son, John Jr., wrote a history of the Baltimore Baptists. One of the John Weishampels, probably the son, was a pronounced anti-Catholic by the 1850s.

45. *American,* Aug. 9, Sept. 7, 11, 16, 1833.

refuted three "pernicious errors" of laissez-faire, Malthusian economists: that sufficient employment opportunities existed to guarantee accessibility to competences; that the poor suffered solely because of their idleness and vice; and that aiding the poor through state or voluntary benevolence created dependence. Directing his comments to the plight of seamstresses, Carey noted that the malignant effects of industrial capitalism induced some to "licentious courses." While decrying those taking "the broad path to destruction," Carey deplored the self-righteous "Phariseeism" of those who would condemn them. Carey also recognized that unchecked competition required employers to keep wages low, but he urged those who could, "with a due regard to their own interest," to raise wages, "according to the dictates of humanity and justice." To meliorate this situation, Carey suggested the voluntary establishment of philanthropic manufactories where livable wages would be paid.[46]

Carey's directives led to the formation at Fell's Point in spring of 1834 a "United Working-Men and Women's Trading Society" to provide reasonably compensated work for seamstresses connected to the Asylum for Widows and Orphans.[47] In late fall, with the project was still struggling to get off the ground, Weishampel urged readers to give to "the poor and now suffering seamstresses," remembering "what you give to the poor, you lend to the Lord."[48] The patronizing attitudes of male leaders toward female recipients of their beneficence was, of course, not atypical for the early nineteenth century, nor was their paternalism contrary to traditionalist ethics,[49] but both elements belied the radical nature of the cooperative economic program planned by Weishampel and the United Workingmen's and Women's Trading Society. "The object," they wrote, "is to have a Clothing Store belonging to the Society" itself, not to a few capitalists or stockholders. Their guiding

46. *American*, Sept. 23, Oct. 1, 2, 4, 7, 1833.

47. *Baltimore Saturday Visiter*, Mar. 15, 1834.

48. *Republican*, Nov. 6, 1834; Jan. 3, 1835; *American*, Oct. 4, 17, 1834. The plight of the seamstresses also attracted the attention of Presbyterian minister Robert Breckinridge, although the exact nature of his remarks remains unclear. His subsequent activity included supporting African-American Presbyterians' efforts in Baltimore to create their own church and promoting fanatical anti-Catholicism in the 1840s. *American*, Sept. 13, 1834. Joseph Mannard, "The 1839 Baltimore Nunnery Riot: An Episode in Jacksonian Nativism and Social Violence," *Maryland Historian* 11 (spring 1980): 16, 21.

49. *Republican*, Apr. 28, 1835. Weishampel and his supporters concluded that "the duties of the Board of Directors" were "too laborious and of too great importance for ladies to attend thereto"; moreover they did not "wish to have ladies in the Board." But, as Sean Wilentz notes regarding contemporary male attitudes toward female operatives, "condescension was not contempt." Wilentz, *Chants Democratic*, 249. The *Republican*, in this light, condemned Louisville tailors for refusing to work with women. *Republican*, Jan. 27, 1836.

principle was the producerist injunction, "Give unto the laborer the produce of his labor." The plan was to provide work at "reasonable compensation" to member seamstresses and to sell at their warehouse the clothes the women made as well as other dry goods at competitive prices. Members would be charged dues of twenty-five cents per month and the surplus over expenses would be distributed by profit-sharing. This was indeed an innovative plan to transcend capitalist accumulation, but the problem of funding it remained.[50]

Despite Weishampel's valiant efforts, the United Working-Men and Women's Trading Society struggled throughout its existence. In an attempt to gain public support, the society felt compelled to assert that "this institution will not be a monopoly, as some think," nor would it "support the indolent and lazy." Instead, the society was "founded upon fair republican principles, and literally gives to each laborer the produce of his labor." Moreover, supporters warned, "if this society is suffered to die away for the want of a few hundred dollars, we shall never again have any prospects of being redeemed from our present state of oppression and poverty." Judging from bipartisan appeals for support appearing in the *Republican*, it is likely that the society became solvent by October 1835. Although it is not known how long the society survived,[51] its importance is clear: it offered an alternative to the dual developments of entrepreneurial exploitation and humanitarian welfare by providing work, wages, and consumer goods outside the capitalist mainstream but dependent on the support and goodwill of the community. Equally noteworthy were the difficulties its proponents encountered in gaining support from a public, increasingly enamored, it would seem, of the promise of individual accumulation.

Weishampel provided the most significant outside contribution to the seamstresses' cooperative activities, but other populist evangelicals also offered their help. Jacob Daley, master chairmaker and Methodist layman, was elected permanent treasurer of the original Female Union Society and advertised his willingness to accept donations at his popular bazaar. John Valiant, cordwainer and Methodist Protestant class leader, was among those who came to the rescue of Weishampel and the seamstresses leadership when they were challenged by an upstart faction. And the initial gatherings of the Female Union Society were held at the Pitt Street (later Aisquith) Methodist Protestant Church, with the blessing of church authorities. The seamstresses were sufficiently grateful for this support that they had their

50. *Republican*, June 8, 1835.
51. *Republican*, Sept. 14, Oct. 16, 1835.

thanks published and continued to meet at the church for months.[52] Throughout their turbulent history, the Female Union Society and their United Workingmen's and Women's Trading Society received invaluable support from Baltimore's populist evangelical community.[53]

In the 1830s artisans were not the only workers struggling with the challenges of industrialization; the transformations and dislocations brought about by modernization were also apparent in the lives of factory operatives. Although the number of operatives in Baltimore was growing, as was the factory system itself, by 1860 only 8 percent of the working population was in manufacturing. The earliest textile factories in the area were converted grain mills, often owned by members of the old Quaker commercial elite. In 1808, spinning operations began in the Powhatan Factory, seven miles outside the city limits. The next year, the wealthy Quaker miller John McKim incorporated the Union Manufacturing Company, and by 1820 he was employing 10 men, 16 boys, and 104 girls. By 1820 the Washington Cotton Factory and Crooks Factory (one of the few within city limits) had opened, and during the next

52. Records of East Baltimore Station Methodist Protestant Leaders' Meetings, 1833–47, Lovely Lane Museum, Baltimore. Jacob Daley was a man of ecumenical spirit. Besides collaborating with the Methodist Protestants in support of the Female Union Society, he allowed the rooms over his bazaar to be used by the Reverend James G. Hamner, a young and vigorous Presbyterian minister who was trying (with only gradual success at first) to establish a New School congregation in a laboring-class neighborhood. *American,* June 22, 1833. For more on Hamner, see *Baltimore Saturday Visiter,* Nov. 19, 1842.

53. With the lack of records for the Female Union Society, the identity of Susannah Stansbury is particularly difficult to unravel and representative of the problems in pinning down the religious and artisanal affiliations of the inarticulate. To exacerbate the problem, the Stansburys were an old Baltimore family and extended throughout all classes of society. In the newspapers (capable of typographical errors), the leader of the seamstresses appears as "Susannah L. Stansbury." In the Methodist class records for November 1829, the following appears: "Stansbury, Susan. P." Other Susans appear in this document, with no period after the name, and other Susannah's appear unabbreviated, although "Susan." definitely implies "Susannah." The different middle initials could point to the existences of two different people, but they could also indicate the use of a maiden name initial in one instance and a given middle name initial in the other. Thus, the evidence establishing a connection between Methodism and Susannah Stansbury is suggestive but inconclusive. As if the above were not sufficiently confusing, a "S. Stansbury" appears (the only one with no complete first name) as one who gives cordwainers their price. *American,* Oct. 23, 1833. Similar problems exist in trying to identify the other leader of the Female Union Society, secretary Hannah Moran Wright. A Hannah Wright is listed as having married a John Wright, with both listed as members of the Bethel Methodist Episcopal Church in later years. A John Wright was a cordwainer trade unionist and a delegate in the nominating process of the original Workingman's ticket in 1833. To attempt to make positive connections between Methodism and worker activism by means of such ambiguous evidence is problematic but plausible.

decade Warren Factory, Gray's Factory, Lanvale (later Hart's) Factory, and Thistle Factory joined the older firms. By the late 1830s, larger cotton duck factories at Woodberry, Mt. Vernon, and Ellicott Mills had been established. Despite this proliferation, making factories profitable was not easy. In 1831, for instance, Samuel Smith, the newly hired overseer from New England of the Warren Factory, complained about the technology and organization of the previous operation ("they are not system-minded"), commented negatively on the inability of the former owners to turn a profit, and set out to correct the situation.[54] With a few notable exceptions, the factory system in Baltimore lagged behind developments in New England.

Artisans continued to outnumber operatives throughout this period, but the number of factory workers in and around Baltimore increased.[55] The backgrounds, experiences, and expectations of these workers—many of them women and children, often rural migrants—differed in many respects from those of the artisans, particularly given the tight-knit social relations of a mill community compared to the open and increasingly depersonalized conditions attendant to metropolitan industrialization. The distinguishing factor in the development of factory village culture was the replacement of artisan mutuality with employer paternalism, wherein wealthy capitalists (with no necessary familiarity with productive operations) owned the means of production and reserved the right to hire, fire, and set workplace rules. Workers, to be sure, were not without agency in this emerging system. In spite of the obvious inequalities in power relations, they were "free laborers" in the sense that they could choose to stay or move on. The workers' willingness to work steadily correlated closely to the owners' ability to meet their basic needs and to respect their essential humanity, but this type of trade-off was rarely a given. And whereas many artisans enjoyed livable wages

54. Laurie, *Artisans into Workers*, 28. Baltimore in the 1830s did not experience the impact of these developments to the same extent that the suburbs of Philadelphia or the mill towns of New England did. John McGrain, *From Pig Iron to Cotton Duck*, 2 vols. (Towson, Md.: Baltimore County Public Library; 1985), 2:15; idem, *Oella—Its Thread of History* (Oella, Md., 1976); Olson, *Baltimore*, 42; Clayton Hall, ed., *Baltimore: Its History and Its People* (New York: Lewis Historical Publishing, 1912), 91; Brooks and Rockel, *History of Baltimore County*, 190; Bilhartz, *Urban Religion*, 96. Samuel Smith to the Reverend Ariel Abbot, in Warren Factory Papers, Maryland Historical Society, Baltimore.

55. The extent of the increase is borne out by the report that seven to eight hundred people were put out of work in 1834 when the Warren Factory just outside of Baltimore burned down. *Republican*, Jan. 25, 1834. A British visitor commenting on the Ellicott Mills in 1840 wrote: "several hundreds of white labourers were said to be employed, at an average rate of a dollar per day, and yielding good profit to the proprietors." J. S. Buckingham, *The Eastern and Western States of America*, 3 vols. (London, 1840), 2:137.

and the existential pride in their work, factory operatives, often drawn to mill communities because of low wages for agricultural labor, might find in their new wages little improvement.[56] But in their exposure to populist evangelicalism and in the problems they encountered from industrialism, artisans and operatives shared much. In addition, strikes among factory workers in the 1840s and labor organizing around the ten-hour day in the 1850s indicate that the same spirit of producerist resistance to oppressive work situations manifested itself in the operatives' consciousness.

Factories, with their relatively large and stable populations of people working in a limited geographical locale, provided a ready-made congregation, and evangelicals soon began to set up regular preaching schedules.[57] In the early 1820s, the young and dutiful Presbyterian Moses Hyde began an individual evangelistic effort at the Crooks Factory, where his father was superintendent, but reported little positive response to his efforts, either as a temperance advocate or as an assistant Sunday School superintendent. Simultaneously (and with much more successful results), Methodist itinerants and local preachers were preaching at Washington and Union factories and gathering Sunday scholars together at Powhatan and Lanvale factories. After the Methodists divided, Methodist Protestants joined the missionary activity at the factories, and during September 1833 (at the height of the WMTU activity), they reported revival successes at the Thistle and Union factories. At the same time, in the community near Powhatan Factory, the Methodist Sunday School "under the charge of the people of that vicinity" was thriving.[58]

56. Bill Harvey, *"The People Is Grass": A History of Hampden-Woodberry, 1802–1945* (Baltimore: Della Press, 1988), 25–27; Brooks and Rockel, *History of Baltimore County*, 201–4.

57. Richard L. Bushman, "Family Security in the Transition from Farm to City, 1750–1850," in *Working Papers of the Regional Economic History Resource Center* (Greenville, Del.: Eleutherian Mills–Hagley Foundation, fall 1980), 32. The Methodists, while the most important evangelical group proselytizing in the mill communities, were not alone. A Baptist church in the vicinity of the Warren Factory preceded the textile mill, and early in the 1820s Presbyterians were attempting to convert operatives at Crooks Factory within the city. Moses Hyde Papers, M1131, Maryland Historical Society, Baltimore. It was not until 1838 that Presbyterians organized for this purpose, sending a minister through their Board of Missions to Ellicott Mills. *Minutes of the Baltimore Presbytery*, Apr. 25, 1838, Presbyterian Historical Society, Philadelphia.

58. If Hyde's preaching was as insipid as his diary keeping, his evangelistic failures need no further explanation. Moses Hyde diary, M1311, Maryland Historical Society, Baltimore. Isaac Cook Papers, Lovely Lane Museum, Baltimore; Slicer, *Journal*, 2:296. The Methodist itinerant Nathaniel Mills reported in 1832 a "large audience" at the Union Factory Sunday School and a "tolerable congregation" at Powhatan Factory for a Sunday night service. Nathaniel Mills diary, June 13, 1832, in Nathaniel Mills Papers, Lovely Lane Museum, Baltimore. *Mutual Rights and Methodist Protestant* 3 (Sept. 27, 1833): 306. Cook, *Early History of Sabbath Schools*, 24; Varle, *Complete View of Baltimore*, 52.

Three factors contributed to the success of these revival efforts. In the first place, to use the economic analogy of supply and demand, enthusiastic itinerants coming from similar backgrounds and speaking a common religious language invigorated by their own religious experience "supplied" a powerful (if circumscribed) message of acceptance and empowerment.[59] Secondly, their audiences were equally proactive, in some cases "demanding" preachers, in other cases taking it upon themselves to organize religious communities. Finally, in these early instances of Methodist missions, itinerant evangelism and popular acceptance of evangelical teaching were independent of owner initiative and control, and like the producer-oriented trade unionist, cognizant of their dependence on public support for success. A letter written by itinerant Luther J. Cox to the *Methodist Protestant* revealed the lack of paternalist intervention in around the Hampden-Woodberry mill communities:

> The greatest difficulty we have to encounter, except the opposition of the Prince of Darkness who sometimes shows his cloven hoof, is the want of means to pay off our debt upon the [Hampden Methodist Protestant] church. Our congregation is poor, composed principally of operators in the factories surrounding us; they can give but little out of their scanty wages, and that by small amounts monthly; we are constrained to look to our friends for help. There is not perhaps within the bounds of the Maryland district a more needy congregation and a place where bounty bestowed is likely to do more good. Who will come up to the help of the Lord against the mighty, and by securing this greatly needed house of worship to His poor children, be instrumental in winning souls to Christ and thereby add many stars to the crown of their rejoicing? Help us brethren; the time for our doing good is short.[60]

The early factory congregations were a product of populist preaching, worker agency, and public donation,[61] giving their members organizational structure

59. For a comprehensive argument presenting the supply-side interpretation of the Second Great Awakening, see Bilhartz, *Urban Religion.*

60. Cox is quoted in Edward D. Stone, *History of Hampden Methodist Protestant Church* (Baltimore, 1917), 16.

61. A Baptist congregation first met in the Hampden-Woodberry mill district in 1836, but community poverty and lack of a meetinghouse hampered its efforts to organize. By 1848, itinerant preacher William Wilder began to hold services in the nearby woods. Wilder's efforts attracted a critical mass of followers as well as the attention of prominent Baptist preacher Dr. Franklin Wilson, who had the stone Rockdale Chapel constructed in Woodberry and paid

and social theology, which either could directly challenge the inequalities of capitalism or could develop self-respect and a certain autonomy.

The evangelical outreach into the mill communities created functioning and nurturing neighborhoods. If this ran counter to the theory that all industrial social organization should lead to class warfare, it was because this message was more attractive to the Baltimore operatives. As in all evangelical efforts, the establishment of order, especially in light of the potential for disorder endemic to the liminal experience of conversion, was paramount. In individual terms, the demands of personal holiness necessitated a high level of self-discipline;[62] the means by which community boundaries were to be developed, however, remained undetermined. In the city, with its relatively depersonalized social relations and the increasingly limited possibilities for achieving harmony, populist evangelicals emphasized the molding of alternative communities, such as congregations and reform organizations. In the mill neighborhoods, however, the ideal of social harmony seemed more attainable, given the proper conditions, which were invariably manifested in a paternalistic system certainly influenced by workers but over time increasingly dominated by owners. The Christian paternalism that developed in Baltimore's mill communites, with owners eventually making contributions to itinerant preaching efforts and church buildings in direct response to worker requests, was thought to be a viable, even preferential option to class-oriented struggle.[63]

Descriptions of later abuses of paternalism in factory life have become commonplace, but in this era of incipient industrialism paternalism was as often a genuine attempt to alleviate the problems accompanying industrialism or to extend the potential for limited upward social mobility as it was a calculated effort to instill rationalized work discipline.[64] And, most important, this paternalism was not the major message of the itinerants

Wilder's salary. The church was an immediate success but floundered in 1855 when fires at two local factories left the operatives without work. [no author], *History of the Hampden Baptist Church in Honor of Her 100th Anniversary* (Baltimore, 1948), 3–5, in the possession of the Baptist Convention of Maryland/Delaware, History Center, Columbia, Md.

62. Howe, "Evangelical Movement," 1220–21.

63. By 1847, paternalism related to church buildings in the villages had grown. The Methodist church in Woodberry had been constructed with one-third of the costs carried by the operatives and two-thirds by mill owner Horatio Gambrill. *Sun*, July 29, 1847, cited by Harvey, "*People Is Grass*," 7–12 (with Harvey's thanks to John McGrain). Despite the obvious temptation to pass judgment indiscriminately on paternalist owners, the issue at stake here is the agency of the operatives who for their own reasons embraced and participated in the construction of mill community paternalism. Harvey, "*People Is Grass*," 26.

64. For owners' attempts to control all aspects of workers' lives, including their religious organizations and theologies, in the twentieth century, see Liston Pope, *Millhands and*

themselves, but rather the by-product of the revamped cosmology that had rejected the traditional limits of human initiative and expanded the boundaries of the morally neutral to include economic systems (if not personal behavior). As a result, wages and work organization in the factories were, for some owners, beyond the realm of ethical consideration. As Michael McBlair of the Maryland Manufacturing Company noted when confronted with the fact that his female workers could not make ends meet on their meager salaries, he had agreed to pay them what pittance their labor was worth on the open market and nothing more.[65] But evangelical factory owners seemed to be still constrained by generic Golden Rule ethics; thus (as it was for evangelical artisans) their emphasis was on creating workable communities where the results of disproportionate power relations were meliorated, not challenged. Preached by itinerants, practiced by workers and owners alike, and appreciated by the majority of operatives when it reflected genuine concern for their social interests and respect for their personal rights, nascent factory paternalism in Jacksonian Baltimore was more complex than the mere rationalization of exploitation.

In the supremely organized approach to evangelism pioneered by the Methodists, young, exuberant exhorters and local preachers like Henry

---

Preachers: A Study of Gastonia (New Haven: Yale University Press, 1942). An archetypical example of paternalism in the Jacksonian era was the Dyottville Glass Works established outside Philadelphia by T. W. Dyott, where the innovative owner sought to guarantee the development of "the happy man, the good citizen, and the valuable operative" and to simultaneously destroy inefficient artisan craft traditions by employing boys, "taking them at so tender an age that their pliant natures could be moulded into habits of temperance, industry, docility, piety, and perfect moral decorum." The proposed pious morality, however, was the antithesis of populist evangelicalism, and the overall tone at Dyottville was one of Enlightenment rationalism run amuck. T. W. Dyott, *An Exposition of the System of Moral and Mental Labor, Established at the Glass Factory of Dyottville, in the County of Philadelphia* (Philadelphia, 1833). Dyott's experiment was ideologically linked to the state guardianship plan (wherein laboring-class children would be educated by the state because workers were not to be trusted with such responsibility) extolled by the antievangelical and erstwhile labor radicals Robert Dale Owen and Fanny Wright. Wilentz, *Chants Democratic*, 178–80. For a description of eighteenth-century Methodist factory paternalism, see Steffen, *Mechanics of Baltimore*, 270–73. I am indebted to James Barrett for the material on Dyottville.

65. Factory work was attractive to male rural migrants because, even including adjustments for room and board, agricultural labor averaged seventy-five cents a day for seasonal work only. The female labor force in McBlair's factory, however, were paid much less; there five dollars a month was average, with a dollar taken out for rent as well as money to maintain a starchy diet of bread, mush, and salted fish. D. R. Adams Jr., "Prices and Wages in Maryland, 1750–1850," *Journal of Economic History* 46 (Sept. 1986): 633–36; Michael McBlair Papers, boxes 3 and 4, MS 1355, Maryland Historical Society, cited in Brooks and Rockel, *History of Baltimore County*, 202.

Slicer trekked to the newly established factory communities outside Baltimore. Henry Slicer was born near the turn of the century in Annapolis, the son of Methodist parents. At sixteen, Slicer came to Baltimore as an apprentice to chairmaker and Methodist master Jacob Daley. A year later, during services at Exeter Street Methodist Church, the young apprentice was converted and joined the church. He became sufficiently active in volunteer church business that Daley willingly granted him time to prepare for the itinerancy. At twenty, Slicer was licensed to preach and sent to western Virginia, where he was responsible for a three-hundred-mile circuit and he preached on average twenty-six times a month. Safely surviving this evangelical rite of passage, he returned two years later to the Baltimore–Washington, D.C., area where he spent the rest of his life in various ministries, including a tour as chaplain of the United States Senate. During the Methodist Protestant upheaval in the 1820s, he stayed with the mother denomination, but he openly opposed the high-handed tactics of the Methodist hierarchy in the expulsions of Dennis Dorsey and William Pool.[66]

Slicer was a typical Second Great Awakening itinerant; unlettered but oratorically powerful, he preached so that "plain men can understand every sentence, and the arguments are so aptly put that no one can fail to feel their force." He was renowned as a revival preacher whose severe denunciation of individual sin was tempered with a deeply held and effectively expressed conviction of the grace of God.[67] Despite the upward mobility available to him through his political contacts, Slicer remained one of the common people he celebrated and spoke out aggressively against actions he deemed socially immoral, especially duelling, lotteries,

66. J. McKendree Reilly, "Rev. Henry Slicer, D.D." (unpub. paper read before the American Methodist Historical Society, Oct. 7, 1874), Slicer Papers, Lovely Lane Museum, Baltimore; J. H. Dashiell, *Memoir of Rev. Henry Slicer, D.D.* (Baltimore, 1875), 3–5. J. E. Snodgrass, editor of the *Baltimore Saturday Visiter* in the 1840s, claimed that Slicer's apprenticeship had been in "the trade of fancy furniture painting," whereas former editor J. H. Hewitt identified Slicer as an apprentice printer, but the other sources agree on Daley. *Baltimore Saturday Visiter*, Oct. 1, 1842; Hewitt, *Shadows on the Wall*, 170–71. For descriptions and statistics on the incredible hardships endured by Methodist itinerants and the high number of early deaths, see Novak, "Perils of Respectability" 16–17; Wigger, "Taking Heaven by Storm," 81–144, esp. 100–109; Hatch, *Democratization of Christianity*, 88–89. Slicer was first elected to the chaplaincy on September 11, 1837. The *Republican* reported favorably upon his reelection in December of that year, by twenty-six out of thirty votes cast. Slicer, *Journal*, 1:243, 253; *Republican*, Dec. 9, 1837. Jennings, *Exposition*, 223.

67. Among his more effective revivalist work were the results of August 5–11, 1830, when two hundred people converted at a revival that was "more extensive than ever before witnessed" in the area." Slicer, *Journal*, 1:22; Dashiell, *Memoir of Henry Slicer*, 6–7, 9–10.

and intemperance.[68] Throughout his career, Slicer was the antithesis of the obsequious minister, never backing off from confrontations, ecclesiastical or secular. In 1848, Slicer was publicly attacked by Congressman John Slingerland of New York, who accused Slicer (and the Methodist Church) of sanctifying the practice of slave-holding because Slicer was seen exchanging pleasantries with an alleged Methodist slavedealer on a train bound for Baltimore. Slicer responded by casting aspersions on Slingerland's bravery, calling his attack on a minister "a very safe experiment . . . as ministers are commanded to be 'no strikers,' and are admonished 'not to return railing for railing.'" But Slicer would have nothing to do with such meekness; after explaining that the meeting with the slavedealer (who was, Slicer maintained, not a Methodist) was incidental, that he would shake hands with "Big Thunder" himself "without supposing that I . . . assumed any of his moral responsibilities," and that he had long labored to better the circumstances of African-Americans, both slave and free, Slicer concluded, "But I 'know my rights; and knowing, dare maintain them.'"[69]

Slicer, as part of his published defense against Slingerland's allegations, described himself as "a plain man . . . being early in life devoted, not to literature, but to an honest mechanical calling." As proud of his artisan origins as he was, however, he was not particularly cognizant of trade union activism and was absent from Baltimore during the rise of the WMTU.[70] Nevertheless, his sermons (especially in his early years) were compatible to

68. Slicer was a personal friend, through his contacts in the Senate, with both James Polk and James Buchanan. Slicer, *Journal*, 2:242 (June 19, 1849), Lovely Lane Museum; Henry Slicer to James Buchanan, Dec. 7, 1858, Slicer Papers, Lovely Lane Museum, Baltimore. When John Hersey, the primitive Methodist known for his outspoken producerism and abolitionism, wrote to rebuke Slicer's moderate antislavery views, he sarcastically apologized, in light of Slicer's connections, for being presumptuous, but was confident that "the fear of man would not deter you from a faithful discharge of this duty" of supporting abolitionism. John Hersey to Henry Slicer, July 18, 1847 in Slicer Papers, Lovely Lane Museum, Baltimore. Hersey misjudged the feisty Slicer; it was fear for the continued viability of the Methodist Church as a unified institution, not the fear of man, that informed all of Slicer's social ethics.

69. *New York Tribune*, May 5, 1848; *Union*, May 1848, in Slicer Papers, Lovely Lane Museum, Baltimore. Slicer was, however, increasingly antiabolitionist and influenced the Baltimore Conference in that direction. John Dixon Long, *Pictures of Slavery in Church and State; Including Personal Reminiscences, Biographical Sketches, Anecdotes, etc., etc., with an Appendix, Containing the Views of John Wesley and Richard Watson on Slavery* (Philadelphia, 1857), 281–82.

70. *New York Tribune*, May 5, 1848. Slicer was preaching on the Potomac District circuit in 1833, so he was not in Baltimore during the journeymen's initial organizing. He was also at this time active in temperance work. Slicer, *Journal*, 1:62, Lovely Lane Museum, Baltimore. His later correspondence with fellow Methodist and *Mechanic's Banner* editor Robert Ricketts was restricted to discussions of Democratic politics. Robert Ricketts to Henry Slicer, Aug. 15, 1840, Slicer Papers, Lovely Lane Museum, Baltimore.

the tenets of producerism and Christian republicanism underlying the journeymen's uprising, and his willingness to span the extremes of American society was reflected in his preaching schedule; in one week in January 1836, he delivered an address to the Senate, spoke at a Methodist church in the Washington area, and preached to an African-American congregation in Baltimore. Equally significant was the invitation tendered to him to speak at the dedication of the plebeian Columbia Avenue Methodist Church in 1844. Slicer's class-inclusive preaching schedule also reflected his vision of creating alternative structures to eased the effects of industrialization—the hallmark of Methodist factory preaching.[71]

Henry Slicer preached without ceasing. During his time on circuits in the Baltimore area from 1829 to 1832, he often ministered to newly formed missions near the Union, Washington, Powhatan, Baltimore, and Warren factories, and he recorded the scriptural texts used in these visits to factory missions. Given the later sermon outlines in his journal and the fact that he often preached from the same texts, we can draw tentative conclusions about the nature, tone, and content of his factory preaching.[72] As expected from an evangelical preacher, the largest number of Slicer's texts concerned calls for conversion. In typical revivalist fashion, Slicer chose scriptures that emphasized the negative motivation of the wrath of God (Hab. 3:2, Rom. 2:4–5, Luke 13:6–9) as well as those that described the mercy and love of God (John 3:16, Rev. 3:20), all in the context of divine affirmation. But the ecstasy of conversion was always tempered by the establishment of order and self-discipline; therefore, Slicer also chose scriptures to introduce sermons reflecting preeminent Methodist concerns with individual and communal sanctification, perfectionism, and holy living (Rev. 3:12, 2 Pet. 3:14, 1 Cor. 1:30).[73]

Slicer's response to the troubles and misfortunes of life as reflected in his sermons was double-edged. On the one hand, he emphasized spiritual consolation (Num. 14:24, Isa. 50:10, Ps. 68:19, Ps. 84:10, Eccles. 9:5, Rev. 7:16);

71. *Sun*, Feb. 9, 15, 1844. The implicit leveling of Slicer's message was evident in his claim that "the most unletter'd African who has been enlightened by the gospel and has felt its saving power knows more of the future world than the most enlightened ancient or modern philosopher who has not been blessed with the gospels light and power." Slicer, *Journal*, 1:120 (Jan. 3, 1836); 1:218 (May 18, 1837).

72. Slicer left a record, albeit spotty at times, of his activities in journals he kept from the late 1820s well into the 1850s. The entries were geographically and chronologically specific, though vague in content; in later years the journals included some sermon outlines and thoughts on contemporary issues.

73. Slicer, *Journal*, 1:19, 20, 27, 29, 39. As early as 1820, Slicer was apparently preaching at the Sabbath School established at the Powhatan Factory. Ibid., 2:296.

he preached that the grace of God could meliorate present distresses and promised hope for both the mediate and eternal futures. Empowerment was another prominent theme, as he appealed to scriptures that demanded the righteous confrontation of social ills (Ps. 40:1–3, John 17:15, 2 Pet. 1:10–11, Rev. 3:12). This combination of consolation and empowerment, for populist evangelicals, was neither surprising nor contradictory; it was an open-ended recognition of unlimited opportunities coexisting with unfulfilled promise, characteristic of early nineteenth century life.[74] The possibilities implicit in the populist evangelical message were surely not lost on Slicer's audiences. And although how they reacted was left to them, the social implications of Slicer's preaching were by no means devoid of direction. Equally significant as what he did preach to factory workers was what he underemphasized. Conspicuous by their absence, particularly in light of the assumption that evangelical preaching to the lower orders stressed quietism and obedience, are the scriptures usually cited to support the ideal of unquestioned submission to authority (e.g., Rom. 13:1–3, Eph. 6:5–8; Col. 3:22–23). Moreover, only two of Slicer's texts (Heb. 11:24–26, Luke 10:42) stress faith-informed resignation (not to be confused with indiscriminate submission) to the unavoidable difficulties of life.[75] This was not accidental. Evangelicals of the early national period, after all, were expected to take advantage of the dynamic of spiritual consolation to actively influence the affairs of the world.

The question remains: what social messages was Slicer presenting to his factory audiences? The empowerment messages offered by preachers like Slicer presents a subtle but significant change in direction for populist evangelicalism. Preoccupation with socioeconomic marginality and suspicion of liberal economics remained pressing issues. Slicer continually reminded his audiences that meaningful commitment to Christ and rejection of worldly ways would result not only in increased self-respect but also in ridicule from elements of the larger community, particularly the well situated. Slicer also reminded his listeners of the problematic nature of wealth: "Israel was in less danger when fed from hand to mouth in the wilderness, than when he had eaten and was full." And in citing Isa. 3:10 in a sermon delivered at the Warren Factory on May 6, 1828, he drew from the same chapter that the journeymen coopers and Mathew Carey had employed in their respective appeals against the oppressors of the poor. Slicer repeated this emphasis six

74. Ibid., 1:22, 26–27, 39.

75. Only one sermon was based on a scripture (Rom. 13:12–14) describing the internal struggle against lust and temptation; the evangelical preoccupation with these issues did not emerge until the Victorian period. Ibid., 1:17, 29.

months later when he used Ps. 15:1–5 to draw attention to the moral dangers of accumulating wealth. Power was as suspect as wealth; in a statement rife with possibilities for radical social upheaval, Slicer encouraged his audience to "renounce all other authority but Christ's."[76] Slicer's commoner pedigree was not to be challenged.

Yet nowhere in Slicer's record are the suggestive social implications of these producer-oriented ideals realized. Instead, Slicer epitomized the gradual mainstream evangelical shift from the communitarian preference for social justice within a producerist context to the psychological concern regarding individual sin within a liberal republican context, and he moved from correction of communal abuses to concern with personal holiness and survival in a depersonalized environment. To be sure, the perception within evangelicalism that moral regeneration must precede meaningful social change had always existed, so this shift in emphasis was not unprecedented. The upward mobility enjoyed by respectable Methodists encouraged this trend. And Slicer's views of power and wealth also reflected new evangelical understandings of authority and economic ethics.

Slicer's use of Psalm 15 included mention of the moral instability of wealth, but his treatment of the passage was more concerned with the necessity of mutual respect and integrity among all social classes. Similarly, his advice to renounce all authority but Christ's was not a call to socio-economic or political leveling but rather expressive of a concern that half-hearted commitments would invariably result in backsliding and endanger the reputation of the church community. Slicer's interpretation of the "authority" to be renounced, therefore, was the power of personal sin: not a social but an internal phenomenon. What social dimension remained in this approach concentrated again on the creation of an alternative community—the congregation—in which the older ideal of social harmony (more difficult than ever to achieve in the context of modernization) could be realized. "By bringing the rich man and poor together and associating them in public," asserted Slicer, "the strong lines that exist in private life are softened, and, engaged in worshiping a common Lord, different ranks meet as brothers."[77] This sentiment, reflecting the traditional producerist emphasis on the harmony of interests, might work until the evangelical rich decided they did not want to be "brothers" in any meaningful sense. In the mean-

76. Ibid., 1:120 (Jan. 3, 1836); 1:218 (May 18, 1837); 1:132 (Apr. 27, 1836). Slicer also alluded to the Prayer of Azur, a passage utilized by both Thomas Branagan and William Cobbett to support their evangelical criticisms of capitalist ethics.

77. Ibid., 1:132, (Apr. 27, 1836); 1:204, (Apr. 9, 1837).

time, Slicer was abandoning the prophetic judgment of these scriptures against the presumption that wealth indicated moral superiority.

This phenomenon became most obvious in the "Jubilee Sermon" which Slicer preached to factory audiences as often as he presented any other. The scripture cited was Ps. 89:15–16, in which the rest and social readjustment of the Sabbath/Jubilee tradition, announced by the blast of Israel's trumpet, was extolled. According to the Jubilee, at the end of every fifty years, the means of economic gain (i.e., land) were to be returned to original owners, but not the profits gained from the industrious use of those means. This plan was designed to recognize and reward personal initiative within limits, while also preventing excessive accumulation and advantage in economic transactions. The Jubilee had long inspired radical Christian critiques of maldistribution of wealth and power, from the seventeenth-century Levelers to the Methodist and Quaker radicals (William Stilwell, James Covel, and Cornelius Blatchly) of the New York Society for Promoting Communities.[78] In contradistinction to this tradition, which identified wealth and power as temptations to sinfulness in and of themselves, however, Slicer's Jubilee was spiritualized. Preaching at a camp meeting on September 1, 1829, Slicer described Psalm 89 in Jubilee terms which "provided for the deliverance of the Captive—for the liberation of the Slave—for the release of the Debtor and his return to his forfeited inheritance or possession—this was typical of the Gospel." Slicer went on to emasculate the prophetic implications of his text relative to capitalist accumulation; all, he claimed, were "Captives to Satan—Slaves to sin—Debtors to divine justice; having forfeited his inheritance" and "must . . . have an experiential knowledge and enjoyment of liberty, etc. as offered by the Gospel."[79] According to this reduction of biblical ethics to spiritual analogies, Slicer ignored the potential for demanding readjustments in keeping with tenets of producerist justice while retaining the possibility of empowering psychological change.

The thrust of this message was clear—the nation would be purified by the internal transformation of individuals, not by the producerist leveling of the economic playing field. Even as Slicer was encouraging his audience to become involved in the sanctification of America (and in keeping with his loyalty to the Democratic Party),[80] he preached that reform was to be

78. Linebaugh, "Jubilating," 143–80; Sutton, "To Extract Poison."

79. Slicer, *Journal*, 1:13–14.

80. Slicer's devotion to the Democratic Party was long-lived; he defended the rights of Irish and Germans to vote and denounced the nativist violence against them in the Know-Nothing riots of 1859. Ibid., 3:204 (Apr. 8, 1859).

established through the agency of moral suasion, not community or governmental coercion. This voluntarist perception was a logical extension of the doctrine of church-state separation, but it also reflected the inability of populist evangelicals to enforce discipline within their own ranks when disestablishment meant transgressors could easily move on to a more lax congregation. In a similar ideological progression, Slicer, while remaining politically active himself, increasingly supported the ideal of separating political agendas from spiritual ones. Thus, by 1842, his interpretation of Matt. 21 and 22 had Jesus refusing to become embroiled in the schemes of either the government or the people. This interpretation, in turn, led him to conclude that Christianity "enjoins a peaceable subjection to the powers that be" and that "the Christian religion is no enemy to Civil Government—but a friend and support."[81] This was quietism with qualifications; nevertheless, it tended to proscribe any number of radical responses to socioeconomic abuses and it signified important points of evangelical accommodation to the emergent culture of liberalism.

Henry Slicer's tendency to spiritualize biblical ethics was wide-ranging. Nowhere was this clearer than in his address in November 1835 at the Wesley Church in Washington, D.C., to the Female Benevolent Association of the Foundry Chapel. In this talk, Slicer acknowledged that preachers were called to specifically spell out and condemn the sins of the populace with no regard for social position. Reflecting the populist evangelical legacy of suspicion toward the privileged, Slicer declared that "the unfortunate drunkard, etc. are readily provided with their portion by the ministry—but who dare charge the rich." Appealing to the authority of Saint Paul, Slicer described the uncertainty and dangers of wealth: "the aristocracy of one generation are the yeomanry or the plebeians of the next—and vice versa" while "riches bring . . . flattery . . . and so engender pride."[82] This last point was critical; the potential immorality of wealth, no longer linked to the socioeconomic

81. Ibid., 2:85, (Mar. 27, 1842). As an indication that discipline in a disestablished milieu was proving difficult to enforce, class meetings began to disappear from the Methodist polity during this period. David Holsclaw, "The Demise of Disciplined Christian Fellowship: The Methodist Class Meeting in Nineteenth Century America" (Ph.D. diss., University of California, Davis, 1979).

82. Ibid., 1:90, (Nov. 30, 1835); 2:85, (Mar. 27, 1842). Slicer also expressed this anti-Whig sentiment toward keeping political and spiritual concerns separated in his outspoken objection to the practice of including the names of secular political leaders on the membership roles of missionary societies with whom they had no real involvement. Ibid., 2:127–28, (Apr. 21, 1844). In the address, Slicer referred to John Wesley who had disapprovingly maintained that "in 60 years he had not heard a sermon expressly on the subject of riches." Ibid., 1:89–90, (Nov. 30, 1835).

sins of exploitation and oppression, had been reduced to the psychological sins of pride and misplaced trust.[83]

Equally profound in Slicer's social theology were the new moral imperatives attached to economics and wealth. Acknowledging that "money is power," Slicer stated that the rich still had social duties; they were to be "high-minded" so that they could "do good" by being willing to "instruct the ignorant—cloathe the naked—visit the sick" and in general be "ready to distribute."[84] This was a fundamental tenet of traditional economic morality: it challenged the ways in which wealth was originally generated and demanded that its distribution be removed from control of the accumulator. The modernized evangelical morality, however, merely wanted to request, through the agency of moral suasion and conscience, that those who accumulated also share, in ways which, of course, the wealthy were to determine. Thus the ethics of wealth were based not on the fairness and justice of its production but on the benevolent distribution of the resulting excess profits, with the latter responsibility denominated "stewardship." As Slicer put it, "To bestow pecuniary relief is the priviledge of the rich."[85] The results, quite obviously, led to various expressions of paternalistic benevolence and had profound implications, for the future of evangelized factory workers and the evangelical community, as the liberal doctrine of stewardship challenged continued allegiance to traditional economic morality. This was not the same, however, as pure and simple accommodation to the laissez-faire abandonment of moral obligations to workers altogether.

Isaac Cook was another young and energetic evangelical preacher. Cook was born in 1810 and raised in Baltimore; his background and subsequent evangelical career were similar to that of Henry Slicer. Cook's mother was raised a Quaker and as a young woman had become a well-known preacher in her own right, but she was disfellowshipped for marrying a soldier (Cook's father who had served with Washington at Valley Forge during the Revolution) and evaded Quaker discipline by joining the Methodists. While the father's occupation remains unknown, according to his son, his "avocations were humble but respectable; an honest struggle for a moderate support, such as poor men often suffer." Cook was one of the original Methodist

83. For a detailed explanation of this tendency, see Robert A. Wauzzinski, *Between God and Gold: Protestant Evangelicalism and the Industrial Revolution* (Rutherford, N.J.; Fairleigh Dickinson Press, 1993).

84. Slicer, *Journal*, 1:89, 90 (Nov. 30, 1835).

85. Ibid., 1:132 (Apr. 27, 1836).

Sabbath scholars in Baltimore, joining the school at age nine. As a young man he worked for the small Methodist printing firm of Armstrong and Plaiskett (publishers of John Hersey's populist manuals on Christian living) and by 1831 was able to open his own bookselling business, which he maintained throughout his life. He was also instrumental in the formation of the Savings Bank of Baltimore, a nonprofit institution established to help working people gain their competences. His real concern, however, was with the fortunes of the Methodist Episcopal Church; discussions at his bookstore were much more likely to concern religion than business. Converted at fifteen, he received permission to exhort two years later, became licensed as a local preacher in 1830, and in 1831 became a charter member of the Local Preachers and Exhorters Association of Baltimore, a group of energetic lay ministers active in supplying missions and establishing new Methodist congregations in the city and surrounding area. By 1836, he was ordained deacon in the Light Street Methodist Church, and for the next forty-eight years he was intimately involved in Baltimore Methodism.[86]

One of Cook's duties as a young preacher was coordinating preaching to the incipient factory congregations in the Baltimore area. Under his direction in the early 1830s, the Local Preachers and Exhorters Association organized a regular schedule of preaching for the factory missions. Cook was one of the preachers, originally spending one weekly assignment out of eight at the factories, preaching and teaching Sunday School, for example, to the 150 hands at Lanvale Factory in the mid-1830s. Cook, as a local preacher, was almost as active as Slicer, the itinerant. It was not uncommon for Cook to spend his day off from the bookstore as he did on April 24, 1836, when he preached morning, afternoon, and evening from Ps. 89:15–16 (the text of Slicer spiritualized Jubilee Sermon) at William Street Church, Gray's Factory, and the Maryland Penitentiary, respectively. Cook's preaching, it seems from the texts chosen, was not as activist as Slicer's, nor did it range as widely; by far his preeminent concerns were to stimulate conversions (Rom. 10:13 and 6:23, 1 Pet. 3:18, 1 Tim. 1:15, Ps. 47:7–9), to encourage spiritual consolation in present times of distress (John 14:27, Rom. 8:32, Matt. 19:27), and to provide self-respect and survival skills for the members of his audience (Dan. 6:21–22, Jn. 5:1–9, Prov. 13:15, 3 John 2). Typical of the message of compen-

86. Isaac Cook to Henry Furlong, May 18, 1841, in Furlong-Baldwin Papers, M193, Maryland Historical Society, Baltimore; Isaac P. Cook's unpublished autobiography and Isaac Cook's Record Book, Isaac Cook Papers, Lovely Lane Museum, Baltimore; *American*, Feb. 16, 1884; *Sun*, Feb. 16, 1884; *Pioneer*, Mar. 1, 1884. For the Savings Bank, see Payne and Davis, *Savings Bank of Baltimore*, 16–21, 32.

sation was a string of sermons Cook delivered at the Union Factory between 1834 and 1840, citing Heb. 10:36, Rom. 8:18, and a passage from Job. Only rarely (citing Amos 6:1) did Cook emphasize the populist theme of divine judgment on the comfortable who neglected stewardship, but, like both Slicer and the journeymen coopers, he did occasionally utilize the anti-oppression message of the third chapter of Isaiah.[87]

The Methodist legacy of cultural marginality (1 Cor. 1:23, 2 Tim. 1:12, Rom. 1:16) was also evident in Cook's sermons, as was the need to embrace the promises of the gospel over the need to gain social status. His clearest statement relative to the contemporary situation in Baltimore came in a sermon based on John 18:36, wherein the arrested Jesus informed Pilate that a political revolution involving his followers was impossible because his kingdom "was not of this world." But Cook's choice of this antimilitant passage (presented as it was in the context of Jesus's complete refusal to submit to the authority of his religious hierarchy) should not be mistaken for docility; if Cook had wanted to preach submission to authority in all situations, he could have cited Jesus' rebuke of Peter in the Garden of Gethsemane earlier in that chapter of John. This sermon, moreover, preached as it was at least four times in 1834 (and apparently not at any other time) in various types of congregations, was probably a reaction to the general conditions of rioting current in the country and not directed at any specific class of Methodists.[88] To recognize in this sermon encouragement to build alternative communities based on shared faith would be a more accurate interpretation of Cook's intent.

The most critical element of Cook's preaching, however, may have had nothing to do with the content; rather, the fact that he preached the same sermon (or at least quoted from the same scriptural texts) to different audiences is symptomatic of the class-inclusive perspective of the Methodists. Of the sixty-four sermons preached to factory congregations from 1829 to 1838, Cook presented almost all of them to other congregations within Baltimore in that same time period. He preached the sermon based on John 18:36, for instance, at the established congregations of Exeter and Eutaw Street churches and at the newly formed William Street church, and at the Union factory, all within the span of six months. Moreover, he often chose scriptures (Col. 3:11, Rom. 1:16 and 10:13, Luke 13:29) that emphasized the New

87. The Record Book of Isaac P. Cook, located in the Lovely Lane Museum, Baltimore, records the locations, dates, and texts of Cook's sermons for approximately fifty years. For a discussion of the sermons offered at Union Factory, see McGrain, *From Pig Iron to Cotton Duck*, 2:335.

88. Isaac Cook Papers, Lovely Lane Museum, Baltimore.

Testament declaration of the inclusive nature of the new covenant underlying the emerging Christian church.[89]

The moral prerogatives of paternalism evident in Slicer's sermons was manifested in Cook's experience with the voluntarist factory preaching system. In the early days Cook and other local preachers walked the fourteen mile round-trip to Powhatan in all kinds of weather. They were rewarded by the operatives' enthusiastic response as well as the kind reception they received from the factory superintendent. In later years, sympathetic factory owners like the Methodist David Carroll sent their carriages into town to transport the preachers to the factory. Carroll had translated the competence he gained as a journeyman ironworker at the Savage Iron Works into co-ownership of the Washington, Whitehall, and Woodberry Cotton factories (purchased in 1832, 1839, and 1842, respectively).[90] The neighborhood that grew up around the last factory, still known as Hampden-Woodberry, became a stable and thriving community, with many workers participating in running local congregations and owning their own homes, all with the help of David Carroll. This cooperation between owners and itinerants was endemic to the paternalism of factory communities like Hampden-Woodberry, and no doubt it helped to blunt evangelical consciousness of economic oppression and worker exploitation. So, however, did the undeniable (if intermittent) generosity of owners like Carroll, and the gratitude felt by the operatives was genuine.[91]

If the records of the experiences and philosophies of Baltimore artisans are difficult to recover, those of Baltimore-area factory operatives in the 1830s are apparently nonexistent. To reconstruct the influence of populist evangelicalism on both groups, we must make conjectures based on the messages of popular preachers like Slicer and Cook, the known activities of producerist artisans and small masters, and the intermittent militancy of Baltimore's artisans and operatives.[92] This much is clear: the notion of evangelical docility in the face of capitalist transformation must be assigned to the historio-

89. Ibid.

90. Cook, *Early History of Sabbath Schools*, 23–24; *American*, July 31, 1881.

91. D. Randall Beirne, "Hampden-Woodberry: The Mill Village in an Urban Setting," *Maryland Historical Magazine* 77 (spring 1982): 6–15. The financial needs of factory congregations were serious. Stone, *History of Hampden M. P. Church*, 16–17. For more on Carroll, see [no author], *Souvenir Book of the Hampden-Woodberry 60th Anniversary Celebration* (Baltimore, 1898), 68, 71.

92. As described in the epilogue, operatives at the Union Factory went on strike for higher wages (in cash) in October 1843 and a decade later, workers in Baltimore area mills staged a massive walkout to demand the ten-hour day. *American*, Oct. 10, 1843; Brooks and Rockel, *History of Baltimore County*, 202.

graphical oblivion it so richly deserves. By discarding untested assumptions, we can recover some of the complexity of evangelical artisan responses, as well as an understandings of the institutional activity that was to follow. In this light, Henry Slicer and Isaac Cook, representative of those preaching at factories, offered an alternative message of populist congregation-building. The new evangelical social consciousness largely ignored explicit allegiance to producerist economic morality even as it insisted on responsible stewardship, benevolent paternalism, and community cooperation.

But Slicer and Cook were not the only ones building artisan and factory congregations. The creation of the Strawbridge Methodist Church in 1842 by laboring-class Methodists in northwest Baltimore illustrates a second influence: that of producerist journeymen and small masters active in the years of the WMTU militancy. Local Methodists, in one of Baltimore's growing artisan neighborhoods, established a Sunday School in a private home on Howard Street, and this steadily grew into the Howard Street Mission by 1839. Three years later the congregation joined nearby Falls Chapel and decided to construct their own building. Located at Biddle and Linden Streets, the church was raised during the depression following the panic of 1837 with material and skill donated by its members, many of them unemployed artisans. The members renamed their congregation the Strawbridge Methodist Church.[93]

The leadership of this congregation included a cross-section of those involved in trade union agitation: Charles Towson, Elisha Carback, Edmund Loane, Jesse Zumwalt (Sumwalt), and John Tilyard. Towson was president of the journeymen hatters in 1836, and Carback and Loane were producerist shoemakers, acclaimed for giving the cordwainers their prices during a strike that same year. Loane, in addition, was a class leader and local preacher, who worked with Isaac Cook and visited the Thistle Factory every four weeks in the mid-1830s. The master plasterer Zumwalt was cited for granting his journeymen the ten-hour day in 1835. Tilyard was also a compatriot of Cook, preaching at the Powhatan Factory three weeks out of four during this time.[94]

93. Strawbridge M. E. Church Records, 1843–54, box 1, MS #1799, Maryland Historical Society. The congregation's namesake, Robert Strawbridge, was recognized as the first Methodist lay preacher in the Baltimore area and one of the first in the American colonies. Strawbridge was a carpenter and a popular preacher who vehemently opposed the creation a bishop-dominated Methodist hierarchy. He was the ideal patron saint of such a populist congregation.

94. Plan of Appointment, Local Preachers Association, in Isaac Cook Papers, Lovely Lane Museum, Baltimore.

The producerist legacy of these evangelical activists would remain as a residual influence on the congregational consciousness.

But increasingly, an alternative evangelical vision—that of church communities serving members as havens from the vicious dislocations of metropolitan industrialization—began to emerge. To be sure, such a drift away from the earlier antagonism toward modernization was operating simultaneously with continued populist evangelical activism; as the Strawbridge congregation grew to maturity, the Columbia Street Methodist Church in another middling-class Baltimore neighborhood was successfully rejecting an attempt by local ecclesiastical authority to control congregational matters. For those with ears to hear, the failure of the trade union movement coupled with the temporary disappointment of artisan militancy questioned the efficacy of direct opposition to cultural change, and the lessons were not lost on evangelicals who had been active as both sympathetic masters and activist journeymen. Thus the militant and righteous counter-hegemonic energy of the early stages of populist evangelicalism in the Second Great Awakening, especially as it supported the moral imperative of producerism and the journeymen's movement, was gradually replaced by the messages of alternative community, individual transcendence, and self-help as typified by Methodist factory preaching. And with the realization that producerist social relations were becoming more difficult to maintain, evangelicals pioneered new methods to meliorate conditions. Although the legacy of traditional economic morality persisted, in the early 1840s, less antagonistic reform efforts were appearing.

Chapter Seven

Evangelical Attempts to Ameliorate Capitalist Dislocation

On August 15, 1840, in the usual list of public notices regarding various religious, educational, and organizational meetings, the *Sun* printed a card from the WMTU. Signed by journeyman hatter activist Adrian Posey, the card announced the public sale of furniture from the Trades' Union Hall and officially signaled the demise of that once vibrant organization. Immediately above this notice was one from trade union sympathizer John F. Hoss representing a hitherto unknown group, the Washington Temperance Society. Hoss's note announced the society's first meeting open to the public.[1] Founded four months earlier as a self-help group by and for problem drinkers in the artisan class, the Washingtonians promised emotional and material support for "reformed drunkards" and invited interested parties from all classes to attend their experience meeting. The symbolic but unplanned juxtaposition of these two notices could not have been more prophetic. Although the WMTU officers continued to meet sporadically and although many of them

1. *Sun*, Aug. 15, 1840. In 1833, Posey had helped John Hawkins publicly articulate the journeymen hatters' complaints that initiated trade union agitation. *Republican*, July 30, 1833. At the same time, Hoss had chaired the mass meeting of Baltimoreans sympathetic to the journeymen hatters. *Republican*, July 29, 1833.

found alternate avenues to success, centralized trade unionism did not mount another serious offensive against capitalist encroachments in Baltimore for decades. In contrast, the infant Washington Temperance Society became arguably the most successful temperance movement in the United States by promoting total abstinence as a solution to socioeconomic difficulties. Whereas anticapitalist trade unionists considered systemic causes for their distress and advocated a varied agenda to moderate capitalist innovation, Washingtonians provided self-help survival skills for dislocated producers to increase their chances of success in the new market economy. Although both groups depended on the leadership of producerist artisans (in many cases the very same leaders) and enjoyed the support of populist evangelicals, their proposals to meliorate capitalist dislocation were significantly different.

The deflation of 1837–43 disrupted the lives of many Baltimoreans,[2] but evangelicalism continued to flourish. And in spite of producerist suspicions of accumulations of wealth and power and biblically inspired anxieties concerning the blurring of economic ethics, the optimistic, liberal sensibilities of modern American culture increasingly invaded mainstream evangelicalism. At this time, when self-discipline was rewarded and economic interdependence was no longer obligatory, some evangelicals began to adapt traditional voluntarist models of social concern to create new reform ideologies of humanitarian philanthropy and self-help.[3] Whereas reform was sometimes the work of elites driven either by conscience or by a desire for social control, artisans in the late 1830s and 1840s developed their own philanthropic and self-help initiatives: the Washingtonian temperance movement, the home missionary outreach to the poor, and the broad-based support for sabbatarianism. Although these efforts were still shaped by the tenets of traditional economic morality and artisan mutuality, the self-help doctrines of the Washingtonians emphasized the efficacy of individual applications to overcome socioeconomic dislocation, the humanitarian benevolence of the home missionary effort aided the poor even as it emphasized character development over environmental inequities, and the largely symbolic reforms

2. Browne, *Baltimore in the Nation,* 130–39; Pearce, "Early Baltimore Potters," xii–xiii, 69–70; Hollander, *Financial History of Baltimore,* 180–81.

3. Watts, *Republic Reborn,* xxii; A. Gregory Schneider, *The Way of the Cross Leads Home: The Domestication of American Methodism* (Bloomington: Indiana University Press, 1993), 196–208. Church groups had always been in the forefront of the effort to address social issues, but in the 1840s, these efforts were less deferential and less paternalistic than previous work. Terry Bilhartz estimated that in the early decades of the nineteenth century, the number of church groups engaged in such activity was more than double that of their secular counterparts. Bilhartz, *Urban Religion,* 100–101.

of the sabbatarians replaced systemic analyses of capitalist dislocation. None of these new labors rejected the producerist legacy; rather, they offered alternative solutions to social problems.

The emergence of a discernible bourgeoisie was a critical element in this development. But in Baltimore, any attempt to discover full-blown class struggle within the context of industrialization remains problematic because of the continued relevance of the ideal of class harmony and the model of entrepreneurial development informed by republican and evangelical conscience; nevertheless, new social perceptions were clearly evident. Middling evangelical populists in the early decades of the nineteenth century had understood themselves to be in solidarity with the lower ranks; increasingly in the 1840s, according to the inculcation of respectable tastes and fashionable consumption, the middle class (evangelical and otherwise) came to share with the wealthy a semipermanent financial security, relatively exalted social positions, and previously unattainable creature comforts. The unpolished but popular Baptist revivalist Jacob Knapp drew attention to this change when he complained of his treatment in December 1841 by what he called Bostonian "wiseacres" who attacked him on cultural not theological grounds. Although it was nowhere made clear how they gained access to such knowledge, his socially respectable opponents circulated rumors concerning the coarse nature of his wardrobe, especially what they deemed a minimal number of changes of underwear.[4] Furthering this trend was the changing ethnic nature of the lower classes themselves, as geographic mobility continued to alter the composition of urban populations and as waves of Irish and German immigrants inundated Baltimore in the 1840s.[5] At the same time, evangelicals of all denominations, as they entered the institutional phase of the Second Great Awakening, began to embrace the common social

4. Laurie, "Spavined Ministers," in Rock, Gilje, and Asher, eds., *American Artisans*, 99–101; Blumin, *Emergence of the Middle Class*, 240–49. Lasch, *True and Only Heaven*, 180; Jacob Knapp, *Autobiography of Jacob Knapp* (New York, 1868), 130.

5. Theodore Hershberg, "Nineteenth-Century Baltimore: Historical and Geographical Perspectives: Commentary," in *Working Papers from the Regional Economic History Research Center* (Wilmington Del.: Eleutherian Mills–Hagley Foundation, 1980), 147. This was particularly pronounced after 1840; in the following twenty-year period, more than 17,000 German and Irish Catholic immigrants poured into Baltimore. John Wemmersten, "Recent Works on the History of Baltimore: Book Review Essay," *Maryland Historian* 11 (fall 1980): 41. For a general discussion of this phenomenon in terms of American workers, see Herbert G. Gutman, "Work, Culture, and Society in Industrializing America, 1815–1919," *American Historical Review* 78 (1973): 537, 540. See also Stanley Nadel, "From the Barricades of Paris to the Sidewalks of New York: German Artisans and the European Roots of American Labor Radicalism," *Labor History* 30 (winter 1989): 47–48.

ground necessary to build an evangelical establishment designed to usher in the Kingdom of God in America.[6] The theological hallmark of this development was the spread of Arminianism, which among other things emphasized individual empowerment and strengthened the idea that the poor were not predestined to poverty but rather possessed the means, through the power of the human will, to break out of downward economic cycles.

The widely noted embourgeoisement and mainstreaming of American evangelicalism in the 1840s was reflected in a number of ways.[7] In general terms (though often with reservations), common Americans across the board moved toward accommodation to liberal culture, and the evangelical center was no exception. As a lay historian of the originally plebeian Columbia Avenue Methodist congregation explained: "It has been the good fortune of the church to ever keep abreast of the times . . . as tastes and views about things external become modified and altered. . . . A wise conservatism contends for the essence and spirit, leaving all else to be changed with the varying mood of the times. So thought those who have shaped the course of this church."[8] The changing architecture of Baltimore's populist churches is a striking example of this tendency. Methodist churches, in particular, raised funds to modernize their buildings, services, and teachings, and Gothic edifices began to replace the simple lines of older Methodist sanctuaries. By 1840, the spontaneous testimonies and the unrestrained emotionalism of communal Methodist worship had given way to decorous behavior, prepared sermons, organs, and paid choirs, in keeping with practices of the more staid Presbyterians and Episcopalians.[9] Such transformations, in the eyes of critics,

6. Marsden, *Evangelical Mind,* 104; Franch, "Congregation and Community," 141–42. In an editorial entitled "Sign of the Times," John Harrod noted that Baltimore evangelicals were treating each other "with increasing friendliness" and less "sectarian bigotry." *Methodist Protestant* 2 (July 15, 1835): 45. See also *Methodist Protestant* 2 (Sept. 30, 1835): 133. Previous to the 1830s, Methodists of all types tended to view the established evangelical network of associations as an ecclesiastical enemy. Charles I. Foster, *An Errand of Mercy: The Evangelical United Front, 1790–1837* (Chapel Hill: University of North Carolina Press, 1960), 127.

7. Cameron, *Methodism and Society,* 277; David Martin, *Tongues of Fire: The Explosion of Protestantism in Latin America* (Cambridge, Mass.: Basil Blackwell, 1990), 41–42. This process has extended into the historiography of antebellum Protestantism, with most religious historians celebrating this phenomenon as indicative of the golden age of American evangelicalism. See Richard W. Pointer, "'Recycling' Early American Religion: Some Historiographical Problems and Prospects," *Fides et Historia* 23 (fall 1991): 31–32.

8. "Historical Sketch of the Columbia Avenue Methodist Episcopal Church," 45. For similar sentiments, see Armstrong, *Old Baltimore Conference,* vi.

9. Franch, "Congregation and Community," 195. A contemporary visitor commented that in Baltimore, architecturally, there were no "great" Methodist churches. Buckingham,

were reflective of respectable expediency over primitive principles. But to their advocates, of course, they were far from apostasy; in fact, the growing Enlightenment-inspired preoccupation with order and rationalized conversion almost demanded those changes.

These innovations were also evident in the socioeconomic realm, with some socially prominent Methodists accepting the formerly anathematized rented pew system. In the early 1840s, no longer willing to bear the social opprobrium of unsophisticated Methodism, elite members in Baltimore, including Jacob Rogers (hat manufacturer), Comfort Tiffany (clothing merchant), and Conrad Fite (bank director), decided that they deserved a more refined congregational experience. These leaders, over the strenuous objection of respected ministers and factory preachers Henry Slicer and Isaac Cook, moved forward with plans to build a new church in Greek Revival style on fashionable Charles Street at Fayette Street, to buy an expensive organ for the new church, and to finance the project by selling conspicuously visible pews to wealthy members. The sale of the pews was advertised in the local papers as open to the public.[10]

Slicer and Cook were not alone in their objections to this break in tradition: the Baltimore Annual Conference expressed its reservations, and J. E. Snodgrass of the *Baltimore Saturday Visiter* was openly sarcastic: "Surely the Trustees of the said 'Pew Church' will not be so *silly* as to accede to the advice of the conference. How can the church expect such refined men to suffer their wives and daughters jostled in 'free pews' by the 'vulgar herd'!" The subsequent vote in the Baltimore City Station was ninety-three to nine against the project, and the Baltimore Annual Conference passed a resolution stating that "the Conference deprecates the system of pew Churches, and considers it an infraction of the discipline, and at variance with the general economy of the Church," yet the erection of the new church went on as planned.[11] Its construction was an indication of the growing power of the

---

America, Historical, Statistic, and Descriptive, 1:413. These were some of the same issues that underlay the Stilwellite secession from the Methodist Episcopal Church in New York City in 1820.

10. Franch, "Congregation and Community," 20, 205; *Sun,* Mar. 16, 1844. For Comfort Tiffany, see Henry Stockbridge Jr., "Baltimore in 1846," *Maryland Historical Magazine* 6 (1911): 23.

11. *Baltimore Saturday Visiter,* Mar. 18, 1843; Armstrong, *Old Baltimore Conference,* 268; *Sun,* May 10, 1843; *Baltimore Saturday Visiter,* Apr. 1, 1843. Isaac Cook commented that "these alleged innovations upon primitive Methodism were strongly objected to." Isaac Cook Papers, Lovely Lane Museum. The church was dedicated on March 25, 1844, by anti-Stilwellite Bishop Joshua Soule. Scharf, *Chronicles of Baltimore,* 511.

wealthy within the Methodist fold and made a mockery of John Wesley's admonition to beware of the overweening influence of rich brethren; it was equally indicative of the inability of voluntary religious organizations competing in a disestablished environment to discipline its own members.[12] The significance of such actions should not be minimized. It would have been one thing for such upwardly mobile types as Rogers, Fite, Tiffany, and others to have outgrown primitive Methodism and moved on to genteel Presbyterian or Episcopalian congregations. Unfortunately for Methodism's continued relations with persons of lesser social status, such was not the case; instead these leaders insisted on dragging the entire denomination up the social ladder with them. But the sustained opposition they encountered indicated that the ideals of populist egalitarianism persisted among Baltimore's Methodists.

Methodist Protestants experienced a congregational situation similar to that of the Charles Street Church stemming from the dissatisfaction of upwardly mobile members of St. John's Methodist Protestant Church. There, well-connected individuals like John Clark and Beale Richardson (the Democratic politician) chafed under the restrictive traditionalism of church polity, and they, too, favored the establishment of rented pews to finance their upscale plans for the church. They recognized, however, that the success of pew rents would depend on preaching that was amenable to the social status and economic practices of the wealthy.[13] Thus, control over the process of choosing the pastor was crucial. St. John's congregation had become accustomed to the erudite (and nonrevivalist) sermons of their favorite preacher, Dr. Augustus Webster, and did not want him replaced with a lesser figure. Retaining Webster, however, was problematic because the so-called Restrictive Rule mandated the transfer of preachers from regularly established congregations at least every three years. But a "mission church,"

12. The largest slavedealer in Baltimore, Georgia merchant Hope H. Salter (or Slater or Slatter), bought a pew in the Charles Street Church, "much to the annoyance of many of the worshippers." J. C. Lovejoy, *Memoir of Rev. Charles T. Torrey, Who Died in the Penitentiary of Maryland, Where He Was Confined for Showing Mercy to the Poor* (Boston, 1847), 132; Stockbridge, "Baltimore in 1846," 26–27.

13. In an argument prefiguring the drift toward modern practices within Methodist Protestantism, Dr. Samuel Jennings argued that lay representation would guarantee, through competition, that the best preachers would emerge from the pack to be rewarded with the choicest pastorates based on their popularity. Jennings, *Exposition*, 135. This tendency was also cited by opponents to indicate how Methodist Protestantism had allegedly failed. "Their itinerancy has degenerated into a local system," wrote Henry Slicer, "and their preachers are in the market waiting for hire." Lewis, comp., *Historical Record of the Maryland Annual Conference*, 17.

because it was still being established and therefore needed pastoral continuity, was not restricted to this pattern. Members of St. John's exploited this loophole: declaring themselves a "mission church," they claimed that Webster could stay as their preacher. By avoiding "the frequent rupture of the tender pastoral relation," as Webster put it, they believed they could guarantee pew rent income and raise their congregation, like that of their Methodist brethren on Charles Street, to new levels of gentility.[14]

Conflict among the St. John's congregants came to a head in 1842. Traditionalists, led by Wesley Starr, a former carpenter and original member of the Baltimore Union Society of Methodist reformers and now a well-established merchant and a director of the Baltimore and Ohio Railroad, were bought out by the modernists and left to build their own church in West Baltimore. Largely funded by Starr's wealth, the new congregation eventually proved unacceptable to him, and entirely at his own cost, he built a third church, appropriately named "Starr's Chapel," on Poppleton Street. Here, his devotion to primitive Methodist simplicity became institutionalized: men and women sat separated in the sanctuary, fundraising fairs and instrumental music were prohibited, and incurring debt to improve the new building was expressly forbidden.[15] Such traditionalism, however, had its price. By leaving no room for congregational autonomy, Starr's dictatorial influence, even as it maintained the forms of evangelical populism, exhibited the new possibilities for considering and using wealth in the service of evangelical ends and prefigured the paternalistic model for later evangelical efforts in factory towns. It was a far cry from the rank-and-file participation that had built the Columbia Avenue and Strawbridge Methodist churches.

The development of independent congregationalism underscored the inherent irony of the populist and republican legacies for evangelicals in a disestablished milieu. Growth, without help from denominational organizations or state taxes, was dependent on a mix of sacrificial giving and excess wealth. When the latter predominated, as it often did, elite control was guaranteed. One way to combat power accruing to the wealthy was through a strong, independent, central authority. But centralized authority was anathema to most populists. The alternative was the creation of an isolated congregation under the strong leadership of dedicated populists resistant to

14. *Baltimore Clipper*, Dec. 15, 1843; Drinkhouse, *History of Methodist Reform*, 2:332; Bucke, *History of American Methodism*, 3:682; Lewis, comp., *Historical Record of the Maryland Annual Conference*, 19–20.

15. Colhouer, *Sketches of the Founders*, 334–35; Bucke, *History of American Methodism*, 3:682–83; Franch, "Congregation and Community," 27.

accommodation, but with little power for broader influence other than that of prophetic moral example. The career of William Stilwell, who repeatedly split with denominational entities until he was left with an independent congregation still true to the populist producerism of early Methodism, illustrates the organizational difficulties for evangelicals attempting to challenge the emergent culture.[16]

The dilution of various Methodist traditions of cultural opposition dovetailed with the trend toward mainstreaming populist evangelicalism in Baltimore in the 1840s, a phenomenon also fostered by the broad evangelical revival of 1839–40. This event brought Baltimore Methodists fully into the social center; as preacher George Little recognized: "A more general religious influence was never felt in this community . . . and a Methodist altar is no longer a bugbear. All are serious and if not engaged in seeking salvation manifest great respect."[17] For Baptists, who to this point had played a minor role in Baltimore's religious life, the coming of itinerant evangelist Jacob Knapp during this period marked a watershed. In a matter of months, their numbers doubled. For the next three years, all Baltimore's evangelical denominations saw remarkable growth.[18] With the internecine strife among denominations limited to sporadic outbursts, the progressive elements among them were ready for an unprecedented level of cooperation in pushing toward the Kingdom of God. Although the agents of this revival, particularly Knapp, were hardly raving liberals, evangelical ecumenism softened the more pointed sociocultural critiques of evangelical producers. As Benjamin

16. Hatch, *Democratization of Christianity*, 208; Sutton, "To Extract Poison."

17. The extended nature and intensity of the revival caused health problems for some preachers. In early 1840, George Little asked Henry Furlong to come to Baltimore to help for a few days because the regular preachers "are nearly broken down." Little claimed that the Methodists had added more than two thousand converts since December 1839. George Little to Henry Furlong, Feb. 19, 1840 in Furlong-Baldwin Papers, M193, Maryland Historical Society, Baltimore.

18. In the early 1830s, Baltimore Baptists became locked in a struggle with their rural brethren over the question of the efficacy of centralized authority, mission societies, and educational institutions. In what became known as the Black Rock declaration, the urban and liberal elements were expelled from the older Baltimore confederation. They went on to form the Maryland Baptist Union Association in 1836, under whose auspices Knapp was called to Baltimore. This group grew from 478 members in 1836 to 1,755 in 1845, compared to more than 40,000 Methodists in Maryland. Norman Maring, "A Denominational History of the Maryland Baptists" (Ph.D. diss., University of Maryland, 1948), 74–75, 90, 95, 100–103, 120. Knapp was a transitional figure, combining the unfashionable characteristics of traditionalism with urban revivalism. Franklin Wilson Journal, Dec. 2, 1839, in Franklin Wilson Papers, Maryland Historical Society, Baltimore; Knapp, *Autobiography*, 99–100; Franch, "Congregation and Community," 146–49.

Kurtz noted in his *Lutheran Observer*, "the subjects of politics and commercial distress have been almost banished from the daily conversation to make room for that of religion."[19] At the same time, the influx of new members, often young and separated from the artisan experience, further undermined producerist concerns. The cumulative result, for evangelical artisans in Baltimore, was less focused critiques of capitalist dislocation and poverty and less antagonistic expressions of activism.

The economic depression of the late 1830s brought on bad times for everyone, but artisans were particularly hard hit. At the same time, social problems related to increased poverty and dislocation were proliferating, including a rising incidence of alcoholism. This trend was not imaginary nor was it simply a recent occurrence. One historian has estimated that per capita consumption of absolute alcohol for those over fifteen reached a peak in 1830 at 7.1 gallons per annum.[20] Convivial drinking had long been a staple of artisan culture, but negative reactions to excessive or even moderate levels of alcohol consumption was, by the 1830s, becoming central to the "radical rectitude" that informed the social ethics of both evangelicalism and artisan activism. This change in attitude stemmed from a number of sources. Protestants had long condemned drunkenness on the basis of scriptural demands. But the desire for rationality, control, and efficiency so central to Enlightenment attitudes played a more important role in this period, as did the tenets of classical republicanism.[21] Temperance advocates argued that for the artisan breadwinner, immoderation in drinking—whether celebrating success or assuaging pain—eventuated in dependence and victimized innocent women and children. Furthermore, one so inclined could neither take advantage of economic opportunities nor avoid the destructive nature of alcohol addiction. In the minds of many, alcohol consumption, long suspected as a major element in the degeneracy of the wealthy, became associated with the depravity of the poor. And in the early national period, such concerns were

19. Franch, "Congregation and Community," 147.

20. This number (7.1 gallons) should be compared to the estimate for 1845 (1.8 gallons), a figure at which consumption levels remained roughly for the rest of the century. William J. Rorabaugh, *The Alcoholic Republic: An American Tradition* (New York: Oxford University Press, 1979), 233.

21. Wilentz, *Chants Democratic*, 255; Marsden, *Evangelical Mind*, 238n15. For an example of the nonreligious expression of temperance advocacy, see *Republican*, Mar. 11, 1834. The original evangelical apostle of temperance, Lyman Beecher, condemned drinking as much on republican grounds as on expressly religious grounds. Lyman Beecher, *Six Sermons on the Nature, Occasions, Signs, Evils, and Remedy of Intemperance* (Boston, 1828), 7, 66.

not always smokescreens for elite attempts to socially control what they perceived to be the unwashed and often besotted masses; by the 1830s, alcohol abuse was emerging as a definite social dilemma and depression circumstances merely made matters worse.[22]

During the Jacksonian period, temperance activity became a central feature of American evangelicalism. Marshaling medical arguments to buttress republican piety, early temperance leaders were usually professionals or elite clergymen. Intemperance was an individual shortcoming with communal implications. According to an address presented to the Baltimore Temperance Society in 1830, alcohol destroyed individuals by "brutalizing their feelings, and dissolving the ties which bind in a common interest, both families and communities." Republican institutions, the address continued, were "based upon the moral and physical soundness of an honest yeomanry," so temperance was necessary to avoid a proliferation of corruptible voters. Recognizing the importance of alcohol to artisan culture, temperance proponents pitched their arguments to workers. "Complete abstinence," they argued (with a lack of appreciation for the rapacious capacities evident in subsequent capitalist development), "would so reduce the price of labour in our country, (and that without injury to the labourer,)" that American manufacturing and commerce could compete globally and thereby insure good wages and steady employment.[23] In all this, however, the Baltimore Temperance Society ignored any systemic examination of environmental causes encouraging alcohol abuse among workers. The problem was the deliberate choice of free Americans, and the solution was to be equally individualistic.

The Baltimore Temperance Society had been formed in 1829, and its leaders included Conrad Fite, Dr. Thomas Bond, Alexander Yearly, Melville Cox, the Reverend Robert Breckinridge, Colonel James Mosher, Thomas Kelso, John Millington, and Isaac Cook. All were socially, politically, or religiously prominent and most were members of Baltimore's emerging elite. Fite and Kelso had risen from common origins to successful business careers and were later leaders in the impressive Charles Street Methodist Church.

22. The immoderate drinking habits of many Baltimoreans was duly recognized by their contemporaries as well as by British visitors. Semmes, *Baltimore As Viewed by Visitors*, 77. John H. W. Hawkins noted that of the eleven apprentices with whom he entered the hatting trade in 1811, thirty years later, eight had died drunks, one was living in the Baltimore almshouse, one was a tavern-keeper, one was unaccounted for, and one was Hawkins himself. These recollections may be exaggerated, but many artisan activists recognized alcohol abuse as a genuine social problem. William G. Hawkins, *Life of Hawkins*, 6.

23. *The Constitution and Address of the Baltimore Temperance Society; to Which Is Added an Address, Delivered Before the Society* (Baltimore, 1830) 15, 35.

Cox, Yearly, and Bond were also Methodists and similarly successful; they had been lay leaders in the expulsion of Methodist Protestants the year before. Breckinridge was a Presbyterian preacher and an outspoken Catholiphobe. In wealth and status, the Methodist exhorter Cook was clearly the anomaly, but he was still a respected small businessman (and factory preacher). Mosher (builder) and Millington (printer) had been active in artisan organizations, but the Presbyterian Mosher had long since moved out of artisan ranks. Only the Methodist Protestant Millington was involved in the WMTU during the mid-1830s. Other important Baltimore temperance advocates included the Methodist itinerant Henry Slicer, the Democratic politician and Methodist Protestant layman Beale Richardson, and the Methodist editor of the *Maryland Temperance Herald*, Christian Keener.[24] Throughout the 1830s, the Baltimore Temperance Society sponsored meetings featuring such eminent authorities as Dr. N. R. Smith of the University of Maryland Medical School and congressmen from Massachusetts and New York. But their efforts were largely unsuccessful among artisans because they depended on shaming the inebriate from a position of self-righteous superiority—as a later temperance advocate explained, "they understand not how to reach his sympathies, and bid him be a man."[25] Moreover, they seemed to have no awareness of the role of capitalist dislocation in exacerbating alcohol abuse. On the eve of the rise of the Jacksonian trade union movement, the Baltimore Temperance Society attributed most contemporary pauperism to intemperance alone, because liquor made workers "less capable of performing labor or enduring fatigue."[26]

Throughout the 1830s, temperance competed with craft traditions of drinking on the job and elsewhere for the allegiance of artisans at the same time that trade union organizing, ten-hour movements, and other efforts were attempting to address artisan dislocation and poverty from producerist

24. *Republican*, Sept. 26, 1835; Slicer, *Journal*, Lovely Lane Museum, Baltimore. In later years, Keener earned the unofficial title "Father," denoting general public approval, as he continued the temperance fight. *Temperance Banner: Sons of Temperance and Rechabite Journal*, June 16, 1849. In the light of artisan temperance leaders' general disrespect for earlier evangelical attempts to link temperance to strict denominational loyalties, Christian Keener enjoyed an unusual range of popularity. John Zug, *The Foundation, Progress, and Principles of the Washington Temperance Society* (Baltimore, 1842), 28–29.

25. *Republican*, Jan. 12, 1837; Zug, *Washington Temperance Society*, 27. Tensions arose between artisans and the older temperance societies over efforts to raise license fees on the taverns. Josiah Bailey, a printer-turned-tavern-keeper who had been very active in the early stages of the WMTU, left that leadership to unite tavern-owners against the temperance efforts. *Republican*, Jan. 26, 1836.

26. *Proceedings of the Baltimore Temperance Society*, Manuscript Division, Maryland Historical Society.

perspectives. With the collapse of Jacksonian unionism and the growing popularity of an individualist ethos, however, temperance arguments gained attention as an reasonable explanation for economic failure. The temperance movement in Baltimore was buttressed in 1839 by the rousing successes of Jacob Knapp, the Baptist revivalist who prided himself on presenting "the government truths of the gospel," one of which was the inherent sinfulness of intemperance.[27] His success was welcomed by other evangelicals, some of whom invited him to address the respectable Young Men's City Temperance Society. Yet Knapp was no temperance elitist; his popular credentials were impeccable. In his autobiography, Knapp wrote about his speech to the society: "On the evening in which I preached on temperance, two men, named Mitchel and Hawkins, together with other hard drinkers, were present." According to Knapp, Mitchel (who in fact was the Baltimore tailor, William Mitchell) went from the church to a grog shop, where he encountered the proprietor railing against Knapp's efforts. Mitchell's mild defense of the temperance speaker escalated into a personal pledge of total abstinence, in which he was allegedly joined by Hawkins and other artisans.[28]

Knapp describes the founding of a new temperance organization—the Washington Temperance Society—in Baltimore in 1840. Although Knapp's story included questionable detail, something remarkable did occur among Baltimore artisans in the wake of his combination revival-temperance effort. In the collective memory of the founders, it was not Knapp but Matthew Hale Smith, a visiting temperance lecturer, who attracted the attention of William Mitchell and five of his artisan friends (none of whom was John Hawkins) on April 2, 1840.[29] The six, who regularly met at Chase's Tavern on Liberty Street, were Mitchell, George Steers (or Stears), David Anderson, Archibald Campbell, James McCurley, and John F. Hoss. Mitchell was a merchant tailor who in 1837 had helped A. I. W. Jackson, Francis Gallagher, and Philip Adams establish the Institution for the Diffusion of Useful

27. Hattam, *Labor Visions*, 108.

28. Knapp, *Autobiography*, 100–101.

29. The agency of Jacob Knapp in the inspiration of the "immortal six," as Mitchell and his friends became known, became the focal point of a public dispute in 1843. It involved those advocating moderate drinking habits and those espousing total abstinence, and it reflected denominational and geographical rivalries, with newcomer Mitchell and Boston Universalist moderates challenging longtime temperance worker Christian Keener and Baltimore Baptist and Methodist absolutists. Methodist Protestant John H. W. Hawkins was enlisted on the side of the total abstinence men, and he claimed that Mitchell, on Nov. 8, 1841, had informed him, with no prompting whatsoever, that Knapp was the predominant influence. Boston opponents of Knapp's Baptist revivalism sought refutation from Mitchell, who provided them with a statement denying that Knapp had anything to do with the

Knowledge among the Working Classes. In tougher times a year earlier, Mitchell had declared insolvency, but five months later he had been able to reopen his store, advertising a "supply of seasonable and fashionable goods." Campbell was a master silversmith, regularly employing, according to one of his advertisements, "several of the very best workmen"; he also sold imported watches and had once advertised for a slave boy to help out at his shop. Little is known about blacksmiths Steers and Anderson, but master coachmaker McCurley was connected to the English Lutheran Church and was one of the producerist employers (like John Curlett) who had readily acceded to United Journeymen Coach Makers' demands for the ten-hour workday in 1833. Even more active in that producerist uprising was carpenter John F. Hoss, who was prominent in Baltimore public affairs for years. A minor officeholder, Hoss's title "captain" referred to his role in the city militia, and he was regularly lauded as an "Old Defender" of Baltimore, stemming from the abortive British invasion of the upper Chesapeake in 1814. He was apparently not part of the carpenters' leadership, but he had chaired the militant meeting of producer-friendly Baltimoreans on July 29, 1833, when a cross section of the citizenry voted to establish a community boycott and a strike fund to support the journeymen hatters. He had also prepared the room for the original meeting of the Female Union Society of Seamstresses and Tailoresses, was vice president of the Jackson Democrats who nominated Joshua Vansant for the state assembly in October 1834, and was one of the assistant marshalls (along with A. I. W. Jackson, John Warner Niles, Samuel Mass, and others) for the funeral parade honoring James Madison in August 1836. As a group, the original six Washingtonians were representative of upwardly mobile, if struggling, producerist artisans.[30]

Discussion at the tavern that night turned to the subject of temperance. The men agreed that abstinence was probably a laudable goal, but they also aired suspicions of well-heeled temperance speakers and ministers. Almost in jest they discussed forming their own temperance society, and, three days later, while drinking and strolling on a Sunday, they actually did. Mitchell, they agreed, should be president and Hoss secretary. The initial membership

---

founding of the Washington Temperance Society. Mitchell subsequently refused to answer Hawkins's public statements about Knapp's role. For a record of this convoluted exchange, see *Baltimore Saturday Visiter*, Mar. 18, 1843; May 20, 1843; May 27, 1843; July 8, 1843; as well as contemporaneous notices in the *Boston Mercantile Journal*, the *New Hampshire Courier*, the *Boston Tetotaler*, and the Universalist *Boston Trumpet*.

30. Zug, *Washington Temperance Society*, 26–27; *Republican*, Oct. 3, 1833; Aug. 23, Apr. 26, Sept. 9, 1836, Feb. 1, 1837; *American*, Aug. 25, 1833; *Republican*, Oct. 15, 1835; *Baltimore Saturday Visiter*, Aug. 24, 1833; *Republican*, July 29, 1833; *American*, Oct. 2, 1834; *Baltimore*

fee was twenty-five cents, monthly dues were twelve and a half cents, and the name, Washington Temperance Society, reflected their allegiance to a mainstream cultural icon. That night Mitchell composed a pledge and in the morning took it to Anderson for his signature. Anderson, hung over from the previous day's frivolity, managed to stagger down to his shop, where he signed the pledge and became the first official Washingtonian. Although this was hardly an auspicious beginning, the other four soon signed as well, as did Mitchell, and the movement—a peculiar amalgamation of producerist masculinity, artisan republicanism, and sentimental emotion—was born.[31] In succeeding years, American artisans with alcohol problems responded in record numbers; by 1843, the parent organization had 5,034 members with related temperance organizations enrolling another 5,000. This work indisputably emanated from the artisan class, although in time the ideological trajectory of the movement proved to have as much in common with emergent liberalism as with producerism.[32]

The Washingtonians began to meet at a rented carpenter's shop and to quietly proselytize within the Baltimore artisan community. After a few weeks, Mitchell suggested that they identify themselves as "reformed drunkards" and tell their stories at meetings in order to recount the beneficent aspects of their temperance freedom. This innovative use of the "experience meeting" technique of revivalism outside the normal channels of evangelicalism was

Saturday Visiter, Aug. 26, 1843. Steers moved on to Hagerstown, Maryland, where he died in late 1842. *Baltimore Saturday Visiter*, Oct. 29, 1842. For mention of McCurley, A. I. W. Jackson, and later Washingtonian official John C. Bokee, see *Register of the First English Lutheran Church, Baltimore* (Baltimore, 1859), 18, 28, 52. When the Washingtonians dissolved, Hoss remained an active officer of the Sons of Temperance. *Baltimore Saturday Visiter*, Apr. 19, 1845.

31. *Eleventh Annual Report of the Maryland State Temperance Society: Embracing an Account of the Origin, Nature, and Extent of the Washington Reform* (Baltimore, 1842), 4; Milton A. Maxwell, "The Washingtonian Movement," *Quarterly Journal of Studies on Alcohol* 11 (1950): 413.

32. Laurie, *Artisans into Workers*, 92–93; *Baltimore Saturday Visiter*, June 17, 1843. John Zug claimed that Washingtonianism was "emphatically a society of working-men." Zug, *Washington Temperance Society*, 49. See also Ian R. Tyrrell, *Sobering Up: From Temperance to Prohibition in Antebellum America, 1800–60* (Westport, Conn.: Greenwood Press, 1979), 159; Wilentz, *Chants Democratic*, 308; and Ruth M. Alexander, "'We Are Engaged as a Band of Sisters': Class and Domesticity in the Washingtonian Temperance Movement, 1840–1850," *Journal of American History* 75 (Dec. 1988): 776. White artisans were not the only populist expression of temperance in Baltimore in the 1840s; also reflecting the tendency to link temperance to populist evangelicalism were the Asbury Total Abstinence Society and the Old Wesley Temperance Sabbath Society, which, along with "other societies of color," attracted three thousand participants to its Fourth of July celebration in 1843. Sun, July 8, 1843. Liberal republican optimism, as well as the conceptions of civil religion, was evident in Washingtonian songs. A. B. Grosh, *Washingtonian Pocket Companion: Containing a Choice Collection of Temperance Hymns, Songs, Odes, Glees, Duetts, Chorusses, &c. with Music*, 4th ed. (Utica, 1845).

not unique to the Washingtonians—Henry Slicer had been using such methods with great effect in Washington, D.C., for the previous three years—but in their hands, it proved highly effective.[33] As artisan advocates of abstinence and self-help put it, where earlier approaches to the drunkard had "been rather to prevent than to cure," Washingtonians "aid him to aid himself back to health, peace, usefulness, respectability, and prosperity." The success of the Baltimore Washingtonians was immediate; within six months, nearly one hundred had taken the pledge and the society was forced to rent church buildings for meetings. During that time, in a typical Washingtonian conversion, the veteran labor activist and Methodist reformer John H. W. Hawkins joined his friends. Hawkins was significantly worse off than the Washingtonian founders; he had failed to become a master and was by this time, still clinging to his Methodist faith, a full-blown drunk. Hawkins later recalled his original Washingtonian encounter: "Well, Monday night I went to the society of drunkards, and there I found all my old bottle companions. . . . The 'six-pounders' of the society were there. We had fished together—got drunk together. We stuck like brothers, and so we do now that we are sober. One said, 'There is Hawkins, the "regulator," the old bruiser,' and they clapped and laughed, as you do now. But there was no laugh or clap in me. . . . The pledge was read for my accommodation. . . . I never had such feelings before. It was a great battle." In the difficult months of drying out to follow, his "old bottle companions" sustained him.[34]

Throughout 1840, the number of Baltimore Washingtonians increased and their successes were chronicled by the old temperance regular and Methodist leader Christian Keener in his *Maryland Temperance Herald*. In February 1841, Hawkins gave his testimony at a Maryland State Temperance Society meeting and was invited to speak to the state legislature, which he did with stunning effect.[35] A month later, Hawkins and four others became the

33. Jed Dannenbaum correctly points out that the original six were not genuine alcoholics, only habitual and serious drinkers. Jed Dannenbaum, *Drink and Disorder: Temperance Reform in Cincinnati from the Washingtonian Revival to the WCTU* (Urbana, University of Illinois Press, 1984), 34. For the experience meeting phenomenon, see Samuel Dickinson, *The New Impulse: or Hawkins and Reform: A Brief History of the Origin, Progress, and Effects of the Present Astonishing Temperance Movement, and of the Life and Reformation of John H. W. Hawkins, the Distinguished Leader* (Boston, 1841), 14–15; *Baltimore Saturday Visiter*, Oct 1, 1842. This work was endorsed by the preeminent revivalist of the time, Charles Finney. Dickinson, *New Impulse*, 26; Zug, *Washington Temperance Society*, 15, 14.

34. Zug, *Washington Temperance Society*, 29; Grosh, *Washingtonian Pocket Companion*, 1; William G. Hawkins, *Life of Hawkins*, 91.

35. Zug, *Washington Temperance Society*, 21; William G. Hawkins, *Life of Hawkins*, 66. Hawkins's impact was described approvingly by Christian Keener. *Sun*, Oct. 23, 1843.

first official Washingtonian missionaries when they came to New York City. Their success was dramatic, and the delegation returned to Baltimore for a huge first anniversary celebration, chaired by George K. Quail, Methodist producerist hatter. Their parade, on April 5, 1841, featured John F. Hoss as chief marshall and included an estimated seven thousand participants. In the tradition of artisan celebrations and complete with bands and groups of "hundreds of marshalls on foot, with their various insignia" (possibly referring to those of the old craft unions), the festively sober crowd was addressed by an orator and various clergy. A few days later, with Hawkins a celebrity and Washingtonianism a national phenomenon, Hawkins and fellow journeyman hatter activist William E. Wright were on their way to Boston. Soon thereafter, the American Temperance Union hired Hawkins as a traveling temperance speaker. It was an unusual way to achieve his competence, and Hawkins never returned to the hatter's trade. For the rest of his life Hawkins served as an indefatigable itinerant, sharing platforms with such elite reformers as Yale theologian Chauncey Goodrich, revivalist Lyman Beecher, and abolitionist Gerrit Smith, yet he never moved far from his artisan roots. For almost two decades, speeches of the "humble Baltimorean" were renowned for their populist authenticity, and he remained effective whereas other temperance speakers soon faded. His death in 1858 was widely mourned, and the Massachusetts State Temperance Convention eulogized 'the noble self-conqueror" for his "truly religious spirit" and his devoted advocacy of the temperance cause.[36]

Hawkins drew and moved audiences with his spellbinding recital of his alcoholic fall from grace.[37] Beneath his sentimental testimony, however, lay

36. Daniel Craig, *Craig's Business Directory and Baltimore Almanac for 1842* (Baltimore, 1842), 41; Zug, *Washington Temperance Society*, 21, 23; William G. Hawkins, *Life of Hawkins*, 64–65, 92, 116–17, 137–39, 218, 417; Tyrrell, *Sobering Up*, 173; *Baltimore Saturday Visiter*, Apr. 15, 1843; June 10, 1843; Sept. 9, 1843. This is not to ignore the fact that his newfound popularity eventually moved Hawkins away from artisan culture into professional circles. Moreover, like all ministers in populist denominations, his financial security was based on voluntary contributions. The impact of this shift in concentration was made evident in Hawkins's memoir, written by his son in 1859. Hawkins's journal and extensive family correspondence makes clear his devotion to both artisan solidarity and populist evangelicalism; nowhere did Hawkins himself see any incompatibility between the two. But his son had a different perspective; the memoir contained no mention of Hawkins's significant trade union activity. Equally interesting was the glossed-over treatment of Hawkins's participation in the Methodist Protestant schism. William G. Hawkins, *Life of Hawkins*, 47–48.

37. *Baltimore Saturday Visiter*, June 10, 1843; Dec. 30, 1843. In hundreds of speeches to follow, Hawkins poignantly described his temperance turning point. Having progressed to an unhealthy quart and a half of whiskey per day by June 1840, and having lost employment, property, and mental equilibrium, Hawkins was contemplating suicide. His daughter Hannah

an oblique acknowledgement of the problems facing artisans in an industrializing situation, not the least of which was the sense of surprise, almost shock, at their deteriorating conditions in light of the optimistic expectations of the early national period. Hawkins's testimonial was unconsciously allegorical: his unexpected alcoholic trauma symbolized his equally unexpected economic despair in a climate where opportunities were supposed to be plentiful. In this context, Hawkins's speeches were geared more to restore self-respect and self-control than to foster upward social mobility, although the advantages of stable living standards and respectable status, gained through temperate living, were also held up to potential recruits.

Hawkins also emphasized the Washingtonian construction of manhood. Over and over in these testimonies, the self-mastery so central to respectable artisan masculinity was presented as the key component of Washingtonian redemption. But this was not the patriarchal dominance of Anglo-American tradition. Nor was it another expression of the alleged feminization of American culture. Rather, it was the empowered demonstration of a reformed man's ability to overcome external domination (in this case, alcohol), thus enabling him to prove his manhood by fulfilling his domestic duties as a breadwinner. As John Zug described the founders of the movement:

> But though these were plain men, they were men of unusual energy. . . . They were in business and five of them had families. They cared for their business, and they loved their families. . . . They looked to their homes, and they saw that much of domestic bliss, which should gather round the fireside, was banished by the inebriating cup. . . . They looked back to the days of their youth, when with free hearts and bounding hopes, they had leaped into life, and had looked forward . . . never dreaming of such a slavery. . . . They looked into the future, and all was clouds and darkness. They deliberately weighed the movement about to be made; and then rising in the energy of their still surviving manhood, they resolved . . . they would drink no more of the poisonous draught forever.[38]

(who was soon elevated to cult status by temperance advocates) came to his bed and begged, "I hope you won't send me for any whiskey today." In a rage, he ordered her out of the room and she left, sobbing, at which point he decided once more to give up his drinking. John Marsh, *Hannah Hawkins, the Reformed Drunkard's Daughter* (New York, 1842), 24–26; William G. Hawkins, *Life of Hawkins*, 71, 91–92. Throughout his testimonials, one is struck by the fact that he considered his condition anomalous. So, apparently, did many in his audience.

38. Zug, *Washington Temperance Society*, 8–11. The historiographical concept of feminization continues to be problematic; see David S. Reynolds, "The Feminization Controversy:

In this sense, Washingtonians like Hawkins expressed a more individualized reconceptualization of similar trade unionist concerns related to family obligations.

Although self-mastery was the key to Washingtonian experience, their environmentalist message identified an evil force (i.e., alcohol) that had acquired an agency of its own and assumed power over its unsuspecting (and therefore nonresponsible) victims. As his son described John Hawkins's condition, "Though he had been educated by a minister of the gospel, he never once thought he could be a drunkard, yet the use of ardent spirit crept upon him and slew him."[39] The clear implication was that individual drunks had been duped into alcoholism and were therefore not deserving of disrespect; nevertheless, they had to assume some responsibility for their plight, if only by acknowledging that individual will power, buttressed by supportive fellow sufferers, was necessary for deliverance. In treating alcoholics sympathetically, Hawkins and the Washingtonians changed the general tone of drunkard reformation from condemnation to empathy because, according to their perspective, drunkards were "the unwilling victims", not the "votaries of the pleasures of the bowl."[40]

For those lost in their own personal fog (socioeconomic as well as existential), temperance served to reduce the entire spectrum of dislocation to a single graspable problem. The Washingtonian rhetoric was steeped in republicanism and resonated with producerist and populist traditions, yet its emphasis on success through self-help championed an individualism more consistent with liberal understandings.[41] The Washingtonian pledge became

---

Sexual Stereotypes and the Paradoxes of Piety in Nineteenth-Century America," *American Quarterly* 52. (Mar. 1980), 96–106. For a powerful argument explaining the constructions of masculinity as formed by men's relationships to other men, especially in terms of escaping domination, see Michael Kimmel, *Manhood in America: A Cultural History* (New York: Free Press, 1996), 6–7 and passim.

39. William G. Hawkins, *Life of Hawkins*, 70–71.

40. Zug, *Washington Temperance Society*, 8; Tyrrell, *Sobering Up*, 171; Murphy, *Ten Hours' Labor*, 107–9; William Breitenbach, "Sons of the Fathers: Temperance Reformers and the Legacy of the American Revolution," *Journal of the Early Republic* 3 (spring 1983): 74.

41. Newly organized Washingtonians were urged to use in the preambles to their constitutions, "a PARODY on our National Declaration of Independence." Masculine egalitarianism ruled; the drunkard "is a man; and all the other classes of society whom we wish to . . . enlist in this blessed cause are neither more or less than men." Washingtonianism also included the craft union welfare legacy, as all societies were urged "to relieve the poor, sick and afflicted members, and families of inebriates," and communitarian producerist tenets were evident in the suggestion that members should "encourage" their fellows "by dealing with and employing them." Grosh, *Washingtonian Pocket Companion*, 5–9. For a discussion of Washingtonian mutual benefit societies, see Alexander, "'We Are All Engaged as a Band of Sisters,'" 776–82.

in popular parlance the "Second Declaration of Independence," reflecting the fact that dependency had long been the bane of both republican and producerist ideologies. Even as they recognized the possibility for conflict between elite-dominated temperance groups, based on their different approaches and constituencies, the Washingtonians desired classless harmony.[42] Most significant, however, was the Washingtonians' redefinition of the causes of the deterioration of the artisan way of life; where a few continued to recognize the unequal power relations inherent in industrial capitalism and others blamed unemployment and low wages on banking practices, in the main, Washingtonians narrowed the cause to one factor—alcohol abuse. Their reorientation toward building individual character was an essential feature of the Washingtonian critique of dependency and its individualistic emphasis on transcending social inequalities was a significant indication of the extent to which liberal tenets were becoming culturally dominant.

Closely connected to this issue was the question of how Washingtonians could achieve temperance transformations in individual alcoholics. The majority position favored persuasion alone, with appeals based on love, empathy, and the promise of self-improvement, apart from government intervention, personal boycott, or even public disapproval of "grog-sellers." "In short," wrote A. B. Grosh, "Moral suasion, not force—love, not hate, are the moving springs in the Washingtonian Creed." In the language of liberalism, Washingtonian publisher John Zug asserted, "The . . . object of the Washington Society is to induce men to quit drinking alcoholic liquors. When they have done this, the rest must regulate itself, and in most cases it will regulate itself. . . . We beseech all men to give up the traffic; . . . and let truth work its own way upon their hearts . . . as in every other reformation of their lives." Founder William Mitchell was adamant in this regard: he refused to back pledges aimed at boycotting merchants who continued to handle alcoholic products, continued to socialize in taverns, and admitted liquor sellers into the society. A spokesmen for the Baltimore Washingtonians summed up the official position: "We do not pass resolutions of nonintercourse with men

42. Miscellaneous papers, July 7, 1841, in Furlong-Baldwin Papers, M193, Maryland Historical Society, Baltimore. Maxwell, "Washingtonian Movement," 435. William Mitchell went to Boston in 1844 to mediate conflicts between the populist Washingtonians and established temperance leaders; in the process he had to set straight the "many *pictures of fancy*" attributed to the original formation of the society. *Sun*, July 1, 1844. In the early years, cooperation was apparently the norm. "In Baltimore . . . the reformed men [Washingtonians] and the old friends of the [Temperance] cause, frequently labour side by side at public meetings in the city, as well as in visiting the surrounding country to advance the common cause." Zug, *Washington Temperance Society*, 46.

who traffic in intoxicating liquors; nor proscribe them . . . , further than advising men not to drink their liquors, may be proscription. . . . Why not require them to abandon every other immoral pursuit in life, which they follow from the love of gain?"[43]

Also present, however, were producerist traditions among Washingtonian artisans—the morality that had informed the pleas of trade unionists for public boycotts of offending masters and had provided the ethical justification for the selective destruction during the bank riot. The connections between Baltimore Washingtonianism and producer-oriented trade unionism were striking and were not limited to Hawkins, Hoss, and McCurley. Accompanying Hawkins in his first visit to Boston in 1841 was William E. Wright, a journeyman hatter who was prominent in the WMTU and particularly active in the mechanics' support for striking carpenters in 1835. Wright went on from Boston to team with David Pollard to bring Washingtonianism to upstate New York and rivaled Hawkins in popularity. Jonah W. Marriott was a leader of the cordwainers who threatened to go out on strike when their wages were cut in 1836. Francis Gallagher and Daniel A. Piper had been delegates to the National Trades' Union conventions in New York and had made significant contributions to that organization. Thomas Bruff and Albert Hall, officials of the Washingtonian spin-off Neptune Temperance Society, led the shipwrights and the tailors, respectively, in the initial demand for the ten-hour workday. Bruff also chaired the meeting of voters planning to nominate only artisans for the 1833 state elections and later served as vice president of the journeymen shipwrights in 1836. John Hawkins and Charles Towson (former president of the journeyman hatters in 1836) were the original president and vice president, respectively, of another Washingtonian auxiliary, the Jefferson Temperance Society. James Morrison, whose testimony was featured in the Eleventh Annual Report of the Maryland State Temperance Society, was also secretary and later president of the journeyman painters in the mid-1830s. Charles B. Purnell had represented the Sixth Ward (with Hawkins) in the abortive Mechanics and Workingmen's political convention in 1833. George K. Quail had distinguished himself as one of the original producerist masters supporting the striking hatters in 1833. Quail, Purnell, Gallagher, Piper, and Marriott were among the twenty-five Washingtonian leaders on the committee to coordinate the commemoration of the first anniversary of the Washington Temperance Society—a celebration that

43. Grosh, *Washingtonian Pocket Companion*, 5; Zug, *Washington Temperance Society*, 31, 51, 53–54; Maxwell, "Washingtonian Movement," 442.

drew members and supporters from around the country. And Quail, Hoss, Purnell, and Morrison continued to lead the Baltimore Washingtonians into the mid-1840s.[44]

Although Washingtonians fixated on the single issue of ending intemperance, participation in the movements did not preclude continued trade union militancy. Francis Gallagher, converted to Washingtonianism after John Hawkins's speech to the Maryland legislature in 1841, was instrumental in the formation of the Legislative Temperance Society, and nine months later he was leading the reorganized Baltimore cordwainers union into another strike for higher wages. When the Danbury, Connecticut, hatters went on strike in 1844 to oppose capitalist reorganization of the trade, their leaders—Joel Clark, H. B. Wildman, William Hinman, and William Schoonmaker—were also Washingtonian leaders.[45] Washingtonian willingness to employ the trade union tactics of boycotts and public humiliation to support their cause was apparent in one of their popular ditties (to be sung, according to its popularizer, to the tune of "Oh, Dear, What Can the Matter Be?"):

The Washington boys are playing the dickens!
The night of confusion around me thickens,
Unless the rum business with some of us quickens,
We'll all have to cut with our rum.

I used to get rich through the toiling mechanic,
Who spent all his earnings in pleasures satanic,
But now I confess I am in a great panic,
Because I can sell no more rum.

44. The central roles played by these trade unionists challenges the assertion that "very few [artisan temperance] leaders had histories of trade union involvement." Laurie, *Artisans into Workers*, 93. For Wright, see *Journal of the American Temperance Movement* 5 (May 1841): 76; *Republican*, July 3, 1835; *National Trades' Union*, July 25, 1835. For Marriott, see *Republican*, Apr. 21, 1836. Gallagher's and Piper's committee work condemning capitalist speculation and the practice of middlemen siphoning profits from producers prefigured similar Populist critiques half a century later. Commons et al. *Documentary History*, 6:291–93. For Bruff and Hall, see *American*, Aug. 2, 1833; Aug. 9, 1833; *Republican*, Sept. 28, 1833; *Baltimore Trades' Union*, May 28, 1836; *Sun*, Apr. 20, 1841. The leadership role of Hawkins and Towson in the Jefferson Temperance Society appears in the *Sun*, Jan. 26, 1841. For Morrison, see *Baltimore Saturday Visitor*, Aug. 24, 1833, and *Republican*, Mar. 28, 1834. Purnell is mentioned in the *American*, Sept. 20, 1833; Quail in the *Republican*, July 22, 1833. The leaders of the Washingtonian anniversary celebration are listed in *Journal of the American Temperance Movement* 5 (Apr. 1841): 49. See also *Baltimore Saturday Visitor*, Mar. 18, 1843.

45. *Clipper*, Jan. 5, 1843; *Sun*, Oct. 23, 1843; *Danbury Times*, Mar. 1, 1843; June 12, June 19, July 10, 1844; July 9, Sept. 10, 1845; Mar. 10, 1847.

I once cloth'd in satin my wife and my daughter,
But now they wear calico! what is the matter?
They give up my rum for the sake of cold water;
Oh what shall I do with my rum?

I'll give up my business, I vow it's no use to me—
It's been a continual source of abuse to me—
The friends of cold water I hope will stick close to me,
So soon as I give up my Rum.

As the song indicated, economic coercion was appropriate in cases where moral suasion had failed. This strain of producerist activism would, in mid-decade, provide direct links between Washingtonianism and labor reform used by striking artisans and ten-hour advocates.[46]

But the previous inability of public pressure tactics to sustain the trade union agenda in the mid-1830s may well have influenced some Washingtonians to abandon confidence in moral suasion alone as sufficient for temperance success. Unlike Mitchell and the moral suasionists, John Hawkins pushed the producerist logic beyond boycotts to place the moral responsibility for alcoholic degradation on those who held control of the trade. He strongly supported state regulation in the form of prohibition and, basing his argument on traditional economic morality, condemned those who produced liquor. "What should we do with a man who sold bad meat . . . or a baker, dishonest in his bread? Put him in the penitentiary. . . . I can see the distiller in his distillery, sitting in his comfortable chair, watching his distilled damnation as it oozes out of his pipe" Later, Hawkins completed the argument, asking, "why in the name of humanity should not the coming Legislature so alter the present law, that the city authorities may be clothed with power so to act that the wicked rum-seller may feel that he shall not be permitted to grow rich upon the poor, and ride rough-shod over the laws of the Commonwealth."[47] In Hawkins's view, communal well-being and concern for the disadvantaged took precedence over the individual rights of entrepreneurial liquor dealers. This disagreement in tactics revealed the ambivalence within

46. Grosh, *Washingtonian Pocket Companion*, 151–52; Murphy, *Ten Hours' Labor*, 177–90.

47. William G. Hawkins, *Life of Hawkins*, 71, 348; Carwardine, *Evangelicals and Politics*, 205. This approach was commonplace for the established temperance groups. One purpose of the October 1829 meeting of the Baltimore Temperance Society was to interest the magistrates in their cause. *Constitution of the Baltimore Temperance Society*, 7. But Hawkins's advocacy of legal sanctions challenges the suggestion that evangelicalism necessarily prevented such perspectives. Murphy, *Ten Hours' Labor*, 164–65.

the Washingtonian movement (and artisan culture in general) regarding the role of government in enforcing restrictions deemed critical to encouraging economic success and social mobility and to regulating liberal opportunities.

Some observers (both contemporaneous and modern) have alleged that the Washingtonians were essentially antireligious, but Ian Tyrrell, the movement's most careful historian, refutes such claims.[48] Clearly, the speaking style and centrality of testimony in the experience meetings indicated similarities to concurrent revival practices; equally central was a generic Arminianism, which identified within human nature "a chord, even in the most corrupt heart, that vibrates to kindness, and a sense of justice." Just as evangelical theologians Nathaniel Taylor, Lyman Beecher, and Charles Finney were locating sin as a force external to the divine creation of human nature but amenable to human attempts to overcome (in the process rejecting traditional doctrines of original sin), Washingtonians identified alcoholism as an evil agency which invaded its victims and required character and self-control to master. Like the Working Men's and Trade Union in Baltimore and the National Trades' Union before them, the Washingtonians were open to a broad-minded populist evangelicalism, as long as sectarian divisions were explicitly eschewed.[49] And although some Washingtonians remained unmoved

48. The contemporary support for such a view, often put forth by nonartisans seeking to control the movement, was expressed in Benjamin Estes, *Essay on the Necessity of Correcting the Errors Which Have Crept into the Washingtonian Temperance Movement* (New York, 1846). Sean Wilentz favors such an interpretation, when he approvingly attributes to the movement a "gruff humanist perfectionism . . . without any mention of Jesus, His love, or attaining grace, and without the slightest hint at what temperance would do for profits. . . . As they departed from the well-beaten temperance path, the Washingtonian societies offered their members more than hope and a hot meal: they brought the idea that ordinary men and women could collectively benefit each other—or at least escape from further degradation—without the assistance of God or their social betters, through patience, toleration, and joy. Wilentz, *Chants Democratic*, 312, 314. Ian Tyrrell dissents, arguing that what mainstream evangelicals objected to among the Washingtonians was the radical evangelicalism of Henry Clapp and others. Tyrrell, *Sobering Up*, 196–97. The best interpretation is offered by Milton Maxwell; he concludes that "many Washingtonians felt that their movement represented a purer form of Christianity than was to be found in the churches. . . . They felt that they were living the principles which the churches talked about." Maxwell, "Washingtonian Movement," 438; Sutton, "Tied to the Whipping Post," 272–77.

49. Grosh, *Washingtonian Pocket Companion*, 5. The interrelations between evangelicalism and Washingtonianism occupied much of Zug's attention in his description of the artisan temperance movement. He scrupulously rejected any effort to tie denominational or doctrinal demands to the Washingtonian cause. Zug, *Washington Temperance Society*, 40–41, 46–47, 59–61. Henry Slicer was equally successful in meeting this demand. His journal records his appearance at the Mechanic's Temperance Society, the Printers' Total Abstinence Society, and the Mechanics' Total Abstinence Society. When the latter called a public meeting for all the friends of temperance in December and foul weather intervened, Slicer was the only speaker

by religious arguments, others felt their evangelical activism to be purer and less otherworldly than devotional withdrawal from earthly concerns, as indicated in this hymn stanza from the *Washingtonian Pocket Companion*:

> This world's not a fleeting show,
> For man's illusion given;
> He that hath sooth'd a drunkard's woe,
> And led him to reform, doth know,
> There's something here of heaven.
>
> The Washingtonian that hath run
> The path of kindness even;
> Who's measur'd out life's little span,
> In deeds of love to God and man,
> On earth has tasted heaven.

Yet, radical evangelical perspectives were clearly circumscribed, as seen in the hymn, "The Jubilee," where socioeconomic reorderings were spiritualized.[50]

The Washingtonians, in fact, filled a kind of parachurch function, providing a haven from the storms of modernization and supplying an implicitly religious group experience that some mainstream evangelical congregations and many established ministers, in their growing preoccupation with decorousness and denial, were ignoring.[51] Accordingly, the Washington Temperance Society of Baltimore held a "reconciliation service" to reunite the Anthony Moffitts in marriage. Presided over by founders William Mitchell (now "Esq.") and John F. Hoss, attended also by officials James Morrison (secretary) and John Bokee (treasurer and Lutheran lay leader), and officiated by Washingtonian missionary James McKnight, this well-publicized service commenced "the winter campaign of the Washingtonians" on October 23, 1843. With the

---

to show up. He also spoke on temperance in his street preaching. Slicer, *Journal*, 2:87–88, 103. In this same light, Washingtonians were welcomed to the Second Presbyterian Church for a concert. *Baltimore Saturday Visiter*, Sept. 3, 1842.

50. This hymn is quoted in Maxwell, "Washingtonian Movement," 438, which included another typical hymn, entitled "Washingtonian Conversation": "When Jesus, our Redeemer, came/To teach us in his Father's name,/In every act, in every thought/He lived the precepts which he taught." See also Grosh, *Washingtonian Pocket Companion*, 11, 13; Sutton, "Tied to the Whipping Post," 274.

51. *Baltimore Saturday Visiter*, Aug. 20, 1842; Dannenbaum, *Drink and Disorder*, 36, 39; Robert H. Abzug, *Cosmos Crumbling: American Reform and Religious Imagination* (New York: Oxford University Press, 1994), 103.

temperance hall full to overflowing, Mr. McKnight opened by reading the fifteenth chapter of Luke (including the parables of the lost sheep, the lost coin, and the prodigal son) and commenting on its message of repentance and restoration.[52]

Following the sermon, an elaborate ritual unfolded, with McKnight conducting Mrs. Moffitt and six bridesmaids "to the charge of Mr. Mitchell" and leading Mr. Moffitt and six Washingtonians to Vice President Charles Purnell. With all parties in place and the audience fully engaged, Secretary Morrison stepped forward to read the reconciliation ceremony as prepared by Mr. McKnight. In the process, Morrison explained Moffitt's initial decline; "you have been one of the victims of the demon of drink; you have been in slavery under his iron yoke, (as well as many of us.)" He went on to recount the story of the alcohol-caused breakup of the Moffitts' marriage, Mr. Moffitt's subsequent alcoholic dissolution, his Washingtonian recovery, and his desire to be reconciled to his wife. In typical melodramatic terms, Morrison then addressed Moffitt on behalf of his wife: "She that still loves you is about to give her hand of love and reconciliation to him that was lost, but now is found, clothed in good resolution, and with his right mind, looking up to God of whom that mind is the judge, and Jesus Christ the Saviour of the world, on whom all the family on earth are dependent. Look unto Him and you will be kept a temperate man unto the day of your death." As the Moffitts repeated their vows, participants and audience erupted into celebration. President Mitchell then gave a short speech "in his usual happy style," the group sang the hymn "Oh, Be Joyful," and the meeting ended with a talk by the old Methodist antireformer Dr. Thomas Bond of the Baltimore Temperance Society on the evils of intemperance and the steadfastness of female love.[53]

The Washingtonian reconciliation service was an explicitly evangelical celebration of nineteenth-century domesticity, yet it was more than the panicked reaction of male artisans "concerned about the way evangelicalism was disrupting their families, displacing them morally and spiritually."[54] On the

52. *Sun*, Oct. 28, 1843. This type of reconciliation service closely resembled the old Methodist love feasts—"special dramas of backsliders returning to the fold." Andrews, "Popular Religion in the Middle Atlantic Ports," 37. The *Baltimore Saturday Visiter* published an announcement of a similar Washingtonian service held in Norwich, Connecticut, and added, "now we venture to say President Mitchell can describe not a few cases in our own city where re-unions have *virtually*, if not formally, taken place." *Baltimore Saturday Visiter*, Nov. 19, 1842.

53. Ibid. This was the same Thomas Bond who led the forces of order during the bank riot of 1835.

54. Murphy, *Ten Hours' Labor*, 101.

contrary, Washingtonianism reflected the longstanding evangelical pattern of blurring gendered roles by combining emotional empowerment with rational consideration of theological propositions, so that a reformed drunk could afterward contemplate the Christian message "with a cool head," in the words of Washingtonian John Zug, and ultimately choose salvation as well as sobriety. This was the outcome of a similar reconciliation effort carried out by temperance missionary John Hawkins in New York City, wherein a separated couple were gradually restored "to social happiness, to society, and to the church."[55] The Washingtonian movement was certainly centered in artisan manly solidarity, but it was more broadly and androgynously developed than the stereotypical image of hyperrationalist masculinity and patriarchal dominance—in fact, Washingtonian openness to expressed emotion and egalitarian social relations was one of its primary attractions.[56] Temperance choirs in Baltimore further broke down gender separation by providing "a little innocent excitement" that enabled "the ladies [to] go oftener" to the meetings. The personal testimony of John Hawkins was powerfully blunt and unapologetically emotional, yet firmly grounded in the manly camaraderie of artisan culture: "We don't slight the drunkard; we love him, we nurse him, as a mother does her infant learning to walk."[57] The reconciliation service was similarly characterized by emotional expressiveness; according to the Sun reporter, not only was the Washingtonian official (James Morrison) in tears as he performed the ceremony, so was much of the audience at this "rejoicing festival" where "the hardest heart was softened."[58]

Emotional release was not the only Washingtonian challenge to gendered traditions. The report of the reconciliation service traced the recovery of Mr. Moffitt and described the stages of his wife's willingness to receive him back—a process throughout which she exercised ultimate authority. First, the Washingtonian representative informed her that her husband had been located and was drying out with them; they asked if she was interested in reestablishing communication as they assisted him "in the mighty struggle for his liberty from under the power and dominion of the king of the worst terrors and cruelties." Mrs. Moffitt remained suspicious ("would to God it would be only true") and apparently demanded further assurance of her

55. Zug, *Washington Temperance Society*, 63; David Harrisson Jr., *A Voice from the Washingtonian Home, . . . Together with a Sketch of the Temperance Reform in America* (Boston, 1860), 58–60.

56. For the "androgynous model of regeneration" characterizing evangelical conversion, see Juster, "'In a Different Voice,'" 36.

57. *Baltimore Saturday Visiter*, July 2, 1842. William G. Hawkins, *Life of Hawkins*, 66, 86.

58. *Sun*, Oct. 28, 1843.

husband's rehabilitation. On a second visit, the Washingtonian "messenger of peace" joined Mrs. Moffitt in prayer "that he who was your partner, protector, and the father of your children, might again be reinstated in his once happy lot." After a third visit, Mrs. Moffitt received her husband only as long as he "gave proof that he was no more a subject to his old tyrant demons." Finally, after having "watched him as a probationer for some days" and becoming "fully satisfied that his situation and present standing are of the true Washingtonian stamp," Mrs. Moffitt decided to receive her husband back. Throughout this process she had been in charge, and during the service the missionary McKnight issued the final admonishment to the rehabilitated drunk: "For a time you have been under a probation which has fixed [your wife's] faith in you," but this happy state was contingent upon Mr. Moffitt's "constancy in virtue and self-denial to last, I trust, until death do you separate."[59] The conditional nature of Anthony Moffitt's reestablishment as husband and father could not have been made more clear: if he were to reclaim his place in the family, he would have to earn it, with divine assistance, through the approval of his wife.

As was evident throughout the movement, many Washingtonians saw temperance and evangelical experience as part of a seamless web of personal empowerment and existential meaningfulness, with the pledge of abstention a crucial step on the path to the choice of salvation. But they were also cognizant of the fact that "respectable" evangelicalism had limited interest in and held little resonance for the displaced artisan, especially if he were alcoholic. Washingtonian piety provided an authentic religious alternative to churches preoccupied with decorousness and worldly success; Washingtonian believers, according to Teresa Murphy, "were drawing on ideals of primitive Christianity which were also a part of popular evangelicalism." As John Zug explained:

> The drunkard is prejudiced against the church and her ministers. Satisfy him that these have nothing to do with your society, and he will listen to you. When he joins and is reformed, and has come to his proper senses and his conscience, no one can doubt the effect his reformation will have on his notions of church matters. Cold water clears the head; and though it does not regenerate, it greatly unwarps the heart. And though a man reformed from intemperance, may still be an unconverted man so far as religion is concerned, yet he is now prepared to view matters in their true light . . . ; and now, if ever, he

59. Ibid.

> will be likely to attend religious worship and become a Christian. Religious influences now have access to him; before they had not.[60]

For if one could choose sobriety through the pledge, according to Washingtonian doctrine, one could equally be expected, according to Arminian doctrine, to choose salvation through Jesus. John Hawkins, for instance, clearly understood his newfound sobriety in soteriological terms. The pledge, he claimed, was worthless outside conversion: "strip me of my salvation, and I am gone," sober or not. Hawkins maintained this tendency to translate sobriety into spirituality and in 1842 was officially ordained as a minister of the Methodist Protestant denomination that he had helped found fifteen years earlier.[61] Many Washingtonians shared this perspective as they searched for a deeper sense of meaning and identity.

Washingtonianism was another indication that American artisans were capable of constructing alternative solutions to their problems. As such, Washingtonianism was as much a populist phenomenon as Methodist egalitarianism or Jacksonian trade unionism and as capable as any other populist expression of maintaining producerist traditions. Yet Washingtonians could also accommodate new cultural perspectives, particularly in redefining the causes of economic dislocation and dependency. Washingtonian preoccupation with demon rum partially deflected artisan attention away from concerns related to capitalist innovation, and the Washingtonian promise of nondependence encouraged individual alcoholics to overcome economic distress through self-help and personal reformation. This is not, however, to negate the possibilities for Washingtonian producerism. Connections between grogseller and capitalist exploitation could be and were made by subsequent labor reformers.[62] But the Washingtonian emphasis on redeeming the character of

60. Zug, *Washington Temperance Society*, 62–63. This tendency was most obvious among black Baltimoreans, whose Methodist-oriented "Temperance Societies of Color" included the Old Wesley Temperance Sabbath School Society and the Asbury Total Abstinence Society. *Sun*, July 8, 1843. The original Washingtonian Society of Baltimore also developed its own Sunday School. *Sun*, July 1, 1844.

61. In a letter to his family written three months after his first missionary trip to New York, Hawkins wrote, "But, mother, although you have been praying for a drunken son for many years, your prayers have been answered, and I am now restored to sobriety, to my friends and family, and to the favor and fellowship of Him who died that I 'might not perish, but have everlasting life.' For years past *I did not expect, when I died, ever to meet you or any of my friends in heaven*; but now my fears and doubts are all gone, and I have a well grounded hope that when I die I shall see you at God's right hand 'where parting shall be no more.'" William G. Hawkins, *Life of Hawkins*, 117.

62. Teresa Murphy draws attention to labor activist Goodwin Wood's reference to the "striking likeness between the rum-drinker and the capitalist" because, as Murphy adds,

lost drunkards, despite the innovative support group context of its meetings, remained essentially individualistic.

The image of the drunkard as a representative type of an unregenerate American evolved during the early years of the republic, but alcohol abusers were not the only group to be "othered." As capitalism developed, increasingly those with few goods, little wealth, and no property were no longer seen as socially neutral and integrated into the lower middle orders of the larger society, but rather as "the poor"—socially regressive and inherently different from the emerging upper- and middle-class consensus. According to old producerist categories, of course, a no-frills material existence coupled with personal skill and labor beneficial to the community at large was sufficient to be considered "middling" and socially positive. But as the general standard of living arose in conjunction with economic expansion, social distinctions became more materially based; disposable wealth mattered more than honest labor as manual labor lost status to white-collar work. In addition (and paradoxically, to many contemporaries), as the economy grew and many common folk began to enjoy a modicum of upward mobility, the pool of those considered poor also grew. Some found themselves in that condition because they were suffering "from misfortunes attributable to causes beyond their immediate controul [*sic*]." These poor, because their poverty was due to environmental factors, were generally to be supported in their efforts to escape or forestall further degradation. Dislocated artisans who had not yet become generationally downtrodden were among this group. Others, however, had wasted their opportunities "in listless indolence and reckless dissipation, instead of providing for the wants of the winter." This group of poor, because their poverty was due to personality defects, were responsible for their plight yet were capable, under the right inspiration, of escaping from chronic apathy or "the chiliasm of despair." During this time, evangelical producerist perspectives on poverty and solutions to its social disruptions began to change.[63]

"neither was able to control his baser urges." The *New England Operative*, reprinted in the *Mechanic*, Aug. 10, 1844, cited in Murphy, *Ten Hours' Labor*, 178.

63. Richard Bushman, *The Refinement of America: Persons, Houses, Cities* (New York: Alfred A. Knopf, 1992). For a contemporary description of the causes of poverty, see *Baltimore Saturday Visiter*, Nov. 30, 1833. The "chiliasm of despair" is, of course, E. P. Thompson's classic but flawed explanation for working-class spirituality. See Thompson, *Making of the English Working Class*, 375–400, and David Hempton, "Motives, Methods, and Margins in Methodism's Age of Expansion," paper presented at Conference on Methodism and the Shaping of American Culture, 1760–1860, Oct. 7–8, 1994, Asbury Theological Seminary, Wilmore, Ky.

Increasingly prominent in the 1840s was a third grouping of the poor: immigrants, especially Irish, less easily acculturated than the British and Scotch-Irish. The plight of this group, especially Irish Catholics, was further complicated by traditional American anti-Catholicism and the expectation that the newcomers would gladly convert to Protestantism or at least submit to Protestant hegemony. Anti-Catholicism based on doctrinal and ecclesiastical differences remained an evangelical staple, but, in Baltimore in the late 1830s, it had not yet evolved into the full-blown nativism that split the ranks of workers in later years or in other cities. Baltimore did, however, experience one episode of anti-Catholic rioting—the so-called Nunnery Riot of 1839—during this period. Sparked by popular Catholiphobia and voyeuristic preoccupation with the secret life of convents and fanned by respectable Presbyterian ministers Robert Breckinridge, Andrew Cross, and George Washington Musgrave, the riot broke out after an unbalanced young nun, complaining vaguely of ill treatment, fled her convent on Sunday, August 18. The Presbyterian anti-Catholics, through the agency of their *Baltimore Literary and Religious Magazine*, had been trying, with only moderate success, to drum up public support for the closing of the Carmelite convent on Aisquith Street since it was built in 1831.[64] Now they saw a new opportunity.

In short order, a crowd—including Breckinridge—gathered at the convent, shouting threats and insisting that the runaway be taken to nearby Washington College for observation by faculty at the medical school. Tensions increased on Monday, when the *Baltimore Post* incorrectly reported that the Washington College physicians had found the nun sane (thereby implying that her complaints were valid), and another crowd attacked the convent, now defended by city guards, the parapolice force established after the bank riots. Despite injuries on both sides, no fatalities occurred and the convent was saved. When the doctors' actual report, declaring the disturbed nun a

64. Mannard, "1839 Baltimore Nunnery Riot," 13–16. The first opportunity for the nativist Presbyterians came in March 1835, when John Bruscup (a tailor and Methodist Protestant class leader), Sophia Bruscup, Lavinia Brown, Hannah Leach, Sarah Baker, and Elizabeth Polk reported hearing cries for help from the Carmelite convent as they came home from a nightly Methodist Protestant meeting. Breckinridge and Cross, the editors of the *Baltimore Literary and Religious Magazine*, made much of this commotion, but the civil authorities ignored it, as there were no other reports of similar problems. *Baltimore Literary and Religious Magazine* 1 (May 1835): 129–32, cited also in Breckinridge, *Tracts to Vindicate Religion and Liberty*, 11–12. Despite his position of authority within the church, Bruscup had previously been disciplined for illegally selling the time of one of his apprentices—a rare instance of an evangelical church disciplining a member for an economic sin. In 1835, the Methodists Protestants expelled Bruscup. Records, West Baltimore Station, Methodist Protestant Church, M1472, Maryland Hall of Records.

victim of "monomania," became known on Tuesday, public outrage quickly subsided, and the nativists found themselves on the defensive. According to Joseph Mannard, there was no obvious socioeconomic factor or producerist rationale involved in this crowd action; rather, it seemed an excuse for young Baltimoreans to let off steam in the direction of an "acceptable" scapegoat and to rationalize their behavior as a defense of republicanism and feminine virtue.[65]

In contrast to the Baltimore Bank Riot, the authorities moved quickly and decisively to protect the convent and property in general. Whereas Baltimore's evangelical community had stayed uninvolved during the bank riot, this episode tended to involve as well as to divide it and further strengthened the law-and-order tendencies so obvious four years earlier. Methodist and Democratic councilman John Seidenstricker and Presbyterian city guard official Peter Fenby played prominent roles in defending the convent, while longtime Methodist Protestant leaders Samuel K. Jennings and Edward Foreman were among the five doctors finding the escaped nun officially insane (thereby defusing the tension). In the aftermath, the socially prominent Presbyterian instigators were tried for inciting to riot and their efforts were publicly condemned, with George C. Addison, Methodist class leader and shoemaker, casting the deciding vote. Nativists began to reassert themselves only in 1843 with the creation of a "Protestant Association" under the leadership of Robert Breckinridge. At the end of 1844, religious and political elements in Baltimore merged to create the fledgling nativist organization, the American Republican Party, supported also by its own local press, as the *Baltimore Clipper* (run by Edmund Bull and William Tuttle) became the *American Republican.* The nativist impulse did not explode in Baltimore until the 1850s, when the bloody Know-Nothing election riots reestablished Baltimore's reputation as "Mobtown."[66]

These changes had profound implications for the relationship between evangelicals and workers, many of whom, under the deskilling impact of

65. Breckinridge, *Tracts to Vindicate Religion and Liberty,* 3–7; Mannard, "1839 Baltimore Nunnery Riot," 14–15, 18–19. For a different dynamic in a similar situation in contemporaneous Philadelphia, see David Montgomery, "The Shuttle and the Cross: Weavers and Artisans in the Kensington Riots of 1844," *Journal of Social History* 5 (summer 1972): 411–46.

66. Mannard, "1839 Baltimore Nunnery Riot," 14, 20, 22; Breckinridge, *Tracts to Vindicate Religion and Liberty,* 14–15. The initial meeting of the Protestant Association was held in the Light Street Methodist Church and included a cross section of evangelical leadership in Baltimore: Benjamin Kurtz (Evangelical Lutheran), Daniel Evans Reese (Methodist Protestant), Elias Heiner (German Reformed), and George Washington Musgrave (Presbyterian), as well as Baptist, Methodist, and Episcopalian representatives. *Baltimore Saturday Visiter,* Apr. 1, 1843.

industrialization, were falling into new categories of the poor. On the one hand, artisans had traditionally excluded from their ranks the unskilled, who lacked both the craft skills and a sufficient stake in society to be considered as anything other than "dependent;" the poor were often rejected as part of the "useless classes."[67] Evangelicals, on the other hand, tended to see the unskilled as poverty-stricken, and they took their responsibility for the welfare of any downtrodden seriously. As J. H. Hewitt reminded his evangelical readers, "we are taught in the sacred volume, that he who gives to the poor lends to the Lord." But, with populist denominations like Methodists merging with respectable mainstream Protestantism,[68] evangelical congregations in the 1840s were not as likely to serve as the same kind of haven for immigrants (especially Catholics) as they had for the native-born artisans only a few years earlier. As a result, the poor were becoming an external mission field rather than an integral part of potential congregational communities.[69]

Delineation of the poor as a distinct social class did not mean they were to be ignored, but removing the causes of their poverty from the realm of producerist critique signified a dramatic departure. Rather than relying on traditional evangelistic efforts from within the community, Baltimore's evangelical establishment developed home missionaries to reach the poor. Made possible by the change in moral considerations of wealth (from denunciations of the inappropriateness of selfish accumulation to explanations of the appropriateness of benevolent dispersal),[70] this system marked the reconciliation of the itinerant tradition to the exigencies of urban life, even as it reflected modern impulses toward efficiency and the division of labor. Like their revivalist predecessors, home missionaries inspired their audiences to concur with the evangelical messages of divine acceptance and holy living and, usually, to join existing congregations. But by the 1840s, these converts had a minimal input because of their low social status and their entrance into an already established institutional setting.[71] The inadvertent

67. Laurie, *Working People of Philadelphia*, 86–87; Hattam, *Labor Visions*, 95.

68. Carwardine, "Unity, Pluralism," in Swanson, ed., *Unity and Diversity*, 329–31.

69. *Baltimore Saturday Visiter*, Nov. 30, 1833.

70. Isaac Cook noted this change in perspective. Disagreeing with the assessment of earlier Methodists who had explained the accidental burning of Cokesbury College in 1796 following the funeral of Patrick Colvin as divine judgment exercised because of his excessive wealth, Cook pointed out that Colvin's daughter had later endowed the Colvin Institute for Girls; thus Colvin's accumulation had been a divine blessing. Cook was active in Methodist relief efforts preceding the home missionary activity. Isaac Cook, unpub. autobiography, in Isaac Cook Papers, Lovely Lane Museum, Baltimore; *American*, Jan. 24, 1834.

71. There continued to be congregational growth, in the pattern of the Columbia Avenue congregation, inspired by the efforts of home missionaries. Daniel McJilton, member

effect of the home missionary impulse, then, was to circumscribe the possibilities of communal empowerment and evaluation of systemic injustice, even as it extended to the poor individualized benefits of self-respect and survival values. Such limitations were obvious in the records of home missionaries. But their efforts were not undertaken to provide employers with a steady supply of docile workers; rather, they were designed to operate, like Washingtonianism, to build character leading to nondependency and to strengthen the individual's ability both to transcend trying economic conditions and to take advantage of the opportunities promised by liberal culture.

The first city missionaries appeared in Baltimore concurrent with the journeymen's upheavals of 1836. Stephen Williams was a Presbyterian minister who, after sensitively canvassing the artisan districts of Fell's Point and Oldtown, published a report that drew attention to Baltimore's poor. Although he promised to later "reveal with exact certainty the defects and dangers of the social system," Williams initially confined himself to describing the degradation of the poor, denouncing intemperance, and, in the tradition of John Weishampel, calling for a wealthy benefactor to found a House of Industry for poor widows "at which, such persons can be furnished with work, at fair prices, while they are in health—and with aid when in sickness." The stage was set for the emergence of voluntarist humanitarianism based on cooperation between wealthy benefactors, small contributors, and incipient social workers.[72]

The other original home missionary in Baltimore was John Hersey, the ascetic Methodist who was hired in April 1836 "to improve the religious condition of the poor and neglected, and to relieve their temporal necessities as far as possible." Hersey epitomized primitive Methodism and his deep-seated

of a fairly prominent Baltimore family who turned his attention to the problems of the poor, was a Methodist local deacon and a city missionary. In 1843, McJilton began a Sabbath School in east Baltimore which, in 1851, became the Harford Avenue Methodist Episcopal Church. McJilton's congregation, however, does not appear to represent the norm. Armstrong, *Old Baltimore Conference,* 172; Cook, *Early History of Sabbath Schools,* 26; Franch, "Congregation and Community," 133.

72. *Baltimore Literary and Religious Magazine* 3 (June 1837): 276–80. Williams's statistics indicated that only one in nine of the poor (including children) were "professedly pious," with one family in four attending church services regularly. The idea of wealthy contributions to the House of Industry was phrased in the language of traditional economic morality; to help the poor would also "rob some profligate heir of a part of the means of dishonoring his memory." Later, the paper asserted that the depression following the panic of 1837 was caused, not by God, but by the "frenzy of speculation." Individualism was the cure: sober, industrious, honest, and fair work habits would pull workers through. *Baltimore Literary and Religious Magazine* 3 (Dec. 1837): 556.

allegiance to producerist ethics led him to condemn capitalist practices in his popular manuals on Christian living, published in Baltimore throughout the 1830s. Despite his producerism, however, Hersey's solution to capitalist dislocation was to offer individual empowerment through conversion and self-help. He received a yearly salary of three hundred dollars (putting him on a financial par with much of his audience), and he obtained the permission of Mayor Samuel Smith to preach in the streets and market places. He was tireless; in little less than a year, Hersey visited more than twenty-one hundred families and recorded their spiritual and material needs for subsequent prayer and action. Hersey's efforts, though restricted to individual cases, were neither ineffective nor unappreciated. Sarah Wilson, for instance, wrote to Hersey thanking him for the barrel of flour he sent her family and for his efforts in getting her son a job with a local merchant. In addition, she asked Hersey to pray that at his new job her son "may be kept from the evil."[73] If at times Hersey lacked tact or sympathy, he did not patronize the poor, and although his approach rarely inspired social activism, his personal attention affirmed them in ways that generated positive reactions from many to whom he preached. Hersey embodied the Methodist understanding of the "Christian virtue of beneficence," which held that "whoever would remedy misery, must himself suffer; and . . . the pains of the vicarious benefactor, are . . . to bear proportion to the . . . malignity of the evils he labors to remove."[74]

Ironically, the home missionary impulse circumscribed the efficacy of that very "virtue of beneficence" by enabling comfortable evangelical contributors to avoid direct contact with the poor, and Hersey did not let his benefactors ignore that tendency. Indicative of this was Hersey's treatment of a contributor judged to be one who "loved the world rather more than became him as a christian." When this man expressed gratitude to God for his prosperity, Hersey offered a challenging parable, which drew attention to the hypocrisy of enjoying wealth while others "have fallen among thieves and have been robbed." Hersey continued, "Sin has mangled many of them dreadfully; many of them are suffering for the necessaries of life," and he encouraged his rich friend to provide more amply to both his servants and any in distress who might come his way. After this rebuke, Hersey noted that his friend "was

73. *Republican*, Mar. 3, 1837. Isaac Cook, "Introduction," in Marine, *Sketch of John Hersey*, iv. At one point, Hersey was sent away unceremoniously by a merchant in Baltimore because he was perceived to be a beggar. When the merchant discovered his error, Hersey asked him for clothes for an impoverished elderly woman and received a large quantity. Ibid., 58–59; Fletcher Marine Papers, MS#1016.3, Maryland Historical Society, Baltimore.

74. *Mutual Rights and Methodist Protestant* 1 (Jan. 7, 1831): 6.

silent, and I hope he profited by the thought. Rich people are in imminent danger. Money has an assimilating influence—it is hard; it hardens the heart; it is blind, it obscures our vision."[75] Hersey's understanding of economics was intensely individualistic as well as moralistic.

Hersey and Williams were among the first city missionaries in Baltimore Another noted street preacher and humanitarian, colporteur Thomas Freeman, appeared later. Freeman was born in England in 1792, the son of prosperous parents who both died before young Thomas was five. The boy was left with an uncaring stepfather, who, in Dickensian fashion, sent his stepson to the workhouse. Soon Freeman became a child laborer in a silk factory outside Manchester. At ten, he was converted (probably to Methodism) at a factory Sunday school, where he also learned to read, and he educated himself by singing to fellow workers who repaid him with donations, which he used to buy more books. Around 1810 he set off for London, but instead he was pressed into the British navy. After surviving a fall overboard and an apparently disastrous trip to "the polar regions" with Sir John Franklin aboard the *Erebus*, he deserted and wound up in Baltimore, where he lived a long life as a tract missionary, to be succeeded by his son James.[76]

His tract reports reveal Freeman's social attitudes, responses directed toward him, and evidences of a muted traditional economic morality. Freeman, like Hersey, did not fit the stereotype of either the middle-class reformer or the opportunistic hypocrite;[77] his long career as a sailor made him particu-

75. Hersey, *Importance of Small Things*, 101–3. Hersey also espoused this voluntarist perspective; at a meeting of the managers of the Humane Impartial Society, he beseeched his audience: "The wants of the widow and orphan speak too loud at this inclement season to make it necessary to say more. Remember, God loves a cheerful giver, and as ye have freely received, freely give." *Republican*, Jan. 12, 1838.

76. Thomas Freeman file, esp. primer owned by Hester Freeman Gordon, Lovely Lane Museum, Baltimore. For a description of the duties of and historical context of colporteurage, see J. T. Crane, "The Tract Movement," *Methodist Quarterly Review* 38 (Jan. 1856): 31; David Paul Nord's "Religious Reading and Readers in Antebellum America," *Journal of the Early Republic* 15 (summer 1995): 241–72, and Carwardine, "Unity, Pluralism," in Swanson, ed., *Unity and Diversity*, 315.

77. A recent description of evangelical efforts in New York is typical of the historiography that assumes evangelical outreach to be part of a capitalist plot to create docile workers: "Although it appeared to be an effort to liberate sailors from a type of bondage, the unspoken agenda of the reformers was to create a more tractable and disciplined labor force." Paul A. Gilje and Howard B. Rock, *Keepers of the Revolution: New Yorkers at Work in the Early Republic* (Ithaca: Cornell University Press, 1992), 194. A more judicious interpretation of this tradition maintains that "humanitarian reform not only took courage and brought commendable changes but also served the interests of the reformers and was part of that vast bourgeois project that Max Weber called rationalization." Thomas L. Haskell, "Capitalism and the Origins of the Humanitarian Sensibility, Part 1," *American Historical Review* 90 (Apr. 1985): 340.

larly comfortable with the conditions and work experience of mariners and other workers.[78] Much of his activity, in fact, was directed to workers in the wharf areas. He was often received kindly, even when his preaching challenged the activities of his audience; when warning those frequenting a grog shop, for instance, that their conduct was dangerous, "they said i [*sic*] was right and they was wrong." On more than one occasion, individuals approached him to thank him for preaching to or praying with them years earlier, and a carpenter near Howard Street told him "my Tracts had been the means of doing a deal of good in this Neighborhood." Responses to his exhorting, however, were by no means uniformly positive; he was also at times ignored, sometimes "laughed to scorn," and one Irish woman vented her displeasure at his intrusion by shaking the contents of her dirty rug on him, and another threatened him with a boiling kettle of water. By 1848, he estimated that he was making five thousand visits annually.[79]

Although each of these visits was, of necessity, brief, much can be learned from the record of them. Freeman's reports revealed the tensions within populist evangelicalism at that time; while retaining plebeian sensibilities, his work, more than that of others, indicated an accommodation of liberal culture. Freeman noted his gratitude toward bankers, merchants, and others who supported his endeavors, yet a populist perspective is also apparent in his expressed distrust of wealth and status. Informing hostile businessmen that he "had as much right to see them as the poor," Freeman was more than willing to remind them "of the language of our lord, what will it profit a man if he gain the whole world and lose his own soul." Describing a typical encounter he wrote: "spoke to one gentleman and oferd [*sic*] him a tract, he

---

See also idem, "Capitalism and the Origins of the Humanitarian Sensibility, Part 2," *American Historical Review* 90 (June 1985): 560. For workers like Hersey and Freeman, as Michael Franch so aptly put it, "fear of the incipient thug seemed to be less of a motivation than compassion for the lost lamb." Franch, "Congregation and Community," 186.

78. "My journeys though attended with a deal of Toil and Labour yet on the whole [h]as been of an encouraging character. I have had to leave the Boats[,] Climb the Rugged Mountains and get into the Clefts of the Rocks to the sun-Burnt Quarry Men [to] give them Tracts and tell them of Christ and his salvation. At a nother [*sic*] time with the Miners working at the ore, then with Furnace Men. [T]hese men of Fire and Heat . . . handle the burning Mettle [*sic*] as a thing of Life. I have been with them at 5 in the morning. Had our friends seen them assemble round me with Pare of Tongs in one hand, a Tract in the other and the Tears in there [*sic*] eyes, they would say our labours were not in vain." Thomas Freeman Papers, n.d., Lovely Lane Museum, Baltimore.

79. Freeman Tract Reports, Sept. 23, 1844; Feb. 13, Apr. 13, June 12, 14, 1845; Dec. 26, 1846; Feb. [undated entry], 1848; Sept. 1, 1850; Lovely Lane Museum, Baltimore. This was the same area which created its own Strawbridge Methodist Church a couple of years earlier (see chap. 6).

said it may do for the lower classes but not for me. i [*sic*] told him with all earnestness suitable to the ocasion [*sic*] to consider his ways and be wise." Another irate recipient informed Freeman that his tracts "were only for negroes." Freeman responded, "some of these would get to heaven before him." He was not awed by those in authority; he noted giving tracts to sailors despite the angry opposition of the mate, and he once visited the mayor's office. He was particularly direct with one group of lawyers he encountered in Baltimore's business district, reminding them of Jesus' "interview with lawyers," wherein the terrors of a higher law were described. Nor was he particularly impressed with the newfound status and respectability of his evangelical brethren. When he discovered a group of well-dressed Methodists chatting outside the Exeter Street Church before church, Freeman freely rebuked their casual approach to worship.[80]

Father Freeman, as he came to be known, could be empathetic, but he could also appear callous, insensitive, and bigoted. When visiting a man who had lost his arm, livelihood, and friends through a rock-blasting accident, Freeman reported that he gave the unfortunate workman "a trifle" and exhorted him "to learn from what he had suffered." Many of Freeman's pronouncements were typically revivalistic—although he was not above reminding his listeners of the dangers of an eternal, unsaved fate, more often he stressed the joys and mercies of reconciliation with God through Christ—but they also reflected individualistic and otherworldly emphases that circumscribed the militant activism implicit in populist evangelicalism. A typical report, in this respect, read "spoke to many in there [*sic*] Work shops about this Religion that will do them good in a dying day." As a rule, Freeman never tried to convert his audience on the spot; rather, he urged them to retreat to their "closets" to wrestle with God, one on one. His simple message, lacking explanation of impoverished conditions in environmental or social terms, was not given to promoting activism. Instead, his portrayal of the godly worker was one who, after a hard day's work, would read his family a chapter in the Bible, give thanks for the mercies of the day, and pray for protection for the night.[81]

Freeman's watered-down critique of contemporary culture was evident in his views on economic morality and was influenced by the ecumenical mainstreaming of populist evangelicalism. The trivial nature of the economic sins he condemned, for instance, indicated a weakening of the producerist legacy,

80. Ibid., Sept. 29, Oct. 1, 2, 1844; Dec. 18, 1845; Apr. 17, June 20, Sept. 9, 1846.

81. Ibid., Aug. 11, Oct. 7, 10, 1844; Apr. 25, 30, 1845. For Freeman's deemphasis on fire and brimstone, see the entry for Oct. 21, 1844.

as Freeman tended to equate all forms of lower-class gaming with "gambling," which he universally attacked. When he found a group of sailors "pitching cents on the ground," Freeman warned them that "for all these things God will bring them into judgement." He also rebuked a poor woman for selling apples on the Sabbath, but, in a visit to a lottery office, he merely "advised them to make there [*sic*] peace with God."[82] And although he warned merchants to consider the fate of their souls, he did not challenge them to consider their current commercial practices. His emphasis on ecumenism, which, except for his anti-Catholic prejudices,[83] was unusually free of sectarian jealousies, reflected the intradenominational sources of his support; he was content to send listeners to the Protestant congregation of his or her choice. In addition, he often steered sailors toward nondenominational mission chapels for mariners (Seamen's Bethels), of which there were two in Baltimore. These missions tended to be manned by two disparate groups: evangelical exsailors like Freeman and Samuel Kramer and, beginning in the 1840s, young, idealistic professionals like Alfred Cookman, whose activism marked both genuine altruism and a peculiarly middle-class evangelical rite of passage to manhood. Their cross-class coordination often reduced the evangelical message to the lowest common denominators of conversion and respectable behavior.[84]

Freeman's work emerged in response to the exigencies of Baltimore's burgeoning population and the dislocations of industrialization. In evaluating the influence of such humanitarian innovations, it is important not to confuse results with motivations. Home missionary work has been accurately described by Thomas Haskell as "an expansion of the conventional limits of moral responsibility that prompted people whose values may have remained as traditional (and unrelated to class) as the Golden Rule to behave in ways that were unprecedented and not necessarily well-suited to their material interests." If it is true, as it has been argued, that America's emerging ruling

82. Ibid., Feb. 12, Apr. 13, 1845; Jan. 27, 1846.

83. Many times, Catholic immigrants treated Freeman with more liberality than he was willing to show them. Freeman wrote of one encounter: "notwithstanding all there [*sic*] Bigotry, they received me with kindness and gave me a cup of cold water." Ibid., Apr. 11, 1846.

84. Ibid., Dec. 7, 1845; Henry B. Ridgaway, *The Life of the Rev. Alfred Cookman, with a Brief Account of His Father, the Rev. George Grimston Cookman* (London, 1876), 101. The Charles Street Methodist Church provided the bulk of the young humanitarians. Their unabashed embrace of upward mobility and identification with the elite—almost unthinkable among Methodists only ten years earlier—was pronounced in the career of Alfred Cookman. Ridgaway, *Life of Alfred Cookman*, 98. Freeman also enjoyed the support of established populist preachers like Henry Slicer. Freeman Tract Papers, Oct. 16, 1845, Lovely Lane Museum, Baltimore.

class of capitalists avoided a serious class confrontation because, in part, of the ameliorative influence of humanitarianism, that perspective was not necessarily the motivating factor for the evangelicals themselves.[85] Freeman, like Hersey, gained only subsistence-level financial support and, it is hoped, a future reward. He was not the willing agent of an evil conspiracy, though that is to say nothing, one way or the other, about the motivations of his wealthy employers. He took the objects of his attention seriously and worked tirelessly to give them what he had—a little money, a little food, and the psychic means to both transcend and change their current circumstances. Like all evangelical populists, he refused to acknowledge the allegedly superior worth of those enjoying more of the fruits of worldly production.

Although neither class nor material benefit may explain Freeman's career, his actions definitely fit within the parameters of the emergent liberal culture. Urban evangelicals encountered problems that were obviously immune to the traditional solutions of face-to-face intervention. Their peculiar and optimistic expectations shaped by perfectionism and millennialism prevented them from ignoring these dislocations; instead, they felt responsible to meliorate conditions. Their primary intentions, therefore, were to inculcate survivalist values, not exploitable ones. In the process, they contributed to the dominance of liberal hegemony.[86] And, as the mainstream evangelical message increasingly lost its prophetic judgment of the evils of industrialization, the messages of self-help and humanitarian benevolence were preferable to no help at all; at least those who benefited from the efforts seemed to appreciate them greatly.

The ambivalence toward producerist legacies exhibited by the evangelicals active in Washingtonian temperance and home missionary efforts was also apparent among Baltimore's trade unionists in the 1840s. Even before the WMTU disintegrated, its leadership cadre had begun to moderate its antagonism toward liberal culture, and many of those leaders remained publicly active throughout the early 1840s. Not surprisingly, their activism turned in the direction of social respectability and voluntary humanitarianism. After the WMTU collapsed, they continued their tradition of mechanics' fancy balls, with the proceeds (ninety cords of wood and seventy-five dollars) of one going to poor relief.[87] Five years later their festivities were ostentatiously

85. Haskell, "Capitalism, Part I," 359.

86. Lears, "Concept of Cultural Hegemony," 572, 576.

87. A public notice announced that coachmen in carriages would be bringing "gentlemen" and that "an efficient police has been procured." *Republican* Jan. 8, 18, 1838.

entitled "Grand Fancy, Military, and Civic Ball for the Benefit of the Poor." Managers of this extravaganza included such leaders of the old trade union movement as A. I. W. Jackson, Joshua Vansant, Edmund Bull, and Samuel Mass, as well as newcomer William Minifee.[88] The addition of Minifee is significant because he had traveled such a different path from that of the WMTU artisans (evangelical and otherwise) of the 1830s. Originally a carpenter and a latitudinarian Protestant who critically judged evangelical revivalism as a mild form of social pathology, Minifee had remained aloof from organized trade union activity in the mid-1830s, pursuing instead his personal agenda of education, social respectability, and upward mobility. In time he became a successful architect and a prominent Baltimore Unitarian. He had not been previously active, except as an organizer of lyceums for upwardly mobile, individualistic craftsmen.[89]

If the expansion of the artisan activist circle to include nonmilitant, entrepreneurial individuals like Minifee was revealing, so too were the nature and perspectives of the continued activities of the trade union leadership. With the demise of the independent labor press following the collapse of the WMTU in 1837 and the departure of Samuel Harker for a career in Democratic Party politics, Edmund Bull and William Tuttle, the former editors of the defunct *Baltimore Trades' Union*, partially filled the void with the *Clipper* (with the *Sun*, edited by John Weishampel's old partner, Thomas Beach, also sympathetic to laborite perspectives). One article describing a performance by fifty scholars of the Methodist Sunday School Union suggests continued compatibility between the old WMTU leadership and new expressions of populist evangelical acculturation. "For ourselves," Bull and Tuttle wrote, "we confess that, although ever impressed with a conviction of the great utility of the Sabbath School system, the gratification we experienced during the evening was far greater than we had anticipated." Furthermore, skeptics should adjust their opinions, since "incalculable benefit must accrue to the rising generation from Sabbath School instruction."[90] This benefit, as was

88. *Clipper*, Jan. 5, 1843.

89. The vaguely liberal religious sentiments that had touched Minifee (and served as his spiritual inspiration) can be found in an anonymous poem he had discovered carved above a window in an old building he was demolishing as a young man in England: "Behold the end ere thou begin/Have mind in death and fear to sin,/For death shall reap where life has sown/And life shall spring where death hath mown./If we do well here we shall do well there/I can tell you no more if I preach a whole year." Minifee Papers, Maryland Historical Society, Baltimore.

90. *Clipper*, Jan. 5, 1843. Indicative of their shifting stance toward worker militance, Bull and Tuttle reported that weavers were rioting in Philadelphia because some of their brethren

becoming the norm, was related more to inculcating survival skills in a competitive economy rather than sustaining systemic critiques of liberal culture, yet Bull and Tuttle extolled the virtues of Sunday School education with no reservations.

The Methodist Sunday scholars cited by Bull and Tuttle presented a series of recitations arguing the merits of evangelical conversion, temperance, and Sabbath-keeping. But Methodist children were not the only ones concerned with keeping the Sabbath; this issue had concerned evangelicals since 1809 when a Pennsylvania postmaster outraged his fellow Presbyterians by bowing to federal pressure to keep his post office open seven days a week. By the late 1820s, Sabbatarianism had become a critical arena of conflict for evangelicals determined to assert at least a minimal amount of control over an open society.[91] If evangelicals, ran the argument, could not control the day ordinarily reserved for their concerns, what chance did they have preserving morality in the rest of the week? Yet, for other evangelicals, distaste for any proposal smacking of the merger of church and state combined with distrust of those established clergy usually in charge of Sabbatarian societies made organized support of Sabbath protection problematic. Similar tensions existed within activist artisan circles. On the one hand, the populist sensibilities of many artisans and their champions instinctively resisted any attempt at outside control of their lives. Thus, in the 1820s and 1830s, radical evangelicals like Cornelius Blatchly in New York City and the Democratic wing of the WMTU in Baltimore condemned Sabbath restrictions. On the other hand, even in the early stages of the activity, some artisans understood Sabbatarianism as one way to ward off the compulsory Sunday work that was sometimes demanded by ambitious employers. Thus, one of the demands of New York City bakers who went on strike in 1834 was mandatory Sunday leisure, and the New York evangelical agrarian and trade unionist Robert Townsend was an avowed Sabbatarian.[92]

In the 1840s, amidst the rapid growth of voluntary associations and political action consortiums, Sabbatarianism in Baltimore took on an institutional form, with the founding of the Convention of the Friends of the Lord's-Day

---

were working below the regular wages. The editors offered no comment on these matters originally, though eventually they referred to the riots as "outrages," without expressing any sort of class solidarity with the concerns of the undercut weavers. *Clipper*, Jan. 12, 14, 1843.

91. Richard R. John, "Taking Sabbatarianism Seriously: The Postal System, the Sabbath, and the Transformation of American Political Culture," *Journal of the Early Republic* 10 (winter 1990): 520, 530; Abzug, *Cosmos Crumbling*, 111–16.

92. Blatchly, *Sunday Tract*, 3; Wilentz, *Chants Democratic*, 232, 225–26. For more on Townsend's evangelical agrarianism, see Sutton, "Tied to the Whipping Post," 268–70.

in 1844. The convention included an interesting cross section of activists. Among its elite leadership were Presbyterian clergymen Robert Breckinridge and George Washington Musgrave, and the Methodist Protestant pillars of the wealthy St. John's congregation, John Clark and Augustus Webster. The Universalists sent Thaddeus Craft, partner of hatter entrepreneur and ringleader of the unpopular masters' combination in 1833, William P. Cole. The First Presbyterian Church denominated Moses Hyde, the unsuccessful factory preacher, and John C. Backus, an outspoken advocate of the voluntarist humanitarian schemes of the Scottish reformer and evangelical apologist Thomas Chalmers.[93] Also prominent, however, were those involved in other efforts commending them more directly to Baltimore's artisans, including temperance advocates Christian Keener and Henry Slicer.

Of greater significance in the Sabbatarian movement was the participation of artisan activists; delegates from all over the artisan evangelical leadership spectrum came to this convention. The Universalist congregation in Baltimore selected Richard Marley, cordwainer, WMTU, and National Trades' Union leader, in addition to Thaddeus Craft. St. John's Methodist Protestant Church, along with Clark and Webster, sent WMTU supporter and Democratic legislator, Beale Richardson, and early Methodist Protestant agitators, John Chappell and John Harrod. Aisquith Street Methodist Protestant Church listed Daniel Perigo, a captain in the Night Watch and leader of the striking journeymen shipjoiners in 1836. Representing the Charles Street Church was George K. Quail, Methodist master hatter consistently sympathetic to journeymen concerns and a Washingtonian leader. Another Washingtonian leader, John Bokee, was chosen by the First English Lutheran Church. Exeter Street Methodist Episcopal Church contributed Daniel Pentz of the butchers' association and Jacob Daley, secretary of the Female Trades' Union of seamstresses, while the Monument Street Methodist Church sent Sterling Thomas and Samuel Pentz, also members of the organized butchers association, and Francis

93. Franch, "Congregation and Community," 140–41; Joseph T. Smith, *Eighty Years of Embracing Presbyterianism in Baltimore, with an Appendix* (Philadelphia, 1899), 21–22. Thomas Chalmers was probably the most prominent Anglo-American evangelical proponent of humanitarian benevolence as the solution to capitalist dislocation. Generally sympathetic to workers, Chalmers was limited by his reliance on Enlightenment doctrines that described the depersonalized causes of economic dislocation as part of the inscrutably wise design of God. Boyd Hilton, *The Age of Atonement: The Influence of Evangelicalism on Social and Economic Thought, 1795–1865* (Oxford: Clarendon Press, 1988), 90, 94; Stewart J. Brown, *Thomas Chalmers and the Godly Commonwealth in Scotland* (New York: Oxford University Press, 1982), 82. For more on Chalmers's ethics, see Sutton, "'To Grind the Faces of the Poor,'" 272–79, and Mark Noll, "Thomas Chalmers in North America," paper delivered to the American Society of Church History, Lisle, Ill., Apr. 13, 1996, 5–6.

Burke, leader of the Baltimore Typographical Society and one of the original organizers of the political wing of the WMTU. The Methodist Wesley Chapel was represented by Christian Keener and George C. Addison, a master shoemaker who had been publicly commended by journeymen cordwainers for maintaining their old wage rates in 1836. From the Eutaw Street Methodist Episcopal Church came Edwin Caldwell, the leader of the journeymen planemakers within the WMTU, while the laboring-class Howard Street (soon to become Strawbridge) M. E. Church selected Elisha Carback, another master shoemaker and like Addison supportive of the journeymen cordwainers, Jesse Zumwalt, a master plasterer who granted his workers the ten-hour day in 1833, and Charles Towson, president of the journeymn hatters in 1836. From the plebeian Columbia Street M. E. Church came Columbus Stewart, a founding layman and one of the striking blacksmiths demanding the ten-hour day in 1833. Finally, Caroline Street M. E. Church sent Henry Slicer and two more activist butchers, John J. and Henry Pentz.[94]

The evangelical churches were not the only contributors to the Sabbatarian effort. Samuel Brady, Joshua Vansant's WMTU-backed running mate for the state legislature in 1835, was sent by the delegation from the Howard Total Abstinence Society of Fell's Point. Addi Pindall, early Methodist factory preacher, Sunday School worker, and temperance preacher, and William D. Ball, WMTU candidate for sheriff in 1836, represented the North Baltimore Total Abstinence Society. Joshua Jones, the original candidate of the politically organized workingmen in 1833, came from the Neptune Temperance Society. The paternalistic White Hall Factory sent owners' sons, Nelson Gambrill and John Carroll. And the Reverend Charles H. A. Dall, a city missionary in the mold of John Hersey and Thomas Freeman, attended as an at-large delegate.[95] The range of representatives at the Lord's-Day Convention was similar to the mix of those active in the various expressions (evangelical and nonevangelical both) of the anticapitalist militancy in the 1830s.

The arguments proposed by the Sabbatarian convention addressed many of the cultural issues under negotiation in the 1840s. In keeping with the evangelical propensity for supporting Scripture with Enlightenment dogma, the convention "gratefully" recognized "the wisdom and goodness of God, in

94. *Convention of Friends of the Lord's-Day*, 9–14. In spite of George Quail's participation and the fact that fourteen other Methodist congregations sent members, the merchant-oriented and affluent Charles Street Methodist Church apparently sent no official delegation.

95. Ibid., 13–16. For more on Charles Dall's home mission efforts, which reflected an unusual level of ecumenism, see *Baltimore Saturday Visiter*, July 1, July, 8, 1843. For the temperance work of Addi Pindall (or Adi Pindel) among Baltimore's firemen, see *Baltimore Saturday Visiter*, Dec. 24, 1842.

the appointment and preservation of the Sabbath" because "the Sabbath . . . is based upon a natural law, and the highest physical, as well as moral good of men," which therefore "requires its universal observance." Much of the Sabbatarian rhetoric was framed in republican language reflecting genuine concern for the welfare of workers, notwithstanding the implied paternalism in the argument. Tying Sabbath observance to maintenance of "the purity and permanence of free institutions," the Sabbatarians condemned engaging in secular business on Sunday; "to interfere with the laboring class, so as to deprive them of the benefit of a due observance of the Sabbath, by requiring or tempting them to labor on that day, is a grievous wrong to that class of people and to the whole community." In summing up, the delegates argued that Sabbatarianism was "for the interest of employers as well as . . . employed."[96] While this approach spoke far more clearly to the producerist harmony-of-interests ideal than to explicit anticapitalist criticism, it presented a clear challenge to the doctrines of unlimited self-interest presented by liberal apologists.

The convergence of these veteran activists around the Sabbatarian cause was further evidence of the modification of producerist tenets. It has been suggested that Sabbatarianism was an attempt by guilt-stricken capitalists to assuage their respective consciences by enforcing the suspension of their normal acquisitive behaviors, but such an interpretation seems unlikely for Baltimore considering that many of the Lord's-Day participants were not capitalists but veteran trade unionists and producerist small masters. It has also been suggested that Sabbatarianism provided a common political symbol for evangelicals at a time when they were being institutionally sundered by the issue of slavery, but that neglects the very real controversy Sabbatarianism inspired among populist evangelicals.[97] According to Richard John, "The Sabbath provided an opportunity for collective renewal, for the encouragement of those ties of family and kin so vital to the emerging cult of domesticity, and for the ritual reaffirmation of the transcendent reality of sacred time." In more mundane terms, Sabbatarianism was an authentic attempt to preserve the producerist traditions restricting exploitation by resorting to communal pressure. In short, Sabbatarians wanted to sublimate purely economic concerns to religious ones—to guarantee, in the traditional language of

96. Ibid., 2–3.

97. John, "Taking Sabbatarianism Seriously," 527; Bertram Wyatt-Brown, "Prelude to Abolitionism: Sabbatarian Politics and the Rise of the Second Party System, *Journal of American History* 58 (Sept. 1971): 335. Richard John notes the universal extent of Sabbatarian popularity in the United States (p. 543).

Calvinist covenantalism, continued national blessing and to avoid, in the words of the Episcopalian minister H. S. Keppler, "exposing us as a Nation to the curse of God." Although stopping short of the position espoused by Presbyterians in 1826, which urged a boycott of transportation companies that operated on Sundays, the Baltimore Sabbatarians were hopeful of enforcing tenets of traditional economic morality, and they commended the local butchers' and drovers' association for enforcing Sabbath restrictions on themselves.[98] Nevertheless, like the home missionary impulse, the Sabbatarian attempt to meliorate the effects of new economic practices ultimatey led to another form of accommodation to the emergent liberal culture.[99]

The most significant aspect of the "Friends of the Lord's-Day" was the lively discussion concerning government intervention. Just as the Washingtonians initially emphasized the efficacy of persuasion alone to establish teetotalism, the Sabbatarians were reluctant to enlist the coercive power of the state. This became evident when the Reverend John A. Collins of the Eutaw Street Methodist Church offered a resolution requesting that "the state Laws and City Ordinances enjoining the observance of the Lord's Day . . . be enforced." After vigorous debate involving Christian Keener, Andrew Cross, and Henry Slicer, among others, Collins withdrew his resolution, and ultimately the convention, through a close vote, refused to go on record advocating any extension of government intervention. The debate made obvious the fact that Sabbatarianism was another theater in the ongoing cultural war, cutting across class lines, regarding the morally appropriate balance between legislation and suasion, between church and state, between evangelical tradition and liberal innovation.[100] The reluctance to resort to

98. Ibid., 531, 535; Carwardine, *Evangelicals and Politics*, 17–22, *Convention of Friends of the Lord's-Day*, 3–7.

99. *Sun*, Jan. 13, 1844; *Convention of Friends of the Lord's-Day*, 3–4. The often-convergent efforts of trade unionists, artisan activists, and populist evangelicals throughout the 1840s to meet the problems of metropolitan industrialization is illustrated by the list of members of ward committees for relief of the poor in 1844 and 1848. Included among them in 1844 were David Parr of the journeymen potters, W. D. Roberts of the National Trades' Union, and Samuel Pentz and Sterling Thomas of the butchers' association. By 1848, the list included John F. Hoss, trade union activist and Washingtonian founder; Richard Marley, Universalist cordwainer and WMTU leader; and Elisha Carback, Methodist class leader and producerist master shoemaker. *Sun*, Feb. 17, 1844; Archibald Hawkins, *Life of Stansbury*, 154–55.

100. *Convention of Friends of the Lord's-Day*, 5–7. The keynote address at the convention, presented by the Honorable Willard Hall of Wilmington, Delaware, emphasized these cultural elements: "In this country law is, it must be, weak. . . . We cannot help seeing the inefficacy. Our security must be in love of order, personal integrity, uprightness of principle, pervading society. . . . To every one there is the open field of business in which he may exercise fully, freely, and without impediment, all his powers—his strength, his skill, his diligence—and for

government restrictions inadvertently encouraged unregulated capitalist development and weakened the prospects of producerist limits.

By the mid-1840s, in the wake of depression and recovery, those whose faith commitments as populist evangelicals throughout the previous decades had inspired them to splinter antidemocratic denominations and to create new congregations in line with their own populist tendencies were also those whose sense of economic morality as producers had led them to challenge unjust labor competition and to condemn certain elements of industrial capitalism as oppressive; now their counterhegemonic energies had been narrowed to denouncing excesses of intemperance, insufficiencies of humanitarian charity, and violations of the Sabbath. With liberal republicanism gradually replacing classical republicanism as the dominant cultural language for many evangelicals, the ethics of limited accumulation and self-denial for the sake of producerist justice and socioeconomic harmony had been transformed into the ideal of voluntary distribution of excess wealth. But if accommodation to liberal culture had enervated the militancy of many of Baltimore's Jacksonian evangelical populists and trade unionists, their message of producerist opposition to the dislocations of metropolitan industrialization was still salient and would emerge again in the 1840s.

The producerist message was not missed by the next generation of Baltimoreans. In October 1843, in the midst of the first strike wave among Baltimore artisans since 1837,[101] a news item appeared in Baltimore's commercial daily newspaper, *Lyford's Price Current*, commending a meeting held in Boston for the support of the United Benevolent Association of Ladies in their attempt to relieve the suffering of grossly underpaid seamstresses and tailoresses. The paper reported that the meeting opened with a reading from Philippians, chapter 2, which concluded with the admonition, "Look not every man on his own things, but every man also on the things of others." The president then laid down her Bible and prayed that the employers

---

these there is all the remuneration that according to reason and justice can be expected. If some are more skillful, more industrious, more frugal, more persevering or better managing that others, there must necessarily be inequality; it is the inevitable result of justice and equity applied in the natural course of things.—But we have not this strong arm of power.—What substitute can we have?—the intelligence and moral principle of the people. . . . This is Americanism." *Convention of Friends of the Lord's-Day*, 24–26.

101. For public notices of organizational meetings for journeymen tailors, cordwainers, cabinetmakers, and oak coopers, see *Sun*, Oct. 2, 7, Nov. 2, 1843; Jan. 6, 1844. The tailors' notices, reflecting the changing ethnic realities of Baltimore artisans, were also published in German. *Sun*, Oct. 9, 1843.

would take this advice seriously so that "they may no longer oppress and grind the poor widow and the needy down to the dust."[102]

This appeal for divine assistance did not mark the end of the tailoresses' efforts. In language and practices reminiscent of the militancy of the 1830s, the ladies adopted a constitution binding themselves together to resist their unlivable wages, thereby implicitly threatening a strike. They called another meeting on the following night at which several addresses were presented, appealing to the implementation of a boycott as an expression of public support for the exploited, both male and female. The meeting was concluded with a resolution: "That we deeply sympathize in the present movement of the journeymen tailors, tailoresses and seamstresses of the city of Boston, and we will withdraw our patronage from those who will not accede to their reasonable terms." Journals throughout the country were quick to pick up the cause of the tailoresses. The *Baltimore Saturday Visiter* reprinted an article from the *Portland Tribune*, which condemned "those . . . growing rich and independent" on the labor of exploited women. "Is it right for mankind to accumulate wealth from the sighs of the poor and unfortunate? Would it not promote the cause of justice and humanity, to give the females what they earn, and be satisfied with a moderate profit? . . . They need it; . . . and while you deny them what justice requires they should have, you are . . . doing an act that will never entitle you to the blessings of the philanthropist or the Christian."[103]

The anomaly of such an article appearing in a commercial journal like *Lyford's* was not lost on the editors. "Probably some of our patrons at first view may look upon this as a subject foreign to the professed object of our paper; but the next moment they may feel otherwise." There may, indeed, have been an ulterior motive to this editorial policy, based on the growing sectional tensions between slave and free states. "This course of proceeding toward poor dependent females affects our sensibility more strongly—because it is in Boston, where such sympathy has been, and continues to be, manifested for a run away slave from the South who seeks covert [*sic*] in that goodly city, that he has been not only protected but almost canonized, while these same slopsellers withhold from honest laborers that which belongs to them the better to enable them to carry into effect their object of stirring up strife among our domestics at the South."[104] But what an audience would do with

102. *Baltimore Commercial Journal and Lyford's Price Current*, Oct. 14, 1843. The editor of this journal, William G. Lyford, was a Lord's-Day Convention delegate and member of the Charles Street Methodist Church.

103. Ibid.; *Baltimore Saturday Visiter*, Dec. 10, 1843.

104. *Lyford's Price Current*, Oct. 14, 1843.

such a message was, of course, beyond the control of its creators. That an avowedly commercial paper would continue to appeal to the producerist labor theory of value indicates its ongoing popular currency.

In early 1844, the wide range of evangelical artisan response to American culture were obvious. On a national scale, the quintessentially populist denominations—the Baptists and Methodists—were splintering over the moral issue of slavery, revealing not only the inherent weakness of church organization in a disestablished milieu, but also an inability to agree on fundamental biblical ethics. The divisions of 1844–45 dwarfed the Methodist Protestant schism of 1828 but replicated the conflict over evangelical understanding of republicanism, individual conscience, and submission to legitimate authority only. In Baltimore, the depression of the late 1830s had finished off a vital but already fragmenting trade union movement, and populist evangelicals continued to wrestle with their relationship to liberal republican culture. By the mid-1840s, some evangelicals participating in trade union organizing, journeyman militancy, small master producerism, and factory preaching had united behind new issues—more symbolic, less systemic—amenable to individualistic and self-help solutions, with cordwainer Richard Marley, chairmaker Jacob Daley, tailor Elisha Carback, planemaker Edwin Caldwell, and minister Henry Slicer joining the Sabbatarian effort even as hatter John Hawkins continued his successful travels on behalf of Washingtonian temperance. But challenges to the presuppositions of capitalist accumulation persisted, and producerist arguments continued to resonate, especially among those who maintained an ethic of limits and hopes for a true moral economy.

Epilogue

In August 1843, the *Sun* reported that shipyards at Fell's Point were "full of busy workmen" and concluded that this "good sign" was "one certain index of returning prosperity."[1] This was of course encouraging news, but the six-year depression had taken a heavy toll, changing lives and modifying traditions. In the 1820s and 1830s, common Americans grounded in the ethical traditions of populist evangelicalism and producerism had challenged the emergent culture of industrial capitalism even as they were questioning long-held habits of deference to socioeconomic and ecclesiastical "superiors." Artisans and their friends who identified themselves as both evangelical and producerist were neither submissive nor docile; rather, their piety was as likely to be culturally confrontational as personally empowering.[2] Yet their opposition was fraught with ambivalence: by the late 1830s, both militant artisans and populist evangelicals were finding ways to accommodate new

1. *Sun*, Aug. 8, 1843. Despite the *Sun*'s optimism concerning the return of prosperity ("the mechanic no longer laments the slow incoming gains of despairing talent—with one hand he gathers, with the other he gathers his dues—happy in the present and confident in the future") workers were not significantly better off financially than they had been before the panic of 1837; by February, for instance, the journeymen caulkers were only reluctantly satisfied with their wages of $1.50 a day. *Sun*, Sept. 28, 1843; Feb. 17, 1844.

2. Hanley, *Beyond a Christian Commonwealth*, 93–103.

cultural realities, a process that expanded in the years following the panic of 1837. Furthermore, swimming against the cultural tide was never simple or straightforward for these individuals. For some, the allure of respectability, opportunity, and upward social mobility coopted their antagonism; for others, circumstances (e.g., disestablishment, surplus labor pools, and self-destructive behavior) crushed their militancy; and for still others, alternative communal, self-help, or symbolic solutions made success more attainable.

The most critical deflection from producerist concerns came from the increased evangelical preoccupation with the question of the morality of slave-holding. But the two issues were related. Antislavery efforts were rooted not only in questions of humanitarian justice and republican ethics, but they also incorporated aspects of producerism, as evident in the writings of John Hersey and others. But evangelicals were coming to realize that internal discipline and moral suasion were simply not equal to the task of eradicating the evil of slavery. Nowhere was this clearer than in the trial of the Reverend Charles Torrey, whose arrest for helping Virginia slaves escape captured the attention of Baltimoreans in 1843 and deeply divided the evangelical community. Torrey was defended by Francis Gallagher and enjoyed the support of antislavery Baltimoreans, but he was ultimately convicted and imprisoned in Baltimore, where he died a martyr's death in 1846. Torrey's efforts and plight were symptomatic of American evangelicals' inability to bring Protestant egalitarianism and humanitarianism to bear on exploitative labor practices. Baltimore Methodists (reflecting circumstances nationally) subsequently divided over the morality of opposing slavery in 1844. Evangelical failure to construct a unified moral response to the issues raised by slavery prefigured an inability to maintain traditional producerist ethics across the board.[3]

The return of the good times hailed by the *Sun* was, as usual, uneven and sparked as much controversy as it fostered harmony. But for some prominent trade unionists, the early 1840s marked the successful completion of their struggles for competences. In addition to the white-collar attainments of Francis Gallagher, John Seidenstricker, Edmund Bull, Samuel Mass, and John Hawkins, advertisements in the local press indicated that A. I. W. Jackson was still captain of the City Guards and that Richard Marley and William L. McCauley (cordwainers), Charles Towson (hatter), and Dennis Wagner

3. For Torrey's interpretation of the negative effects of slavery on the circumstances of the southern laboring classes, see Lovejoy, *Memoir of Rev. Charles T. Torrey*, 133. When the Baltimore Methodists could not agree on an appropriate settlement of their profitable book concern, they went to court, with Reverdy Johnson representing the Southern Methodists.

(hatter) had all achieved master status.[4] But these individual accomplishments do not reflect the full extent of Baltimore artisan experience. The deteriorations of industrialization continued to hit some workers particularly hard and handloom weavers complained of large-scale unemployment, having seen their former wages of a dollar a day cut to fifty cents by 1843. Summer 1843 saw a resurgence of trade union reorganization (under new leadership for the most part) and significant strike activity, but no central structure. The first to strike were the seamen, who turned out in September demanding no less than fifty cents a day (fifteen dollars a month). They promised to name strike-breaking seamen and, in an innovative twist on maintaining a closed shop, to publicly expose the landlords with whom the scabs lived. Such threats led at least one landlord to take out a notice claiming he was being unfairly accused of exploiting seamen and extending his personal support to "the sons of the ocean." One week later, the Sun was "pleased" to report that the seamen's strike was "marked by perfect order and sobriety" with none "of those acts of violence which have recently disgraced the operatives of other cities whilst endeavoring to obtain an advance in their rates of compensation."[5]

Less than a week after the seamen's strike began, the journeymen tailors, who had just begun meeting again at the Washington Temperance Society Hall, announced their intention to call upon "the Merchant Tailors (vulgarly called Master Tailors)" with a new bill of prices. This action was predicated on changes in fashion and reflected the difficulties in maintaining traditional set rates of work. The rate for plain coats was not to change; only rates covering "the little etceteras" were to increase. It appeared that the tailors would be immediately successful, but on October 9, the journeymen called a one-day strike in order to discuss the matter further, hoping to broaden their ethnic base by printing their announcements in German as well as in English. This led to a full-blown turnout a few days later. The resultant establishment of an organization of master tailors suggested that the conflict was expected to be bitter and prolonged. Instead, under the leadership of Methodist class leader John Patterson, the masters association worked for reconciliation, and on October 27, the journeymen tailors proudly announced that the strike had

4. *Sun*, Jan. 2, 1843; *Sun*, Aug. 27, 1840. William McCauley bragged on his new invention, the "pegged cork sole boot," which he was selling at a price "so low all can wear them." *Sun*, Dec. 29, 1839. Charles Towson, former president of the journeymen hatters, a force in the creation of the populist Strawbridge Methodist Church, and a Washingtonian official, was offering hats made "under his own instruction" at costs based on the prevailing "scale of prices." *Sun*, Nov. 3, 1843. And Dennis Wagner, president of the journeymen hatters during the seminal strike of 1833, opened his own hat emporium early in 1844. *Sun*, Jan. 4, 1844.

5. *Sun*, Sept. 7, 15, 22, 25, 1843.

been "amicably settled." That same day, however, in a new and alarming development in capitalist labor relations, six journeymen tailors were indicted for conspiracy. In the following days, those arrested "conducted themselves with much decorum and propriety, and stated their readiness to comply cheerfully." When an important witness failed to appear in court a month later, the petit jury was asked to reconvene in February 1844. By then the strike had long been settled, public attention had faded, and the trial, if ever held, received no coverage in the local papers.[6]

As the tailors were struggling to establish new rates, the cordwainers of the ladies' branch met to discuss their circumstances. As early as July 1843 under the leadership of Francis Gallagher, they had reestablished their union, and now they were offering the olive branch to those recently expelled for delinquency even as they explained why such action had been necessary: "The time has arrived when the journeymen cordwainers should take a firm . . . stand against the oppressive hand of avarice. Our brethren of New York, Philadelphia, Wilmington and in the Eastern States, have come out in their strength and triumphed. Then why do we of Baltimore submit, as passive drudges, to our bosses who are enriching themselves by the fruits of our toil? Let [us] . . . now, uniting in our strength, assert our undoubted right: the right of fixing the price on our labor." A few days later they did just that by turning out "for competence." They called on the community to sustain them in "putting a stop to that unjust, cold, and heartless competition . . . so ruinous to every honest employer and journeyman" and reminded Baltimore cordwainers to forswear traveling to New York for work, as cordwainers of the men's branch there were also on strike.[7] At the same time, other journeymen were reorganizing, including cabinetmakers (who promised to "never again . . . suffer ourselves to be broken up," and who "earnestly" called for other associations of cabinetmakers in the country to communicate with them); saddlers, trunk and harness makers; bricklayers (with employers invited to join); and oak coopers—with the last group going out on strike in early November. As usual, the results of these strikes remain

6. *Sun*, Sept. 11, 20, 25, 26, Oct. 9, 13, 27, 1843. The journeymen also placed their notices in Annapolis, Frederick, Norfolk, Richmond, Philadelphia, and New York papers. *Sun*, Oct. 23, 1843. The apparent unwillingness of Baltimore authorities to prosecute the tailors may have been a result of the precedent-setting *Commonwealth vs. Hunt* case, settled in the Massachusetts Supreme Court in 1842, which reversed the earlier pattern of automatically disallowing journeymen's combinations as unfairly restricting individual trade. Tomlins, *State and the Unions*, 36–44.

7. *Sun*, Oct. 9, 23, 1843.

obscured, but the oak coopers, who called a meeting to announce "Glorious News" on November 13, won theirs.[8]

In spite of these signs of renewed producerist consciousness, the widespread militancy of the previous decade did not repeat itself. Increased corporate consolidation, growing pools of immigrant and rural laborers, creeping public apathy, and artisan self-help alternatives played a role in this, but so did an ambivalence toward capitalist opportunity. This confusion was most apparent in the hatters' strike that broke out in February 1844, less than a month after the Convention of Friends of the Lord's-Day had instituted Baltimore Sabbatarianism. Hard-pressed journeymen, again threatened by employers who refused to pay mutually agreed-upon wages, went public for support as they had successfully done in 1833. Deploring the pernicious effects of underemployment, competition, and "the disposition on the part of men engaged in the business to grind the face of the laborer" by underselling their "more scrupulous" competitors, the hatters bemoaned their lowered wages (which had decreased 50–60 percent since 1839), and their plea reflected more desperation than militancy. But the identification of industrial capitalism as the oppressor remained foundational to their appeal, as did their reliance on the ethically informed support of the public.[9]

In calling on the public to patronize employers who gave the wage and to boycott those who refused, the journeymen were simply repeating a tactic effectively employed before. But the leadership of the movement was new and the position of the principals had changed dramatically because most leaders in the 1830s, such as Joshua Vansant, Charles Towson, Dennis Wagner, John Hawkins, William E. Wright, and Philip Adams, were no longer journeymen. The first three were now master hatters, with Vansant serving as postmaster and Towson working as a Sabbatarian and Washingtonian leader; Hawkins and Wright continued their Washingtonian work; and Adams embraced a Whig political career. Furthermore, the list of masters cited by the new journeymen's organization as friendly or hostile indicated the depths of the ambiguity of early capitalist development. Among those granting the wages were familiar figures: Vansant; George Quail, Washingtonian, Sabbatarian, and Methodist layman outspoken in his support of the journeymen in 1833; and the heirs of the late Methodist leader Jacob Rogers, who had refused to participate in the earlier exploitative masters' combination. Cited

8. *Sun*, Oct. 24, 26, Nov. 4, 10, 13, 27, 1843. By November 2, the cabinetmakers were 125 strong and their secretary, Martin Haynie, was calling for a national organization. *Sun*, Nov. 16, 1843. Boston tailors also turned to cooperationism at this time. *Sun*, Oct. 3, 1843.

9. *Sun*, Feb. 15, March 2, 1844.

as refusing to honor the agreement were William Cole, one of the founders of the offending masters association, and his new partner, the Sabbatarian Universalist Thaddeus Craft, but also Towson and Wagner, both former presidents of the journeymen hatters! Equally significant, in terms of tracing the ambiguities within populist evangelicalism, were the respective alignments of Towson and the sons of Rogers. Towson was a founder of the populist Strawbridge Methodist congregation, while the Rogers family was instrumental in the erection of the controversial and ostentatious Charles Street Methodist Church, with the patriarch Jacob influential in the expulsion of the Methodist Protestant reformers sixteen years earlier as well.[10] Such a reversal of expectations suggests the complexity of tracing persistent allegiance to producerist ethics among upwardly mobile populist evangelicals.

Despite this confusion, the producerist legacy continued to find its champions. Moreover, artisan organization and strike activity were not the only expressions of populist producerism to survive the depression years. Artisan sympathizers at the *Sun* commended a cooperative effort begun by Rochester widow seamstresses who had "formed a society to protect themselves from the rapacity of employers" and suggested that Baltimore would be better off with similar efforts. The *Sun* also printed a number of articles from its sister paper, the Philadelphia *Public Ledger*, decrying the growing abuses of unchecked consumerism and finance capitalism: "All the wealth of the world that feeds the indispensable wants of humanity, is drawn from the land, the ocean, or the workshop," but the producer received only "a small portion of his produce, the exchanger receiving the rest, and the consumer . . . paying enhanced prices for what he receives." Further complicating matters was the "associated wealth" of "corporations and paper money," which allowed one capitalist to receive "as much for one year of light labor, as thirty women for one year of severe and exhausting toil." Part of the solution depended in large part on the consumer: "the public should patronise those employers only who paid a fair compensation for labor."[11]

10. Rogers had died in 1842 while attending Methodist services, but his sons maintained his operation. *Sun*, Apr. 11, 1842, cited in Brigham, *Baltimore Hats*, 61. Towson's advertisements reflected his embrace of consumerism over producerism; he bragged of having the cheapest prices in town. *Sun*, Mar. 2, 1844. Quail, in contrast, advertised that he paid "highest wages" and employed the producerist vernacular to entitle his ad "Live and Let Live" and "No Combination." *Sun*, Feb. 10, 1844. Towson and Quail were both prominent Methodist laymen.

11. *Sun*, Dec. 5, 1843; Feb. 24, 1844. This action reflected difficult conditions for journeymen hatters throughout the country. See the call for a national convention of hatters to be held in New York City on July 10, 1844, in *Danbury Times*, June 12, 1844.

These articles, published in both Baltimore and Philadelphia, repeated the familiar strictures of traditional economic morality: "We forget, when we eulogize sudden wealth as a great gift of Providence, that man has other and higher objects than to eat, sleep and die. . . . We are naturally weak, irresolute, and prone to become attached to the things of this world. The ease of opulence is a fearful peril . . . and few who have no check of poverty or religion can successfully resist her alluring strains." The article suggested ways in which industrialization could enrich workers morally and financially, but only if emergent consumer practices were rejected.

> We do not recommend a return to the old-fashioned slow spinning wheel and loom; for all the modern improvements of machinery can be used in families as well as in factories, and machinists could reap a rich harvest in making mules and jennies and looms for family use, to spin and weave wool and flax and cotton. But this, says the economist, will cost more than the cloth of the factories; and what intelligent farmer will employ his daughters in making shirting that costs him twelve cents per yard, when he can buy it from the factory at six cents? But if it be made at home, his daughters live in peace, plenty, security, and become useful, respectable and happy as wives and mothers. But if he buy it from a factory, his daughters must fly to the cities for employment, and drudge and starve for wholesale dealers. . . . The fashion of the day is to commend everything for its cheapness, and to commend as the cause of this cheapness the extreme concentration of labor. But this cheapness is very dear. It is enormously expensive in human health, happiness and life.[12]

The article continued by citing the growing habit among capitalists to associate themselves even as they anathematized worker attempts to do the same: "Employers agree among themselves about wages, and lawyers and physicians about fees. Then why should not laborers agree about wages?" The problem had always been that when one trade went on strike, underpaid workers in other trades gladly became strikebreakers. The proposed solution prefigured later arguments for industrial unionism and the general strike: "if all classes of laborers combine and devise a tariff for each, calculated upon a just distribution of reward between laborer and employer, they will rescue labor from its present degradation. If all trades stop at once, society

12. *Sun*, Nov. 11, 1843.

must stand still, for employers must yield to just demands. But as each class of rich employers can hold out longer than each class of poor laborers, strikes in detail must end in the defeat of the strikers and the continued degradation of labor." Equally despicable was the capitalist dependency on banks. When calculated together, these conditions, "we are told by . . . political economists, promotes national strength and glory." But in reality this system "furnishes soldiers for armies and sailors for fleets; it promotes concentration of power in the hands of politicians, and sends them to seek new quarrels and subdue distant communities, in search of means to sustain the system. Through injustice, blood, and devastation, the market of China is opened. For whose benefit? For that of the capitalist: the manufacturer, the merchant, the politician who kindly condescends to govern the world. But where is the reward to labor? It drudges and starves for wages just as it did before."[13]

This set of articles, published in the mainstream Baltimore press, indicates that traditional economic morality and the evangelical artisan propensity for opposing oppression continued to thrive by combining producerist consciousness, union organization, and consumer responsibility in a broader critique of emerging economic power relations. Similar sentiments were expressed by "Old Honesty," the anonymous writer of a series of articles for the *Sun.* "Old Honesty's" ramblings covered a number of contemporary labor and populist evangelical topics, but the activity of workers at the Union Factory outside Baltimore was of particular interest to him. The Union Factory had struggled throughout the depression of 1837, and its assets were mortgaged to Moses Sheppard for $27,000 on May 8, 1837.[14] In spring 1843, the factory workers were reduced to taking their wages in goods from the company store, with no money changing hands. Six months later they turned out "for higher wages and payment in cash," temporarily closing the mills. This action, at the site of concentrated Methodist factory preaching, warranted the approval of "Old Honesty," complete with typical biblical allusions: "I am sorry to say—no I am glad to mention—that a little *disunion* is happening at the Union Factory in this vicinity, hoping apostolically, that '*these things are working together for good*' of the hands employed there. They are *striking* for higher wages and, hoping that they will *strike* the rock and bring out the *silver* stream,

13. *Sun,* Oct. 27, Nov. 1, 1843.

14. The material on the sale of Union Factory comes from John McGrain's notebooks on Baltimore area mills, in his personal possession. Moses Sheppard was a longstanding member of the Quaker commercial elite and one of the wealthy Baltimoreans who financed John Hersey's trip to Liberia with the American Colonization Society.

and not *strike* with their fists the conductors of the establishment,—I wish them success. To suit the hard times they worked for lower wages, which I presume fed their bodies without clothing them, and now, while the country is reviving, they justly claim more."[15]

The female operatives at the Union Factory were emphatically militant. At an earlier strike they had tarred and feathered a scab ("Mrs. or Miss Benedict Arnold"), or at least threatened to do so. Another *Sun* correspondent, "Come-Back," was equally friendly to the cause and explained again that not only were operatives poorly paid, but they were forced to purchase necessities at the company store. In its treatment of operatives, the Union Factory was contrasted to the Thistle and Gray's factories (also scenes of intense Methodist and Methodist Protestant proselytization), with the Thistle Factory extolled by "Old Honesty" as "one of the most flourishing in the country, . . . not in the practice of starving . . . boys and girls into almshouses and dwellings of prostitution." In subsequent columns, "Old Honesty" was unsparing in his producerist condemnation of the Union Factory, and with great satisfaction he announced that the strikers "in Consequence of some revolutionizing sentiment" had won—not only did they gain wages commensurate to the other factories but they were also paid in cash.[16] Producerist ethics and worker militancy had by no means disappeared during the depression of the late 1830s.

"Old Honesty" concluded his summary of social relations in Baltimore with a celebratory dialogue between "Mr. Baltimore" and himself. Heartily commended in this discussion was the *Sun* itself, boasting of a daily circulation of 18,000 and exhibiting general editorial "brilliancy." Equally appreciated were Baltimore's "one hundred sanctuaries, giving a 'church-going' character to your children, showing that they feel confident the city is built in vain and cannot prosper unless the Lord influences, sanctions, and directs!" Also celebrated were the "'Six Original Washingtonians'—a half dozen that's equal to a baker's dozen in many places who commenced that glorious reformation that" revolutionized "public sentiment, turning the wheel of general prosperity by water power, and not whiskey." According to this source, "Mr. Baltimore" was "getting on his legs again, recovering from the national pestilence which

15. *Sun*, Apr. 17, Oct. 10, 14, 24, 1843; *American*, Oct. 10, 1843. The scriptural allusion is to Rom. 8:28. Old Honesty cast his net wide. Ridiculing Millerite prophecies of impending doom, he praised the *Sun* for reflecting the "brightness" of our "common Saviour." Likewise he condemned the solutions of Mike Walsh's Shirtless Democracy as "blackguardism" mixed "so heterogeneously that it comes out an incomprehensible balderdash." For a more sympathetic view of Mike Walsh, see Wilentz, *Chants Democratic*, 327–35.

16. *Sun*, Oct. 10, 14, 18, 24, 1843.

has been desolating . . . our land, being successfully physicked by a pill of several hundreds of buildings in the course of erection, and a revival of commerce . . . in the form of restored public credit, administered . . . in the latest Brandrethian style."[17] Baltimore was indeed reviving, but it was a different city than the one that had been staggered by the panic six years earlier, and none knew that better than the artisan activists still fighting to maintain their producerist rights and dignity.

Although liberalism had become the dominant expression of American culture by the mid-1840s, evangelical producers continued to inspire alternatives to unregulated capitalism. Their moral critiques would inform American labor dissent throughout the nineteenth century, from the ten-hour movement of the 1840s and the post–Civil War emergence of the Knights of Labor to the producerist militancy and American radicalism undergirding the People's Party and Debsian socialism.[18] "Old Honesty," anonymous friend of factory operatives and defender of evangelical producerism summed up the inspirational power of this tradition in a benediction directed toward himself and the producerist ethic he espoused: "'Old Honesty': When your time comes may you not die, but live to cheer other's hearts as you have the deepest recesses of mine!"[19] Throughout the subsequent development of American labor militancy and producerist opposition to capitalist exploitation, such hopes proved not to be in vain.

And continuing to provide prophetic insight and energy for Christian populists, trade unionists, and other producers was their faith. Perhaps journeyman printer William Johnston's testimony at the end of his life best summarizes the empowering capabilities of evangelical spirituality for believ-

17. *Sun*, Oct. 24, 1843. The "Brandrethian" reference is to a popular health pill regularly advertised in the Baltimore papers.

18. "Drawing upon traditional ideals of artisan independence and republican equality, the postwar labor movement mobilized the skilled and unskilled, the native and the foreign-born. To the reigning economic orthodoxy that preached the virtues of acquisitive individualism and the iron law of supply and demand, labor counterposed an ethic of mutuality and what one mechanic called a 'moral economy' that insisted economic activity, like other endeavors, must be judged by ethical standards." Eric Foner, *Reconstruction: America's Unfinished Revolution, 1863–1877* (New York: Oxford University Press, 1988), 477–78. For examples of evangelical producerist contributions to subsequent labor radicalism, see Lazerow, *Religion and the Working Class*; Murphy, *Ten Hours' Labor*; Laurie, *Working People of Philadelphia*, 168–87; Gutman, "Protestantism in the Gilded Age"; Fones-Wolf, *Trade Union Gospel*; Craig, "Underside of History;" Wauzzinski, Between God and Gold; David P. Demarest, ed., *"The River Ran Red": Homestead, 1892* (Pittsburgh: University of Pittsburgh Press, 1992), 107–12; and Nick Salvatore, *Eugene Debs: Citizen and Socialist* (Urbana: University of Illinois Press, 1982), 62–68, 151–52, 229–31, 236–40, 311–12.

19. *Sun*, Oct. 24, 1843.

ing artisans. In 1836 Johnston had been the recording secretary for both the Baltimore Typographical Society and the Working Men's Trades' Union, as well as a faithful Methodist layman. As part of the core leadership of Baltimore's central labor organization along with such men as Francis Gallagher, Richard Marley, Philip Adams, and A. I. W. Jackson, he had experienced the alienating confusions of capitalist transformation and the heady successes of Jacksonian trade unionism. When the WMTU went into decline after 1837, Johnston moved to Annapolis to help publish "a political paper." He died there in February 1843, following a painful illness. In the days before his passing, he gently urged his frequent and sympathetic visitors "to seek an interest in the Savior," as one friend remembered it. According to this witness, Johnston left him and others some significant advice. "If you value your immortal soul, oh do not delay until a dying hour to prepare for death. I have suffered more than I ever imagined human nature could bear; but I have been sustained through the power there is in religion."[20] One would be hard pressed to envisage a more fitting epitaph for Baltimore's evangelical artisans.

20. *Baltimore Trades' Union,* May 28, 1836; *Sun,* Feb. 15, 1843.

BIBLIOGRAPHY

PRIMARY SOURCES

Manuscript Collections

ptist Convention of Maryland/Delaware, History Center, Columbia, Maryland

nutes. Maryland Baptist Union Association.

nutes. Second Baptist Church, Baltimore.

story of the Hampden Baptist Church in Honor of Her 100th Anniversary. Baltimore: 1948.

och Pratt Public Library, Baltimore

eland, Evelyn. "An Economic History of Warren, Maryland." Typescript.

ryland Diocesan Archives (Maryland Historical Society), Baltimore

ittington, William. *The Voice of the Lord: A Sermon, Preached in St. John's Church, Washington . . . on Occasion of the Death of William Henry Harrison* (Washington, 1841), in William R. Whittingham Papers.

ryland Hall of Records, Annapolis

rch register and minutes, male members meeting. Columbia Street Methodist Episcopal Church.

rch register. East Baltimore Station, Methodist Episcopal Church.

story of Columbia Avenue Methodist Church."

t Baltimore Station Methodist Protestant Church Records.

utes. Black Rock Baptist Church.

utes. Ebenezer Baptist Church.

bationers list and minutes. North Baltimore Station, Methodist Episcopal Church.

ords. East Baltimore Station, Methodist Protestant Church.

ryland Historical Society, Baltimore

rch records. Fifth Presbyterian Church, Baltimore.

ong-Baldwin Papers.

Gallagher, Francis, Papers.
Hyde, Moses, Papers.
Kauffman Daybooks.
Leakin-Sioussat Papers.
Marine, Fletcher, Papers.
Methodist Class Meeting records.
Minifee, William, Papers.
Shriver Family Papers.
Warren Factory Papers.
Wilson, Franklin, Papers.

Peabody Library, Baltimore

Minutes of the Convention of the Friends of the Lord's-Day, from Maryland, Delaware and the District of Columbia, Held in Light-street Church, Baltimore, January 10th and 11th, 1844. Baltimore: 1844.

Presbyterian Historical Society, Philadelphia

Data file. First Presbyterian Church, Baltimore.
Minutes. Baltimore Presbytery.

United Methodist Historical Society–Lovely Lane Museum, Baltimore

Cook, Isaac P. Unpublished autobiography.
Cook, Isaac P., Papers.
Forsyth, Susanna A. "Strawbridge Methodist Episcopal Church." Typescript.
Freeman, Thomas. File.
Freeman Tract Reports in Thomas Freeman Papers.
Hartman, A. Z. "Methodism in Maryland, 1770–1912." Typescript.
"Members Admitted to Classes." Baltimore City Station records, Methodist Episcopal Church.
Methodist Discipline.
Methodist Episcopal Church class registers.
Mills, Nathaniel. *Journal.*
Records. East Baltimore Methodist Episcopal Church.
Records. East Baltimore Methodist Protestant Church.
Slicer, Henry. Unpublished Journal, 3 vols.
Slicer, Henry, Papers.

Wesley Theological Seminary, Washington D.C.

Journal of the General Conference of the M. P. Church. Baltimore: 1831.
Journal of the . . . Quadrennial Session of the General Conference of the Methodist Protestant Church.
Minutes. Maryland Conference, Methodist Protestant Church.

Personal Collections

John McGrain, scrapbook on Baltimore-area factories, in possession of John McGrain.

Books and Articles

Address of the Maryland Ten Hour Association to the Working Men of the State. Ellicott Mills, Md., 1850

Arfwedson, C. D. *The United States and Canada in 1832, 1833, and 1834.* London, 1834.

Bangs, Nathan. *A History of the Methodist Episcopal Church.* 4 vols. New York, 1845.

Beach, Thomas J. *A Full and Authentic Account of the Rise and Progress of the Late Mob in the City of Baltimore.* Baltimore, 1835.

Beecher, Lyman. *Six Sermons on the Nature, Occasions, Signs, Evils, and Remedy of Intemperance.* Boston, 1828.

Blatchly, Cornelius. *An Essay on Common Wealths.* New York, 1822.

———. *Some Causes of Popular Poverty, Derived from the Enriching Nature of Interests, Rents, Duties, Inheritances, and Church Establishments, Investigated in Their Principles and Consequences, and Agreement with Scripture.* New York, 1817.

———. *Sunday Tract.* New York, 1828.

Boehm, Henry. *Reminiscences, Historical and Biographical, of Sixty-four Years in the Ministry.* New York, 1866.

Branagan, Thomas. *Avenia, or a Tragical Poem, on the Oppression of the Human Species; and Infringement on the Rights of Man in Five Books with Notes Explanatory and Miscellaneous. Written in Imitation of Homer's Iliad.* Philadelphia, 1810.

———. *A Beam of Celestial Light, in a Dark, Deluded, and Degenerate Age; or Epistles, Consolatory, Argumentative, and Instructive: Addressed to the Church of Christ in the Wilderness.* Philadelphia, 1814.

———. *The Beauties of Philanthropy, Extracted from the Writings of Its Disciple.* New York, 1839.

———. *The Excellency of the Female Character Vindicated; Being an Investigation Relative to the Cause and Effects of the Encroachments of Men upon the Rights of Women, and the Too Frequent Degradations and Consequent Misfortunes of the Fair Sex.* 2d. ed. Philadelphia, 1808.

———. *A Glimpse of the Beauties of Eternal Truth, Contrasted with the Deformity of Popular Error. Intended As a Preliminary to the Grand Centurial Jubilee of the Reformation of the Year 1517, to Be Celebrated in Denmark and North America, October 31, 1817.* Philadelphia, 1817.

———. *The Guardian Genius of the Federal Union; or, Patriotic Admonitions on the Signs of the Times, in Relation to the Evil Spirit of Party, Arising from the Root of All Our Evils, Human Slavery.* New York, 1839.

———. *The Penitential Tyrant; or Slave Trader Reformed: A Pathetic Poem in Four Cantos.* New York, 1807.

———. *The Pleasures of Contemplation, Being a Desultory Investigation of the Harmonies, Beauties, Benefits of Nature: Including a Justification of the Ways of God to Man, and a Glimpse of His Sovereign Beauty.* Philadelphia, 1817.

———. *A Preliminary Essay on the Oppression of Exiled Sons of Africa.* Philadelphia, 1804.

———. *The Pride of Britannia Humbled; or, the Queen of the Ocean Unqueen'd, "by the American Cock Boats"* . . . Philadelphia, 1815.

———. *Serious Remonstrances, Addressed to the Citizens of the Northern States, and Their Representatives: Being an Appeal to Their Natural Feeling & Common Sense: Consisting of Speculations and Animadversions, on the Recent Revival of the Slave Trade, in the American Republic: with an Investigation Relative to the Consequent Evils Resulting to the Citizens of the Northern States from That Event, Interspersed with a Simplified Plan for Colonizing the Free Negroes of the Northern, in Conjunction with Those Who Have, or May Emigrate from the Southern States, in a Distant Part of the National Territory: Considered As the Only Possible Means of Avoiding the Deleterious Evils Attendant on Slavery in a Republic.* Philadelphia, 1805.

Breckinridge, Robert J. *A Plea for the Restoration of the Scriptures to the Schools.* Baltimore, 1839.

———. *Tracts to Vindicate Religion and Liberty. No. 1. Containing the Review of the Case of Olevia Neal, the Carmelite Nun, and the Review of the Correspondence Between the Archbishop and Mayor of Baltimore. With Important Additional Matter to Both Reviews.* Baltimore, 1839.

Brigham, William T. *Baltimore Hats, Past and Present.* Baltimore, 1890.

Brooks, Richard A. E., ed. *The Diary of Michael Floy Jr., Bowery Village, 1833–1837.* New Haven: Yale University Press, 1941.

Brown, George. *Recollections of Itinerant Life: Including Early Reminiscences.* Cincinnati, 1866.

Buckingham, James. *America, Historical, Statistic and Descriptive.* 3 vols. London, 1841.

———. *The Eastern and Western States of America.* 3 vols. London, 1840.

Carey, Mathew. *Autobiographical Sketches in a Series of Letters Addressed to a Friend.* Philadelphia, 1829.

Chalmers, Thomas. *The Christian and Civic Economy of Large Towns,* abr. by Charles R. Henderson. New York: Charles Scribner's, 1900.

Cobbett, William. *Twelve Sermons.* London, 1823.

Colhouer, Thomas H. *Sketches of the Founders of the Methodist Protestant Church and Its Bibliography.* Pittsburgh, 1880.

Constitution and Address of the Baltimore Temperance Society; to Which Is Added an Address, Delivered Before the Society. Baltimore, 1830.

Constitution and By-Laws of the Baltimore Typographical Society, Adopted June 2, 1832; to Which Is Added, the List of Prices. Baltimore, 1832.

Constitution and By-Laws of Masons and Bricklayers Beneficial Society of Baltimore City and Precincts. Baltimore, 1822.

Constitution and Discipline of the Methodist Protestant Church. Baltimore, 1830.

[Cook, Isaac P.]. *Early History of Methodist Sabbath Schools, in Baltimore City and Vicinity; and Other Interesting Facts Connected Therewith.* Baltimore, 1877.

Cooke, C[ornelius]. *Discourse on the Life and Death of the Rev. Asa Shinn.* Pittsburgh, 1853.

Craig, Daniel. *Craig's Business Directory and Baltimore Almanac for 1842.* Baltimore, 1842.

Crane, J. T. "The Tract Movement." *Methodist Quarterly Review* 38 (Jan. 1856): 31.

Dashiell, J[ohn] H. *Memoir of Rev. Henry Slicer, D.D.* Baltimore, 1875.

Dickinson, Samuel. *The New Impulse: or Hawkins and Reform: A Brief History of the Origin, Progress, and Effects of the Present Astonishing Temperance Movement, and of the Life and Reformation of John H. W. Hawkins, the Distinguished Leader.* Boston, 1841.

Doughty, Samuel Stilwell. *The Life of Samuel Stilwell, with Notices of Some of His Contemporaries.* New York, 1877.

Douglass, Frederick. *Narrative of the Life of Frederick Douglass, an American Slave: Written by Himself.* New York: Signet Books, 1968.

Dunn, Thomas, and William Whitesides. *A Reply to the Address of the Male Members of the Methodist Episcopal Church in Baltimore, Who Held a Meeting on the 7th of August, 1827.* Philadelphia, 1827.

Dyott, T. W. *An Exposition of the System of Moral and Mental Labor, Established at the Glass Factory of Dyottville, in the County of Philadelphia.* Philadelphia, 1833.

Emory, John. *Defense of "Our Fathers," and of the Original Organization of the Methodist Episcopal Church, Against the Rev. Alexander McCaine and Others: with Historical and Critical Notices of Early American Methodism.* 5th ed., New York, 1840.

———. *History of the Discipline of the Methodist Episcopal Church.* New York, 1844.

Estes, Benjamin. *Essay on the Necessity of Correcting the Errors Which Have Crept into the Washingtonian Temperance Movement.* New York, 1846.

Gobright, John C. *City Rambles, or Baltimore As It Is.* Baltimore, 1857.

Grosh, A. B. *Washingtonian Pocket Companion: Containing a Choice Collection of Temperance Hymns, Songs, Odes, Glees, Duetts, Chorusses, &c. with Music.* 4th ed. Utica, 1845.

Hall, John. *The Cabinet-makers Assistant.* Baltimore, 1840.

Harrisson, David, Jr. *A Voice from the Washingtonian Home . . . Together with a Sketch of the Temperance Reform in America.* Boston, 1860.

Hawkins, Archibald. *The Life and Times of Hon. Elijah Stansbury, an "Old Defender" and Ex-Mayor of Baltimore; Together with Early Reminiscences, Dating from 1662, and Embracing a Period of 212 Years.* Baltimore, 1874.

Hawkins, William G. *Life of John H. W. Hawkins.* Boston, 1859.

Hazen, Edward. *The Panorama of Professions and Trades; or Every Man's Book.* Philadelphia, 1836.

Hersey, John. *Advice to Christian Parents.* Baltimore, 1839.

———. *An Appeal to Christians, on the Subject of Slavery.* Baltimore, 1833.

———. *The Importance of Small Things; or, A Plain Course of Self-Examination to Which Is Added, Signs of the Times.* Baltimore, 1833.

———. *The Privilege of Those Born of God; or A Plain Rational View of the Nature and Extent of Sanctification.* Baltimore, 1841.

Hewitt, John H. *Shadows on the Wall, or Glimpses of the Past.* Baltimore, 1877.

History of Baltimore, Maryland. Baltimore: S. B. Nelson, 1898.

Instrument of Association, Together with the General Rules of Messrs. John and Charles Wesley, and the Additional Regulations Prepared by the Associated Methodist Reformers in Baltimore. Baltimore, 1828.

Jennings, Samuel K. *An Exposition of the Late Controversy in the Methodist Episcopal Church; of the True Objects of Parties Concerned Therein, and of the Proceedings by Which Reformers Were Expelled, in Baltimore, Cincinnati, and Other Places; or, A Review of the Methodist Magazine and Quarterly Review, on Petitions and Memorials.* Baltimore, 1831.

———. *The Married Lady's Companion or the Poor Man's Friend.* New York, 1808.

Johnson, Reverdy. *The Memorial of Reverdy Johnson to the Legislature of Maryland, Praying Indemnity for the Destruction of His Property in the City of Baltimore by a Mob in August 1835.* Annapolis, 1836.

Knapp, Jacob. *Autobiography of Jacob Knapp.* New York, 1868.

Long, John Dixon. *Pictures of Slavery in Church and State; Including Personal Reminiscences, Biographical Sketches, Anecdotes, etc., etc., with an Appendix, Containing the Views of John Wesley and Richard Watson on Slavery.* Philadelphia, 1857.

Lovejoy, J. C. *Memoir of Rev. Charles T. Torrey, Who Died in the Penitentiary of Maryland, Where He Was Confined for Showing Mercy to the Poor.* Boston, 1847.

Luther, Seth. *An Address on the Origin and Progress of Avarice, and Its Deleterious Effects on Human Happiness, with a Proposed Remedy for the Countless Evils Resulting from an Inordinate Desire for Wealth.* Boston, 1834.

Marine, Fletcher E. *Sketch of Rev. John Hersey, Minister of the Gospel of the M. E. Church.* Baltimore, 1879.

Matchett, Richard J. *Matchett's Baltimore Directory for 1825.* Baltimore, 1825.

———. *Matchett's Baltimore Directory.* Baltimore, 1833.

———. *Matchett's Baltimore Directory.* Baltimore, 1847.

McCaine, Alexander. *An Appeal to the Public, from the Charges Contained in the "Reply of the Rev. James Smith, to the Strictures of the Rev. Alexander McCaine"; Accompanied with Remarks upon the Government of the Methodist Episcopal Church.* Baltimore, 1826.

———. *A Defence of the Truth, As Set Forth in the "History and Mystery of Methodist Episcopacy," Being a Reply to John Emory's "Defence of Our Fathers."* Baltimore, 1829.

———. *The History and Mystery of Methodist Episcopacy, or, A Glance at "The Institutions of the Church, As We Received Them from Our Fathers."* Baltimore, 1827.

Member's Manual of the First Baptist Church in Baltimore. Baltimore, 1836.

Member's Manual of the First Baptist Church in Baltimore. Baltimore, 1843.

Minutes of the Convention of the Friends of the Lord's-Day, from Maryland, Delaware and the District of Columbia, Held at Light-street Church, Baltimore, January 10th and 11th, 1844. Baltimore, 1844.

Moore, Henry. *An Account of the Lord's Dealings with the Rev. Thomas Rutherford, the Greater Part Written by Himself.* Baltimore, n.d.

Musgrave, George Washington. *A Vindication of Religious Liberty, or the Nature and Efficiency of Christian Weapons.* Baltimore, 1834.

Proceedings of the Baltimore Typographical Society at Their Anniversary Supper. Baltimore, 1833.

Proceedings of the General Conference of Delegates from the Members and Local Preachers of the Methodist Episcopal Church, Friendly to Reform, Assembled in the First English Evangelical Lutheran Church, in the City of Baltimore, Nov. 15, 1827. Baltimore, 1827.

Reilly, J. McKendree. "Rev. Henry Slicer, D.D." Unpublished paper read before the American Methodist Historical Society, Oct. 7, 1874 (in Slicer Papers, Lovely Lane Museum, Baltimore).

Reese, Daniel E. *Rev. D. E. Reese's Protests, Arguments, and Address, Against the Whole of the Proceedings of His Prosecutors, &c. in the Baltimore City Station, Who Have Combined to Prefer Charges Against Him and Others.* Baltimore, 1827.

Reese, Levi R. *Levi R. Reese's Argument and Protests Against the Whole of the Proceedings of His Prosecutors, &c. by the Baltimore City Station, Who Have Combined to Prefer Charges Against Him and Others.* Baltimore, 1827.

———. *Thoughts of an Itinerant.* Baltimore, 1847.

Ridgaway, Henry B. *The Life of the Rev. Alfred Cookman, with a Brief Account of His Father, the Rev. George Grimston Cookman.* London, 1876.

Roszel, Stephen George. *The Substance of Sermon Delivered in the White Marsh Meeting House, Lancaster City, Virginia, on the 15th of May, 1825.* Baltimore, 1826.

Seaman, Samuel A. *Annals of New York Methodism, Being A History of the Methodist Episcopal Church in the City of New York.* New York, 1892.

Sewell, Benjamin T. *Sorrow's Circuit, or Five Years' Experience in the Bedford Street Mission, Philadelphia.* Philadelphia, 1859.

Shinn, R. F. *A Tribute to Our Fathers: Being A Vindication of the Founders of the Methodist Protestant Church.* Cincinnati and Baltimore, 1854.

A Short Scriptural Catechism Intended for the Use of the Methodist Society. Baltimore, 1826.

Smith, Joseph T. *Eighty Years Embracing a History of Presbyterianism in Baltimore, with an Appendix.* Philadelphia, 1899.

Snethen, Nicholas. *Snethen On Lay Representation, or Essays on Lay Representation and Church Government, Collected from the Wesleyan Repository, the Mutual Rights, and the Mutual Rights and Christian Intelligencer, from 1820 to 1829 Inclusive, Now Republished in a Chronological Order, with an Introduction by the Rev. Nicholas Snethen.* Baltimore, 1835.

———. *The Identifier of the Ministers and Members of the Methodist Protestant Church.* Philadelphia, 1839.

Sprague, William B. *Annals of the American Pulpit.* 7 vols. New York, 1859.

A Statement of the Facts Alluded to in "An Address to the Ministers and Members of the Methodist Protestant Church in the Maryland District." Baltimore, 1844.

Stockton, T[homas] H. *A Discourse on the Life and Character of the Rev. Samuel K. Jennings, M.D.* Baltimore, 1855.

Torrey, Jesse, Jr. *The Moral Instructor, and Guide to Virtue and Happiness in Five Parts.* Ballston Spa, 1819.

Varle, Charles. *A Complete View of Baltimore As It Is with a Statistical Sketch.* Baltimore, 1833.

Wakeley, J. B. *Lost Chapters Recovered from the Early History of American Methodism.* New York, 1889.

Wesley, John. *The Works of the Reverend John Wesley, A.M.* 7 vols. New York, 1831.

Williams, James R. *History of the Methodist Protestant Church.* Baltimore, 1843.

Zug, John. *The Foundation, Progress, and Principles of the Washington Temperance Society of Baltimore.* Baltimore, 1842.

SECONDARY SOURCES

Books

Abzug, Robert. *Cosmos Crumbling: American Reform and Religious Imagination.* New York: Oxford University Press, 1994.

Ahlstrom, Sydney E. *A Religious History of the American People.* New Haven: Yale University Press, 1972.

Appleby, Joyce. *Capitalism and a New Social Order: The Republican Vision of the 1790s.* New York: New York University Press, 1984.

Armstrong, James E. *History of the Old Baltimore Conference from the Planting of Methodism in 1773 to the Division of the Conference in 1857.* Baltimore: King Brothers, 1907.

Ashworth, John. *Slavery, Capitalism, and Politics in the Antebellum Republic.* New York: Cambridge University Press, 1995.

Baker, Gordon Pratt, ed. *Those Incredible Methodists: A History of the Baltimore Annual Conference of the United Methodist Church.* Baltimore: Commission on Archives and History, The Baltimore Conference, 1972.

Bensman, David. *The Practice of Solidarity: American Hat Finishers in the Nineteenth Century.* Urbana: University of Illinois Press, 1985.

Berman, Marshall. *All That Is Solid Melts into Air: The Experience of Modernity.* New York: Simon and Schuster, 1981.

Bestor, Arthur E. *Backwoods Utopias: The Sectarian and Owenite Phases of Communitarian Socialism in America, 1663–1829.* Philadelphia: University of Pennsylvania Press, 1950.

Bilhartz, Terry D. *Urban Religion and the Second Great Awakening: Church and Society in Early National Baltimore.* Rutherford, N.J.: Fairleigh Dickinson University Press, 1986.

Blumin, Stuart M. *The Emergence of the Middle Class: Social Experience in the American City, 1760–1900.* Cambridge: Cambridge University Press, 1990.

Bonomi, Patricia. *Under the Cope of Heaven: Religion, Society, and Politics in Colonial America.* New York: Oxford University Press, 1986.

Bradley, David Henry. *A History of the A. M. E. Zion Church: Part 1, 1796–1872.* Nashville: Parthenon Press, 1956.

Brooks, Neal A., and Eric G. Rockel, *A History of Baltimore County.* Towson, Md.: Friends of the Towson Library, 1979.

Browne, Gary L. *Baltimore in the Nation, 1789–1861.* Chapel Hill: University of North Carolina Press, 1980.

Bruchey, Stuart W. *The Roots of American Economic Growth, 1607–1861.* New York: Harper and Row, 1968.

Brugger, Robert J. *Maryland: A Middle Temperament.* Baltimore: Johns Hopkins University Press, 1988.

Bucke, Emory Stevens, ed. *The History of American Methodism.* 3 vols. New York: Abingdon Press, 1964.

Calhoun, Craig. *The Question of Class Struggle: Social Foundations of Popular Radicalism During the Industrial Revolution.* Chicago: University of Chicago Press, 1982.

Cameron, Richard M. *Methodism and Society in Historical Perspective.* New York: Abingdon Press, 1961.

Cantor, Milton, ed. *American Workingclass Culture: Explorations in American Labor and Social History.* Westport, Conn.: Greenwood Press, 1979.

Carwardine, Richard. *Evangelicals and Politics in Antebellum America.* New Haven: Yale University Press, 1993.

———. *Trans-Atlantic Revivalism: Popular Evangelicalism in Britain and America, 1790–1865.* Westport, Conn.: Greenwood Press, 1978.

Cassell, Frank A. *Merchant Congressman in the Young Republic: Samuel Smith of Maryland, 1752–1839.* Madison: University of Wisconsin Press, 1971.

Cherry, Conrad. *Nature and Religious Imagination: From Edwards to Bushnell.* Philadelphia: Fortress Press, 1980.

Click, Patricia C. *The Spirit of the Times: Amusements in Nineteenth-Century Baltimore, Norfolk, and Richmond.* Charlottesville: University of Virginia Press, 1989.

Cochran, Thomas C. *Frontiers of Change: Early Industrialism in America.* New York: Oxford University Press, 1981.

Cohen, Charles L. *God's Caress: The Psychology of Puritan Religious Experience.* New York: Oxford University Press, 1986.

Commons, John R., et al. *A Documentary History of American Industrial Society.* 10 vols. Cleveland: Arthur H. Clark, 1910.

———. *History of Labour in the United States.* 2 vols. New York: MacMillan, 1918.

Conkin, Paul K. *The Uneasy Center: Reformed Christianity in Antebellum America.* Chapel Hill: University of North Carolina Press, 1995.

Cooke, Raymond W. *One Hundred Years of Christian Service, 1833–1933.* Baltimore, 1933.

Crowley, John E. *This Sheba, Self: The Conceptualization of Economic Life in Eighteenth Century America.* Baltimore: Johns Hopkins University Press, 1974.

Dannenbaum, Jed. *Drink and Disorder: Temperance Reform in Cincinnati from the Washingtonian Revival to the WCTU.* Urbana: University of Illinois Press, 1984.

Davis, Caroline Franks. *The Evidential Force of Religious Experience.* Oxford: Clarendon Press, 1989.

Dawley, Alan. *Class and Community: The Industrial Revolution in Lynn.* Cambridge: Harvard University Press, 1976.

Dayton, Donald W. *Discovering an Evangelical Heritage.* New York: Harper and Row, 1976.

Dayton, Donald W., and Robert K. Johnston, eds. *The Variety of American Evangelicalism.* Knoxville: University of Tennessee Press, 1991.

DeLeon, David. *The American As Anarchist: Reflections on Indigenous Radicalism.* Baltimore: Johns Hopkins University Press, 1978.

Dilts, James D. *The Great Road: The Building of the Baltimore and Ohio, the Nation's First Railroad, 1828–1853.* Stanford: Stanford University Press, 1993.

Dorfman, Joseph. *The Economic Mind in American Civilization, 1606–1865.* 2 vols. New York: Viking Press, 1946.

Drinkhouse, Edward J. *History of Methodist Reform, Synoptical of General Methodism, 1703 to 1898, with Special and Comprehensive Reference to Its Most Salient*

Exhibition in the History of the Methodist Protestant Church. 2 vols. Baltimore and Pittsburgh, 1899.

Dublin, Thomas. *Women at Work: The Transformation of Work and Community in Lowell, Massachusetts, 1826–1860.* New York: Columbia University Press, 1979.

Faler, Paul G. *Mechanics and Manufacturers in the Early Industrial Revolution.* Albany: State University of New York Press, 1981.

Fee, Elizabeth, Linda Shopes, and Linda Zeidman, eds. *The Baltimore Book: New Views of Local History.* Philadelphia: Temple University Press, 1991.

Finke, Roger, and Roger Stark. *The Churching of America, 1776–1990: Winners and Losers in Our Religious Economy.* New Brunswick: Rutgers University Press, 1992.

Foner, Eric. *Free Soil, Free Labor, Free Men: The Ideology of the Republican Party Before the Civil War.* New York: Oxford University Press, 1970.

Foner, Philip S. *William Heighton: Pioneer Labor Leader of Jacksonian Philadelphia.* New York: International Publishers, 1991.

Fones-Wolf, Ken. *Trade Union Gospel: Christianity and Labor in Industrial Philadelphia, 1865–1915.* Philadelphia: Temple University Press, 1989.

Foster, Charles I. *An Errand of Mercy: The Evangelical United Front, 1790–1837.* Chapel Hill: University of North Carolina Press, 1960.

Fowler, Robert Booth. *Unconventional Partners: Religion and Liberal Culture in the United States.* Grand Rapids, Mich.: William B. Eerdmans, 1989.

Freyer, Tony A. *Producers vs. Capitalists: Constitutional Conflict in Antebellum America.* Charlottesville: University of Virginia Press, 1994.

Genovese, Eugene D. *Roll, Jordan, Roll: The World the Slaves Made.* New York: Pantheon Books, 1974.

Gilchrist, David T., ed. *The Growth of Seaport Cities, 1790–1825.* Charlottesville: University Press of Virginia, 1967.

Gilje, Paul A., ed. *Wages of Independence: Capitalism in the Early American Republic.* Madison, Wis.: Madison House, 1997.

Gilje, Paul A., and Howard B. Rock, eds. *Keepers of the Revolution: New Yorkers at Work in the Early Republic.* Ithaca: Cornell University Press, 1992.

Gitelman, Howard M. *Workingmen of Waltham: Mobility in American Urban Industrial Development, 1850–1890.* Baltimore: Johns Hopkins University Press, 1974.

Glickstein, Jonathan A. *Concepts of Free Labor in Antebellum America.* New Haven: Yale University Press, 1991.

Goodman, Paul. *Towards a Christian Republic: Antimasonry and the Great Transition in New England, 1826–1836.* New York: Oxford University Press, 1988.

Goodwyn, Lawrence. *Democratic Promise: The Populist Moment in America.* New York: Oxford University Press, 1976.

Gordon, David M., Richard Edwards, and Michael Reich. *Segmented Work, Divided Workers: The Historical Transformation of Labor in the United States.* Cambridge: Cambridge University Press, 1982.

Graham, Leroy. *Baltimore, the Nineteenth Century Black Capital.* Washington, D.C.: University Press of America, 1982.

Gusfield, Joseph R. *Symbolic Crusade: Status Politics and the American Temperance Movement.* Urbana: University of Illinois Press, 1963.

Haggerty, William A. *150th Anniversary of the East Baltimore Station, Methodist Episcopal Church, 1773–1923.* Baltimore, 1923.

Hall, Clayton, ed. *Baltimore: Its History and Its People.* New York: Lewis Historical Publishing, 1912.

Hall, David D. *Worlds of Wonder, Days of Judgment: Popular Religious Belief in Early New England.* Cambridge: Harvard University Press, 1989.

Hanley, Mark Y. *Beyond A Christian Commonwealth: The Protestant Quarrel with the American Republic, 1830–1860.* Chapel Hill: University of North Carolina Press, 1994.

Harris, David. *Socialist Origins in the United States.* Assen, The Netherlands: Van Gorcum, 1966.

Harvey, Bill. *"The People Is Grass": A History of Hampden-Woodberry, 1802–1945.* Baltimore: Della Press, 1988.

Hatch, Nathan O. *The Democratization of American Christianity.* New Haven: Yale University Press, 1989.

Hattam, Victoria. *Labor Visions and State Power: The Origins of Business Unionism in the United States.* Princeton: Princeton University Press, 1993.

Heilbroner, Robert L. *The Economic Transformation of America.* New York: Harcourt, Brace, Jovanovich, 1977.

Hempton, David. *Methodism and Politics in British Society, 1750–1850.* Stanford: Stanford University Press, 1984.

Hilton, Boyd. *The Age of Atonement: The Influence of Evangelicalism on Social and Economic Thought, 1795–1865.* Oxford: Clarendon Press, 1988.

A Historical Sketch of Exeter Street Methodist Episcopal Church, Baltimore, Maryland. Baltimore: Thomas and Evans, 1902.

Hobsbawm, Eric. *Labouring Men: Studies in the History of Labour.* New York: Basic Books, 1964.

Hoffman, Ronald, and Peter J. Albert, eds. *Religion in a Revolutionary Age.* Charlottesville: University of Virginia Press, 1992.

Hollander, J. H. *The Financial History of Baltimore. Baltimore, 1899.*

Hoopes, James. *Consciousness in New England.* Baltimore: Johns Hopkins University Press, 1989.

Horwitz, Morton J. *The Transformation of American Law, 1780–1860.* Cambridge: Harvard University Press, 1977.

[Hubbard, E. L.] *The Baltimore Century Plant: History of Eutaw Street Methodist Episcopal Church and the Relation of Eutaw Church to the Downtown Problem.* Baltimore: Lowenthal-Wolf, 1908.

Hugins, Walter E. *Jacksonian Democracy and the Working Class: A Study of the New York Workingmen's Movement, 1829–1837.* Stanford: Stanford University Press, 1960.

Industries of Maryland: A Descriptive Review of the Manufacturing and Mercantile Industries of the City of Baltimore. New York, 1882.

Innes, Stephen. *Creating the Commonwealth: The Economic Culture of Puritan New England.* New York: W. W. Norton, 1995.

Isaac, Rhys. *The Transformation of Virginia, 1740–1790.* Chapel Hill: University of North Carolina Press, 1982.

Jacob, Margaret, and James Jacob, eds. *The Origin of Anglo-American Radicalism.* London: George Allen & Unwin, 1984.

Jaggers, F. Y. *The Story of My Life: Fayette-Bennett Methodist Episcopal Church.* Baltimore, 1933.

Johnson, Curtis D. *Islands of Holiness: Rural Religion in Upstate New York, 1790–1860.* Ithaca: Cornell University Press, 1989.

Johnson, Paul E. *A Shopkeeper's Millennium: Society and Revivals in Rochester, New York, 1815–1837.* New York: Hill and Wang, 1978.

Joyce, Patrick, ed. *The Historical Meanings of Work.* Cambridge: Cambridge University Press, 1987.

Kahn, Philip, Jr. *A Stitch in Time: The Four Seasons of Baltimore's Needle Trades.* Baltimore: Maryland Historical Society, 1989.

Katznelson, Ira, and Aristide A. Zolberg, eds. *Working-Class Formation: Nineteenth-Century Patterns in Western Europe and the United States.* Princeton: Princeton University Press, 1986.

Kimmel, Michael. *Manhood in America: A Cultural History.* New York: Free Press, 1996.

Kurtz, Don. *South of the Big Four.* San Francisco: Chronicle Books, 1995.

Land, Aubrey C., Lois Green Carr, and Edward C. Papenfuse, eds. *Law, Society, and Politics in Early Maryland.* Baltimore: Johns Hopkins University Press, 1977.

Laqueur, Thomas W. *Religion and Respectability: Sunday Schools and Working Class Culture, 1780–1850.* New Haven: Yale University Press, 1976.

Larkin, Jack. *The Reshaping of Everyday Life, 1790–1840.* New York: Harper and Row, 1988.

Lasch, Christopher. *The True and Only Heaven: Progress and Its Critics.* New York: W. W. Norton, 1991.

Laurie, Bruce. *Artisans into Workers: Labor in Nineteenth Century America.* New York: Noonday Press, 1989.

———. *Working People of Philadelphia, 1800–1850.* Philadelphia: Temple University Press, 1980.

Lazerow, Jama. *Religion and the Working Class in Antebellum America.* Washington: Smithsonian Institution Press, 1995.

Levering, Rosalind R. *Baltimore Baptists, 1773–1973: A History of the Baptist Work in Baltimore During 200 Years.* Lutherville, Md.: Baltimore Baptist Association, 1974.

Lewis, Thomas H., comp. *Historical Record of the Maryland Annual Conference of the Methodist Protestant Church.* Baltimore: Methodist Protestant Book Concern, 1918.

Licht, Walter. *Industrializing America: The Nineteenth Century.* Baltimore: Johns Hopkins University Press, 1995.

Livengood, James W. *The Philadelphia-Baltimore Trade Rivalry, 1780–1860.* New York: Arno Press, 1970.

Luxon, Norval N. *Niles' Weekly Register: News Magazine of the Nineteenth Century.* Baton Rouge: Louisiana State University Press, 1947.

McCoy, Drew R. *The Elusive Republic: Political Economy in Jeffersonian America.* Chapel Hill: University of North Carolina Press, 1980.

McGrain, John. *From Pig Iron to Cotton Duck.* 2 vols. Towson, Md.: Baltimore County Public Library, 1985.

———. *Oella—Its Thread of History.* Oella, Md., 1976.

McLoughlin, William G. *Revivals, Awakenings, and Reform.* Chicago: University of Chicago Press, 1978.

Marsden, George M. *The Evangelical Mind and the New School Presbyterian Experience.* New Haven: Yale University Press, 1970.

———. *The Secularization of the Academy.* New York: Oxford University Press, 1992.

Martin, David. *Tongues of Fire: The Explosion of Protestantism in Latin America.* Cambridge, Mass.: Basil Blackwell, 1990.

Mathews, Donald G. *Religion in the Old South.* Chicago: University of Chicago Press, 1977.

May, Henry F. *The Enlightenment in America.* New York: Oxford University Press, 1976.

Montgomery, Charles F. *American Furniture: The Federal Period.* New York: Viking Press, 1966.

Moody, J. Carroll, and Alice Kessler-Harris, eds. *Perspectives on American Labor History: The Problems of Synthesis.* DeKalb: Northern Illinois University Press, 1989.

Moore, R. Laurence. *Religious Outsiders and the Making of Americans.* New York: Oxford University Press, 1986.

Morgan, Edmund S. *Visible Saints: The History of a Puritan Idea.* Ithaca: Cornell University Press, 1963.

Murphy, Teresa Anne. *Ten Hours Labor: Religion, Reform, and Gender in Early New England.* Ithaca: Cornell University Press, 1992.

Murray, J. T., and T. H. Lewis, *Historical Sketch of the Maryland Annual Conference of the Methodist Protestant Church.* 5th ed., rev. Baltimore, 1939.

Noll, Mark A., ed. *Religion and American Politics: From the Colonial Period to the 1980s.* New York: Oxford University Press, 1990.

North, Douglas C. *The Economic Growth of the United States, 1790–1860.* Englewood Cliffs, N.J.: Prentice-Hall, 1961.

Norwood, Frederick A. *The Story of American Methodism.* Nashville: Abingdon Press, 1974.

Nye, Russel B. *Society and Culture in America, 1830–1860.* New York: Harper and Row, 1974.

Olson, Sherry H. *Baltimore: The Building of an American City.* Baltimore: Johns Hopkins University Press, 1980.

O'Neill, William L., ed. *Insights and Parallels: Problems and Issues of American Social History.* Minneapolis: Burgess, 1973.

Payne, Peter Lester, and Lance Edwin Davis. *The Savings Bank of Baltimore, 1818–1866: A Historical and Analytical Study.* New York: Arno Press, 1976.

Pope, Liston. *Millhands and Preachers: A Study of Gastonia.* New Haven: Yale University Press, 1942.

Rabinowitz, Richard. *The Spiritual Self in Everyday Life: The Transformation of Personal Religious Experience in Nineteenth-Century New England.* Boston: Northeastern University Press, 1989.

Richey, Russell E. *Early American Methodism.* Bloomington: Indiana University Press, 1991.

Richey, Russell E., and Kenneth E. Rowe, eds. *Rethinking Methodist History: A Bicentennial Historical Consultation.* Nashville: Kingswood Books, 1985.

Rock, Howard, Paul A. Gilje, and Robert Asher, eds. *American Artisans: Crafting Social Identity, 1750–1850.* Baltimore: Johns Hopkins University Press, 1995.

Roediger, David R. *The Wages of Whiteness: Race and the Making of the American Working Class.* London: Verso, 1991.

Roediger, David R., and Philip S. Foner. *Our Own Time: A History of American Labor and the Working Day.* New York: Greenwood Press, 1989.

Rorabaugh, William J. *The Alcoholic Republic: An American Tradition.* New York: Oxford University Press, 1979.

———. *The Craft Apprentice: From Franklin to the Machine Age in America.* New York: Oxford University Press, 1986.

Rosenberg, Carroll Smith. *Religion and the Rise of the City: The New York City Mission Movement, 1812–1870.* Ithaca: Cornell University Press, 1970.

Roth, Randolph A. *The Democratic Dilemma: Religion, Reform, and the Social Order in the Connecticut River Valley of Vermont, 1791–1850.* Cambridge: Cambridge University Press, 1987.

Rothman, David J. *The Discovery of the Asylum: Social Order and Disorder in the New Republic.* Boston: Little, Brown, 1971.

Runyon, Theodore, ed. *Sanctification and Liberation: Liberation Theologies in Light of the Wesleyan Tradition.* Nashville: Abingdon Press, 1981.

Ryan, Mary P. *Cradle of the Middle Class: The Family in Oneida County, New York, 1790–1865.* Cambridge: Cambridge University Press, 1981.

Salvatore, Nick. *Eugene Debs: Citizen and Socialist.* Urbana: University of Illinois Press, 1982.

Scharf, J. Thomas. *The Chronicles of Baltimore: Being a Complete History of "Baltimore Town" and Baltimore City from the Earliest Period to the Present Time.* Baltimore, 1874.

———. *History of Baltimore City and County from the Earliest Period to the Present Day: Including Biographical Sketches of Their Representative Men.* Philadelphia, 1881.

Schneider, A. Gregory. *The Way of the Cross Leads Home: The Domestication of American Methodism.* Bloomington: Indiana University Press, 1993.

Schultz, Ronald. *The Republic of Labor: Philadelphia Artisans and the Politics of Class, 1720–1830.* New York: Oxford University Press, 1993.

Sellers, Charles. *The Market Revolution: Jacksonian America, 1815–46.* New York: Oxford University Press, 1991.

Semmel, Bernard. *The Methodist Revolution.* New York: Basic Books, 1973.

Semmes, Raphael. *Baltimore As Seen by Visitors, 1783–1860.* Baltimore: Maryland Historical Society, 1953.

Silver, Rollo. *The Baltimore Book Trade, 1800–1825.* New York: New York Public Library, 1953.

Smith, Billy G. *The Lower Sort: Philadelphia's Laboring People, 1750–1800.* Ithaca: Cornell University Press, 1990.

Smith, Timothy L. *Revivalism and Social Reform in Mid-Nineteenth-Century America.* New York: Abingdon Press, 1957.

Stansell, Christine. *City of Women: Sex and Class in New York, 1789–1860.* New York: Oxford University Press, 1986.

Steffen, Charles G. *The Mechanics of Baltimore: Workers and Politics in the Age of Revolution, 1763–1812.* Urbana: University of Illinois Press, 1984.

Stephens, D. S., comp. *Defense of the Views of the Reformers.* Indianapolis, 1884.

Stephenson, Charles, and Robert Asher, eds., *Life and Labor: Dimensions of American Working-Class History.* Albany: State University of New York Press, 1986.

Stokes, Melvyn, and Stephen Conway, eds. *The Market Revolution in America: Social, Political, and Religious Expressions, 1800–1880.* Charlottesville: University of Virginia Press, 1996.

Stone, Edward D. *History of Hampden Methodist Protestant Church.* Baltimore, 1917.

Stout, Harry S. *The New England Soul: Preaching and Religious Culture in Colonial New England.* New York: Oxford University Press, 1986.

Sweet, Leonard I., ed. *The Evangelical Tradition in America.* Macon, Ga.: Mercer University Press, 1984.

Taylor, George Rogers. *The Transformation Revolution, 1815–1860.* New York: Rinehart, 1951.

Tholfsen, Trygve R. *Working Class Radicalism in Mid-Victorian England.* New York: Columbia University Press, 1977.

Thomas, George M. *Revivalism and Social Control: Christianity, Nation Building, and the Market in the Nineteenth-Century United States.* Chicago: University of Chicago Press, 1989.

Thompson, E. P. *The Making of the English Working Class.* New York: Vintage Books, 1966.

Tomlins, Christopher L. *Law, Labor, and Ideology in the Early Republic.* Cambridge: Cambridge University Press, 1993.

———. *The State and the Unions: Labor Relations, Law, and the Organized Labor Movement in America, 1880–1960.* Cambridge: Cambridge University Press, 1985.

Toner, Carol N. *Artisan Work and Culture in Bangor, Maine, 1820–1860.* New York: Garland Press, 1995.

Turner, James. *Without God, Without Creed: The Origins of Unbelief in America.* Baltimore: Johns Hopkins University Press, 1985.

Turner, Victor W. *Dramas, Fields, and Metaphors: Symbolic Action in Human Society.* Ithaca: Cornell University Press, 1974.

Tyrrell, Ian R. *Sobering Up: From Temperance to Prohibition in Antebellum America, 1800–1860.* Westport, Conn.: Greenwood Press, 1979.

Valeri, Mark. *Law and Providence in Joseph Bellamy's New England: The Origins of the New Divinity in Revolutionary America.* New York: Oxford University Press, 1994.

Wallace, Anthony F. C. *Rockdale: The Growth of an American Village in the Early Industrial Revolution.* New York: Alfred A. Knopf, 1978.

Watts, Steven. *The Republic Reborn: War and the Making of Liberal America, 1790–1820.* Baltimore: Johns Hopkins University Press, 1987.

Wauzzinski, Robert. *Between God and Gold: Protestant Evangelicalism and the Industrial Revolution.* Rutherford, N.J.: Fairleigh Dickinson University Press, 1993.

Weishampel, John F., Jr. *History of Baptist Christians in Maryland, Connected with the Maryland Baptist Union Association.* Baltimore, 1885.

Wells, Ronald. *History Through the Eyes of Faith: Western Civilization and the Kingdom of God.* San Francisco: Harper and Row, 1989.

Wilentz, Sean. *Chants Democratic: New York City and the Rise of the American Working Class.* New York: Oxford University Press, 1984.

Williams, Harold A. *The Baltimore Sun, 1837–1987.* Baltimore: Johns Hopkins Press, 1987.

Wills, Joshua. *Historical Sketch of the Second Baptist Church of Baltimore, Maryland.* Philadelphia: George F. Lasher, 1911.

Wilmore, Gayraud. *Black Religion and Black Radicalism: An Interpretation of the Religious History of Afro-American People.* 2d ed. Maryknoll, N.Y.: Orbis Books, 1983.

Wind, James P. and James W. Lewis, eds. *American Congregations.* 2 vols. Chicago: University of Chicago Press, 1994.

Working Papers from the Regional Economic History Research Center. Wilmington, Del.: Eleutherian Mills–Hagley Foundation, 1980.

Zweig, Michael, ed. *Religion and Economic Justice.* Philadelphia: Temple University Press, 1991.

Articles and Papers

Abbott, Collamer L. "Isaac Tyson, Jr., Pioneer Mining Engineer and Metallurgist." *Maryland Historical Magazine* 60 (Mar. 1965): 15–25.

Alexander, Ruth M. "'We Are Engaged As a Band of Sisters': Class and Domesticity in the Washingtonian Temperance Movement, 1840–1850." *Journal of American History* 75 (Dec. 1988): 763–85.

Appleby, Joyce. "Republicanism in Old and New Contexts." *William and Mary Quarterly*, 3d ser., 43 (Jan. 1986): 20–34.

Banner, Lois W. "The Protestant Crusade: Religious Missions, Benevolence As Social Control: A Critique of an Interpretation." *Journal of American History* 60 (June 1973): 23–41.

Banning, Lance. "Jeffersonian Ideology Revisited: Liberal and Classical Ideas in the New American Republic." *William and Mary Quarterly*, 3d ser., 43 (Jan. 1986): 3–19.

Bates, Thomas R. "Gramsci and the Theory of Cultural Hegemony." *Journal of the History of Ideas* 36 (Apr.-June 1975): 351–66.

Beirne, D. Randall. "Hampden-Woodberry: The Mill Village in an Urban Setting." *Maryland Historical Magazine* 77 (spring 1982): 6–15.

Bernard, Richard M. "A Portrait of Baltimore in 1800: Economic and Occupational Patterns in an Early American City." *Maryland Historical Magazine* 69 (winter 1982): 341–60.

Berthoff, Rowland. "Peasants and Artisans, Puritans and Republicans: Personal Liberty and Communal Equality in American History." *Journal of American History* 69 (Dec. 1982): 579–98.

Billings, Dwight B. "Religion As Opposition: A Gramscian Analysis." *Journal of American Sociology* 96 (July 1990): 1–31.

Blumin, Stuart M. "The Hypothesis of Middle-Class Formation in Nineteenth-Century America: A Critique and Some Proposals." *American Historical Review* 90 (Apr. 1985): 299–338.

Boles, John B. "John Hersey: Dissenting Theologian of Abolitionism, Perfectionism, and Millennialism." *Methodist History* 14 (July 1976): 215–34.

Brannan, Emora T. "From Right to Expedience: Lay Representation and Thomas Emerson Bond." *Methodist History/A. M. E. Z. Quarterly Review* (Apr. 1975): 123–44.

Bratt, James D. "Religious Alienation and American Culture." *Evangelical Studies Bulletin* 3 (Oct. 1986): 1–2.

Breitenbach, William. "Sons of the Fathers: Temperance Reformers and the Legacy of the American Revolution." *Journal of the Early Republic* 3 (spring 1983): 69–82.

Bushman, Richard L. "Family Security in the Transition from Farm to City, 1750–1850." *Journal of Family History* 6 (fall 1981): 238–56.

Carroll, Douglas. "A Botanist's Visit to Baltimore in 1835." *Maryland State Medical Journal* 23 (Apr. 1974): 49–55.

Carwardine, Richard. "The Second Great Awakening in the Urban Centers: An Examination of Methodism and the 'New Measures.'" *Journal of American History* 59 (1972): 327–40.

Coll, Blanche D. "The Baltimore Society for the Prevention of Pauperism, 1820–1822." *American Historical Review* 61 (Oct. 1955): 77–87.

Craig, Robert. "The Underside of History: American Methodism, Capitalism, and Popular Struggle." *Methodist History* 24 (Jan. 1989): 73–88.

Davis, Mike. "Why the U.S. Working Class Is Different." *New Left Review*, no. 123 (Sept.-Oct. 1980): 3–46.

Dawley, Alan, and Paul G. Faler. "Workingclass Culture and Politics in the Industrial Revolutions: Sources of Royalism and Rebellion." *Journal of Social History* 9 (1976): 466–80.

Faler, Paul G. "Cultural Aspects of the Industrial Revolution: Lynn, Massachusetts, Shoemakers and Industrial Morality, 1826–1860." *Labor History* 15 (summer 1974): 367–94.

Fink, Leon. "The New Labor History and the Powers of Historical Pessimism: Consensus, Hegemony, and the Case of the Knights of Labor." *Journal of American History* 75 (June 1988): 115–36.

Finke, Roger, and Rodney Stark. "How the Upstart Sects Won America, 1776–1850." *Journal for the Scientific Study of Religion* 28 (1989): 27–44.

Franch, Michael S. "The Congregational Community in the Changing City, 1840–70." *Maryland Historical Magazine* 71 (fall 1976): 367–80.

Garonzik, Joseph. "The Racial and Ethnic Make-up of Baltimore Neighborhoods, 1850–70." *Maryland Historical Magazine* 71 (fall 1976): 392–402.

Gilje, Paul A. "The Baltimore Riots of 1812 and the Breakdown of the Anglo-American Mob Tradition." *Journal of Social History* 13 (summer 1980): 547–64.

Griffin, Clifford S. "Religious Benevolence As Social Control." *Mississippi Valley Historical Review* 44 (Dec. 1957): 423–44.

Grimsted, David. "Ante-bellum Labor: Violence, Strike, and Communal Arbitration." *Journal of Social History* 18 (fall 1985): 5–28.

———. "Rioting in Its Jacksonian Setting." *American Historical Review* 77 (Apr. 1972): 361–97.

Gutman, Herbert G. "Protestantism and the American Labor Movement: The Christian Spirit in the Gilded Age." *American Historical Review* 72 (Oct. 1966): 74–101.

———. "Work, Culture, and Society in Industrializing America, 1815–1919." *American Historical Review* 78 (1973): 531–87.

Hagensick, A. Clarke "Revolution or Reform in 1836: Maryland's Preface to the Dorr Rebellion." *Maryland Historical Magazine* 57 (Dec. 1962): 346–66.

Haller, Mark H. "The Rise of the Jackson Party in Maryland, 1820–29." *Journal of Southern History* 28 (Aug. 1962): 307–26.

Hartz, Louis. "Seth Luther: The Story of a Working-Class Rebel." *New England Quarterly* 13 (Sept. 1940): 401–18.

Haskell, Thomas L. "Capitalism and the Origins of the Humanitarian Sensibility, Part 1." *American Historical Review* 90 (Apr. 1985): 339–61.

———. "Capitalism and the Origins of the Humanitarian Sensibility, Part 2." *American Historical Review* 90 (June 1985): 547–66.

Howe, Daniel Walker. "The Evangelical Movement and Political Culture in the North During the Second Party System." *Journal of American History* 77 (Mar. 1991): 1216–39.

John, Richard R. "Taking Sabbatarianism Seriously: The Postal System, the Sabbath, and the Transformation of American Political Culture." *Journal of the Early Republic* 10 (winter 1990): 517–67.

Juster, Susan. "'In a Different Voice': Male and Female Narratives of Religious Conversion in Post-Revolutionary America." *American Quarterly* 41 (1989): 34–62.

Kealey, Gregory S. "Gutman and Montgomery: Politics and Direction of U.S. Labor and Working-Class History in the 1980s." *International Labor and Working Class History*, no. 37 (spring 1990): 58–68.

Kloppenberg, James T. "The Virtues of Liberalism: Christianity, Republicanism, and Ethics in Early American Political Discourse." *Journal of American History* 74 (June 1987): 9–33.

Kohl, Lawrence F. "The Concept of Social Control and the History of Jacksonian America." *Journal of the American Republic* 5 (1985): 21–34.

Kornblith, Gary J. "The Artisanal Response to Capitalist Transformation." *Journal of the Early Republic* 10 (fall 1990): 315–21.

Lasch, Christopher. "Conservatism Against Itself." *First Things: A Monthly Journal of Religion and Public Life*, no. 2 (Apr. 1990): 17–23.

Laurie, Bruce. "'Nothing on Compulsion': Life Styles of Philadelphia Artisans, 1820–1850." *Labor History* 15 (summer 1974): 337–66.

Lazerow, Jama. "Religion and Labor Reform in Antebellum America: The World of William Field Young." *American Quarterly* 38 (summer 1986): 265–86.

———. "Religion and the New England Mill Girl." *New England Quarterly* 60 (Sept. 1987): 429–53.

———. "Spokesmen for the Working Class: Protestant Clergy and the Labor Movement in Antebellum New England." *Journal of the Early Republic* 13 (fall 1993): 323–54.

Lears, T. J. Jackson. "The Concept of Cultural Hegemony: Problems and Possibilities." *American Historical Review* 90 (June 1985): 567–93.

Leary, Lewis. "Thomas Branagan: Republican Rhetoric and Romanticism in America." *Pennsylvania Magazine of History and Biography* 77 (July 1953): 332–52.

Lefurgy, William D. "Baltimore's Wards, 1797–1978: A Guide." *Maryland Historical Magazine* 75 (June 1980): 145–53.

Linebaugh, Peter. "Jubilating; Or, How the Atlantic Working Class Used the Biblical Jubilee Against Capitalism, with Some Success." *Radical History Review,* no. 50 (1991): 143–80.

Mannard, Joseph. "The 1839 Baltimore Nunnery Riot: An Episode in Jacksonian Nativism and Social Violence." *Maryland Historian* 11 (spring 1980): 13–27.

Mathews, Donald G. "The Second Great Awakening As an Organizing Process, 1780–1830." *American Quarterly* 21 (spring 1969): 23–43.

Maxwell, Milton A. "The Washington Movement." *Quarterly Journal of Studies on Alcohol* 11 (1950): 412–27.

Mayer, Arno J. "The Lower Middle Class As Historical Problem." *Journal of Modern History* 47 (Sept. 1975): 409–36.

Montgomery, David. "The Shuttle and the Cross: Weavers and Artisans in the Kensington Riots of 1844." *Journal of Social History* 5 (summer 1972): 411–46.

———. "The Working Classes of the Pre-Industrial American City, 1780–1830." *Labor History* 9 (winter 1968): 3–22.

Moorehead, James. "Social Reform and the Divided Conscience of Antebellum Protestantism." *Church History* 48 (Dec. 1979): 416–30.

Morris, Richard B. "Labor Militancy in the Old South." *Labor and Nation* 4 (May-June 1948): 32–36.

Muller, Edward K., and Paul Groves. "The Changing Location of the Clothing Industry: A Link to the Social Geography of Baltimore in the Nineteenth Century." *Maryland Historical Magazine* 71 (fall 1976): 403–15.

Muraskin, William A. "The Social-Control Theory in American History: A Critique." *Journal of Social History* 9 (June 1976): 558–68.

Neufeld, Maurice F. "The Size of the Jacksonian Labor Movement: A Cautionary Account." *Labor History* (fall 1982): 599–607.

Noll, Mark A. "Republicanism, Liberalism, and the Languages of Northern Protestant Theology in the Early American Republic." Paper delivered at American Historical Association meeting, New York, Dec. 1990.

Nord, David Paul. "Religious Reading and Readers in Antebellum America." *Journal of the Early Republic* 15 (summer 1995): 241–72.

Novak, Stephen J. "The Perils of Respectability: Methodist Schisms of the 1820s." Paper delivered at American Historical Association meeting, 1980.

Nutt, Rick. "'The Advantages of Liberty': Democratic Thought in the Formation of the Methodist Protestant Church." *Methodist History* 31 (Oct. 1992): 16–25.

Palmer, Bryan D. "Classifying Culture." *Labour/Le Travailleur* (autumn/spring 1981/1982): 153–83.

Pals, Daniel L. "Reductionism and Belief: An Appraisal of Recent Attacks on the Doctrine of Irreducible Religion." *Journal of Religion* 66 (Jan. 1986): 18–36.

Pessen, Edward. "We Are All Jeffersonians, We Are All Jacksonians: or A Pox on Stultifying Periodizations." *Journal of the Early American Republic* 1 (spring 1981): 1–26.

Pocock, J. G. A. "Virtue and Commerce in the Eighteenth Century." *Journal of International History* 3 (1972): 119–34.

Pointer, Richard W. "'Recycling' Early American Religion: Some Historiographical Problems and Prospects." *Fides et Historia* 23 (fall 1991): 31–42.

Prince, Carl E. "The Great 'Riot Year': Jacksonian Democracy and Patterns of Violence in 1834." *Journal of the Early Republic* 5 (spring 1985): 1–19.

Ridgway, Whitman H. "Community Leadership: Baltimore During the First and Second Party Systems." *Maryland Historical Magazine* 71 (winter 1976): 334–48.

———. "McCulloch vs. the Jacksonians: Patronage and Politics in Maryland." *Maryland Historical Magazine* 70 (winter 1975): 350–62.

Rosenmeier, Jesper. "John Cotton on Usury." *William and Mary Quarterly*, 3d ser., 47 (Oct. 1990): 548–65.

Ross, Steven J. "The Transformation of Republican Ideology." *Journal of the Early Republic* 10 (fall 1990): 323–30.

Salvatore, Nick. "Response to Sean Wilentz, 'Against Exceptionalism': Class Consciousness and the American Labor Movement, 1790–1920." *International Labor and Working Class History*, no. 26 (fall 1984): 25–30.

Samuel, Raphael. "Workshop of the World: Steam Power and Hand Technology in Mid-Victorian Britain." *History Workshop* 3 (spring 1977): 1–77.

Schantz, Mark S. "Religious Tracts, Evangelical Reform, and the Market Revolution in Antebellum America." *Journal of the Early Republic* 17 (fall 1997): 425–66.

Schneider, A. Gregory. "Social Religion, the Christian Home, and Republican Spirituality in Antebellum Methodism." *Journal of the Early Republic* 10 (summer 1990): 163–89.

Schultz, Ronald. "The Small-Producer Tradition and the Moral Origins of Artisan Radicalism in Philadelphia, 1720–1810." *Past and Present* 127 (May 1990): 84–108.

Shalhope, Robert E. "Republicanism and Early American Historiography." *William and Mary Quarterly*, 3d ser., 39 (Apr. 1982): 334–56.

Sheller, Tina H. "Artisans, Manufacturing, and the Rise of a Manufacturing Interest in Revolutionary Baltimore Town." *Maryland Historical Magazine* 83 (spring 1988): 3–17.

Stearns, Peter N. "The Middle Class: Toward a Precise Definition." *Comparative Studies in Society and History* 21 (1979): 377–96.

Steffen, Charles G. "Changes in Artisan Production in Baltimore, 1790–1820." *William and Mary Quarterly*, 3d ser., 36 (Jan. 1979): 101–17.

Stockbridge, Henry, Jr. "Baltimore in 1846." *Maryland Historical Journal* 6 (1911): 15–20–34.

Sutton, William R. "Benevolent Calvinism and the Moral Government of God: The Influence of Nathaniel W. Taylor on Revivalism in the Second Great Awakening." *Religion and American Culture* 2 (Feb. 1992): 23–47.

———. "Tied to the Whipping Post: New Labor Historians and Evangelical Artisans in the Early Republic." *Labor History* 36 (spring 1995): 251–81.

Thompson, Edward P. "The Making of a Ruling Class." *Dissent* 40 (summer 1993): 375–82.

———. "Time, Work Discipline, and Industrial Capitalism." *Past and Present* 38 (Dec. 1967): 56–97.

Tucker, Bruce. "Class and Culture in Recent Anglo-American Religious Historiography: A Review Essay." *Labour/Le Travailleur* 6 (autumn 1980): 159–69.

Valeri, Mark. "The Economic Thought of Jonathan Edwards." *Church History* 60 (Mar. 1991): 37–54.

Vickers, Daniel. "Competency and Competition: Economic Culture in Early America." *William and Mary Quarterly*, 3d ser., 47 (Jan. 1990): 3–29.

Wiener, Martin J., ed. "Humanitarianism or Control? A Symposium on Aspects of Nineteenth-Century Social Reform in Britain and America." *Rice University Studies* 67 (winter 1981): 1–84.

Wigger, John. "Taking Heaven by Storm: Enthusiasm and Early American Methodism, 1770–1820." *Journal of the Early Republic* 14 (summer 1994): 167–94.

Wilentz, Sean. "Artisan Origins of the American Working Class." *International Labor and Working Class History*, no. 19 (spring 1981): 1–22.

Williams, Raymond. "Base and Superstructure in Marxist Cultural Theory." *New Left Review* 82 (Nov.-Dec. 1973): 3–16.

Wyatt-Brown, Bertram. "Prelude to Abolitionism: Sabbatarian Politics and the Rise of Second Party System." *Journal of American History* 58 (Sept. 1971): 316–41.

Yeo, Eileen. "Christianity in Chartist Struggle 1838–1842." *Past and Present* 91 (May 1981): 109–39.

Dissertations

Andrews, Doris E. "Popular Religion and the Revolution in the Middle Atlantic Ports: The Rise of the Methodists, 1770–1800." Ph.D. diss., University of Pennsylvania, 1986.

Clark, Dennis R. "Baltimore, 1729–1829: The Genesis of a Community." Ph.D. diss., Catholic University of America, 1976.

Franch, Michael S. "Congregation and Community in Baltimore, 1840–1860." Ph.D. diss., University of Maryland, 1984.

Gorochow, Anita. "Baltimore Labor in the Age of Jackson." Master's thesis, Columbia University, 1949.

Holsclaw, David. "The Demise of Disciplined Christian Fellowship: The Methodist Class Meeting in Nineteenth Century America." Ph.D. diss., University of California, Davis, 1979.

Jentz, John B. "Artisans, Evangelicals, and the City: A Social History of Abolition and Labor Reform in Jacksonian New York." Ph.D. diss., City University of New York, 1977.

Lazerow, Jama. "A Good Time Coming: Religion and the Emergence of Labor Activism in Antebellum New England." Ph.D. diss., Brandeis University, 1982.

Maring, Norman. "A Denominational History of the Maryland Baptists." Ph.D. diss., University of Maryland, 1948.

Pearce, John N. "The Early Baltimore Potters and Their Wares, 1763–1850." Master's thesis, University of Delaware, 1958.

Phillips, Christopher W. "'Negroes and Other Slaves': The African-American Community of Baltimore, 1790–1860." Ph.D. diss., University of Georgia, 1992.

Ridgway, Whitman H. "A Social Analysis of Maryland Community Elites, 1827–1836: A Study of the Distribution of Power in Baltimore City, Frederick County, and Talbot County." Ph.D. diss., University of Pennsylvania, 1973.

Sisson, William A. "Bell Hours: Work Values and Discipline in the American Textile Industry, 1787–1880." Ph.D. diss., University of Delaware, 1984.

Wallock, Leonard Syd. "Chapel, Custom, Craft: The Transformation of the Struggle to Control the Labor Process among the Journeymen Printers of Philadelphia, 1850–1886." Ph.D. diss., Columbia University, 1984.

Wigger, John. "Taking Heaven by Storm: Methodism and the Popularization of American Christianity, 1770–1820." Ph.D. diss., University of Notre Dame, 1994.

INDEX